Women in Missouri History

Women in

IN SEARCH OF

Edited by LeeAnn Whites,

Missouri History
POWER AND INFLUENCE

Mary C. Neth, and Gary R. Kremer

University of Missouri Press   Columbia and London

Library of Congress Cataloging-in-Publication Data

Women in Missouri history : in search of power and influence /
edited by LeeAnn Whites, Mary C. Neth, and Gary R. Kremer.
    p. cm.
  Includes bibliographical references and index.
  ISBN 0-8262-1526-2 (alk. paper)
  1. Women—Missouri—History. 2. Women—Missouri—Social
conditions. I. Whites, LeeAnn. II. Neth, Mary. III. Kremer,
Gary R.
  HQ1438.M8W65 2004
  305.4'09778—dc22
                                            2004002549

♾ This paper meets the requirements of the
American National Standard for Permanence of Paper
for Printed Library Materials, Z39.48, 1984.

Designer: Kristie Lee
Typesetter: Crane Composition, Inc.
Printer and binder: Thomson-Shore, Inc.
Typefaces: Sabon and Gillies Antique

For photo credits, see p. 275.

Contents

Introduction
  LeeAnn Whites and Mary C. Neth 1

French Women in Colonial Missouri, 1750–1805
  Susan Calafate Boyle 15

Esther and Her Sisters: Free Women of Color as Property
Owners in Colonial St. Louis, 1765–1803
  Judith A. Gilbert 31

German-Speaking Women in Nineteenth-Century Missouri:
The Immigrant Experience
  Linda Schelbitzki Pickle 45

"May We as One Family Live in Peace and Harmony": Relations
between Mistresses and Slave Women in Antebellum Missouri
  Diane Mutti Burke 64

City Sisters: The Sisters of St. Joseph in Missouri, 1836–1920
  Carol K. Coburn and Martha Smith 82

The Tale of Two Minors: Women's Rights on the Border
  LeeAnn Whites 101

The Changing Role of Protection on the Border: Gender and
the Civil War in Saline County
  Rebekah Weber Bowen 119

Her Will against Theirs: Eda Hickam and the Ambiguity of
Freedom in Postbellum Missouri
  Kimberly Schreck 134

Sedalia's Ladies of the Evening: Prostitution and Class in a
Nineteenth-Century Railroad Town
  Rhonda Chalfant 152

Domestic Drudges to Dazzling Divas: The Origins of African
American Beauty Culture in St. Louis, 1900–1930
  De Anna J. Reese 168

"We Are Practicable, Sensible Women": The Missouri Women
Farmers' Club and the Professionalization of Agriculture
  Rebecca S. Montgomery 180

Euphemia B. Koller and the Politics of Insanity in Ralls County,
1921–1927
  Gregg Andrews 200

Breaking into Politics: Emily Newell Blair and the Democratic
Party in the 1920s
  Virginia Laas 219

The Doctor's Wife: Fannie Cook and Social Protest in Missouri,
1938–1949
  Bonnie Stepenoff 236

Bibliography of Secondary Works 253

Contributors 261

Index 265

Acknowledgments

Coordinating the computer programs of our many contributors was a challenge that was ably met by Patty Eggleston, staff member of the University of Missouri–Columbia Department of History, and Kristine Stilwell, a Ph.D. candidate in history, who not only stepped in at a crucial time to put all of the manuscripts into the same format, but also went beyond the call of duty and did some editing as well. We thank both of them for making our work on this manuscript much easier. We also would like to thank Sandy Rubinstein Peterson, also a Ph.D. candidate in history, who compiled and prepared the bibliography for the anthology.

For many of the contributors to this volume, interest in the history of women in Missouri began with a request on the part of the Cooper County American Association of University Women to research the history of women for the 125th anniversary of the founding of their county. We would like to thank the members of that organization, especially Mary Ellen McVicker, as well as the Missouri Humanities Council, for their funding of that initial project. We would also like to thank the staffs of the State Historical Society of Missouri, the Western Historical Manuscript Collection, and the Missouri State Archives for their generous research assistance over the years.

Women in Missouri History

Introduction

LeeAnn Whites and Mary C. Neth

In 1971, the University of Missouri Press published the first volume of *A History of Missouri,* the beginning of what would culminate in 1997 as a five-volume, multiauthored survey of the history of the state. In the close to thirty years that the authors—Lawrence O. Christensen, William E. Foley, Richard S. Kirkendall, Gary R. Kremer, Perry McCandless, and William E. Parrish—labored over the writing of this milestone achievement, our very understanding of the nature of history itself was simultaneously being radically reassessed and redefined. The rise in social activism in the 1960s, beginning with the Civil Rights movement but moving on to other social movements, percolated into the thinking and writing of historians, causing us to look at our state histories anew and ask, Where are the workers? Where are the women? Where are the ethnic, racial, and religious minorities?[1]

We can see the impact of this new, more inclusive way of thinking about what constitutes the proper subjects for historical study in the way this five-volume history varies from the first volume, which was published in 1971, to the last, which was published in 1997. Nowhere is the contrast more apparent than in the treatment of the history of women. Reflecting the prevailing historiography of the time, the initial three volumes (published in the early 1970s) included no subject entries in the index at all for "women." However, by the publication of volume 5 in 1987, there were more than twenty-five. Indeed, prior to the great watershed of the 1960s,

1. William E. Parrish et al., *A History of Missouri,* vols. 1–5 (Columbia: University of Missouri Press, 1971–1997).

the history of the state was arguably conceived of as corresponding largely to the activities of class- and race-privileged men, those who held formally constituted political and economic power and therefore presumably controlled the important events and transactions that made up the very warp and woof of the state's history. The only time women as a social group entered into this narrative was when they attempted to empower themselves as these men were empowered. In Missouri history books published prior to the 1980s, the subentries under the index subject "women" generally only pertain to women's efforts to acquire the vote through the woman suffrage movement.[2]

Although contributions of women as a social group were overlooked in the history of the state, some few "notable" women, such as Jessie Benton Frémont, Marie Chouteau, Philippine Duchesne, or Susan Blow have always appeared on the pages of various volumes. This practice was so widespread in the historical profession that historians of women understand it as one of the earliest stages in the development of the field. If we consider why these particular women were included, we can see that frequently, historians' perceptions of their importance lay in their connections to politically or economically powerful men. In some state histories, for example, Jessie Frémont's name is presented, per the old custom, as "Mrs. J. C. Frémont," underscoring the importance of her relationship to John Charles Frémont, the Civil War military general of the state. Her father, Thomas Hart Benton, was also a prominent political figure in the state—a leader of the Democratic party and a longtime state senator in the antebellum period. By virtue of these familial connections, Jessie Frémont was located close to traditional centers of white male political power and positioned to at least influence some of the state's most important political decision makers and, on occasion, to even make some important decisions in her own right. Similarly, "Madame Chouteau"—Marie Chouteau—is frequently mentioned in early state histories, for she was the matriarch of the powerful Chouteau family, the founders of St. Louis.[3]

2. For index subject listings, see Frederick Arthur Culmer, *A New History of Missouri* (Mexico, Mo.: McIntyre Publishing, 1938), 594; Edwin C. McReynolds, *Missouri: A History of the Crossroads of the State* (Norman: University of Oklahoma Press, 1964); Duane G. Meyer, *The Heritage of Missouri: A History* (Hazelwood, Mo.: State Publishing, 1970), 826; Paul C. Nagel, *Missouri: A Bicentennial History* (New York: Norton, 1977), 205; and Floyd C. Shoemaker, ed., *Missouri: Day by Day* (Columbia, Mo.: State Historical Society, 1943), 2:499.

3. Gerda Lerner, "Placing Women in History: Definitions and Challenges," in Lerner, *The Majority Finds Its Past: Placing Women in History* (Oxford: Oxford University Press, 1979), 145–59. For "Mrs. J. C." Frémont and "Madame" Chouteau, see Culmer, *New History of Missouri*, 588–89.

The invisibility of women as a group and the scarcity of notable women arguably have the same root. As a group, women were invisible to historians because most women became wives and mothers. The place of women as wives and mothers was not to make history in their own name, but rather to assist (or to use the nineteenth-century terminology, "to influence") their husbands, fathers, and sons in their exercise of economic and political power. "Notable" women in this system are the ones fortunate enough to be attached to men with political and economic position; in assisting these men they occasionally find their way onto the stage of history, if only through "influence." Most women, however, whether poor or just middling in economic terms, or members of racial or ethnic minorities, or single or widowed, fall through the sieve of this approach to determining what is historically significant.

Although the appearance of women on the pages of the state histories, whether as a group or as notable individuals, may have been scant, many state history volumes have been dedicated to the author's wife and daughters, presumably for the contributions they made to the author's life and work. For example, in 1938, Frederick Arthur Culmer dedicated his one-volume survey of the state's history, *A New History of Missouri*, to "my wife and daughter," and in 1963, Duane Meyer dedicated *The Heritage of Missouri: A History* to his wife, Andrea, and their children. Although women warranted only a single entry in the indexes of both Culmer's and Meyer's books, as individuals these authors certainly recognized the deep significance of their own female relations to the fabric of their lives and to the writing of their histories. At first glance, it seems contradictory that an entire volume of history might be dedicated to female individuals, when the actual text rarely affords any women even a page to recognize their historical contributions. If women could make such a great contribution to historical scholarship, why not recognize the contributions women had made in other areas, and to the development of the state in general? This paradox, however, reflects an understanding of "history" that was widespread at the time. While professional historians, who were mostly male in this time period, might clearly recognize the importance of their wives and daughters in their own lives, they generally did not see women's contributions, their "influence," as being properly the stuff of history. The "personal" was not recognized as "political" by historians in 1938 or even in 1963.[4]

4. For a discussion of the history of women in the historical profession, see Jacqueline Goggin, "Challenging Sexual Discrimination in the Historical Profession: Women Historians in the AHA, 1890–1940," *American Historical Review* 97, no. 3 (June 1992): 760–802.

The assumption that women's contributions to the social order were of secondary importance, through their "influence" upon men, helps to explain the almost total exclusion of women from the state's history, and from history more broadly at this stage of its development. Indeed, almost all other social groups, regardless of their exclusion from formal political or economic power, find more coverage in the older histories of the state than did women. While seriously underexplored to this day, we nevertheless always find entries in old histories for Native Americans and African Americans, for example. While the discussion of these groups is generally framed in terms of the policies exercised in relation to them by the white men who held formal political power, they are nonetheless recognized as a separate or discrete social group in a way that women are not. Their relationship to white men was viewed as public, political, and about power, while women's matters were assumed to be in the realm of the private and the personal—domestic issues with no direct ties to the public world except through the mediation of male relatives. Early in the development of women's history, people who wanted to study women had not only to identify what women did in the past, but also to learn how to analyze these activities and assert that they are a proper subject of "history."

Thus women are particularly problematic for the historian writing a general historical survey, first, because they have lacked formally vested political and economic power (like other groups whose history is underrepresented in the state), and second, because they suffer from perceptions about the very kind of power they *do* have. The very "influence" that they exert as wives and daughters causes them to disappear from "history," as many historians have defined it. While this circumstance is problematic for race- and class-privileged women, they at least occasionally may exercise "notable" influence on men who make the formal political policy. For women outside the privileged categories of race and class, the approach taken by the older state surveys becomes a kind of double historical submersion. As the women members of already-overlooked racial and ethnic groups, they simply disappear from the story. For even when these groups appear in the written history of the state, they have generally been described, and therefore conceived of, using the generic *men*. Thus we find twentieth-century historians repeating the nineteenth-century term *freedmen*—not "freedpeople" and certainly not "freedwomen."[5]

5. For example, see this term in the index of Lorenzo J. Greene, Gary R. Kremer, and Antonio F. Holland, *Missouri's Black Heritage*, rev. ed. (Columbia: University of Missouri Press, 1993), 250.

One way that some historians of women have responded to this absence of women from history is to emphasize the ways in which women have gradually emerged out of the obscurity of "influence" and into the limelight of "power." This approach accepts the traditional biases of history and attempts to make a case for the significance of women as historical actors, using the definition of *power* as the exercise of public political or economic agency. That state histories have long recognized Susan Blow, who led the nation to establish kindergarten programs, reflects this way of thinking about women's history. The assumption is that the development of a more urban and industrial economy in the nineteenth century allowed women to move from their privatized domestic status into ever-wider forms of waged labor. As women acquired higher levels of education, were able to take up professional occupations, and began to organize formally and work for changes in the legal and political status of women, they then finally emerged on the historically significant plane of public political and economic power.[6]

If we followed this approach, the subtitle of this anthology would read, "From Influence *to* Power." We have, however, chosen instead the subtitle "In *Search* of Power *and* Influence." Here we indicate several things about our thinking concerning the history of women in the state. In the first place, we indicate that we do not see the basic line of women's history as a triumphant march out of domestic obscurity into ever-increasing public power and personal autonomy. While we are interested in discussing the ways in which women have gained formal political power and economic autonomy, we also want to document the ways in which power has remained elusive for women, the ways women continue to search for power, perhaps more often than they acquire it. By including *influence* as well as *power* in our title, we also indicate that we understand "influence"—the realm of the personal, women's traditional contribution to their households—as a significant contribution to the history of the state in its own right.

In this respect the anthology reflects the changes in the way historians of women have understood women as historical actors. Initially, women's historians asked questions about what women did within their "domestic" realm and how they moved from it into the "public" world. This led to

6. This approach was called "contribution history" because it studied the way women "contributed" to what had already been defined as "history" when men were its primary focus. This phase of women's history was a significant "transitional" stage because it helped lead to new concepts and approaches; see Lerner, "Placing Women in History," 149–50. For early discussions of Susan Blow's contributions to the history of the state, see Shoemaker, *Missouri: Day by Day;* and Meyer, *Heritage of Missouri.*

two lines of inquiry: one that focused on "women's sphere" or "women's culture," and another that examined women's political activism and economic participation. Soon historians were considering the links between the two. Eventually, the notion of "women's culture" itself became fractured as our historical knowledge of the differences among women expanded. Our understanding of "separate spheres" also became less absolute as we began to redefine the meanings of *politics* and *public* in ways that included women, to reconsider the meaning of the *domestic* and *personal* for men, to identify the many links that crossed the divide of "spheres," and to analyze "gender" as a relational system that shaped the lives of both men and women. By the late 1980s, women's historians were moving in new directions that attempted to put the "old" history of men and the "new" history of women into the same page in order to create new general historical narratives.[7]

While historians of women at the national level were finding new historical approaches, historians of women in Missouri also expanded their efforts; however, much of this work reflected the uncovering of women's lives and activities, the initial stages of any history of women. For example, in 1989, Mary K. Dains published a pathbreaking essay on "Missouri Women in Historical Writing" that surveyed what had been written on the history of women in the state. She also called for historians to find "the role of women" in Missouri history and to give women "a larger share of

7. For a discussion of the initial stage in women's history, see Ellen Carol DuBois, Mary Jo Buhle, Temma Kaplan, Gerda Lerner, and Carroll Smith–Rosenberg, "Politics and Culture in Women's History: A Symposium," *Feminist Studies* 6, no. 2 (1980): 28–64. Two discussions of how our understandings of the differences among women have reshaped women's history are Nancy Hewitt, "Beyond the Search for Sisterhood: Women's History in the 1980s," *Social History* 10, no. 3 (October 1985): 299–321; and Elsa Barkley Brown, "What Has Happened Here? Politics of Difference in Women's History and Politics," *Feminist Studies* 18, no. 2 (summer 1992): 295–312. Three historiographical essays that indicate these new directions in women's history are Linda Kerber, "Separate Spheres, Female Worlds, Woman's Place: The Rhetoric of Women's History," *Journal of American History* 75, no. 1 (June 1988): 9–39; Joan Wallach Scott, "Gender: A Useful Category of Historical Analysis," *American Historical Review* 91, no. 5 (December 1986): 1053–75; and Paula Baker, "The Domestication of Politics: Women and American Political Society, 1780–1920," *American Historical Review* 89, no. 3 (June 1984): 620–47. In our own work, we have used this approach to reconsider the historical narratives of the Civil War and the history of the rural Midwest. See LeeAnn Whites, *The Civil War as a Crisis in Gender: Augusta, Georgia, 1860–1890* (Athens: University of Georgia Press, 1995); and Mary Neth, *Preserving the Family Farm: Women, Community, and the Foundations of Agribusiness in the Midwest, 1900–1940* (Baltimore: Johns Hopkins University Press, 1995).

the history," a plea that echoed the earliest stages in the development of women's history. Important works of the 1990s, such as Carla Waal and Barbara Oliver Korner's collection of primary source writings by Missouri women, *Hardship and Hope,* and Kathleen T. Corbett's excellent survey of the history of St. Louis women (and the sources available to study them further), *In Her Place,* have continued to advance the study of Missouri women's history.[8]

The essays in this volume will continue in this path, carved out by previous historians, of uncovering the lives of diverse women in Missouri. However, our approach also attempts to incorporate the kinds of questions that redefine the terms of history and to create new approaches that move us toward a more inclusive narrative of the history of the state. A more nuanced and expansive understanding of both power and influence in women's lives not only enables us to see women as historical actors, but also expands our understanding of the nature of power itself. For when we consider the question of power from the location of women in the social order, perhaps not surprisingly we learn that it was not necessarily located where previous historians of the state have assumed it to be. If we begin in the statehouse, we find power in the statehouse, but if we begin elsewhere—for instance, in the family—we find power *there.* Indeed, prior to the industrial revolution and the centralization of power that accompanied it—whether it was the centralization of economic power in corporations, the consolidation of political power at any level, or the concentration of power in urban populations as they grew—power was actually structurally organized in a more decentralized fashion, at the level of the individual household. In other words, although women were more clearly excluded from public political power prior to the industrial revolution—they could not vote, hold office, serve on juries, or sue or be sued—power itself did not rest as entirely on the political level as the old histories of the state have assumed. The essays herein build on these ideas.

In her essay on Ste. Genevieve in the French colonial period, Susan Calafate Boyle considers the extent of women's power within their households. She discusses two major factors that gave married women of this time and place economic control over those households. First, the conditions of frontier settlement intensified the location of power on the level of

8. Mary K. Dains, "Missouri Women in Historical Writing," *Missouri Historical Review* 83, no. 4 (July 1989): 417–28; Carla Waal and Barbara Oliver Korner, eds., *Hardship and Hope: Missouri Women Writing about Their Lives, 1820–1920* (Columbia: University of Missouri Press, 1997); and Katharine T. Corbett, *In Her Place: A Guide to St. Louis Women's History* (St. Louis: Missouri Historical Society Press, 1999).

the household; second, the French society, unlike the American system that would replace it, offered particular conditions and customs that bestowed upon women a relative amount of power within the household.

The women that Boyle considers tended to be race and class privileged, but in her essay "Esther and Her Sisters," Judith A. Gilbert considers the experience of free women of color in St. Louis and finds that even given their race and gender disadvantages, free women were able to amass considerable wealth and gain significant public standing through their ownership of property.

Gilbert and Boyle are not suggesting that women were not disadvantaged or excluded based on their race or their sex in the French colonial social order, but they do propose that we might understand power differently than we have in the past, vesting it more on the level of the household, where women were able to exercise power. By shifting our focus in this manner, away from the statehouse and the courthouse to what stood at the center of the larger social order—the household—our authors open the door to an exploration of a wide range of structures and strategies and a discussion of the various contributions that households made to the initial founding and development of the state.

In her essay "German-Speaking Women in Nineteenth-Century Missouri," Linda Schelbitzki Pickle considers the role that immigrant German women played in the establishment and the perpetuation of the German culture and community in the early nineteenth century. Next, Diane Mutti Burke, in her essay "May We as One Family Live in Peace and Harmony," analyzes the role that women, both white and black, played in the success of the slaveholding household of the antebellum period. In a state in which slaveholding was characterized by its small-household form, Burke analyzes the ways in which the viability of slavery depended directly upon the ability of black and white women to work closely together in the household. Considered as a pair, the Pickle and Burke essays suggest that sometimes—through their outright control of property, but more often in their roles as household managers or as laborers in the household workforce—women played a role not simply in the economic survival of the population but in the very construction and perpetuation of a myriad of cultures in the state. These essays consider the ways in which various factors, such as frontier life, immigrant status, or the demands of a slave-labor system, increased the significance of women's role in the household as a whole.

But what about those women who never married or who were widowed? How did they fit into this world of the household economy? While we are perhaps not inclined to think of nuns in this regard, one can argue that they stood at the head of the largest and most influential female-headed "households" in the state. Indeed, Mother Philippine Duchesne, as the head of the state's Ursuline order, has long appeared in state histories as a "notable woman." In their essay "City Sisters," Carol K. Coburn and Martha Smith detail the contributions of the Sisters of St. Joseph of Carondelet, and of nuns more generally, to Missouri history. The order could be seen as a household form writ large, but it was also a public household, serving as "mother" to the larger community. In this way it was also transitional, anticipating the process through which various aspects of the household and household responsibility became public. Nuns led the way in the nineteenth century as "public women" as they founded hospitals, schools, and social welfare institutions, performing work in public that corresponded to women's traditional "cultural" and "influential" work in the household economy.

Indeed, the nineteenth century represents a long period of transition from the rural household economy of the early nineteenth century to the urban, industrial structures of the twentieth century. This transition created unstable and shifting relationships between "public" power and "private" influence for the state's women. LeeAnn Whites's essay, "The Tale of Two Minors," explores the origins of women's rights activism in the state. Here we see public political power connected in unexpected ways to the "influence" women hold within the household. Through a close examination of the inner workings of the particular household of two of the state's earliest and most prominent women's rights advocates, Francis and Virginia Minor, Whites suggests that it was the very companionability of their household, the very extent of Virginia Minor's "influence" over her husband, Francis, that created the basis for their long and dedicated struggle for the public political and economic empowerment of women in the state.

The ways in which public and private, power and influence, shift over time in unexpected ways is also revealed in the history of Missouri in the middle 1800s. The Civil War in general and emancipation in particular served to open the door to expansion of a more urban, industrial society in Missouri. The growth of the waged work force and of urban areas further destabilized the household as the organizing rubric of the social order in the state. In her essay "The Changing Role of Protection on the Border," Rebekah Weber Bowen considers how the fighting of the war itself contributed to this destabilization of the household. Given Missouri's divided loyalties as a slaveholding state that remained within the Union, much of the fighting occurred on the level of the community and guerrilla actions. In these circumstances, women were frequently transformed into the protectors of their men and their families, as the men took to the bush and the women were left to head up the households. In the war's aftermath, Kimberly Schreck finds that historians have seriously overestimated the extent to which black women and children were able to acquire power and autonomy in relation to their previous owners. In her essay "Her Will against Theirs," she instead finds a persistence of the dependent status of black women that caught them within the framework of the old white slaveholding household much longer than we might imagine.

By the late nineteenth century and increasing dramatically into the twentieth century, a changing economy spurred growth in economic opportunities for women outside of the household. While waged work created a greater potential for economic independence and increased power, this potential was limited by the continued control of most economic resources by powerful men and by gender segregation in the workplace, which limited the types of work women could do and justified lower pay. Within the parts of the economy designated as "female," women could often gain the skills and resources to exert larger control in their communities. However, women who gained some forms of control of economic and cultural capital still had difficulty wielding this power because the larger systems of economic control were still dominated by men.

One early form of women's employment was prostitution. Rhonda Chalfant's study of prostitutes in a mid-Missouri railroad town, "Sedalia's Nymphs du Pave," suggests that some women used this economic opportunity to gain entrepreneurial skills and to control property. As owners of brothels, women became "businessmen." However, they could assert their power only so far. Although men could participate in and profit from the business of prostitution and keep their social status, respectability, and political power, women could not. While prostitutes manipulated the systems of law, business, and middle-class respectability, their access to broader community power and acceptance was limited by their association with being "public" women whose work and prominence challenged the ideals of middle-class Sedalians. In gender terms, they could not assert power as respectable "businessmen" and property owners, nor could they gain influence as middle-class women because they lacked the key element of women's ability to influence men—respectability.

The successful African American businesswomen of St. Louis described by De Anna J. Reese in "Domestic Drudges to Dazzling Divas," illustrate how women's entrepreneurial activities could support rather than challenge a community, particularly when that community is not empowered within the larger society. Annie Malone and Madam C. J. Walker found their economic opportunities through the beauty industry, a field that created new markets and served female consumers. While empowered more like men in terms of their public business acumen, their businesses and their markets were both deeply raced and deeply gendered. These women used their business savvy to build economic institutions that not only gave other African American women more economic opportunities, but also provided facilities and resources for the entire black community of St. Louis. Because of Jim Crow segregation and racial discrimination in employment, these businesses met crucial community needs, and these women became recognized and respected leaders.

While Sedalia's prostitutes and the successful African American entrepreneurs of St. Louis worked within the female-defined segment of the economy, other women attempted to move into economic or professional activities that were part of the male-defined economy and found different kinds of obstacles. The women farmers of Rebecca S. Montgomery's "We Are Practicable, Sensible Women" owned property and planned to manage these farms independently. Empowered as men were in terms of property ownership, they attempted to gain access to knowledge that would help them manage their farms according to the best new tenets of scientific agriculture. As they attempted to gain this knowledge, they found their access to it limited both by the gendered assumption that farmers were *male* and that women on farms were farmers' wives, not farmers, and by the active gender segregation of the newly emerging fields of agricultural education that separated agriculture as a business from home economics. Even with access to some means of privilege in male terms—land ownership—these women had to organize in order to attempt to break down these newly emerging gender barriers of professionalization.

Gregg Andrews's study of Euphemia Koller further illuminates the difficulties of property-owning women becoming fully independent and socially or politically powerful. In "Euphemia B. Koller and the Politics of Insanity in Ralls County, Missouri, 1921–1927," Andrews explores how Koller engaged in a long battle with the dominant corporation in a company town for control of land that she and her sister owned. Despite her legal skills and her economic and social status, the powerful economic interests could manipulate ideas of gender to make Koller's tenacity and willingness to use the legal system to assert her right to control her property seem like an "obsession" that disqualified her from retaining control of this property and ended in her confinement in a mental institution. In this case, a woman who had economic resources and knowledge of the law could be viewed as unreasonable and then insane because she fought to keep those resources by using that knowledge.

If increased economic opportunity provided one avenue to redefined contests over women's empowerment, women's organized political activism also increased their access to power, and it redefined the arenas in which women could exercise it. Virginia Laas's study of Emily Newell Blair, "Breaking into Politics," examines the ways women attempted to capitalize on their newly gained access to the franchise. Blair, a leader of Missouri's suffrage movement and of the Democratic party, attempted to leverage women's organizational strength in the state as voters, into greater power within the male-dominated political party system. Just as Montgomery's women farmers gained access to property but had to fight for access to scientific farming education, women gained a new route to power that had previously been defined as male-only—the vote—but this led to a struggle to gain power in a new arena, the male-dominated political party, where women met new barriers and found themselves negotiating for greater influence.

Like Blair, Fannie Cook, the subject of Bonnie Stepenoff's essay "The Doctor's Wife," was a political activist; however, she also was a novelist who used her art to exert a cultural influence that complimented her social vision of a just society. Writing and publishing was certainly not a new avenue of political influence for women (one need only think of Harriet Beecher Stowe's *Uncle Tom's Cabin,* published in 1852), but Cook's writing reveals a varied political agenda that was deeply engaged with the issues of her time, including equality for women, economic justice for workers, and opposition to racism and anti-Semitism. As the Depression deepened, her work shifted in focus from increased opportunities for middle-class women to issues of poverty and economic injustice and discrimination against African Americans, particularly regarding the sharecroppers' protests in Southeast Missouri. By World War II, her identity as a Jew became more prominent in her novels as she focused on the impact of anti-Semitism. Stepenoff shows the interconnections between political contexts and the issues Cook chose to address, and she suggests that women's "influence" and voice were deeply tied to the contexts in which they spoke and to the shifting political struggles of their times.

In this anthology, then, we discuss those moments in the history of the state in which women actually exercised formal political power, the kind of power recognized in existing histories of the state. We find that kind of power in both expected and unexpected historical moments and contexts. The historical moments in which women are most likely to break into the "traditional" narrative are covered in our history. We see this in the frontier, when men are frequently absent and the household is particularly empowered, when women's "influence' frequently slides into "power" as women take up the tasks of running their households, making the critical difference in survival, and doing "men's" work. We see these situations extending longer than we might have expected, beyond the initial colonial period, deep into the nineteenth century. Each new immigrant group in the state had to rely upon the resources of the individual household as their ethnic culture was tested by the challenges of a new settlement in a new society.

Another historical moment in which women are likely to move into positions of power is during wars. Again because men are called away, the door is opened to women's "formal" assumption of power. In Missouri, the Civil War constituted such a moment with a vengeance, because of the nature of guerrilla warfare, the continued importance of the household, and the slaveholding nature of many of those households.

The end of slavery marked the beginning of a new era, when women would increasingly enter into the arena of waged labor and public political influence in their own right. The opportunities of the market have much wider impact than the three pages on women's suffrage included in most state histories. Power seeped in unexpected ways through the social order— women as farmers, as prostitutes, as nuns, as entrepreneurs, as lawyers and politicians, as social reformers, and as novelists. But power also remained illusive, as new conditions also created new barriers.

In a variety of ways, in widely different historical periods and social and cultural contexts, these essays explore how Missouri's women have engaged and participated in formally organized systems of power, on the one hand, and exercised their own forms of power, that is, "influence," on the other. Part of the reason we do not see an equal inclusion of women in histories grounded in the principle of "power" is that women in the state, for various reasons, continue to exercise "influence." In these essays we attempt to include this role and to recognize that women's "influence" had, and has, an impact on the larger events of the state. We also analyze the relationship between power and influence in women's lives and in the development of the state and its history. It is precisely because women in the twenty-first century have more open access to formally constituted political power and personal autonomy that we increasingly acknowledge the importance and significance of their "influence"—their continued domestic contribution to their families. Indeed it seems no accident that the practice of dedicating volumes to wife and family by various historians of the state seems to peak in the years between the two women's movements. At that time women had acquired the formal political power of the vote and

some public visibility, but it was still prior to the Women's Liberation movement, when a critique of women's subordination in the household was
fully articulated and women's history became a part of the profession.

In this anthology we hope to accomplish two things. First, we hope to
move closer to the kind of general historical overview of women that we
already have for other social groups in the state. Second, we hope to increase the visibility of women's historical contributions by also problema-
tizing our understanding of the roles that both power and influence have
played in the history of the state and in the writing of this history. In doing
so, we hope this volume will not only make women more visible in the history of Missouri, but also reconceptualize the questions we ask about the
state in ways that make women's absence impossible.

French Women in Colonial Missouri, 1750–1805

Susan Calafate Boyle

Ste. Genevieve, a community on the west bank of the Mississippi River, about sixty miles south of St. Louis, was one of a number of French settlements in a region that extended from Quebec to Louisiana. During the eighteenth century, the territory on both sides of the Mississippi River, between the Ohio River and the Great Lakes, including present-day Missouri, was called the Illinois Country.[1] Like other communities in the Illinois Country, the population of Ste. Genevieve was highly mobile and included French, Spanish, Americans, blacks, and several Indian groups.

French settlement began in Ste. Genevieve in the middle of the eighteenth century, when *habitants* (resident farmers) trickled in from Kaskaskia, Cahokia, Post Vincennes, Prairie du Rocher, Nouvelle Chartres, and other communities in the vicinity, along with some from Canada, particularly the province of Quebec. Cession of the Mississippi's east bank to Britain in

---

This article was published in slightly different form in *William and Mary Quarterly,* 3d ser., 44, no. 4 (October 1987): 775–89.

1. William E. Foley, *The Genesis of Missouri: From Wilderness Outpost to Statehood* (Columbia: University of Missouri Press, 1989), 1. Originally, the term *Illinois Country* designated the territory occupied by the Illinois Indians, but by the eighteenth century, it consisted of the territory claimed by the French from the mouth of the Ohio River to the Great Lakes, including the valleys of the Mississippi, Missouri, and Ohio rivers. See Carl J. Ekberg, *Colonial Ste. Genevieve: An Adventure on the Mississippi Frontier* (Gerald, Mo.: Patrice Press, 1985), 2; and Carl J. Ekberg, *French Roots in the Illinois Country: The Mississippi Frontier in Colonial Times* (Urbana: University of Illinois Press, 1998), 1–2.

1763 prompted French settlers to cross the river, as did the advance of Americans into the region after the Revolutionary War. Then, from 1766 on, the river's west bank was Spanish territory, but Spanish rule was only lightly felt.

During the eighteenth century, Ste. Genevieve remained small and predominantly male. It expanded from 23 settlers, according to the 1752 census, to 1,170 in 1800. In 1803 a French visitor, M. Perrin du Lac, reported that it had reached a population of about 1,300, including blacks and a number of white Americans.[2]

Travelers in the Illinois Country noted that French women, whom one described as "by no means prone to consider themselves in the light of goods and chattels of their liege-lords," tended to assume greater responsibilities than we might expect. In 1811 Henry Marie Brackenridge revisited the town where he had spent three years of his childhood. A man of letters, a lawyer, a diplomat, and a perceptive observer, he remarked that the women of Ste. Genevieve "will not be considered secondary personages in the matrimonial association. The advice of the wife is taken on all important, as well as on less weighty concerns, and she generally decides."[3]

A year later, Amos Stoddard, the first U.S. civil commandant of the area, offered a strikingly similar assessment:

> The women have more influence over their husbands than is common in most other countries. Perhaps this arises in part from the example of the parent state; in part from the respect, which the men entertain for their wives; and perhaps still more from the almost ex-

2. M. Perrin du Lac quoted in Edmund Flagg, *The Far West; or, A Tour beyond the Mountains* . . . , in Reuben Gold Thwaites, ed., *Early Western Travels, 1748–1846* . . . , (Cleveland, 1906), 27:53–54. Nine censuses survive for eighteenth-century Ste. Genevieve: 1752 (Loudon Papers at the Huntington Library, San Marino, California); 1766 (Archivo General de Indias, Audiencia de Santo Domingo, legajo 2595 [87–1–5]) (photocopy at the Library of Congress); 1772, 1787, 1795, 1796, and 1800 (Missouri Historical Society, St. Louis); and 1791 (published by Louis Houck in *The Spanish Regime in Missouri* [Chicago, 1909], 2:365–70). Additional information on population growth and on the 1770 census comes from A. P. Nasatir, "The Anglo-Spanish Frontier in the Illinois Country during the American Revolution, 1779–1783," *Journal of the Illinois State Historical Society* 22 (1928): 291–358; A. P. Nasatir, "The Anglo-Spanish Frontier on the Upper Mississippi, 1786–1796," *Iowa Journal of History and Politics* 29 (1931): 155–232; and M. Perrin du Lac, *Voyage dans les deux Louisianes et chez les nations sauvages du Missouri* . . . (Paris: Capelle et Renand, 1805), 36.

3. Henry Marie Brackenridge, *Views of Louisiana: Together with a Journal of a Voyage up the Missouri River, in 1811* (1814; reprint, Chicago: Quandrangle Books, 1962), 135.

clusive right, which the women have to the property, in consequences
of marriage contracts. . . . Even in most instances of purchases and
sales, the women are consulted; and they not unfrequently assume the
management of property.[4]

Few studies have focused on Missouri women during the French colonial period, but general histories of the area tend to support these travelers'
observations.[5] This study tests their validity and explores how demographic, legal, and economic factors interacted in Ste. Genevieve to allow
French women a stronger role in decisions affecting themselves, their families, and their community.

Since the French in the Illinois Country left virtually no surviving diaries,
reminiscences, or personal correspondence that might provide intimate
glimpses of their activities or attitudes, this analysis is based on official
records—marriage contracts, wills, estate records, land sales and transfers,
petitions, and legal proceedings. Although these documents are not numerous, they include all the known surviving official papers of the community
of Ste. Genevieve. A few travelers' accounts round out the body of evidence.[6] These records are the main source to study women of French descent,
principally wives and widows. While this study focuses on Ste. Genevieve,
it is likely that conditions in other communities in the Illinois Country
were substantially similar.[7]

4. Amos Stoddard, *Sketches, Historical and Descriptive, of Louisiana* (Philadelphia:
A. Carey, 1812), 323, 328.

5. Foley, *Genesis of Missouri*, 107–77; Katharine T. Corbett, *In Her Place: A Guide to
St. Louis Women's History* (St. Louis: Missouri Historical Society Press, 1999), 3–19.

6. This study is mostly based on the Ste. Genevieve, Missouri, Archives, 1756–1930,
microfilm collection C3636, in Joint Collection, Western Historical Manuscript
Collection–Columbia, State Historical Society of Missouri, University of Missouri–
Columbia, folders 1–1474 (hereinafter cited as SGA). Additional information comes
from the Kaskaskia Manuscripts, Randolph County Clerk's Office, Chester, Illinois.
Other valuable papers are at the Missouri Historical Society in St. Louis (MHS), in-
cluding the Schaaf, Siegler, and Guibourd collections. Visitors' accounts include Henry
Marie Brackenridge, *Recollections of Persons and Places in the West* (1834; reprint,
Philadelphia: J. B. Lippincott, 1868); Timothy Flint, *Recollections of the Last Ten Years
passed in occasional residences and journeyings in the valley of the Mississippi . . .*
(1826; reprint, New York: Da Capo Press, 1968); Thomas Ford, *A History of Illinois . . .*
(New York: Ivison and Phinney, 1854); Benjamin Henry Boneval Latrobe, *Impressions
Respecting New Orleans: Diary and Sketches, 1818–1820,* ed. Samuel Wilson Jr. (New
York: Columbia University Press, 1951); and Christian Schultz Jr., *Travels on an Inland
Voyage,* 2 vols. (New York: Isaac Riley, 1810).

7. This is V. Baker's conclusion in "Cherchez les Femmes: Some Glimpses of Women in
Early Eighteenth-Century Louisiana," *Louisiana History* 31, no. 1 (winter 1990): 21–37.

Throughout the eighteenth century, males outnumbered females in Ste. Genevieve by a considerable margin, the number of white women in the population rising from 25 in 1752 to 430 in 1800. The census of 1766 showed that even though the proportion of females was low (30 percent), the imbalance would prove temporary, since over half (54 percent) of the individuals aged fourteen and older were females. Among those younger than fourteen, however, males were heavily preponderant (68 percent). The census of 1779 revealed a similar pattern, listing 178 adult males fourteen or older for 90 adult females of the same age range. The more detailed 1787 census recorded slight changes. The percentage of females increased to 34 (and for the first time females are listed as heads of households), but the gap between males and females of marriageable age widened even more. There were 111 men aged eighteen years or older for 21 women aged fourteen years or older. Comparing the 1766 and 1787 censuses also shows a decline in the proportion of adult women, from 42.2 percent in 1766 to 37.9 percent in 1787.[8]

Sexual imbalance resulted in a considerable discrepancy in the ages of the marriage partners. In 1787, sixty-one of eighty households were headed by married couples. In fifty-three of these, the husband was older than the wife, the average difference being 10.1 years. Thirty-three husbands were at least eight years older than their wives, and thirteen were more than sixteen years older. These circumstances were not limited to 1787. Analysis of age at first marriage for all couples who drew contracts between 1754 and 1805 reveals that the average bride was almost nine years younger than her husband (18.8 years of age for women versus 27.8 years of age for men). Brides were as young as fourteen years of age, but the majority of women (83.7 percent) got married between the ages of fifteen and twenty-one. Men began to wed at eighteen; however, the age at first marriage for most men (86.7 percent) ranged much more widely, from twenty to thirty-six.[9]

Dramatic sexual imbalance combined with wide age discrepancy between many spouses understandably produced a large number of widows and a higher rate of second and third marriages for women than for men. Almost 20 percent of the brides who drew marriage contracts were widows, but fewer than 10 percent of the grooms were widowers. Some wives who were very young when their husbands died enjoyed considerable influence and independence for many years of their lives. Examination of the

8. The 1766 census does not give the age of individuals for each household.
9. For marriage contracts, see SGA, 356–75, 453.

notarial register, which was maintained from 1766 to 1805 and lists many of the community's legal transactions, reveals a high rate of participation by widows. Of the seventy-five women noted, fifty-six were widows and six were legally separated. Although close to 25 percent of these women remarried, they continued to be active in social and economic affairs.[10]

The presence of a small but influential group of mature females characterized eighteenth-century Ste. Genevieve. Maturity was the distinctive feature of the wives and widows who initiated legal proceedings, the average age of such women being close to forty. It is doubtful that the very young Ste. Genevieve brides could have had much influence in the early years of marriage. The evidence suggests that newly married women kept a low profile; unless acting jointly with their husbands, they seldom participated in significant socioeconomic activities. Their days were devoted to child rearing and learning to manage their households. With time, however, they became involved in more varied transactions, acquired experience and greater responsibility, and improved their status vis-à-vis their husbands.

Demographic factors do not totally explain the circumstances of women in the Illinois Country. Equally influential were elements of the French legal system that survived there throughout the eighteenth century. The French colonies in North America were governed according to laws compiled in the *coutume de Paris* (Custom of Paris), which adopted the form of property devolution traditionally used in the western regions of France: equality among all heirs regardless of sex. According to students of French inheritance laws, the system contributed to high rates of celibacy and late marriage because it delayed the final division of parents' property. At the same time, by giving all the children a share of the patrimony, it encouraged them to remain close to the paternal home. Especially in times of high mortality, this system of *lignage* (descent) served as an important element in organizing the relationship between generations by providing guidelines for property transfer and by ensuring some measure of financial security for descendants. In Ste. Genevieve this became crucial.[11]

10. For the Ste. Genevieve notarial register, see SGA, 448–52.

11. Jean Yver, "Les caractères originaux du groupe de Coutumes de l'Ouest de la France," *Revue historique de droit français et étranger*, 4th ser., 30 (1952): 18–79. Yves F. Zoltvany, "Esquisse de la coutume de Paris," *Revue d'histoire de l'Amérique française* 25 (1971): 365–84, provides an analysis of the effects of the Custom of Paris on French society. The only work that discusses legal practices in the middle Mississippi Valley is Hans W. Baade, "Marriage Contracts in French and Spanish Louisiana: A Study in 'Notarial' Jurisprudence," *Tulane Law Review* 53 (1979): 3–92. For more on French inheritance practices, see Lutz K. Berkner and Franklin F. Mendels, "Inheritance Systems, Family Structure, and Demographic Patterns in Western Europe, 1700–

Marriage contracts, *partages* (divisions of estates), and wills record the system of property transfer used in the Illinois Country. Marriage contracts are the most important. One hundred and fifty survive. When these are checked against the parish register, which contains the most complete list of marriages for the overwhelmingly Catholic community of Ste. Genevieve, we find that for the whole period 1752–1804, 63 percent of couples who married in the parish church drew marriage contracts, with fluctuations as follows: 1760s, 47 percent; 1770s, 88 percent; 1780s, 58 percent; 1790s, 61 percent. Most of the long-standing French families in Ste. Genevieve, regardless of their economic position, drew such documents, even for illegitimate daughters. Couples of mixed ethnic background, particularly when the wife was an Indian, were less likely to resort to this formality. Contracts were also rare among those who had not lived long in the community.[12]

Contracts followed the French tradition of community property to which both husband and wife made contributions, mostly their *propres*—the property inherited from parents or other relatives. Drawn up at the moment of marriage, these contracts regulated the distribution of property at the marriage's dissolution. The system granted each spouse half of the estate upon the death of the other, with the remaining half to be divided equally among the couple's children. If they had no offspring, the survivor was entitled to enjoy the couple's property for life. In addition, the wife was entitled to a *douaire* (dower), a sum of money stipulated in the contract that she would receive when her husband died.

Ste. Genevieve contracts show concern about protecting the property of the descent line and in so doing safeguarded the bride's property from mismanagement by her husband. In eight instances a distinction was made be-

---

1900," in Charles Tilly, ed., *Historical Studies of Changing Fertility* (Princeton: Princeton University Press, 1978), 209–23; Robert Wheaton, "Affinity and Descent in Seventeenth-Century Bordeaux," in Robert Wheaton and Tamara K. Hareven, eds., *Family and Sexuality in French History* (Philadelphia: University of Pennsylvania Press, 1980), 111–34; and Jack Godoy, "Inheritance, Property, and Women: Some Comparative Considerations," in Jack Godoy, Joan Thirsk, and E. P. Thompson, eds., *Family and Inheritance: Rural Society in Western Europe, 1200–1800* (Cambridge: Cambridge University Press, 1976), 10–36.

12. Hubert Charbonneau, *Vie et mort de nos ancêtres: Étude démographique* (Montreal: Université de Montréal, 1975), 151–52, found almost the same rates for seventeenth-century Canada. Marriage contracts are invaluable for any analysis of French society. See Peter N. Moogk, "Rank in New France: Reconstructing a Society from Notarial Documents," *Histoire sociale–Social History* 8 (1975): 34–53; and Paul Lachance, "Economic Rank, Occupational Status, Ethnicity, and Marital Choice in New Orleans, 1804–1819" (paper presented at the Social Science History Conference, Washington, D.C., October 1983).

tween the property that would remain hers or her relatives' and that which was to become part of the couple's communal assets. Was this an attempt to protect the property of these women from the vagaries of the local economy, or did it reflect fear of mismanagement of their estates by their husbands? Only for women who had been previously married do contracts systematically identify the value of the property brought into the spousal community—usually their share of the community of the first marriage. The *douaire* and the *preciput* (another sum listed in the marriage contract that normally went to the surviving spouse) from the bride's first marriage were sometimes excluded from the community of the second one. In some cases, grooms provided their wives-to-be with additional shares.[13]

A wife had the option of renouncing the community property if, upon the death of her husband, their estate was burdened with debts. In such cases the widow received her *douaire,* her *propres,* her personal effects, and the *preciput,* while creditors vied for the remaining assets. In cases of separation, the wife could also renounce the community property. Thus a wife's property was protected from a husband's rapacity or fecklessness. The system provided women with financial security, while at the same time it tended to discourage risky economic activities.[14]

Commentators on French customary law believe that the right to renounce the community property was a privilege accorded women as a counterbalance to the limitations that marriage placed on them. Having little say in the success of her family's economic enterprise, a woman in France was free to disclaim its failures. This privilege was also maintained in the Illinois Country, although in Ste. Genevieve the contribution of the wife to the welfare of her family was more significant than in France.[15]

Partages also shed light on inheritance practices. Of almost four hundred surviving sets of estate records for the 1752–1830 period, twenty-five

13. Moogk, "Rank in New France"; SGA, 356–75, 453. Wealthy French families were particularly careful to itemize property. See marriage contracts of Joseph Decelle Duclos and Marianne Placet, 1781, SGA, 362; Joseph Loisel and Louise Marguerite Levasseur, 1782, SGA, 365; Charles Normand and Catherine Billeron, 1777, SGA, 368; Nicolas Paquin and Marie Descoux, 1783, SGA, 368; and Louis Lacroix and Françoise Lebeau, 1781, SGA, 365.

14. See the estate of Marie Magdeleine Ridre Robinet, 1770–1780, SGA, 267, 347–48; and Schaaf Collection, MHS; separation proceedings of Jean Baptiste Hubardeau and Marguerite Mellon, 1756, Kaskaskia Manuscripts, 56:5:22:1; Charles Valle and Pelagie Carpentier, 1783, SGA, 372, 399; Charles Chauvin Charleville and Marie Louise Despins, 1787–1788, SGA, 128, and Marie Josephe Deguire Tirat *dit* St. Jean, 1779, SGA, 285.

15. Barbara B. Diefendorf, "Widowhood and Remarriage in Sixteenth-Century Paris," *Journal of Family History* 7 (1982): 379–95.

contain such divisions, pertaining mostly to estates of medium to above-average size. Legal expenses probably discouraged the less well-to-do from taking such formal measures. The poor are apt to have relied on a different, extralegal system to hand down property to their children. It is unlikely that men or women who owned only one arpent (about 0.85 of an acre) of land, a cow, and a few tools would have resorted to the same inheritance strategy as the more affluent.

Numerous other estate documents, dealing with such matters as appointments of guardians, repartitions among debtors, and separations, offer direct and indirect evidence that confirms the existence of a single system of property division—division by halves and equality among heirs. First, the share of the surviving spouse was established. The *preciput* and the *douaire*, if the survivor was the wife, were deducted from the total assets of the estate. The remainder was halved, with one half going to the surviving spouse and the other half to the offspring. Divisions reveal that all children received similar portions of the various kinds of property the family held—slaves, land, stock, tools, furniture. There was no discrimination against female offspring.

Wills were rare in the Illinois Country; only forty-five survive for the period examined. Such low numbers are understandable in that the *coutume* did not require that heirs be named or their shares specified. Twenty-three testators were single men or widowers who bestowed their property on surviving kin. Testaments from five widows followed the same pattern. Wills drawn jointly by couples, of which there were seven between 1752 and 1830, granted the surviving partner the entire estate regardless of sex and without any reservations. Also during this time, the ten documents drawn by married men placed the wife in complete charge of the couple's property until the children came of age. When that time came, the widow got at least half of the property and in some cases an additional share, while the remainder was equally divided among the children. Even if she remarried, a widow did not lose her half of the community property, and in no case was she deprived of her dower. The evidence indicates that the customary law was followed in Ste. Genevieve. Only one will, that of François Leclerc, shows disregard for the provisions of the *coutume*. He not only made his wife his sole heir and administrative executor, but also established that when his two sons came of age, she was to give each only 1,500 livres, a very small share of the couple's property, which was assessed at over 50,000 livres.[16]

16. For wills, see SGA, 297–301. See also will of François Leclerc, 1789, SGA, 299, and his estate in 1792, SGA, 226. Americans who settled in the area did not follow the

Residents of Ste. Genevieve maintained the basic aim of French law—to protect the property right of the descent line—and in so doing protected the property rights of all family members, including females. But it was the peculiar nature of the socioeconomic system that evolved in the region that allowed women to "not infrequently assume the management of property."[17]

Despite encouragement by French and Spanish authorities, few *habitants* of either sex became full-time farmers. The people of Ste. Genevieve produced more food than they consumed and exported the surplus, but the surplus owed less to their efforts than to the extraordinary fertility of the soil. Anglo-Americans and even some French visitors called them indolent; they took eight or ten days for planting and then did nothing else until harvest time, leaving the crops untended, the weeds uncut.[18] In addition, the women of Ste. Genevieve may have appeared idle because they seldom engaged in such typically female activities as sewing, spinning, weaving, knitting, and embroidering. The inventories of more than three hundred families list few of the tools—spinning wheels, looms, knitting needles—that made such endeavors possible; both French and American travelers noted the absence of home industries.[19]

Frenchmen in the Illinois Country did not want to depend on the slow profits derived from agriculture; most hoped for the quicker gains to be made from other activities, especially production of salt and lead, and the fur trade. They made large profits by bringing manufactured necessities and other commodities from New Orleans and other major ports for sale to settlers and nearby Indian tribes. Their type of business required sizable investments of capital or at least substantial credit, and it entailed considerable risk. In addition to the funds tied up in the procurement of furs and

French practices. In a 1786 will, William Scott left his property to his wife, Mary, but stipulated that should she remarry the estate would revert to his nephews and nieces (SGA, 298).

17. Stoddard, *Sketches of Louisiana,* 323.

18. Nasatir, "Anglo-Spanish Frontier," *Journal of the Illinois State Historical Society* 21 (1928): 291–358; Brackenridge, *Views of Louisiana,* 20–26; Ford, *History of Illinois,* 37–39; John Bradbury, *Travels in the Interior of America, 1809–1811,* in Reuben Gold Thwaites, ed., *Early Western Travels* (Cleveland: A. H. Clark, 1904), 4:257–61.

19. Travelers and historians of the Mississippi Valley agree that domestic industries were nonexistent. See Brackenridge, *Views of Louisiana,* 134, 136–37; and Clarence W. Alvord, *The Illinois Country, 1673–1818* (Springfield: Illinois Centennial Commission, 1920; reprint, Urbana: University of Illinois Press, 1987), 217. For the contents of inventories, see SGA, 108–296. French authorities had imposed a ban on home weaving; see Natalia Belting, *Kaskaskia under the French Regime* (Urbana: University of Illinois Press, 1948), 47.

in the production of salt and lead, it was necessary to outfit convoys going up and down the Mississippi River and to pay for large amounts of merchandise. The trips were long, and the weather limited the time when shipments could be made. Boats often capsized or were seized by Indians or "pirates." Goods could be lost, spoiled by the humidity or for lack of proper care, or eaten by rats. Many in Ste. Genevieve still found the risks worthwhile. Their serious commitment to such commerce is evidenced by the huge sums of money that were tied up in numerous notes and obligations, and the large quantities of merchandise stored in many of their homes.[20]

Enterprising *habitants* understood that diversification was crucial to their success, for it allowed them to cushion their wealth against the volatile circumstances resulting from changing colonial administrations and also inherent in the economic system in which they were involved. And diversify they did. They were fur traders, merchants, miners, and farmers. They acted as bankers, middlemen, retailers, and outfitters. They traded directly and indirectly, legally and illegally, with Indians, Spaniards, French, English, and Americans. Their economic dealings tied them not only to communities across the river, such as Kaskaskia, Cahokia, and Prairie du Rocher, but also to St. Louis, Post Vincennes, Detroit, Quebec, New Orleans, and even Philadelphia, New York, Puerto Rico, and the West Indies.

Such system required well-to-do men to spend considerable time away from home, exchanging merchandise, ensuring that operations ran smoothly, maintaining business connections, and tending to legal affairs. Records in St. Louis and New Orleans, as well as those of Ste. Genevieve and Kaskaskia, document their frequent trips. Louis Bolduc, for example, made at least four trips to New Orleans between 1775 and 1781, each for more than four months. Less-wealthy men, like Jean Jaulin, were also away from

---

20. A similar conclusion has been reached in examining conditions in the lower Mississippi Valley; see Daniel H. Usner Jr., *Indians, Settlers, and Slaves in a Frontier Exchange Economy: The Lower Mississippi Valley before 1783* (Chapel Hill: University of North Carolina Press, 1992), 147–48, 274–86. See also estates of Matthew Kennedy, 1772, SGA, 197; Jean Baptiste Labastille, 1770–1776, SGA, 189–200; Mathieu Laffite, 1780–1781, SGA, 212; and Silvestre Cantrel *dit* Filibustier, 1776–1779, SGA, 137. Numerous paper notes listed in inventories document the widespread geographic connections of many in Ste. Genevieve. For specific references to their travels, see litigations procedures, SGA, 302–55. See also the estates of Jean Datchurut, 1789–1790, SGA, 156–57; Jean Baptiste Deguire, 1781, SGA, 160–61; Jean Baptiste Laffont, 1789–1790, SGA, 213; and Louis Lambert *dit* Lafleur, SGA, 217. See also Frederic L. Billon, *Annals of St. Louis in Its Early Days under the French and Spanish Dominations, 1764–1804* (1886; reprint, New York: Arno Press and New York Times, 1971), 110–13; François Milhomme, 1783, SGA, 239; and François Leclerc, 1792, SGA, 226.

their families for long periods, for they were the *voyageurs*—the hunters, the overseers, the boatmen, the soldiers—who made the entire system function.[21]

What was the impact on women's lives? The prolonged absences of their menfolk gave wives additional power and ample opportunity to function as deputy husbands, protecting their own interests and those of their families. Some women undertook further responsibilities when the men in their family were absent. Marie Descoux not only was in charge of the farm chores of her own household, but also handled those of her son-in-law, Louis Gelie. Others, like Anne Normand Gadobert, Catherine Bardon Chamard, and Isabel Rodríguez Peyroux, empowered as proxies, shrewdly fended off creditors while managing their families' businesses. Quick, decisive action was often required. Thus Ann Normand Gadobert requested legal authority to place a lien on the property of a nonresident trader, one of her husband's debtors. She realized that unless she acted promptly, her chance of recovering what was owed would diminish because the trader was not likely to stay long in Ste. Genevieve. Madame Larochelle initiated a similar procedure against a *voyageur* indebted to her family. And while her husband was away, Marie Magdeleine Tirat made an agreement with Louis Boucher to repair a fence and build an enclosure, and she quickly initiated legal action against Boucher when she realized the job would not get done.[22]

Legal actions by Ste. Genevieve wives show awareness of the rights to which they were entitled under the French legal system. They understood that a wife's economic contribution to the couple's community property was essential and had to be protected, so they kept themselves informed of their families' finances. Marie Veronneau, Marie Louise Lalande, Charlotte Jassin, Louise Perthuis, Marieanne Billeron, Cecile Choquet, Marie Louise Valle, Françoise Phillipeaux, Françoise Lebeau, and others accurately listed the outstanding credits and liabilities of their estates upon termination of their marriages by either separation or husband's death. The case of Marie Magdeleine Ridre is the exception that proves the rule. Her husband apparently

21. For Bolduc's travels, see SGA, 1818, 310–12.

22. Laurel T. Ulrich used the term "deputy husband" in *Good Wives: Image and Reality in the Lives of Women in Northern New England, 1650–1750* (New York, 1982), 9. See estates of Louis Chamard, 1771–1780, SGA, 142, 392; Pierre Gadobert, 1772–1778, SGA, 326, 395; litigation proceedings of Marie Descoux against Louis Gelie, 1798, SGA, 341; Isabel Rodríguez Peyroux against John Coffee, 1800, SGA, 314; Anne Normand against Catalan, 1769, SGA, 449; Madame Larochelle against Simon, 1778, SGA, 450; and Marie Magdeleine Tirat against Louis Boucher, 1779, SGA, 310.

kept her in ignorance, for she declared that she did "not follow the affairs of her husband" and had "nothing to do with his debts." But when she realized that he was mismanaging their holdings, she filed for legal separation and then joined a proceeding against her former spouse to obtain her share of the community property before creditors could collect their due. The separation procedure of Pelagie Carpentier and Charles Valle reveals that even when couples were at odds, wives managed to keep up with their husbands' transactions.[23]

Examination of economic activities suggests that coverture, the control of women's legal activities by their husbands, was not strictly enforced. Was this the result of the men's extensive traveling or of women's financial independence? It is clear that wives were often involved in transactions seldom associated with their marital status. They participated in public sales, bid on property, and made substantial purchases. They were listed as co-owners in land exchanges and sometimes canceled land purchases their husbands had made. Like Helen Blouin, they petitioned the court to enforce payment of debts owed to their spouses. Like Catherine Bardon, they spoke and acted on behalf of their husbands and testified in court. Like Anne Normand, they held powers of attorney authorizing them to manage and sell their property. Like Isabel Rodríguez, they developed a sound understanding of their husbands' trade, in this case the production and distribution of salt. Like Marie Louise Despins, they delayed payments to creditors when their husbands were unable or unwilling to take care of affairs. Like Marie Magdeleine Ridre, they ran successful businesses.[24] While

23. Estates of Marie Veronneau–Antoine Aubuchon, 1803, SGA, 110; Marie Louise Lalande–Louis Boucher, 1781, SGA, 138; Charlotte Jassin–Antoine Hunau, 1773, SGA, 192; Louise Perthuis–François Lalumandiere, 1784, SGA, 216; Marieanne Billeron–François Diel, 1784, SGA, 494; Cecile Chouquet–François Thomure dit Lasource, 1783, SGA, 694; Marie Louise Valle–François Leclerc, 1792, SGA, 226; François Dorlac–Françoise Phillipeaux, 1772–1789, SGA, 167–70; Louis Lacroix–Françoise Lebeau, 1781, SGA, 208–9; separation proceedings of Louis Robinet and Marie Magdeleine Ridre, 1770–1780, SGA, 267, 347–48; Charles Valle and Pelagie Carpentier, 1783, SGA, 372, 399.

24. Wives commonly made purchases at public auctions. See SGA, 102–5, 108–296; the notarial register, SGA, 448–52; and the land sales, SGA, 86–96. See also sale by Angelique Lafleur Perodot to Joseph Tellier, 1783, SGA, 93. Marie Jeanne Perthuis canceled a purchase of land arranged by her husband, 1777, SGA, 56. See the legal proceedings of Helene Blouin against Daniel McElduff, 1789, SGA, 308; proceedings of creditors against L. Chamard, 1771–1780, SGA, 142, 392; proceedings against Pierre Gadobert, 1772–1774, SGA, 326, 395; proceedings of Isabel Rodríguez Peyroux against John Coffee, 1800, SGA, 314, and against John and Andrew Price, 1798–1800, SGA, 342, 345; and proceedings of Hugh Howard against Charles C. Charleville,

managing their households, wives at all socioeconomic levels gained the practical experience they would need if their husbands should die.

This apprenticeship, as it might be called, was the result of local circumstances, but it also accorded with French tradition. Barbara Diefendorf has pointed out that widows in sixteen-century Paris assumed important responsibilities for the administration of their deceased husbands' affairs. The experience qualifying women to take on these duties, she argues, could only have been acquired after years of informal participation in, or even supervision of, their family's economic activities. This also happened among the French in America. Canadian studies show that in New France, as in the Mississippi Valley settlements, wives and widows exercised considerable power and came to be excellent administrators of their families' rural and commercial property.[25]

It was not uncommon for married women in the Illinois Country to undertake economic activities that went beyond laundering, mending clothes, and providing room and board to the bachelors who crowded the area. Isabelle Bisette Vachard, wife of Louis Vachard *dit* Lardoise, exemplified this spirit of enterprise. She brought from her home in St. Louis to the saltworks near Ste. Genevieve a boat laden with articles of clothing and dry goods, which she traded to slaves and other workers for salt, cornmeal, and grain. The St. Louis authorities curtailed her activities when the owners of the saltworks complained that her trading caused the slaves to steal from their masters and, in one instance, to run off to avoid punishment.

1788, SGA, 229. Marie Magdeleine Ridre was an established merchant in her own right, SGA, 267, 347–48. See also evidence from the estate of Marie Fouillard, 1773, SGA, 250.

25. Barbara Diefendorf, "Widowhood and Remarriage," *Journal of Family History* 7 (1982): 379–95. See also, for example, Liliane Plamondon, "Une femme d'affaires en Nouvelle-France: Marie-Anne Barbel, veuve Fornel," *Revue d'histoire de l'Amerique française* 31 (1977): 165–85; Jan Noël, "Les femmes favorisées: Women in New France," *Atlantis* 6 (1981): 80–98; Micheline Dumont, "Les femmes de la Nouvelle-France étaient-elles favorisées?" *Atlantis* 8 (1982): 118–24; Marie Lavigne and Yolande Pinard, *Les femmes dans la société québécoise: Aspects historiques* (Montreal, 1977), 5–19; Louise Dechene, *Habitants et marchands de Montréal au XVIIe siècle* (Paris: Plon, 1974), 434–39; Isabel Foulché-Delbosc, "Women of New France (Three Rivers: 1651–63)," *Canadian Historical Review* 21 (1940): 132–49; Vaughan Baker, Amos Simpson, and Mathé Alain, "Le mari est seigneur: Marital Laws Governing Women in French Louisiana," in Edward F. Haas, ed., *Louisiana's Legal Heritage* (Pensacola, Fla.: Perdido Bay Press, 1983), 7–17; and Winstanley Briggs, "The Enhanced Status of Women in French Colonial Illinois," in Clarence A. Glasrud, ed., *The Quiet Heritage/Le Heritage Tranquil* (Moorhead, Minn.: Concordia College, 1987).

Other women, like Marianne Richelet, unintimidated by the ruling, continued to make trading voyages to Ste. Genevieve and Kaskaskia.[26]

According to Diefendorf, sixteenth-century attempts to limit widows' freedom to dispose of their properties underscore the significant autonomy that widows possessed in French society. Such autonomy existed in Ste. Genevieve, where widows were always appointed guardians of their children, where they lent and borrowed money, and where they bought and sold slaves. They traded real estate with special zeal, owned or had shares in mills or boats, and leased and rented property. Some of them were guarantors for the purchases of other widows, like Marie Descoux, who guaranteed the purchase of a mill by Marie Louise Gauvreau, a possible indication of a form of women's network. Others became executors of estates, their husbands' or even those of other men, as in the instance of Marie Louise Valle, who administered the estate of Louis Largeau. Some, like Madame Manuel, were in charge of the property of *voyageurs,* and others managed the affairs of absent male tenants.[27]

Widows shared their late husbands' understanding that economic success required a diversified economic base. The numerous requests for extensive concessions of land made by Marie Louise Valle, widow Leclerc, show awareness of the lucrative potential of lead mining and the increasing profitability of raising cattle. Nor was she an exception. Other wealthy widows, such as Madame Robinet and Madame Lacroix, farmed, mined, milled, and traded. Some went into partnerships like that of Marie Louise Gauvreau with her brother-in-law Louis Lacroix. In most instances, widows continued the same type of business that their husbands had operated, an indication that during their spouses' lives French wives likely helped to manage their families' affairs.[28] This was even more necessary for women in the Illinois Country than in France owing to the frequent absence of men.

26. Billon, *Annals of St. Louis,* 227–29.

27. Diefendorf, "Widowhood and Remarriage," 394. In Ste. Genevieve, women always were entrusted with the guardianship of their children, except when the mother was seriously ill. See estate of Jean Baptiste Lacroix–Marie Louise Gauvreau, 1781, SGA, 206–7; proceedings of Walter Fenwick against Louis Largeau, 1805, SGA, 515; and proceedings of James Cooper against Thomas Bedford, 1803, SGA, 315.

28. The following is a partial listing of widow Leclerc's land transactions: 1792, SGA, 56; 1795, SGA, 57; 1798, SGA, 44; 1800, SGA, 96; 1801, SGA, 95; 1799; *American State Papers: Documents, Legislative and Executive of the Congress of the United States,* 38 vols. (Washington, D.C.: U.S. Government Printing Office, 1832–1861), *Class VIII: Public Lands,* 6:770–71. The estate of Marie Fouillard (1773, SGA, 250) documents some of the trading activities of Marie Magdeleine Ridre; the estate of Jean Baptiste Lacroix (1781, SGA, 206–7) and sale transactions (1793, SGA, 55) show the

Possession of wealth underscores variations in the experience of women in Ste. Genevieve. Widows from the most affluent families were the ones who became active in the local economy. Wealthy wives and widows were also more likely to file grievances before the legal authorities, as widow Tessier successfully did in 1773, when she requested and secured an additional share of the estate of her father-in-law. Less-affluent women recognized that lack of money shrank their options. Marie Joseph Deguire, the illegitimate daughter of Jean Baptiste Deguire and an Indian woman, pleaded that unless she were given her share of her father's estate, she would be forced to marry for the third time since she was unable to provide adequately for her children. Her preference for widowhood is understandable, for widows had greater freedom and fuller control of their daily lives than did married women.[29]

Wealthy women were also more aware of their rights and less hesitant to petition the authorities concerning their grievances. The case of Jeanne Saucier, the wife of Antoine Duclos, is a good example. Virtually at the mercy of their numerous creditors, Saucier begged the local authorities to stop them from seizing the couple's property lest she be unable to take of her young children. As a result, only two slaves owned by the couple were sold to satisfy a portion of their debts.[30]

Even the rights of black women were sometimes upheld. Elizabeth Datchurut, for twenty-six years the common-law spouse of Antoine Aubuchon and the mother of his ten illegitimate children, upon his death successfully claimed a portion of his personal property and of his crops.[31]

French women in Ste. Genevieve and the Illinois Country as a whole benefited from the special demographic circumstances that characterized the settlement and early development of the area. The legal system, particularly inheritance practices, provided wives appreciable economic independence by protecting their property. The economic system encouraged women at all social levels to act on their interests and to become well

---

various enterprises in which Marie Louise Gauvreau became involved. Other active widows were Marie Louise Lalande, 1784, SGA, 31; 1796, SGA, 56; Cecile Choquet, 1783, SGA, 40; Elizabeth Villier, 1797, SGA, 44; Marguerite Prudhomme, 1779, SGA, 72; Marieanne Billeron, 1792, SGA, 56; 1795, SGA, 52; 1803, SGA, 97; Marie Tirat, 1804, SGA, 55; Catherine Lalumandiere, 1803, SGA, 63; Marie Campos, 1787, SGA, 65; Marie Carpentier, 1804, SGA, 74; and Elizabeth Aubuchon, 1774, SGA, 97.

29. Estates of Jean Baptiste Tessier, 1766, 1775, SGA, 282, and Jean Baptiste Deguire, 1781, SGA, 161. Even though the local authorities decided in her behalf, Marie Joseph Deguire still went ahead and married for a third time.

30. Estate of Antoine Duclos, 1777, SGA, 394.

31. Proceedings of Elizabeth Datchurut against the Aubuchon heirs, 1798, SGA, 317.

acquainted with their families' assets and liabilities. Wives, and especially widows, free to participate in various kinds of transactions, showed a thorough understanding of the region's economy and legal system. Possession of wealth gave women greater opportunity to control their lives. It is likely that men were well aware of the essential role played by the women of Ste. Genevieve and the Illinois Country and showed their appreciation by consulting them, taking their advice, and allowing them generally to decide.

Esther and Her Sisters

Free Women of Color as Property Owners in Colonial St. Louis, 1765–1803

Judith A. Gilbert

In 1764 in Cahokia, from which his unit was soon to move to St. Louis, a French captain named Pierre Devolsey spent a sleepless night wrestling with a question of honor. Word had come to him that the slave Magdelon, nurse of his wife's invalid brother, had died. What would become of her two-year-old daughter, the adorable little Françoise? Should he confess to his wife that he was the father of Françoise, and take her into his house? Or, to protect his already troubled marriage, should he allow his daughter to be placed with another slave family?[1]

On October 4, 1770, a free black woman known as Jeannette watched as the crude coffin holding the remains of her husband was lowered into a freshly dug grave. Standing beside her were four small, bewildered children. As the sexton began spilling clods of dirt into the grave, a handful of neighbors clasped her hands and murmured words of condolence. For all their sympathy, however, an unspoken question hung in the autumn air.

This article was published in slightly different form in *Gateway Heritage* 17, no. 1 (summer 1996): 14–23.

1. Françoise Devolsey, writ of manumission, June 22, 1872, in Slave Files, Missouri Historical Society (hereinafter cited as MHS), St. Louis; Pierre François Devolsey, wills, November 12, 1768, and October 3, 1782, in St. Louis Archives (hereinafter cited as SLA), 3:86–87, in MHS; J. Thomas Scharf, *History of Saint Louis City and County*, 2 vols. (Philadelphia: Everts, 1893), 1:175–76.

Without Gregory and his blacksmith shop, how was Jeannette going to provide for her family?[2]

In 1784 a mulatto slave named Esther, who had come to Kaskaskia from Virginia with the Ichabod Camp family, kissed her eleven-year-old daughter goodbye and set off for St. Louis with a new owner. Camp had borrowed money from St. Louis merchant Jacques Clamorgan, putting up his slaves as collateral; when the debt became past due, Clamorgan paid a visit and crooked a finger at Esther. On the long trek to St. Louis she thought of Camp, who was a relatively lenient master, and wondered what her life would be like with the brusque, impatient Clamorgan.[3]

None of these three—Françoise, Jeannette, or Esther—seemed to have any likely prospects for success, and certainly not for the accumulation of substantial amounts of property. Yet like a number of other women of color, they acquired a remarkable amount of real estate and left their marks on St. Louis history. Françoise married well and held property in common with her husband, and then later inherited all her father's property, including 240 arpents (about 204 acres) at the village of Little Prairie.[4] Jeannette acquired one house—possibly two—and owned two farms, one of forty arpents and another of eighty arpents.[5] Esther, the best known of the trio, became owner of an entire city block, two other lots with houses, a forty-arpent farm in the St. Louis Prairie (the common grazing land adjoining the village), and an immensely valuable eighty-arpent tract north of town.[6]

It was not unusual for women of color to own property in colonial

2. SLA, 3:147, Instr. 2031, and 3:351, Instr. 2286; Frederic E. Billon, *Annals of St. Louis in its Early Days under the French and Spanish Dominations, 1764–1804* (1886; reprint, New York: Arno Press and New York Times, 1971), 78.

3. Plaintiff's petition, October 15, 1810, in *Ester v. Clamorgan,* St. Charles Historical Society (hereinafter cited as SCHS), St. Charles, Mo.; Ester, complaint, July 5, 1809, and deposition of Catherine [Camp] Dodge, May 10, 1832, both in *Ester v. Carr,* SCHS; biographical note of Camps in Billon, *Annals of St. Louis,* 461–64.

4. Devolsey will, SLA, 3:30, 86–88; *American State Papers, Public Lands* (hereinafter cited as *ASP*), 6:802; St. Louis Deed Book F:152, in City Hall, St. Louis; testimony of William Carr Lane in *Cabanne v. Walker,* court papers in MHS.

5. Billon, *Annals,* 38 (Laclède grant); Valentine's estate inventory in SLA, 5:182, Instr. 2433; LT, 3:111 (Grand Prairie); LT, 2:207 (half of Desnoyers tract), and Valentine's estate inventory, above (other half of Desnoyers tract). See also "Memo of Title to Jeanette Tract," and *Berthold v. MacRee,* both in Gamble Papers, MHS.

6. Respectively, Livres Terreins (hereinafter cited as LT), 4:168, in MHS; SLA, 2:376, Instr. 592; SLA, 1:405, Instr. 754, and St. Louis Deed Book K:379; SLA, 1:451, Instr. 602; LT, 5:10. For the history of these holdings, see *Ester v. Clamorgan* (1811) and *Ester v. Carr* (1830–1833), court papers in MHS and SCHS; "Opinion of Gamble and Spalding" and *Maguire v. Tyler,* both in Gamble Papers, MHS; and "Opinion of Title to Old Esther Claim," in Todd Papers, MHS.

St. Louis. Many of these women were former slaves or the daughters of slaves, and for them property ownership represented security: a home that could not be taken away, a stable environment for their children, a base of operations for various kinds of work, an opportunity to supplement their income with boarders, a capital asset that lenders would accept as collateral. Moreover, owning property brought with it a certain status in the community, recognition by others that one "belonged" and was, in one crucial respect at least, a peer.

In addition, owning a lot in St. Louis entitled one to petition the government for a piece of farmland in the city's common fields. Laid out in the French fashion in strips one arpent wide and forty arpents deep (about 192 feet by a mile and half long), these tracts were offered to lot owners on condition they would turn them into productive use as cropland. One of the great problems the Spanish authorities had was finding residents who were willing to work as farmers; a perennial complaint of the commandants was that the local Frenchmen all fancied themselves fur traders and merchants and would not turn a hand to plowing and tilling. It was an excellent opportunity for black women, many of whom were skilled farmers, and they made the most of it. They acquired tracts, either by themselves or with a husband, from the government, or bought them from former owners. A few assembled more than one tract and consolidated their holdings into sizable farms—land that had no great value to others at the time but would later become prime St. Louis real estate.[7]

The exact number of African American women who owned property in colonial St. Louis is difficult to determine. In its records of real estate transactions, the Spanish government usually identified nonwhites as such, but not always. And while under French and Spanish law a woman owned marital property equally with her husband ("in community"), the record does not always reflect this ownership. The husband usually managed the couple's property, and it was generally recorded (and thus indexed) under his name alone; as a result, unless the wife survived him, her ownership is often obscured. And finally, many owners held their property by unrecorded

7. McCune Gill, "The Beginning of Title in St. Louis," *St. Louis Law Review* 7 (1922): 69–84, 72–77; McCune Gill, "Title to St. Louis Real Estate" (pamphlet; no date), in MHS; Lamont K. Richardson, "Private Land Claims in Missouri," *Missouri Historical Review* (hereinafter cited as *MHR*), 50:132–44, 271–86, 387–99; "Report of Don Pedro Piernas to Gov. O'Reilly," in Louis Houck, comp., *The Spanish Regime in Missouri*, 2 vols. (Chicago: R. R. Donnelley and Sons, 1909; reprint, New York: Arno Press, 1971), 1:71–73; and de Leyba letter of November 16, 1778, in Lawrence Kinnaird, ed., *Spain in the Mississippi River Valley, 1765–1794* (Washington, D.C.: U.S. Government Printing Office, 1949), 2:312.

deeds or simply "by possession," and are missing from the official record. Although many later had their titles confirmed by the American land commissioners, they are generally absent from the colonial archives.[8]

Even so, several African American women can be identified with certainty as property owners in colonial St. Louis. Besides Françoise, Jeannette, and Esther, two other African American women owned impressive amounts of real estate: Flore, who owned a house and lot and twenty arpents at the edge of town, and Marie LaBastille, who owned a house and lot and an entire city block by unrecorded deeds. Others held lesser amounts, generally a house and a lot—still a substantial amount of real estate, inasmuch as the typical lot was one-fourth of a city block. Among those owning homes in their own name were Elizabeth (or Zabetta) Datchurut, her daughter, Isobel Datchurut, and an ex-slave known as LouLou. Others, such as the wives of Carlos Leveille and Augustin Amiot, owned homes in common with their husbands. Quite probably other African American women owned property as well, but their ownership cannot be documented as well as that of these women.[9]

Esther and her sisters, of course, were not typical of their time. The typical African American woman of colonial St. Louis was poor, did not own property, and was most likely a slave; rather than owning property, she probably *was* property, subject herself to being bought and sold, mortgaged and replevined. The free women of color who owned property were elite among the African American community, just as the Chouteaus, the Cabannes, the Sarpys, and others were elite among the French. They were, in a sense, the colonial equivalent of Cyprian Clamorgan's nineteenth-century "colored aristocracy.[10] Yet their lives show the social mobility that was possible for those who did achieve freedom—and who had the good for-

8. The Spanish government recorded land grants in the Livres Terreins and also recorded deeds of private buyers and sellers in the St. Louis Archives, both of which are held in the MHS. See also Edward F. Haas Jr., "Louisiana's Legal Heritage: An Introduction," 1–6, and Vaughan Baker, "Le Mari est Seigneur: Marital Laws Governing Women in French Louisiana," 7–17, both in Edward F. Haas Jr., ed., *Louisiana's Legal Heritage* (New Orleans: Tulane University Press, 1983); and Gustavus Schmidt, *The Civil Law of Spain and Mexico* (New Orleans: n.p., 1851), 11–17. On unrecorded deeds, see Gill, "Beginning of Title in St. Louis," 69–84; and Henry W. Williams, *History, Abstracts of Title, Evidences of Location, &c, Relating to the Common Field Lots* (St. Louis: Republican, 1854), 6–9.

9. Flore: SLA, 2:112, Instr. 138; and LT, 2:77. Marie LaBastille: SLA, 2:372, Instr. 583; SLA, 2:373, Instr. 58; SLA 2:477, Instr. 781B; SLA, 4:22, Instr. 1063, and *ASP* 2:638. Zabetta: SLA, 2:463, Instr. 775. Isobel: SLA, 2:518, Instr. 901. LouLou: SLA, 2:392, Instr. 632. Leveille: LT, 5:159; and St. Louis Deed Book N:474. Amiot: LT, 4:98.

10. Cyprian Clamorgan, "The Colored Aristocracy of St. Louis" (St. Louis, 1858); reprinted in *MHS Bulletin,* October 1974, 1–31.

tune to live when and where they did, in a fur-trading entrepot that was a unique blend of French culture and Spanish government. Several factors contributed to this mobility. First, the Spanish government was so eager to strengthen its presence in Upper Louisiana that it granted property in and around St. Louis to petitioners regardless of race or sex. Women's labor was as welcome as that of men, and in some ways even more so for women of color. Black women, many of whom were former plantation workers, had the agricultural background so lacking among French traders and trappers. As a result, the Spanish commandants did not hesitate to grant women of color both city lots and outlying strips of farmland.

A second factor has to do with their social acceptance by the community itself. The French and French Canadians who made up most of the population of St. Louis were, at least compared with the English, a racially tolerant group who took blacks and Indians into their midst with only moderate discrimination. Because the ratio of men to women was around three to one in 1767 and remained two to one in 1794, French men often took black or Indian women as wives or mistresses and accepted the racially mixed offspring as their own.[11]

In addition, these women benefited from a legal system that, quite unlike the system prevailing in the English colonies, allowed women to hold property on essentially equal terms with men. Under French law (which, in most private matters, continued to be observed in St. Louis under Spanish rule) a married woman retained title to any property she brought into a marriage, and owned "in community" with her husband any property acquired by either during the marriage. Upon the death of one of the partners, the community property went half to the surviving spouse and half to any children; when there were no children, that half went to the nearest blood relatives of the deceased. It was customary under French law, however, for couples to modify this arrangement with a prenuptial agreement—the marriage contract—that provided for most, or even all, of the marital assets to pass undivided to the surviving spouse. In that way, the survivor would have the immediate and full use of all funds for the family's well-being.[12]

Third, these women benefited from the fact that slavery in Upper

11. Tanis Chapman Thorne, "People of the River: Mixed-Blood Families in the Lower Missouri" (Ph.D. diss., University of California–Los Angeles, 1987), 26–56, 92; Sylvia Van Kirk, *Many Tender Ties: Women in Fur-Trade Society, 1670–1870* (Norman: University of Oklahoma Press, 1980), 3–7.

12. Haas, "Louisiana's Legal Heritage: An Introduction," 1–6, and Vaughan Baker, "Le Mari est Seigneur: Marital Laws Governing Women in French Louisiana," 7–17, both in Haas, *Louisiana's Legal Heritage;* see also Schmidt, *The Civil Law of Spain and Mexico,* 11–17.

Louisiana was far more benign than in the American South. The French Code Noir ("black code"), which regulated the rights and treatment of black people, and the closely related Spanish slave code did not treat slaves as mere chattel, but instead encouraged slaves to marry and forbade masters to break up families. The law mandated humane treatment, made it possible for industrious slaves to accumulate purchase money, and to a certain extent encouraged manumission. Even though slaves might lead hard lives, they lived in relatively stable families and were accepted within the community as fellow human beings who, rather unfortunately, happened to owe someone lifetime service. As a result, freed slaves generally emerged from servitude with the social skills, self-confidence, and personal drive that enabled them to make their own way and to find a successful niche in the community.[13]

Of all the women of color who owned property in colonial St. Louis, the most successful was Esther, the slave taken in 1784 by Jacques Clamorgan when her master defaulted on his debt. About thirty-one years old at the time, the strikingly beautiful woman quickly became Clamorgan's mistress and business confidante. Clamorgan was a legendary frontier character— proprietor of over a million arpents in Spanish land grants, manager of a far-flung fur-trading empire, developer of lead and salt mines, pioneer of the Santa Fe trade, and promoter of endless dreams and schemes. In Esther he found a high-spirited woman with a will as strong as his own, and a cleverness that matched his. He installed her as mistress of his household, where she oversaw a staff of servants and entertained business associates and prominent visitors. Clamorgan traveled extensively, and he trusted Esther to handle his personal affairs in his absence. She seemed, to one astonished observer, to have virtually taken over his house. She "seemed to have the control within the premises when Clamorgan was absent," marveled Gabriel Cerré, "and very much so when he was at home."[14]

But she was more than simply a mistress and housekeeper. When they later came to a bitter parting of the ways, Esther demanded—and won— recompense in court for her "work, labour, care and diligence in and about

13. Herbert S. Klein, *Slavery in the Americas: A Comparative Study of Virginia and Cuba* (Chicago: University of Chicago Press, 1967), 58–85; Hans W. Baade, "The Law of Slavery in Spanish Louisiana," in Haas, *Louisiana's Legal Heritage*, 43–86.

14. A. P. Nasatir, "Jacques Clamorgan," in Leroy Hafen, *The Mountain Men and the Fur Trade of the Far West*, 10 vols. (Glendale, Calif.: A. H. Clark, 1965–1972), 2:81–94; Deposition of John Hay, May 2, 1810, in *Ester v. Clamorgan*, shown in Plaintiff's Exhibit A, *Ester v. Carr*, SCHS; Gabriel Cerré, Deposition, April 14, 1832, *Ester v. Carr*, SCHS.

the business of him." A glimpse into how closely involved they were can be seen in a flurry of transactions in 1793, when Clamorgan took one of his greatest plunges and founded the ambitious and financially risky Missouri Company. To safeguard at least part of his assets, he freed Esther—thus making her capable of owning real estate—and shifted certain properties into her name, Clamorgan granted Esther the house and lot adjoining his own house, and he used his influence with the Spanish commandant to secure for her the entire city block across the street from the two properties, as well as an eighty-arpent tract north of town. His hand can also be seen in her purchase about the same time of a forty-arpent tract in the common fields; in an unusually complicated transaction she bought the property from Joseph Brazeau, a silent partner in several of Clamorgan's speculations.[15]

During the same few months in 1793, Clamorgan also sold Esther her daughter, Sile, whom he had bought about a year after bringing Esther into his house. By 1793 Sile had a four-year-old son, Edward Fitzgerald, whose father—a British military officer—was a frequent guest in the Clamorgan house. Clamorgan freed Edward, made him his personal ward, and arranged for an associate to give him a half interest in a four-hundred-arpent coal-mining tract. Clamorgan obviously trusted not only Esther but also her entire family; his personal finances had to a great extent become entwined with theirs.[16]

Clamorgan later insisted that Esther was only a straw party in these transactions, but she clearly did not see her role that way, nor did others in the community. She farmed Brazeau's old ground and raised cattle on the eighty-arpent Spanish grant; her neighbors always considered her the owner of the land, and they later testified to this understanding, adding that the cattle "were always called Esther's cows." She also tended an orchard on the city block granted her by the government, an undertaking that Clamorgan first encouraged and then later wanted to claim as his own. "That wench," he complained to Brazeau, "wants to take away the one-half of my orchard."[17]

Shortly after 1793 Clamorgan began a series of flagrant affairs with younger mulatto women, not only infuriating Esther but also alarming her

15. Complaint, *Ester v. Clamorgan*, October 4, 1809, SCHS (citing a signed agreement between the two); SLA, 2:376, Instr. 592; SLA, 1:451, Instr. 602; LT, 4:168; LT, 5:10.

16. SLA, 2:379, Instr. 597; SLA, 1:403, Instr. 587.

17. Clamorgan's claim is given in Deed Book A:207, and is disputed in *ASP* 6:820, and in Joseph Brazeau, Deposition, *Ester v. Clamorgan*, April 4, 1810, in SCHS.

into giving serious thought to her future. Unable to read or write, she became suspicious of any paper put before her, fearing that Clamorgan was trying to cheat her. Instead of obligingly affixing her mark, she began refusing to sign anything—at one point cursing at Clamorgan before an astonished notary and hurling a brush across the room. Clamorgan responded with beatings and verbal abuse, until in 1797 she found it necessary to leave his house for good.[18]

Esther did not leave empty-handed. She took with her the deeds to her various properties, secure in the knowledge that her title was protected by the Spanish government. She continued to farm and to raise cattle, supporting Sile and eventually three grandchildren with her work. She eventually lost much of this property after the American accession in 1804, defrauded both by Clamorgan and—in her view at least—the lawyer she hired to protect herself against him. Even so, she managed to hold onto her house at Third and Popular and, more importantly, the eighty-arpent tract, which was confirmed to her by the American land commissioners. Esther litigated her various claims until her death in 1833, leaving both her property and several pending lawsuits to her grandchildren. In 1848 they sold their interest in all her property, including that still in litigation, to a real estate dealer for $10,000 in cash.[19]

Esther's accomplishments seem remarkable, but only in retrospect; by the time she acquired her property in 1793, women of color who owned substantial amounts of real estate had ceased to be a novelty in St. Louis. In a sense, Esther was only following a path first blazed by an African American known as Jeannette, or, as she is sometimes called in Spanish documents, Juanita Forchet. Jeannette's origins are uncertain, but she was probably one of the slaves freed by a French priest, Father Francis Forget, in Cahokia in 1763. At any rate, she was given one of Pierre de Laclède's original grants of a city lot in 1765—on Church Street, between Myrtle and Elm—and shortly thereafter married an African American blacksmith, Gregory. They settled on her lot and built on it, in the French fashion, a sturdy, twenty-by-twenty-five-foot "house of posts in the ground."[20]

18. Depositions of Marie Philippe Leduc, January 4, 1832, in *Ester v. Carr,* and John Hay, May 2, 1810, in *Ester v. Clamorgan,* both in SCHS. Cyprian Clamorgan, "The Colored Aristocracy," 5–7 (Clamorgan's children).

19. The commissioners rejected Clamorgan's claim to the tract in 1806 and finally confirmed Esther's shortly before her death in 1833, in *ASP* 6:819–20. The complicated litigation can be followed in *Ester v. Clamorgan* in MHS, *Ester v. Carr* in SCHS, and papers relating to Esther in the Gamble Papers and Todd Papers, both in MHS.

20. Billon, *Annals,* 38, and inventory of assets in 1773 in SLA, 5:338, Instr. 2319.

When Gregory died in 1770, it was this property that enabled Jeannette and her three children to survive. They had a roof over their heads, enough ground for a garden, a cow, a few chickens, and a base of operations for a small business. Jeannette seems to have supported her family for the next three years by running a laundry business out of her home; when she mar-ried again in 1773 and listed her assets in a marriage contract, prominent among them were five large iron kettles, four brass kettles, and three pairs of smoothing irons.[21]

Moreover, judging from this inventory, hers was no poverty-stricken household. "The said Jeannette produced a featherbed," the appraisers re-ported, "covered with ticking, a paillaise covered with linen, two sheets, a blanket, three-point, another large blanket, a couch, [and] a bolster, half-worn." They went on to list other items that hinted at prosperity: a smaller feather bed, more blankets, another bolster, eight place settings of pewter tableware, two copper candlesticks, a crystal saltcellar, and various other items.[22]

The most impressive portion they saved for last. Jeannette had only months earlier been awarded by the Spanish government a forty-arpent tract in the Grand Prairie, the common grazing land, and she now listed as assets seven cows, seven calves, four sows, a dozen hens, and a rooster. Altogether, she brought into her marriage a net worth estimated at 1,349 livres—somewhat more than the bridegroom, a free black gunsmith named Valentine, who claimed business and personal effects worth some 1,220 livres.[23]

Consequently, Jeannette was in an excellent negotiating position, and the marriage contract reflects this. Valentine made her a gift of three hun-dred livres, promised to help support and educate her children, and agreed to make her his sole heir if they had no children of their own. This latter provision proved to be crucial. In 1790 Valentine died while on a hunting trip among the Osage, and his estate—that is, his half of their community property—went directly to her rather than to his nearest relatives. From the inventory that was made of these assets, it is apparent that he and Jeannette had prospered in their marriage. The big featherbed now rested on a walnut bedstead, and other walnut pieces adorned the house: a large armoire with lock and key, a smaller armoire, two tables, and a kneading

21. SLA, 3:147, Instr. 2031; SLA, 5:338, Instr. 2319.
22. Ibid.
23. Ibid. Beginning in 1766, the Spanish government divided the Grand Prairie, a large grazing area west of the older St. Louis Prairie, into tracts of cropland. As the vil-lage grew, other common fields and pastures were added to the south and west, among them the Little Prairie and Prairie Desnoyers.

trough. The house itself was described as being covered with shingles and floored above and below, with a gallery all around. Outside were two substantial outbuildings, a large garden, and an orchard with a variety of fruit trees.[24]

Moreover, Valentine and Jeannette had acquired more land in the common fields. In 1788 they received a grant of eighty arpents in the Prairie Desnoyers to go along with the forty acres Jeannette already had in the Prairie. They were evidently doing more crop farming than raising livestock, for their assets in the estate inventory showed a yoke of oxen for plowing but only two cows and a calf and a small flock of poultry.[25]

After Valentine's death, Jeannette mortgaged her house for 1,372 livres; she lived on the proceeds until her death in 1803. In her will, she left the house to her daughter, Susanne, who had begun making payments on the mortgage, and she left the rest of her estate, in equal parts, to Susanne, her son, Augustin, and a grandchild named Jean Baptiste Marly. There was little demand for the farmland at the time of her death; her heirs let the forty-arpent piece go for forty dollars, and they later sold the eighty-arpent tract for slightly more than five hundred dollars. In time, however, the home lot—one-fourth of a city block—became extremely valuable; Jeannette's heirs and their children divided it among themselves and eventually sold it in bits to speculators. They did not become rich from the property (that good fortune would come later, to the speculators who bought from them), but thanks to Jeannette's foresight, they had the financial security to enjoy comfortable lives in the free black community of nineteenth-century St. Louis.[26]

At the time that Esther and Jeannette were amassing their property, young Françoise, the mulatto daughter of Pierre Devolsey, was acquiring hers. After the death of her slave mother in 1764, Pierre—at the time, commandant of the French garrison at Cahokia—took the two-year-old into his home, explaining her presence to his wife, Elizabeth, by means that can only be guessed. He arranged the purchase of the child for five hundred livres and brought her to St. Louis when he moved there with Elizabeth in 1765. In a joint will executed in 1768, he and Elizabeth mention "the little girl named Françoise" whom they have adopted, and declare that she shall be sole heir of "all goods acquired during their com-

24. SLA, 3:147, Instr. 2031; SLA, 5:182, Instr. 2433.
25. LT, 2:107; SLA, 5:182, Instr. 2433; and Gill, "Title to St. Louis Real Estate," map on pp. 18–19.
26. SLA, 4:380, Instr. 1791 (mortgage); SLA, 3:348, Instr. 2286 (will); St Louis Deed Book A:119, R:220, S:264, O:396, 439, Q:22, R:220, and S4:264.

munity." In 1772 the couple signed a writ of manumission freeing Françoise.[27]

Over the next few years, the Devolsey marriage became increasingly
troubled, and it fell apart completely in 1774 when Pierre went to France
on a two-year business trip and Elizabeth began an affair with the church
choirmaster. On his return Pierre filed for a dissolution of their marriage
and a severing of their finances, a process that took some three years. Elizabeth left town with her lover, allowing Pierre custody of the teenage Françoise. In 1782—then twenty years old—Françoise married a French Canadian
named Paul Dupuis; she is identified in the marriage record simply as "colored," and although his parents are listed by name, hers are not. Together
they had a daughter named Julia, who later adopted the same surname as
her mother.[28]

In 1788 Pierre wrote a new will, for the first time formally acknowledg-
ing Françoise as "his natural daughter" and again making her his only heir.
By that time their roles had become reversed; he had fallen into alcoholism
and chronic illness, and she had become his caretaker. The extent of his dependence on her is revealed in yet another will, dictated by Pierre to the
Spanish commandant in 1792; once again leaving all his assets to Françoise, he speaks affectionately of her as one "of whom he has received the
best services, having attended him in all his sickness, by her cares, her fac-
ulties and means, giving him as present, lodging, food, and personal services."[29]

Pierre died in 1795. No inventory of his estate survives, so exactly how
much Françoise inherited is unknown; much of it had been wasted away
during his lifetime, but at least some was left, including 240 arpents of
farmland at Little Prairie. It was enough, at any rate, to allow Françoise to
free herself from her bad marriage to Paul Dupuis, to take a lover named
Louis Bosaillon, and to begin a new life for herself. While her husband was
away on a business trip to Florissant (then known as St. Ferdinand),
Françoise cleaned out their savings and, in her husband's outraged words,
"fled with the said Bosaillon, taking with her two hundred ninety-nine
hard dollars, and all the furniture, beds, household utensils which she was
able to take, together with the table and bed clothes, axes and muskets of

27. SLA, 3:87; Writ of manumission, June 22, 1772, in Slave Files. For Devolsey's
life, see Billon, *Annals,* 435–36; and Scharf, *History of St. Louis,* 1:175–76.
28. Oscar Collett, comp., *Index to St. Louis Cathedral and Carondelet Church Marriages* (St. Louis: Missouri Historical Society, 1918), April 24, 1782, and Devolsey will,
codicil, in SLA, 3:30.
29. SLA, 3:86, 88.

the Petitioner, leaving him with no other clothes but those which he took on his journey." The couple fled to Vincennes Post on the American side; in time Bosaillon disappeared from the picture, and Françoise settled there permanently with her daughter.[30]

Françoise and Julia became the toast of the military community there. William Carr Lane, later to become mayor of St. Louis, recalled socializing with them at "French balls" and enjoying their company; she apparently had enough money to be received in the better society there and to maintain her daughter in some comfort. Françoise held onto the 240 arpents in the Grand Prairie until 1817, when she sold it to fur trader John Cabanne for an undisclosed amount; thirty years later, his heirs retailed it to the developer Thomas Allen, who made it into one of St. Louis's first and most profitable subdivisions.[31]

In general, the colonial women of color who owned property in St. Louis displayed, despite their universal illiteracy, a remarkable level of legal and financial sophistication. A free black woman named Flore, who supported herself and her daughter by dressing furs and skins, had little money but wanted to own a home. In 1774 she made a proposal to the trader Louis Dufresne: She would use a "deerskin mortgage" to buy his house, delivering 100 livres' worth of hides as a down payment and another 150 livres' worth over time. As security she pledged both the house and "all her goods, real and personal, actual and future." Flore paid off the mortgage in 1780 and eight years later acquired more property, a grant of twenty arpents in the Prairie Desnoyers near Jeannette's tract. After she died, around 1805, her daughter sold the farmland to Charles Gratiot for forty dollars but kept the more valuable town property, gradually subdividing it among her children and providing comfortable homes for them.[32]

Elizabeth Datchurut, a free mulatto, had ten children with her lover, Antoine Aubuchon, a Ste. Genevieve planter who "avowed constantly" that he would provide for them after his death. But when he died in 1798 without a will, under Spanish law his entire estate—worth almost five thousand livres—went to his wife and legitimate children. Although Elizabeth had no legal claim as an heir, she sued his estate and recovered at least part of what she considered rightly hers: the crop that she had put in on lands belonging to him at Ste. Genevieve, several items of personal property, and a

---

30. Paul Dupuis, Complaint and Inventory, July 20, 1797, in SLA, 5:271, and William Carr Lane testimony in *Cabanne v. Walker* (1856), transcript in MHS, pp. 6–8.
31. St. Louis Deed book F:152.
32. SLA, 2:112, Instr. 138; LT, 2:106 (survey at 2:77); St. Louis Deed Book A:197, H:150, P:24, P:86, X2:246, M:61, N:474, M:255, A:494, and A:342.

formal acknowledgment by the Aubuchon family that Antoine was the father of her children. She used the proceeds to move to St. Louis and buy a house on Church Street for herself and her children.[33]

Marie LaBastille claimed ownership of an entire city block under the Spanish government, as well as her own home at Third and Walnut. The American land commissioners found her title to the block to be invalid, but she held onto her home and its 120-by-150-foot lot and in 1812 shrewdly sold it on terms that amounted to a lifetime annuity. Reserving the right to continue living in the home, she deeded it to her neighbor John Beaufils "for and in consideration of 20 pounds of coffee, 25 pounds of sugar, 300 pounds of flour, 25 loads of firewood, 80 pounds of pork, and 20 pounds of beef, which said John Baptiste Beaufils promises and obligates himself to deliver to me annually during my life." Marie lived another fourteen years in the house rent free while Beaufils provided her with groceries and firewood and waited fretfully for possession of the property.[34]

The women of color who owned property in colonial St. Louis were a diverse group, but they had a number of traits in common. They were, almost without exception, energetic and hardworking; either working alone or with other members of their households, they made their own way in life and could point with pride to their accomplishments. A great many of them were entrepreneurs who were quick to recognize opportunity and to seize it, whether this opportunity was a place in the fur-trading business, a chance to farm one's own land, or an opening for a small home business. As a group these women were remarkably sophisticated about legal affairs, protecting themselves with recorded deeds, marriage contracts, wills, and other documents and never hesitating to assert their rights in court.

If there is one constant in the lives of these women, however, it is the strength of their family ties. Time after time we find these women and their kin sharing burdens and taking crucial action on one another's behalf. Pierre Devolsey risked his marriage to take Françoise into his home, and she in her turn nursed him through illness and alcoholism. As a young widow Jeannette took in laundry to hold her family together, and later a loving husband left her everything in his will; in her old age, her daughter took over mortgage payments for her. Although Esther's relationship with Jacques Clamorgan ended badly, for a decade or more she enjoyed his love

33. See "Complaint of Elizabeth Datchurutt," in *Elizabeth Datchurutt, free negress, v. heirs of Antoine Aubuchon*, 11, in Ste. Genevieve Archives, Litigations, no. 80, (microfilm in MHS); and SLA, 2:463, Instr. 775.

34. *ASP* 2:638; deed, Labastille to Beaufils, June 13, 1812, in Bates Papers, MHS; St. Louis probate book A:253 (1826), City Hall, St. Louis.

and support; without him, ironically, she would never have amassed the property that afforded her the means to leave him. Elizabeth Datchurut sued her lover's estate not just for money but for the right of her children to use his name; their relationship had been close enough that she insisted on having it recognized publicly. The closeness of other families can also be seen in their choice of names. Flore's daughter, Florence, adopted Flore as a surname and was often confused in legal documents with her mother. And although she had been married to their father, Gregory, Jeannette's children called themselves Susanne Jeannette, Maria Jeannette, and Augustin Jeannette, and a grandson, Jean Baptiste Marly, often signed his name "Jean Baptiste Jeannette." These women derived their strength from family ties woven with threads of mutual respect and sacrifice. They were, in the truest sense of the word, an aristocracy—not of birth or privilege, but of merit and accomplishment.

German-Speaking Women in Nineteenth-Century Missouri

The Immigrant Experience

Linda Schelbitzki Pickle

German-speakers were the largest group of non-English-speakers to immigrate to Missouri in the nineteenth century. Unlike the French fur trappers and traders who came in the late 1700s, these immigrants arrived chiefly in family groups, so women were always present in significant numbers. Yet we know relatively little about their specific roles in the contributions this group made to Missouri history and culture, since most women's influence was felt primarily in the home and family, where few records were kept. Among the many public ways in which nineteenth-century German-speaking women assisted in the settlement of Missouri, the most conspicuous are those that can be attributed to nuns, who founded schools, hospitals, and social organizations. The history and experiences of these religious women are also relatively well recorded because of the institutional and personal manuscripts collected in archives. It is a different story with laywomen, however. We can document the experiences of only a small number of secular German-speaking women through their personal writings. We also have, for the most part, only indirect evidence of how they furthered their family's goals and the more public accomplishments of the men in their families. And yet we know that their efforts were considerable, for without them the German-speaking immigrants in Missouri could not have been as successful as they were in persisting as family-based units. The present study offers an overview of the first century of German-speaking women's residence in the state. It also seeks to offer insights into general patterns of immigrant women's experiences, in Missouri and elsewhere.

Timothy Flint was the first to record the presence of German-speakers in the territory that became Missouri. In the early 1820s he visited a settlement along the Whitewater River in southeastern Missouri and wrote: "[A]mong the races in this country, the Germans succeed decidedly the best; better, even, than the Anglo-Americans. They have no vagrant imaginations; and they cast a single look over the forest or prairie which they have purchased, and their minds seize intuitively the best arrangement and division, and their farming establishment generally succeeds. They build a good house and barn. They plant a large orchard. Their fences, their gates, all the appendages to their establishment, are strong and permanent. They raise large horses and cattle. They spend little, and when they sell will receive nothing in pay but specie. Every stroke counts toward improvement." Flint also acknowledged the contributions of the "good, laborious, submissive, and silent housewives" toward the farming success of the German-speaking immigrants: "Their wives have no taste for parties and tea. Silent, unwearied labour, and the rearing of their children, are their only pursuits; and in a few years they are comparatively rich." We know that not all German-speakers were such intuitively successful farmers and businesspeople and that not all women among them were as Flint described those of the Whitewater River area. Nonetheless, the qualities of frugality, hard work, and submission of self-interest to family goals were probably characteristic of most women in this immigrant group. Such "invisible" contributions were important in the role that German-speakers played in building the communities and the culture of Missouri.[1]

Flint was certainly correct about the persistence of the German-speakers. They were the most numerous non-English-speaking immigrant group in nineteenth-century Missouri. Although Anglo-Americans lumped all the immigrants together as "Germans" or "Dutch," the German-speakers differed by regional heritage, religious affiliation, social class, and dialect and were very conscious of these distinctions among themselves. One commonality among them, however, was that most had immigrated for economic reasons, with religious or political reasons sometimes playing a role.[2] By

1. Timothy Flint, *Recollections of the Last Ten Years, Passed in Occasional Residences and Journeyings in the Valley of the Mississippi* (1826; reprint, New York: Knopf, 1932), 228–29. See also Linda S. Pickle, *Contented among Strangers: Rural German-Speaking Women and Their Families in the Nineteenth-Century Midwest* (Urbana: University of Illinois Press, 1996), 23–40.

2. Mack Walker, *Germany and the Emigration, 1816–1885* (Cambridge: Harvard University Press, 1964), is the classic work on the background of German emigration.

1880, more than 293,000 Missouri residents were German-speaking immigrants or the children of such immigrants. The long-term effects of this influx are still evident in the state's demographics. In spite of the degree to which German-speakers seemed to "disappear" into the American mainstream within two or three generations, it is clear upon closer investigation that the conservation of a sense of group identity persisted, and not only in the preservation of cultural traditions. The integration of an immigrant group, even one that had so much in common with the dominant American culture as the German-speakers, is a slow process, especially if members of the group succeed in settling in close proximity to each other.[3]

Missouri German-speakers primarily immigrated with or joined Old World family and friends and often formed immigrant neighborhoods in cities and rural areas, hoping to prosper in the New World. Many responded to formal and informal invitations to settle in the state, like Gottfried Duden's influential *Report of a Journey to the Western States of North America and a Stay of Several Years along the Missouri* (1829).[4] Others, the so-called Dreissiger and Achtundvierziger, were middle-class intellectuals alienated by the repression of nascent democratic movements in German-speaking Europe during the 1830s and after the revolutions of 1848, who formed emigration societies to establish ideal German communities within the United States. The town of Hermann, along the Missouri, was planned as such a colony where true "Germanness" could be fostered. Leaders of these societies became important forces in Missouri education,

---

Walter Kamphoefner, *The Westfalians: From Germany to Missouri* (Princeton: Princeton University Press, 1987), is a seminal work on the history of German speakers in nineteenth-century Missouri. See the maps showing the dispersal of German-born immigrants in the United States between 1850 and 1900, reprinted from Max Hannemann, *Das Deutschtum in den Vereinigten Staaten*, Petermanns Mitteilungen, Ergänzungsheft no. 224 (Gotha, Germany: Perthes, 1936), 11, 62, in Pickle, *Contented*, 10–11.

3. U.S. Census Office, *U.S. Census Reports, Tenth Census, 1880* (Washington, D.C.: U.S. Government Printing Office, 1883), table 27, 680–92. In 1990, 36 percent of the population of Missouri (1,844,192 individuals) claimed German ancestry, testifying to the persistence of German self-identification over several generations. Of these persons, 44.5 percent stated that they had only German ancestry, an indication of the extent to which ethnic Germans married only within their own ethnic group during a century and a half of residency in Missouri (Bureau of the Census, *1990 Census of Population and Housing: Summary Tape File 3A* [Washington, D.C.: U.S. Government Printing Office, 1992]).

4. Gottfried Duden, *Report of a Journey to the Western States of North America and a Stay of Several Years along the Missouri (During the Years 1824, '25, '26, and 1827),* ed. and trans. James Goodrich et al. (Columbia: University of Missouri Press, 1980). William G. Bek translated selected writings of several of the most important "followers of Duden" for the *Missouri Historical Review* between 1919 and 1925.

politics, and journalism. Their rationalistic, antireligious bent found expression in free-thinker societies and publications. They and German-speaking immigrants in general opposed slavery, and in the German American newspapers they founded they rallied the immigrant community to the Union in war-torn Missouri. The Achtundvierziger also founded Turner Societies, clubs dedicated to physical fitness and the nurturing of social bonds within the ethnic community; these supplied the North with significant numbers of Missouri recruits and whole German-speaking regiments.

But intellectuals and rationalist anticlerics were always in the minority among the German-speaking immigrants in Missouri. Most of the immigrants founded or associated themselves with German-language churches, and for them, as for the Americans around them, the church became one of the most important social institutions in their lives. Religion was a prime reason for ministers, priests, monks, and nuns to come from Europe to establish churches, tend to German-language congregations, and teach the immigrants' children. Some laypersons came to escape religious oppression in their homeland or to gain the freedom to practice religion as they wished. The so-called Old Lutherans established four settlements in Perry County in the winter of 1839 in order to continue to practice the version of conservative Lutheranism forbidden them in Saxony. They eventually founded the Missouri Synod Lutheran Church, which identified the conservation of German culture and the German language as necessary underpinnings to its religious identity. Bethel, a settlement founded by German immigrant Wilhelm Keil in accord with his ideas of Christian communistic economic principles, survived from 1844 until its formal dissolution in 1879 and so is the longest-lived of the fourteen known Missouri utopian communities founded in the nineteenth century. Like Hermann, Bethel retained its German identity and continues to cultivate that heritage.[5]

Women clearly were present in all of these groups. Given the complexity of the history of German-speakers in nineteenth-century Missouri, the life of a single woman cannot completely represent the experience of them all, but Henrietta (Jette) Geisberg Bruns's story can tell us a good deal. For

5. See Walter O. Forster, *Zion on the Mississippi: The Settlement of the Saxon Lutherans in Missouri, 1839–1841* (St. Louis: Concordia Publishing House, 1953); Charles Nordhoff, *The Communistic Societies of the United States* (1875; reprint, New York: Schocken, 1965); and Robert J. Hendricks, *Bethel and Aurora: An Experiment in Communism as Practical Christianity* (New York: Press of the Pioneers, 1933; reprint, New York: AMS Press, 1971). In the 1990 census, 71.9 percent of the residents of Perry County stated that they had German-speaking ancestors, and 67.6 percent claimed to be full-blooded German Americans (Bureau of the Census, *1990 Census of Population and Housing: Summary Tape File 3A* [Washington, D.C.: U.S. Government Printing Office, 1992]).

more than sixty years after she followed her husband to a farm in the Missouri woods, Jette Bruns (1813–1899) wrote letters to the family she left behind in Westphalia. These lengthy documents, detailed, personal, and often passionate, tell us much about the realities of immigration and what it could cost educated middle-class women, especially those who came to frontier areas with small children and without the support of female relatives in their immediate surroundings. The letters also reveal how immigrant women fostered and supported their families' new lives.

Jette Geisberg was the oldest child of the mayor of Oelde, a medium-sized city in Westphalia. At the age of nineteen she married a physician, Bernhard Bruns, who, seeing the opportunities created by immigration, bought a homestead along the Maries River in Osage County in a community nostalgically named Westphalia. In 1836 Jette, her young son, and her brothers Franz and Bernhard Geisberg joined her husband on the Missouri frontier. Jette wrote years later: "For me it was a hard struggle between inclination and duty . . . but I had given my husband my promise to follow him to the New World." Taking two of her brothers with her in order to give them opportunities that they might not have had in Oelde turned out to be as much of a burden as a blessing. Both Bernhard and Franz Geisberg often argued with Bernhard Bruns as well as with their sister about the best way to go about establishing themselves in Missouri. Jette was a loving but exacting older sister, who hoped much for her brothers but also expected a good deal of them. A few years after immigrating, Franz Geisberg married a neighbor girl from a peasant family, whom Jette had employed as a domestic for a time. In Jette's Old World view, this was a step down for him and for her entire family. Meanwhile, Bernhard Geisberg had contracted a "brain fever" in 1838 that recurred several times in the next years and increasingly affected his behavior. In 1843 Jette regretfully agreed to his return to Germany, where he had to be committed to an asylum. Eventually Jette and her husband had to take over her brothers' business affairs and the care of Franz's three small children after he went to California in 1849 to search for gold, his wife having died of tuberculosis in 1847. Thus, the presence of these family members was not always a consolation to her, particularly as she lacked the company of sympathetic women with similar backgrounds. Thinking of old friends of her youth, she wrote in 1840: "Here, how lonely I am; there is not another congenial female being with whom I could exchange now and then my feelings when I need some relief and would forget the daily worries and cares and set these aside for a short time."[6]

6. Adolf E. Schroeder and Carla Schulz-Geisberg, eds., *Hold Dear, as Always: Jette, a German Immigrant Life in Letters* (Columbia: University of Missouri Press, 1988), 46, 107, 113, 105.

Indeed, although she was amply busy caring for husband, children, and brothers, as well as helping with her husband's various business enterprises, Jette seems to have felt lonely much of the time. "Often I think I don't want to write anymore and don't like to think of you all anymore, but that is not possible. You all always stand before me, fresh and alive, and always there is the ocean and the world between us. There can never be hope for a reunion. You are constantly growing deeper into the situation over there and we into the situation here." The pain of Jette's isolation was particularly evident when she wrote of the loss of three of her four young children to dysentery. She told her family in Oelde of the sad events in a letter written in stages over three months:

> "There rest now, my sweet, my beloved in God; there rest now, in peace, free of all troubles."
> And then I stroke the pale cheek and kiss the cold mouth. I want to look once more at little Rudolph. Then they may bed him next to Max and Johanna.—In the house here it is very quiet. Hermann, the only one, is skulking around, still lacking his strength; however, he is almost well now. We have been afflicted by dysentery. My three little angels have been taken away by the Good Lord. Yesterday morning sweet little Rudolph passed away. Since that time his mother has had peace. Peace to nourish her grief, peace to capture resignation. (October 3, 1841)
>
> Now all wishes, all striving have been quieted! I even no longer wish to go back to you, to Germany! It is so painful to me. Up there where the angels live and where the Almighty is enthroned, it's probably singularly beautiful. There I will also find you all again! Until then we shall postpone our reunion. There it will be happier. —How I wish I could have said farewell to the world six weeks ago, if only the Good Lord would have considered it my time. I had been provided with the last sacrament. Even though my life, full of sin and weakness, made me fear, yet the hope was strong to find a gracious judge. I believe I could have been able to take leave of my husband and son. (October 17, 1841)
>
> I feel deeply that I have to communicate with you. But it takes such a long time for us to exchange our emotions with each other. You think that I am now happily in the circle of my beloved ones—that is over forever. (December 7, 1841)[7]

The temporal disjunction between experiencing life-altering events and sharing them with loved ones in the homeland was emotionally difficult for

7. Ibid., 110, 111–13.

immigrants. Women may have felt this more strongly than men, accustomed as most of them were to ongoing intimate exchanges within the family. In lieu of real human contact, letters were the only available substitute. Much as Jette Bruns had done, Käthchen Hamm wrote a moving letter from Ste. Genevieve to her sister Christine Venus in Iowa, describing how she prepared her infant daughter for burial:

> [We] washed her and I had her dressed as if she were alive, her white underclothes and a short white dress with short sleeves. Her little arms were still just as chubby and white as in life. She had the same small, beautifully formed arms as you. I often said to Hamm that she would probably resemble you in everything. Then I had them put a wreath all around the baby and one of little white flowers around her little head and wrists and shoes and [she] looked just as if she were alive.[8]

Apparently these two sisters never saw each other again after separating in St. Louis, a year or two after they arrived there together in 1849. But the loving bonds they sought to maintain and the longing for old family relationships are evident in the letters they wrote for almost two decades after parting.

Homesickness was a common experience for immigrants, whatever their regional and social background. Female German-speakers may have felt freer to admit it, however, than the men in their communities. Henry Bode remembered his mother, Elizabeth Kirsch Bode, sitting by the window of their Femme Osage parsonage on many occasions, weeping with homesickness. A visitor to Missouri in the 1830s reported that his parents' former maid burst into tears when she recognized him and then complained of her isolation on a farm outside of Hermann. A woman who had immigrated to Missouri at the age of thirteen with the Saxon Old Lutherans still thought her homeland the best place on earth forty years later and asserted that the finest American pastry could not match her mother's Christmas kuchen. In 1853 Jesse Benton Frémont witnessed a sudden attack of homesickness suffered by a woman who had resided in Missouri for twenty-four years. Reminded by Mrs. Frémont's genteel apparel of her former life in Kassel, she burst into tears, complaining that she had never left the little town of Washington since coming to America.[9]

---

8. Undated letter (probably spring or summer 1860), "Correspondence received, 1849–70," Joseph Venus Collection, Iowa State Historical Department, Historical Society, Iowa City, Iowa. Unless otherwise indicated, all translations from the German are my own.

9. Henry Bode, *Builders of Our Foundation* (Webster Groves, Mo.: privately printed, 1940), 162; Frederic Trautmann, "Missouri through a German's Eyes: Franz von Löher

And yet we must remember that most immigrant women, including Jette Bruns, persevered in their new lives in spite of bouts of loneliness and homesickness. They tried to make things as good as possible for those around them. Women who lived in larger communities near extended family or in faith-based groups generally had an easier time adjusting to their new lives than did Jette Bruns. Christiane Loeber's 1839 letters from Perry County show how membership in a group could help arm an educated, middle-class woman against despair and cultural alienation. She mentioned the miserable living conditions, the scarceness of food, and the illness and death that were so prevalent in the colony in the first winter. But she also expressed a firm conviction that God was overseeing the venture and asserted that God had sent the abundant harvest of 1839 so that neighboring Americans could be especially generous to the starving colonists. Christiane Loeber paid back the Americans with needlework and shared her room and money with an impoverished widow with two children. Although she died in April 1840, before she could implement her plans to help support the colony by earning money by spinning and weaving, the tone of cheerful confidence in God's grace and in the sustaining power of the Perry County religious community speaks clearly through her letters.[10]

Like the Saxon Old Lutherans, the shared religious convictions and communal life of the nuns and priests who came to Missouri in the nineteenth century were usually a strong support in their adjustments to America. A good example of this is the Ursuline community founded in St. Louis in 1848. For the next forty years, the Ursulines continued to recruit new members from their originating convent in Bavaria while running a successful boarding school in St. Louis and later a second one in Iron Mountain. Well into the twentieth century, they trained and sent German-speaking nuns out as teachers for many Missouri ethnic parishes and supported the

---

on St. Louis and Hermann," *Missouri Historical Review* 77 (1983), 388; Margarethe Lenk, *Fühnzehn Jahre in Amerika* (Zwickau: Johannes Hermann, 1911), 54–55; Jesse Benton Fremont, *The Story of the Guard: A Chronicle of the War* (Boston: Ticknor and Fields, 1863), 56–57.

10. Christiane Loeber's letters of fall 1839 and December 4, 1839, are found in *Von Altenburg (Sachsen-Altenburg) nach Altenburg in Nordamerika (Missouri). Ein Briefwechsel aus den Jahren 1838–1844*, ed. Heinrich Loeber-Eichenberg (Kahla, Germany: J. Beck, 1912), 28–32, 38–43. See also Stella Wuerffel, "Women in the Saxon Immigration," *Concordia Historical Institute Quarterly* 35 (fall 1962): 81–95; Pickle, "Women of the Saxon Immigration and Their Church," *Concordia Historical Institute Quarterly* 57 (winter 1984): 146–61; and Louise Buenger Robbert, "Lutheran Families in St. Louis and Perry County, Missouri, 1839–1870," *Missouri Historical Review* 82 (July 1988): 424–38.

efforts of other German-speaking religious orders to found communities in the state. The letters that the first immigrant sisters wrote back to their motherhouse in Landshut contain many passages that reveal the bonds of affection among the sisters and their dependence on each other for support in the new environment. For example, in February and March 1850, Mother Isabella Weinzierl wrote a series of messages to all of the Landshut sisters, in which she addressed things of particular interest to each. She described her seasickness to the four nursing sisters. She described how American ladies and Indians dressed for the fancy needlework teacher Mother Fortunata. She reminded Sister Borgia of the time they had spent together in Lucerne and addressed this special friend as "little bug of my heart." The immigrant nuns used their correspondence to continue personal bonds, describe their new experiences, seek sympathy for difficulties in adjustment, and ask advice on how to deal with the demands of a different church hierarchy. As was the case with many secular women, the support Catholic nuns sought from one another and in their letters home helped them attain their primary purposes in coming to Missouri. In their case, this was to support the Roman Catholic Church's ministry to the growing number of parishes in the state. The archives of the foundations made by German-speaking nuns in Missouri are rich repositories of fascinating material that offers insights into the immigrant experience in general and that of female immigrants in particular. As one Ursuline chronicler has written, women in such groups played an important role "in a particularly nineteenth century American setting of a predominantly German ethnic community."[11]

The support of others who shared one's religious beliefs and purposes in emigrating was not always enough to ensure that women could adjust to and be successful in America, however. An example is Luise Marbach, whose husband, Franz, was a leader among the Saxon Old Lutheran immigrants. She succeeded in getting her husband to return to Germany, but only after losing five of her seven children. Another example of failed immigration is Sophie Luise Duensing. She fled a forced marriage and was determined never to wed when she boarded a ship to America in 1848. But during the trip she met a missionary minister, Gotthilf Weitbrecht, and agreed to become his wife to help him in his work. During the year and a

11. "Letters to Landshut Ursuline Convent," German TS, Ursuline Archives, Central Province, Crystal City, Mo., box II H, Kirkwood, folder 2, pp. 105–25. Sr. Ignatius Miller, *Ursulines of the Central Province* (Crystal City, Mo.: Ursuline Provincialate, 1983), 92. See also Pickle, "German and Swiss Nuns in Nineteenth-Century Missouri and Southern Illinois: Some Comparisons with Secular Women," *Yearbook of German-American Studies* 20 (1985): 61–82.

half they spent serving three country parishes in the woods outside St. Louis, they were afflicted with illness:

> The summer was terribly hot. Large trees surrounded the little parsonage, so that no fresh air could get through. Water had to be fetched far away in the forest. I was sick, Father came back from a visit to people sick with dysentery. He had to get up often out of bed, but then was too weak to climb back in, remained kneeling in front of the bed, asking for water. There wasn't any in the house; I didn't have the strength to fetch it. We thought we were going to die; little Gotthilf, two years old, ran from one bed to the other. Thus the day passed.

Finally toward evening a neighbor woman looked in on them, gave them water, and sent for a doctor. The Weitbrechts recovered, but Sophie Luise was so weakened that she had to stay in bed six weeks. A daughter born soon after died within two months. Although always convinced of the importance of her husband's calling, both Sophie Luise and her husband struggled with the physical conditions of the frontier, the lack of a supportive church structure, and the lack of a homogenous religious culture among German immigrants in America. They were happy to return to their Swabian homeland nine years after immigrating.[12]

The Missouri climate and geographic environment also posed challenges to German-speaking immigrants. In September 1837 Jette Bruns wrote:

> We have also had some very warm days here, warmer than I have ever experienced, but not so sultry. One can sit quietly on a chair and the perspiration runs quietly down one's cheeks in drops, and I often wonder that I am so warm and feel it so little. . . . However, this summer is said not to be equal to the ones in former years; the last few weeks we again had cooler nights. The change in the weather is so sudden here that it is really amazing. Now it is again very warm, but last week I wanted to have somebody go and fetch our featherbeds.

In her more negative moods, Jette also found the lush Missouri landscape uncongenial: "At home I could take pleasure in the outdoors, and I became happy as a child after a walk. Here it makes me melancholy to see the wild, desolate abundance of plants and trees. The disadvantages make

---

12. Forster, *Zion on the Mississippi,* 175, 284, 529–30. Sophie Luise Weitbrecht, "Neun schwere Aufbaujahre in deutschen Gemeinden der Vereinigten Staaten von Nordamerika (1848–57)," comp. Hans-Thorald Michaelis, *Genealogie* 2 (1980): 57.

walking disagreeable, the ticks, all kinds of hindrances such as burrs, the lack of well-built roads." Some immigrants adapted to the heat and the difficult conditions of frontier life by lowering the standards of dress and cleanliness that they had brought with them from Europe. Their countrymen were appalled and often gave no regard to the poverty that was also a likely factor in such cases. Riding between Union and Washington, Missouri, in the summer of 1835, Friederich Gustorf noted in his diary the filthy living conditions of immigrant farmers from Osnabrück. He refused to drink the water offered by one woman because she and her naked children were so dirty. He was even more repulsed by the next woman he encountered, who was dirtier than the first and dressed only in her shift.[13]

Nuns could not shed exterior layers of their clothing in a similar fashion. An Ursuline wrote that in the intense St. Louis heat of July 1849 she changed her perspiration-drenched habit three times a day and that she and other sisters suffered from a miserable heat rash. The Swiss Benedictine sisters who opened a school in Maryville in 1874 reported the snow that sifted into the attic dormitory and the prairie winds that rocked the shabby rectory that they shared at first with the parish priests. Although one wrote of the grandeur of American sunrises and sunsets and the starry skies over the vast prairie, she also noted the dirty path to the church and the many pigs searching in the garbage. Another praised the charms of the rolling hill country around Maryville, but she and others also missed the mountainous landscape of their homeland. In one of her first letters back to Switzerland, their leader wrote of their homesickness: "In the evening it would do us good to spend some time in our beloved mountains!" Later she thanked her Mother Superior for sending them a picture of the mountains of their Swiss homeland.[14]

German-speaking nuns came to Missouri to continue work that they had carried out in Europe. The Ursulines, the Benedictines, the Sisters of the Adoration of the Most Precious Blood, and the School Sisters of Notre

13. Schroeder and Schulz-Geisberg, *Hold Dear,* 82, 144; Frederick Julius Gustorf, *The Uncorrupted Heart: Journal and Letters of Frederick Julius Gustorf,* ed. and trans. Fred Gustorf and Gisela Gustorf (Columbia: University of Missouri Press, 1969), 131.

14. "Letters to Landshut," 54, 70–71; M. Beatrice Renggli, OSB, "From Rickenbach to Maryville: An Account of the Journey," *American Benedictine Review* 27 (1976), 266; *Letters from Mother M. Anselma Felber, OSB, and Others,* trans. M. Dominica Bonnenberg, OSB (St. Louis: Benedictine Sisters of Perpetual Adoration, 1977; manuscript letters of Mother Anselma and others, Archives of the Benedictine Sisters of Perpetual Adoration, St. Louis, photocopies of German originals with English translations), letters of September 12, 1874, February 15, 1875, May 29, 1875, July 12, 1876, July 17, 1876.

Dame all founded schools in larger communities and sent sisters to German-speaking rural and small-town parishes to educate children. Mother Odilia Berger founded a new order, the Sisters of St. Mary, that opened a refuge for unwed mothers (1874–1877), ran an orphanage (1876–1882), and established St. Mary's Infirmary (1877), beginning a tradition of health care that is still important in the state today. But all of these immigrant sisters had to make adjustments to their accustomed work and lives. American bishops pressured them to send small groups of sisters away from the convent to establish schools, to accept boys as well as girls in those schools, and to modify their strict traditions of prayer, contemplation, and enclosure. In remote or frontier regions, nuns often had no priests to administer the sacraments. If priests were present, they were sometimes as much a burden as a comfort to the sisters. One of the Benedictine sisters at Maryville taught school, was in charge of the church choir, had additional household duties in the rectory, and was given the responsibility of caring for the priests' two horses. Her confessor reported back to the Swiss motherhouse that she was "greatly tested—temptations of suicide, of running away, so that she can barely stand it." Another sister reported a month after her arrival in Maryville: "In the evening I am so tired that I can hardly stand or kneel during prayer."[15]

Statements of this sort contrast with men's reports on the labor performed by middle-class immigrant women. Gert Goebel, who came to Missouri as a boy, asserted of the immigrant women of his mother's generation "that precisely the most educated German women became the best farmers' wives. They were the least demanding and the most modest and never demanded comforts and unnecessary advantages, to which they certainly were accustomed but which went beyond the financial powers of their husbands. These women, who never lost sight of the value of their genuine female dignity, did not consider it a scandal to wash, scour, and milk cows with their own hands, in other words, to do work that they never needed to do earlier." Writing earlier than Goebel, Friedrich Muench, who had bitter personal experience of the hard labor that frontier conditions demanded of women and men, acknowledged that some educated

15. *Letters from Mother M. Anselma Felber, OSB, and Others,* letters of March 5, 1877, July 17, 1876. Other rich sources on immigrant nuns include M. Pascaline Coff, OSB, et al., *100 Years for You: The Story of the Benedictine Sisters of Perpetual Adoration* (St. Louis: Congregation of Benedictine Sisters of Perpetual Adoration, 1974); "Chronicles, O'Fallon, Missouri, 1870–1881," Archives of the Sisters of the Adoration of the Most Precious Blood, Collection I, D, Transition to America, folder 9; Mary Gabriel Henniger, SSM, *Sisters of St. Mary and Their Healing Mission* (St. Louis: Sisters of St. Mary of the Third Order of St. Francis, 1979).

immigrant women were "disconsolate" because of what they had lost by coming to America. But he nonetheless declared: "Yet the great majority of German women accustom themselves with that good and upright will, which is characteristic of the better among them, to their new conditions, and while the former force their husbands to spend extravagantly, the latter are their husband's most essential support. . . . Our women here have a significant and difficult task, but they sense its importance, are never plagued with boredom, and are content with what they accomplish every day for the good of their loved ones."[16]

We get a different picture from the testimony of Jette Bruns. One of her earliest negative experiences in Missouri was during a visit to the neighbor who had led her husband to the Westphalia settlement and convinced him of its advantages. Jette wrote:

> Our first visit to Mr. Hesse's upset me very much. The lady took Bruns aside, cried, and complained that she couldn't stand it here. They were the only refined family in the settlement. No doubt Mr. Hesse himself was to be blamed that he wasn't doing so well. He had brought with him a teacher, a secretary, workmen, and a maid. He wanted to establish a distillery at a time when there weren't even fields there. As soon as the people began to claim American wages, it didn't work.[17]

Five months after the Brunses arrived in Missouri, the Hesses returned to Germany. Jette's letter reporting this confirmed the importance of family harmony and cooperation for successful immigration:

> Mr. Hesse toiled honestly in his field, but he alone, with his quick temperament, could not accomplish enough. The children were not directed to do anything; the mother lived only for her children and wished nothing more than to return. And here sat Mr. Hesse, without means, without help, without a prospect. It is true that only after long resistance did he decide to give in finally to the will of his wife. Perhaps in the end he secretly longed to return himself; however, without the strong urging of the latter he probably would never have decided to do it.[18]

16. Gert Goebel, *Länger als ein Menschenleben in Missouri* (St. Louis: C. Witter, 1877), 68; Friedrich Muench, *Der Staat Missouri, geschildert mit besonderer Rücksicht auf teutsche Einwanderung* (New York: Press of the Farmers' and Vinegrowers' Society, 1859), 99–100.

17. Schroeder and Schulz-Geisberg, *Hold Dear,* 71.

18. Ibid., 80.

Jette herself was determined to do her part to make her husband's dreams of betterment come true. In the first months of immigration, she tried to put the best face possible on the unaccustomed work she had to do: "You cannot believe how satisfying it is to work. I probably have had few days in which I was ever as busy as I am here, that is, having to do hard work, but I'm quite happy in doing it, and like all the others I have a tremendous appetite and sleep soundly." Later, however, she wrote of the burdensome aspects of this labor, which often had to do with the many extra men she cooked and cleaned for: her brothers, hired hands, and workers on various construction projects. Having domestic help and, for a time, slaves did not reconcile her to her own work and the supervision of a large and extended household. On one occasion, she complained about cooking for weeks for the men building the Brunses' mill and wished that her brother would marry to make her own burden less. Ten years after immigrating, she wrote: "I do not like farm life at all anymore. I long for peace. It does not bring me anything but a great deal of trouble."[19]

Women's labor in the home and for family businesses was crucial for material success in America. Jette Bruns was often left in charge of running the family store in Westphalia and supervising the workers who built their house and the mill that they also established there. In 1851 the Bruns family moved to a farm with a ferry across the Osage River. This brought Jette new work: lodging strangers. All of these activities took their toll on the woman who had come to Missouri as a cultivated young wife. Shortly after the new year in 1853, in a letter to her brother, Jette described herself at thirty-nine years of age: "There is none of the youthful freshness left, but instead a stiff, sad, indifferent figure, without manners, without interest, with aged features, a mouth without teeth." A year later, the family decided to move to Jefferson City, where Jette's husband could establish a medical practice without lengthy absences and where the children (by this time the Brunses had had seven more children and lost two of them) would be better educated. Jette's husband and brother eventually established a successful store in the center of the capital city and Bernhard Bruns even became mayor. But he died suddenly in April 1864 while still in office, leaving Jette alone with three half-grown children plus two of her brother's. Then she discovered that her husband's estate was in disarray and heavily in debt: "I am now constantly studying in what way I might be able to earn something. My strength is giving out, I work a lot in the garden and the house, but often the hardest work pays least." She decided to take

19. Ibid., 67, 101, 135.

in boarders in order to "keep up appearances." But first she had to satisfy her husband's creditors. Her comments on how she faced these difficulties tell us a great deal about the reservoirs of strength and pragmatism that no doubt many women relied on in similar trying circumstances:

> I have had a hard time to live through. On 8 March [1865] I had a public sale, and then I repurchased what I believed I could not do without. Since that time we have tried to get settled again, and this means vacating as many rooms as possible in order to rent them out. Our bedroom was the first—the most beautiful, the most airy room in the city. In the beginning I was constantly shaking my head and did not know where to begin. Then I wanted to be strong and I attacked it, and then I suddenly got to crying until I was quite dull, and then it worked. Now I have been almost completely settled in my living room for the past two weeks, but since that time I have had a cold and fever, etc. And now during the most beautiful spring weather I have to stay inside. And there is the garden to take care of, and making soap, and the girls can't do anything. If I want to hire a man to help me, that costs two dollars per day. Well, I'll practice patience.

Such dogged patience, hard work, frugality, and attention to detail helped Jette Bruns persevere through those difficult days. Prominent German American congressmen of the day boarded with her during the legislative sessions of the next years, so that her home became known as "the radical corner." She eventually saw her daughters well married and her sons settled.[20]

Negative testimony about physical labor, especially from women like Jette Bruns and the missionary nuns who did not come from a peasant or working-class background, may give a lopsided impression that all German-speaking women resented the hard work they had to do to help their families settle in Missouri. We must remember, however, that women sometimes used their letters to relieve their frustrations. It is likely that most immigrant women were used to such work and accepted it as necessary and not worthy of complaint or even comment. Margaret Blauff Hillenkamp may serve as an example. No documents written by her survive, although we know something about her life from letters her husband wrote to Germany and from public records. Born in 1810, she came to St. Charles County from Warstein and in November 1835 married Frederick Hillenkamp, who had come to Missouri from Velmede in the Rhine area a year earlier. Unlike

20. Ibid., 159, 157, 13–14, 196, 201–2, 197–98.

her husband, Margaret Blauff does not seem to have been an educated person. We know that she was hardworking and that her contributions were vital to the economic success that she and her family attained in Missouri. Her husband stated in his first extant letter (May 1843) that his wife had helped him clear and cultivate about twenty acres of his 145-acre forested land for crops. They had also planted an orchard, and he regularly took the fruit it produced, along with several hundred eggs from Margaret's chickens, to St. Louis to purchase all their necessary household goods. In January 1846 Hillenkamp wrote that his wife had helped him "in every kind of work when her circumstances allowed" (that is, when she was not pregnant). He also mentioned that they kept twelve sheep "for their own use," probably to produce wool for weaving. The Hillenkamps listed the same number of sheep in the 1860 agricultural census, along with five horses, two work oxen, four milk cows, ten head of cattle, and thirty pigs. The census did not count poultry or the value of eggs produced (an indication of the lack of attention paid to women's labor and moneymaking enterprises), so we cannot know if Margaret continued to pay for much of the ongoing family expenses. But it is likely that this was so. By 1860 the Hillenkamps' landholdings had almost doubled to 260 acres, 120 of these improved. They had three daughters and two sons living at home, ranging in age from twelve to twenty-three. One daughter had died in 1847, but with these five children, Frederich and Margaret Hillenkamp had the help that in January 1846 he had written was necessary for farming success in America. We cannot be sure that Margaret Hillenkamp was happier in her life than Jette Bruns. Compared to Jette, Margaret probably worked harder in physical terms, and without the benefit of hired help. But Margaret may well have been more content with her lot. Unlike Jette, she is likely to have had expectations about her life in terms of physical conditions, social contacts, and material progress that corresponded closely to the reality that she helped shape.[21]

Women of the educated classes no doubt also had more difficulty than those from peasant or craftsmen families in adjusting to certain aspects of the new culture around them, especially if they settled in rural areas. Jette Bruns chafed generally under the lack of genteel society and sophisticated culture that she had grown up enjoying and worried that her family was

21. Friedrich Gillet Hillenkamp, "Briefe 1843–1847," German TS, Bochumer Aus-wandererbriefsammlung, Ruhr University, Bochum, Germany; *Marriage Records of St. Charles County, Missouri, 1805–1844,* comp. Lois Stanley et al. (St. Louis, 1978), 43; *1860 U.S. Agricultural Census Manuscript Record,* Dardenne Township, St. Charles County, Missouri (U.S. Census Office, 1860).

declining in social status in America. She fretted about the lack of educational opportunities for her children in the Missouri woods and, a devout Roman Catholic, she also found religious education and pastoral care especially wanting on the rural Missouri frontier. Other women noted similar lacks in American society and culture. On their trip to Missouri, the women in the families of the colony-founding Solingen Society leaders found the casual and rude behavior of tobacco-chewing male American travelers offensive. In a conversation with Friedrich Gustorf, a Mrs. Tappe, recently arrived in Missouri from Bielefeld, wondered if Americans "had religion," since they always walked around with long bowie knives in their belts. Julie Turnau, on her way to St. Louis to meet her betrothed, the Evangelical pastor George Wall, was taken aback by the unconcerned behavior of the American river pilot sent to guide her ship into dock at New Orleans. This gentleman, no doubt accustomed to dealing with the southern climate, took off his coat to nap at midday on the bare boards of the ship's deck. German-speaking nuns wrote that Americans were generally careless, their children too independent and unruly, their buildings and goods cheaply made, and their culture too materialistic. But female immigrants from peasant or working-class families had other cultural and social expectations. If they could see that their new lives offered promise of economic betterment for their children, this was the most important consideration and a justification for the loss of their accustomed surroundings.[22]

Immigrant women who were forced to interact with Americans experienced additional stress in their adjustment to their new lives. Those who stayed at home and lived in close-knit ethnic communities could often avoid learning English; they only needed enough English to use in shops. Other women found it necessary to learn it quickly. The immigrant nuns who ran schools or tended to the sick, especially in communities that were not dominated by German-speakers, were under particular pressure to acquire sufficient English language skills as quickly as possible. The stress this caused is especially clear in the letters that the Swiss Benedictines wrote from Maryville. Jette Bruns also came in frequent contact with Americans because of her husband's business ventures and her family's general position

22. Schroeder and Schulz-Geisberg, *Hold Dear,* 92n35, 80, 103–4, 113, 116, 199, 125, 128, 136–37, 171; Frederick Steines, letter of September 15, 1834, in Wilhelm Bek, trans., "Followers of Duden," *Missouri Historical Review* 15 (1921), 530; Gustorf, *Uncorrupted Heart,* 129; Diary of Julie Turnau Wall, 1842, trans. Armin Saeger, TS, p. 28, Eden Theological Seminary Archives. On "culture shock," see also "Letters to Landshut," 7, 17–18, 81, 123–24. For a discussion of peasants' attitudes toward immigration, see chapter 2 of Pickle, *Contented.*

in the community. In 1837 she wrote of her embarrassment at not knowing English better: "I have progressed with my English speaking so far that I can understand occasionally a few common little sentences and can reproduce them. I must really learn more, for it annoys me tremendously when I stand there like a blockhead and cannot answer." Ten years later, in a blue mood at the end of a long, hard winter, she said: "You cannot imagine how hard it is to become accustomed to things here. The customs, the morals, the language, people without feeling, everything is foreign and cold." With time, Jette did learn English tolerably well. Particularly after her family moved to Jefferson City and her husband became a successful businessman and eventually the city's mayor, she was forced to use it more and more. But like many other German-speakers, the Brunses spoke German at home into the third generation and associated the use of their native tongue with education and culture.[23]

Other immigrants connected the German language to religious practice. Missouri religious communities founded by German speakers clung to the use of German for this reason. Some communities of immigrant nuns regarded using German as part of their religious mission. Several orders continued to speak German within their communities, even for liturgical purposes, until World War I. Convent archives also contain records indicating that immigrant nuns retained their foreign citizenship for many years after coming to America. The Missouri Synod Lutherans were particularly tenacious about retaining their language. They continued to hold church services in German until after World War II in many Missouri communities.[24]

In all immigrant families, women played a central role in language and cultural retention. The same woman who hosted Jesse Frémont in Washington and burst into tears of homesickness in her presence had also managed to recreate some of her old life in the New World. Mrs. Frémont commented on the German atmosphere of her lodgings, enhanced by German-style food and furnishings and culminating in an evening of German music performed by the entire immigrant family. German-speaking women

23. "Letters from Mother Anselma," September 12, 1874, November 7, 1874, February 15, 1875, late March 1875, Easter 1875, April 30, 1875, November 1875, April 5, 1876; Schroeder and Schulz-Geisberg, *Hold Dear,* 77, 144.

24. On the language retention of immigrant religious women, see Pickle, "German and Swiss Nuns," 78; and Mary Ewens, OP, "The Role of the Nun in Nineteenth-Century America: Variations on the International Theme" (Ph.D. diss., University of Minnesota, 1971), 136. German cultural values of "plain simplicity, good morality, and . . . the beloved German language" were considered central underpinnings of the Synod's conservative faith (Lenk, *Fühnzehn Jahre,* 34).

left their most obvious mark, both within and outside of the ethnic community, by handing down foodways and holiday practices. Some customs, such as erecting Christmas trees, were adopted by non-German neighbors, and pre-Christmas visits by Belsnickel—a stern St. Nicholas dressed in furs who warned children they had better be good—continued into the twentieth century in some Missouri German American areas. The sausages and sauerkraut, the dumplings and roast goose that were mainstays of the immigrant table came to be accepted outside the ethnic communities as well. Missouri breweries and vineyards in the nineteenth century owed their existence to German-speaking immigrants. Except for the minority of immigrants who joined American Protestant denominations, German speakers, both male and female, Protestant and Catholic, considered wine and beer dietary mainstays and were staunch opponents of prohibition in Missouri as elsewhere. Women also supported the tradition of Sunday family excursions to wine and beer gardens. While this practice shocked and angered Anglo-Americans, it was a welcome opportunity for women as well as men to socialize in a setting reminiscent of their homeland. Today, Missouri residents of many ethnic backgrounds enjoy this aspect of the German speakers' heritage, as is evidenced by the popularity of Maifest and Oktoberfest celebrations throughout the towns of Missouri's Rhineland.[25]

In retrospect, we know that the German-speaking immigrants to Missouri had much in common with other immigrant groups in the state and elsewhere. Women's documents and experiences give us insights into the nature, costs, and advantages of immigration on an intimate level. It is important that we understand the immigrant experience in all its ramifications, for it will continue to affect public and private life in Missouri and the United States. It has shaped our culture in significant and lasting ways and is, after all, one of the quintessential American experiences. The history of nineteenth-century German-speaking women in Missouri helps illustrate the complexity and the importance of that experience.

---

25. Frémont, *Story of the Guard,* 57. Elizabeth Ewen has said that the female world in an immigrant community "created a web of personal, social, and familial relationships that mediated the world of culture left behind and the alien culture they had stepped into" (*Immigrant Women in the Land of Dollars: Life and Culture on the Lower East Side, 1890–1925* [New York: Monthly Review Press, 1985], 37). Steve Parsons, "A German-Style Ozarks Christmas: Before Santa There Was Scary Old Belsnickels," *Ozarks Mountaineer* 40 (November/December 1992): 32–35. On the retention of German customs, see Adolf E. Schroeder, "The Survival of German Traditions in Missouri," in *The German Contribution to the Building of the Americas,* ed. G. K. Friesen (Hanover, N.H.: Clark University Press, 1977), 289–313.

"May We as One Family Live in Peace and Harmony"

Relations between Mistresses and Slave Women in Antebellum Missouri

Diane Mutti Burke

After two weeks of conflict between the slave and slaveholding members of her household, Paulina Stratton pleaded to God in her diary, "[M]ay we as Christians forgive one another and as one family live in peace and harmony." Stratton not only described her family as including both white and slave members, but her words also evoked a highly personal system of economic and social relations, much more "domestic" than that which prevailed in the plantation South. Such a description would have rung true to many of her contemporaries, for in Missouri most slaveholding farmers owned only one family of slaves, living and working alongside them in their homes and fields.[1]

1. Missouri slave mistress Paulina Stratton wrote these lines shortly before migrating from the Kanawha Valley of western Virginia to central Missouri. She expressed the same kind of sentiments after moving to Missouri, for the nature of her relationship with her slave women did not change dramatically after their move. Like Missouri, western Virginia was also a region of small-slaveholding and yeoman farmers. Slaveholding migrants brought to Missouri methods of slave management they had learned in the small-scale slavery districts of the Upper South. See Fall 1852, Pauline Stratton Collection (hereinafter cited as Stratton Collection), Western Historical Manuscript Collection–Columbia, University of Missouri–Columbia (hereinafter cited as WHMC-C). See also Harrison Trexler, *Slavery in Missouri, 1804–1865* (Baltimore: Johns Hopkins University Press, 1914), 19.

Plantation slavery never developed in Missouri, in part because the state was unsuitable for large-scale cotton production, but also because Missouri's geographic position on the northwestern border of the slave South made slavery appear vulnerable. Most slaveholding migrants to Missouri were small holders who came from the backcountry areas of the Upper South rather than the region's plantation districts. In a majority of Missouri's counties, over 90 percent of the slavcholders owned ten or fewer slaves, and a small percentage of the state's farmers ever achieved planter status: few owned over twenty slaves, and almost none owned more than fifty. By the 1830s, Missouri had emerged as a magnet for southern slaveholding families of limited means, who were attracted by a climate in which they could replicate the patterns of diversified agriculture found in their original homes. By 1860, slaveholders had settled throughout the state, but most lived in the counties bordering the Missouri and Mississippi Rivers.[2]

Although slavery was firmly entrenched in the state as an economic, political, and social institution, the profile of Missouri's slaveholding households often better reflected that of the family farm than of the plantation. Instead of concentrating on a single cash crop, most farmers produced a wide variety of products for household and market use, such as grains, livestock, tobacco, and hemp. The modest size of these farms meant that few required a large number of laborers. Each day the farm family toiled together with its small slave workforce to maintain both agricultural and domestic operations. The master and his sons worked alongside his slave men, boys, and occasionally women, and together they cleared the land, planted, harvested, and tended the livestock. The mistress and her daughters, meanwhile, labored with the slave women and small children to complete their daily household duties. Slaves performed the most arduous tasks, and because overseers were rare most slaveholders directly supervised and assisted this labor.

The unique working and living conditions found on small-slaveholding farms in Missouri profoundly shaped the experiences of slaveholding families and their slaves. The lives of mistresses and slave women were particularly affected by the conditions of small-scale slavery because the intimacy of farm life fostered a personal relationship between the women and allowed them the extraordinary power to influence the quality of one another's

2. See R. Douglas Hurt, *Agriculture and Slavery in Missouri's Little Dixie* (Columbia: University of Missouri Press, 1992), 219–22; Sam Bowers Hilliard, *Atlas of Antebellum Agriculture* (Baton Rouge: University of Louisiana Press, 1984), 37–38; and Russel L. Gerlach, *Settlement Patterns in Missouri: A Study of Population Origins with a Wall Map* (Columbia: University of Missouri Press, 1986), 15.

lives. While slave women were provided with unique opportunities to resist their enslavement, the lack of individual autonomy and family and community support found on most Missouri farms also complicated their existence.

In Missouri, the lives of slaveholding and slave women were defined by more conventional divisions of labor than were found on the South's plantations. As on plantations, the mistress's role as supervisor of domestic operations—preparing food, keeping the house clean, being in charge of clothing, and taking care of children—was crucial to the economic well-being of the household. Due to a small slave workforce, Missouri's mistresses engaged in more actual labor and were less involved in leisure pursuits than were their plantation counterparts. Slaveholding women supervised and augmented the labor of their slave women, who performed the most backbreaking of the household tasks, while mistresses devoted much of their time to child care and needlework. Many slave women worked in the house at domestic chores and moved to the fields only during periods of peak agricultural activity.

Since in Missouri most slaveholders owned only one, or at most two, adult female slaves, rarely were they assigned to specific household or field duties, as was the custom on plantations. Instead, most Missouri slave women worked within the small-slaveholding household, performing a wide variety of domestic tasks under the supervision and often with the assistance of mistresses. Slave women labored as cooks, housekeepers, and laundry women, but they assisted the mistress with cloth production, sewing, and child care when these primary chores were done. Former slave Marilda Pethy remembered, "Mother done everything. Dey had two cooks but both of dem done all kinds of work." And former slave Mollie Renfro Sides recalled, "Mah mammy done de cookin' an' 'twen time she'd weave on de loom, an' spin an' knit." Maintaining a small-slaveholding household required tremendous labor from slave women. "Old Miss Howard" never allowed her slave woman, Sarah Waggoner, to work in the fields, believing that her labor was much more valuable in the home. Waggoner explained, "Oh Lordee, but I worked hard since I was twelve years old. But not in de fields. Old Miss she say dere was plenty for me to do in de house, and dere was, sure 'nough."[3]

While most slave women worked primarily in their owners' homes, it was nonetheless common for slave women to move to the fields, especially

3. Marilda Pethy interview, in George P. Rawick, ed., *The American Slave: A Composite Autobiography* (Westport, Conn.: Greenwood Press, 1972), 11:277–82 (hereinafter cited as *AS*). Mollie Renfro Sides interview, in ibid., 11:310. Sarah Waggoner interview, in ibid., 11:355–64.

during planting and harvesting. Although a few large Missouri slaveholdings included female field hands, most households were too small for exclusive assignments of slave women to field labor. Melinda Discus remembered, "My mother was a fine cook and worked indoors mostly, though she did some work in the fields too." Whether or not slave women spent much time in the fields depended upon the demographic makeup of the slaveholding and the presence of grown sons in the master's family. On the Stratton and Napton farms, there were enough slave men, older slave boys, and slaveholding sons to maintain the agriculture enterprises of the farms without much labor from slave women. But on many smaller slaveholdings, the work of slave women in the fields was crucial. On Joe Lane's farm, the only adult male slave was elderly, and therefore his slave woman, Allie Ann Lane, worked in the fields rather than in the house. As Allie Lane's son, James Monroe Abbot, recalled, "My Muthuh wuz big an' strong . . . dey warn't nothin on de place dat she couldn' do. She cud cut down a big tree en chop off a rail length an' use a wedge an' maul an' make rails as good as anybody."[4]

Slave women labored not only in their owners' homes and fields, but also for their own husbands and children. After work, slave women often cooked their families' evening meals and completed chores around their cabins. Care of their children consumed much of their free time and it was not unusual for slave women to watch their young children and babies in the house or field while they labored throughout the day. Other slave women, such as Sarah Graves's mother, tended their personal crops or livestock at night in order to generate spending money for their families' use. It was also common for slave women, like William Nelson's mother, to supplement their families' meager diets through the cultivation of their own garden plots.[5]

Although slave women performed most domestic tasks, the few female slaves owned by most Missouri slaveholders made the labor of mistresses necessary. While a plantation mistress's role was largely supervisory, Missouri's small-slaveholding women were unable to keep from getting their hands dirty. Most mistresses merely managed slave women as they cooked, cleaned, and washed, performing these strenuous chores themselves only

4. Melinda Discus interview, in ibid., supp., ser. 1, 2:166–70; Stratton Collection; William B. Napton Papers (hereinafter cited as Napton Papers), Missouri Historical Society, St. Louis, Missouri (hereinafter cited as MHS); James Monroe Abbot interview, in *AS* 11:1–5.

5. Annie Bridges interview, in *AS* 11:43–50; Mattie Jackson, *The Story of Mattie J. Jackson* (Lawrence, Kans.: Sentinel Office, 1866), 12–13; Sarah Graves interview, in *AS* 11:126–38; William Nelson interview, in *AS* 16:74–75.

while slave women recovered from sickness and childbirth. In fact, mistresses so rarely engaged in this type of labor that it elicited special remarks in their diaries and letters. Elvira Weir Scott, the wife of a Miami, Missouri, merchant, wrote that she did "the cooking & most of the housework for a family of 10" for two weeks while her only slave woman, Margaret, recovered from childbirth. Mistresses were more directly involved with tasks such as sewing, child care, and maintenance of the barnyard and kitchen garden. The amount of work performed by small-slaveholding women depended on the household size and circumstances, including factors such as the number of female slaves owned by the family; the number of children in the family; the employment of husbands; and whether the family lived on a farm or in town. However much mistresses and their daughters labored in homes and barnyards, small-slaveholding women did not toil in the fields as did slave women and the wives and daughters of some non-slaveholding farmers. Owning slave women protected small-slaveholding women, like Paulina Stratton, from this type of labor. Only after emancipation did Stratton and her young children work in the fields.[6]

Most Missouri mistresses spent hours in the production of cloth and in sewing for both the white family and their slaves. Although by the middle of the nineteenth century women in many parts of the United States were buying their cloth rather than producing homespun, much cloth was still woven on Missouri's farms. Slave women frequently assisted mistresses in the production of homespun, which was often used for slave clothing. While a number of former slaves remembered their mothers sewing, the records indicate that it was most often the mistress who engaged in the bulk of the needlework for both the white family and its slaves. Melinda Napton constantly complained about her many hours of sewing, claiming that she barely had time to write her absent husband a letter. Manie Kendley remembered seeing her mother, Mary Jane Kendley, exhausted from sewing, asleep in her chair with garments scattered around her on the floor. One of Paulina Stratton's primary occupations was preparing clothing for the members of her household. Rather than use the labor of her slave women, Stratton invited her neighbors to a "sewing" to assist her with the preparation of the slaves' clothing. Although they also engaged in sewing for their households, plantation mistresses delegated more of this work to slave seamstresses than did the mistresses on Missouri's farms.[7]

6. March 1860, Elvira Ascenith Weir Scott Diary, 1860–1887, WHMC-C; Stratton Collection.

7. Melinda Napton to William B. Napton, November 4, 1857, and March 26, 1858, Napton Papers; Louis Filler, ed., *The New Stars* (Yellow Springs, Ohio: Antioch Press,

The most important job of small-slaveholding women was the care of their children. Although slave nurses sometimes assisted white mothers, most women did not own enough slaves to assign a slave woman to this specific task. On many farms, the only slave nurse was a young slave child who watched over the white children. Usually most of the care of the children fell to their mothers. In addition, in a state with scanty opportunities for public education, many women, like Melinda Napton and Manie Kendley's mother, spent hours overseeing the education of their children. Although the record is largely silent on the issue, it is also likely that some mistresses watched over slave children while their mothers worked. If the case of Sarah Graves Crowdes is indicative, it is probable that this care was not always vigilant. Sarah Graves's mother chose to take her to the field rather than leave her under the careless supervision of her mistress, Emily Crowdes. This decision was reached after the slave baby was nearly burned by a curtain that had caught fire near where she lay.[8]

The daily labor of slave women and their mistresses defined their days, and their relationship with one another was crucial to the quality of their lives. Slave and slaveholding women were bound together by common gender and work experiences, but their intimate relations were more likely to result in conflict than accord. The unique circumstances found on Missouri's small-slaveholding farms afforded slave women tremendous opportunities for resistance and at the same time eroded the already limited power of mistresses. Although this resistance provided some slave women with the means to improve their lives, small slaveholding exposed others to the worst forms of abuse. While many of the same issues plagued the relations between small-slaveholding men and male slaves, the complexities of this interaction were intensified among women, who were confined to the often-cramped quarters of the small-slaveholding household and lacked the space provided men, who labored in the fields and greater community.

Although it sometimes proved a double-edged sword, the close proximity in which Missouri's slave women and their mistresses lived and worked often benefited slaves. Small-scale slavery provided slave women with the

1949), 30; February 1856, November 27, 1856, February 1860, November 1860, and December 1860, Stratton Collection. See also Jeanette Leonard to Abiel Leonard, September 11, 18[40], Abiel Leonard Papers, WHMC-C.

8. For examples of slave children as nurses, see Margaret Nickens interview, in *AS* 11:263; and Marie Askin Simpson interview, in ibid., supp., ser. 1, 2:230–34. For the household education of slaveholding children, see Melinda Napton to William B. Napton, January 26, 1858, Napton Papers; and Filler, *New Stars*. For care of slave children by small-slaveholding mistresses, see Sarah Graves interview, in *AS* 11:126–38.

tools to shape their relationships with their owners in ways that generally were not possible for the average plantation slave. By virtue of their close daily relations with their mistresses, slave women were well placed to understand their owners' personalities and to use this knowledge to their advantage, notably by exploiting their mistresses' personal weaknesses in order to gain greater control over their circumstances. While slaves throughout the South used various forms of resistance as a means of negotiating their situation, resistance on farms was especially effective because it was directed at the individuals with whom slaves shared such a great part of their lives. Because slaves and owners knew one another so well it was often difficult to maintain the kind of distance between the parties needed to instill the respect and authority that made paternalism possible. Already operating with limited power, the negative impact on a mistress's ability to govern was often striking.

The case of Paulina Stratton dramatically reveals the masterful strategies many slave women employed to gain an upper hand in the small-slaveholding farm's power structure and the effects of this struggle on the relations among the slaveholding and slave members of the household. In 1855, the Strattons migrated to Cooper County, Missouri, from western Virginia, with their four children and their nine slaves, including two adult slave women. During the early years of Paulina and Thomas Stratton's married life, the couple lived with his mother, Mary Ann Stratton, on her Roanoke County, Virginia, farm. A power struggle developed between Mary Ann and Paulina Stratton over control of the household, which eventually undermined Paulina Stratton's authority over her slaves. The slave women learned to use the strained relations among Stratton family members to their advantage. For example, during Mary Ann Stratton's lifetime, the slaves knew that there were two mistresses, often with conflicting ideas about running a household and managing slaves, and frequently the female slaves attempted to play one mistress off of the other. An often-used tactic of the slave women involved telling one mistress stories about the other in order to cause trouble. Paulina Stratton recorded one such incident: "Patience spun the two days it rained and as usual told stories enough to keep her Mrs in hot water the rest of the week." Paulina Stratton's influence over her slaves, already irreversibly damaged, continued to decline well after Mary Ann Stratton's death and the family's move to Missouri. In addition, her husband, Thomas, constantly undermined her, which did little to bolster her authority in the household. Capitalizing on their mistress's weakness, the Stratton slaves used resistance to register their displeasure and occasionally to improve their circumstances. Throughout the years, the slaves often were insolent and disobedient and occasionally even verbally threatened their owners. Despite Paulina Stratton's best efforts, the relations between mistress and slaves were never harmonious.[9]

The Stratton slave women were not the only slaves who used the intimate conditions found in Missouri's small-slaveholding households to influence their lives for the better. Many Missouri slaveholders echoed the Strattons' complaints about unruly servants. Sallie Bedford described the slaves on her mother's farm as acting as if they were "entirely without a master, and serve us through their own good or bad will." When Mary Cox threatened to sell her slave woman, Polly, down the river for performing a task incorrectly, Polly told the mistress that she did not care to live there anyway. Other slaves openly made demands on their owners, as when one slave woman refused to go with a new mistress who had purchased her. Her owners acquiesced and called off the sale. Melinda Napton's elderly slave woman, Jinney, saucily challenged Napton's right to own her. She said that she had never wished to be brought from Napton's father's home in Tennessee to Missouri and that the Naptons "required work of her that she was unable to do." Jinney further claimed that she and her children were actually freepersons. Napton was so appalled by the slave woman's impudence that she wrote her husband: "I will not be imposed upon by her any longer, and Papa must either give me another or consent for her to be sold."[10]

As in the case of the Stratton slaves, it was especially common for slave women to use knowledge of the dynamics of the white family to manipulate a situation in their own favor. Cooper County slave Delicia Patterson took vengeance upon her difficult mistress when her master returned from an extended journey. The master asked Patterson to report to him if his in-laws, whom he disliked, came to visit in his absence. Disgruntled with waiting on the mistress's many relatives, Patterson tattled on the mistress to the master. Esther Easter also sought revenge against her master and mistress, both of whom she considered cruel. When her master returned on a furlough during the Civil War, Easter informed him that his wife was having an affair with a neighbor.[11]

Although slaves also resisted masters, both male and female slaves resisted

9. 1860 U.S. Census, Cooper County, Missouri. For quotation, see July 1853, Stratton Collection.

10. Sallie Bedford to dear sister, June 27, 1851, Charles Yancey Letters, 1839–1865, WHMC-C; Lucy Delaney, *From the Darkness Cometh the Light, or Struggles for Freedom* (St. Louis: J. T. Smith [1891]), 21; Smokey Eulenburg interview, in *AS* 11:109–12; Melinda Napton to William B. Napton, Friday evening [1840s], Napton Papers.

11. Delicia Patterson interview, in *AS* 11:269–76; Esther Easter interview, in ibid., 7:88–91.

the authority of mistresses because they perceived white women's weaker position in the power structure of the slaveholding household. Mistresses throughout the South lived with the problem of slave resistance, but the intimate relations found on farms in Missouri exacerbated its negative effects on white women's authority. Slave men often tested their mistresses' authority, knowing that the women physically were unable to punish them. Resistance was particularly acute when slaveholding men left the farm on business, whether for a few hours or for days; the scarcity of overseers in Missouri often left the mistress as the sole and final authority in her husband's absence. Judge Charles Yancey traveled frequently, leaving the management of the farm in the hands of his capable wife, Mary, whose letters to her husband chronicled constant struggles with her servants, particularly a male slave named Mose. As Charles Yancey observed, "Mose as usual finds it convenient to cut up some shines whenever I leave home." When Thomas Stratton was away from the farm, the family's one slave man, Ike, frequently used the opportunity to test Paulina's weak authority. But slave women, like Melinda Napton's Jinney, were just as likely to test their mistresses when their husbands were nearby as they were when they were away and unable to reinforce their authority.[12]

While most resistance was subtle, some slaves used more dramatic forms of resistance to register their displeasure. It was quite common for slave women to temporarily run off and hide if they were angry with their owners or were threatened with punishment. Most slaves returned within a few days to face the consequences. When she was a slave, Cynthy Logan often used this form of resistance to influence her treatment by her owners. She hated her master because he had bought her in Arkansas and separated her from her husband and twins. Logan's daughter, Rachal Goings, claimed her mother was half-Cherokee and was always "mad and had a mean look in her eye. When she got her Indian up de white folks let her alone. She usta run off to de woods till she git over it. One time she tuk me and went to de woods an' it was nigh a month fore dey found her." A Greene County woman recalled that as a small child she was left in the charge of a slave woman while her parents were away on a trip. The slave woman ran off with the white child when the man who had been left to manage the farm told her to work in the fields rather than allow her to watch her white

12. Charles Yancey to Mary Yancey, October 16, 1855, November 1, 1855, and October 27–28, 1857, and Mary Yancey to Charles Yancey, October 13, 1854, and Sunday evening, 1855, in Yancey Letters, 1839–1865, WHMC-C; January 1857 and March 1863, Stratton Collection; Melinda Napton to William B. Napton, Friday evening [1840s], Napton Papers.

charge. Slave women were more likely to run away temporarily as a means of resisting their owners' authority than they were to leave permanently in search of freedom. Despite the close proximity to the free states, the odds of a slave woman's successful flight were not great, because she often had her children in tow.[13]

It was not unusual for slave women's resistance to become violent, especially when their mistresses attempted to discipline them. William and Polly Cleveland gave their slave girl, Mary Armstrong, to their kind daughter, Olivia Cleveland Adams, upon her marriage. Earlier, when Polly Cleveland had attempted to whip her, Armstrong had picked up a rock and hit her in the eye. Adams felt that her mother had gotten what she deserved. When the Strattons' slave Aga refused to do work requested of her, Paulina Stratton hit her with a stick. Paulina Stratton wrote: "Aga caught hold of the stick and would not let it go[;] I then picked up the poker and we had a scuffle for it[.] She either hit her temple against the house or I hit her[,] I do not know[,] but she got a good knock and a black eye and let the poker go." Stratton regretted the incident, not because Aga was hurt or because her actions were unbecoming for a Christian, but because she "was wrong in contending with her[;] she had double my strength and might have hurt me."[14]

While the intimacy found in small-slaveholding households was the primary influence on the quality of the relations between mistresses and their slave women, the economic conditions of Missouri's farms provided slaves with additional opportunities for resistance. Economic resistance in Missouri did not differ significantly from that found in the plantation South, although its impact was often greater. On a large plantation, one slave's slow performance, or a number of chickens killed by slaves, did not substantially affect the unit's overall economic stability. Slaves understood, however, that economic resistance had more immediate and destructive consequences on farms, and many became expert at undermining their economy. Thus, slaves often performed their tasks in a slow or shoddy manner. Many slaveholders, like Paulina Stratton and Melinda Napton, interpreted this as laziness rather than resistance. Slaves also damaged farm implements and

13. Rachal Goings interview, in *AS* 11:121–24; Margaret Montgomery Zogbaum, "The Life of Mary Ann Phelps Montgomery, 1846–1942," 1967, WHMC-C. See also Donnie Duglie Bellamy, "Slavery, Emancipation, and Racism in Missouri, 1850–65" (Ph.D. diss., University of Missouri–Columbia, 1971), 82–85, 91; and Deborah Gray White, *Ar'n't I a Woman?* (New York: Norton, 1985), 70–74.

14. Mary Armstrong interview, in *AS* 4:25–30; January 12, 1856, Stratton Collection.

stole livestock or provisions from their owners. Eliza Overton stole meat from her owner, both by hitting a hog over the head and by stealing the keys to the smokehouse. Ann Smith Richardson cooked flapjacks made from ingredients stolen from the big house. Other slave women perfected behaviors that allowed them brief respite from an otherwise grueling existence. It was Melinda Napton's inquiry into a feigned illness that precipitated the previously described hostile encounter with her slave Jinney. Katie Cherry cooked for her owner but was often assigned to the fields after she finished her work. She habitually hid in her cabin to keep from being sent to the fields. It was in the best interest of all slaveholders to compromise with slaves in order to keep them happy and working; this was particularly true on the more vulnerable farms of Missouri.[15]

Some mistresses found the responsibility of managing unruly slaves so trying and the relationship with female servants so acrimonious that they claimed that they would prefer to own no slaves. Elizabeth Coleman wrote to her parents that she would rather make do with her daughters' help than use that of her family's two unreliable slave women. Priscilla Patton hoped to convince her husband to move to the North and free their slaves because "constant worry with the servants" annoyed her. Although these protestations sound similar to those of plantation mistresses, the impact of resistance was greater on small-slaveholding women whose daily lives were defined by slaves with whom they shared so much time. It was difficult for mistresses like Paulina Stratton not to be emotionally hurt by the resistance they encountered from slaves rather than see that much of it was due to the unique circumstances of Missouri's small-slaveholding farms.[16]

While small-scale slavery provided slave women with ample opportunities to carve out some degree of influence over their lives, many slave women benefited in other ways from the intimacy they enjoyed with their mistresses. On farms, it was common for mistresses and slave women to become concerned with one another's lives because of the confined living conditions. Some mistresses expressed a sincere and profound interest in their slave women and treated them well. They went beyond caring for the

15. November 14, 1855, and early 1862, Stratton Collection; Melinda Napton to William Napton, Friday evening [1840s], May 28, 1840, December 5, 1857, Napton Papers; Eliza Overton interview, in *AS* 11:266–68; Charlie Richardson interview, in *AS* 11:290–97; Tishey Taylor interview, in *AS* 11:342–43. See also Mary Rollins to James Rollins, February 7, 1862, James S. Rollins Papers, WHMC-C.

16. Elizabeth Coleman to James and Sarah Hayter, February 19, 1855, Coleman-Hayter Family Papers, 1839–1900, WHMC-C; Priscilla Patton Diary, October 18, 1855, Patton-Scott Papers, WHMC-C; Stratton Collection.

sick and supplying basic needs, and they acknowledged their slaves' humanity. A Ste. Genevieve slave, Peter Corn, claimed he could not say a negative word about his old mistress because she treated her slaves almost like white people.[17]

Slaveholding women assisted slaves in many ways that revealed their affection and concern. Some mistresses held individual slaves in such high esteem that they gave certain rewards and privileges to them. Katie Leonard petitioned her father, Abiel Leonard, on behalf of a slave named Ann to grant her request for a closet in her newly constructed cabin. Illiterate slaves often used their owners as conduits through which to relay information to their family members who lived far away. Mary Belt's slaves sent messages in her letters to a slave relative named Penelope, who had accompanied Belt's parents when they moved to Texas. Some mistresses extended kindness even after their deaths by specifying in their wills that certain slaves be kept within the family or occasionally even emancipated. Hiram Sloan's widow asked her friends to purchase her slaves at auction in order to keep them in the neighborhood. Occasionally this interest persisted even after Missouri's slaves were emancipated in 1865. When Louisa Hayes and three small children were left homeless after emancipation, Pethy's former mistress took them in. Paulina Stratton worried over her former slave women and their children even after slavery ended. Stratton made sure that they had proper clothing and decent employment situations. Mrs. Charles Douthit claimed that her mother's former mistress gave her mother land and built her a house that still remained in the family. In the years following the Civil War, hundreds of pension claims were filed by former slaves from Missouri who served in the federal army and by their family members. More often than not the former owners who were asked to provide evidence toward a claim did so willingly, suggesting their feelings of obligation toward and even affection for their former servants.[18]

17. Peter Corn interview, in *AS* 11:85.

18. Katie Leonard to Abiel Leonard, April 13, 1856, and April 15, 1856, Abiel Leonard to Jeanette Leonard, April 19, 1856, and Abiel Leonard to Katie Leonard, April 20, 1856, in Abiel Leonard Papers. For examples of slaves who sent family members messages, see Mary Belt to Elizabeth Coleman, December 1, 1859, February 18, 1860, April 3, 1860, October 14, 1860, December 14, 1860, and Sunday, [no month] 27, 1861, Coleman-Hayter Family Papers. Hiram Sloan Slaves interviews, in *AS* supp., ser. 1, 2:236–39. Marilda Pethy interview, in *AS* 11:277–82; August 28, 1866, July 27, 1867, February 23, 1868, and March 29, 1869, Stratton Collection; Charles Douthit interview, in *AS* 11:107; Missouri Civil War Pension Claims, 65th U.S. Colored Troops (hereinafter cited as USCT), National Archives, Washington, D.C. (hereinafter cited as NA).

While many actions were arguably altruistic, more complex motivations drove most "kind" mistresses. It is sometimes difficult to distinguish between acts of kindness and acts of economic pragmatism. For example, small slaveholders in Missouri took great care of sick slaves. Slaveholders' writings are filled with discussions of steps taken to save slaves, and doctors' ledgers record the expenses of slaves' medical treatments. Although concerned with the welfare of slaves, slaveholders also hoped to preserve valuable property and keep workers healthy. Similar stories told by three different women—two mistresses and one former slave woman—reveal the ambiguity that accompanied the interaction of slave women and mistresses on the farms of Missouri. Paulina Stratton, Melinda Napton, and Sarah Graves's mistress, Mrs. Crowdes, nursed slave children alongside their own. Stratton nursed a slave infant because it would not take its mother's milk; Napton nursed a slave baby whose mother was dying; and Crowdes nursed Graves so that her mother could continue working in the fields. These white women nursed slave children because no slave women on their farms were lactating at the time. Economic considerations clearly played a role in their behavior, but Paulina Stratton's diary suggests additional motivations. Having recently suffered the death of an infant daughter, Stratton hoped to spare the baby's mother similar heartache. There were limits nonetheless to these women's compassion. Melinda Napton put the slave baby on a bottle when she realized that it was too physically straining to nurse both her own baby and the slave infant. When a white family member became gravely ill and needed care, Stratton stopped nursing the slave child, who then died.[19]

In general, most Missouri slaveholders understood that in their situation kindness was more pragmatic than cruelty. It was not in their best interest to exploit or abuse their slaves to the extent that they were no longer productive. In addition, slaves worked harder when treated well and were less susceptible to rebellion or flight. The close interaction on small-slaveholding farms also heightened slaveholders' psychological need to be liked by their slaves, and to have their acts of kindness acknowledged and appreciated. Many slaveholders, like Paulina Stratton and Priscilla Patton, were disap-

19. For examples of the medical treatment of slaves, see Henry E. Rice Jr., Notes, WHMC-C; file 706, Ste. Genevieve, Missouri, Archives, 1756–1930, WHMC-C; and Estate of Russel Farmhan, 1827, and B. Jones Estate, 1837–1839, Slaves and Slavery Collection, 1772–1950, MHS. Melinda Napton to William Napton, October 31, 1858, Napton Papers. The nursing incident occurred within months of the Strattons' migrating to Missouri from Virginia; see January 1855, Pauline Stratton Diary, WHMC-C. Sarah Graves interview, in *AS* 11:138.

pointed to receive indifference or contempt rather than gratitude. Stratton took her slaves' acts of resistance personally, and she never understood why her slaves did not like her better when she, in her own opinion, had done so much for them. Patton wrote in 1855, "Negros are the bane of my life. I wish to be kind and do right with them[,] but they will not let me[;] they will not appreciate my motives. . . . It has caused me more unhappiness than everything else in this world." The very nature of the intimacy found on small-slaveholding farms made it unlikely that the relations between mistresses and slave women would be anything but fraught with tensions.[20]

But while small slaveholding allowed slave women latitude in altering their relationships with their owners through resistance, this intimacy also had profoundly negative consequences. On balance, the close living and working conditions were at least a nuisance for slave women, who had little time free from the watchful gaze of the mistresses who worked alongside them. In the absence of plantation slave quarters, many Missouri slave women also lived inside their owners' homes or in slave cabins nearby, leaving slave families little time alone together. Worse, many mistresses believed that they had the right to interfere directly in their slaves' lives. The fact that mistresses felt a sense of intimacy with their slave women, which they oftentimes naively believed was reciprocated, exacerbated this problem. For example, Paulina Stratton constantly attempted to convert her slaves to her evangelical faith and closely monitored their moral behavior, even confronting them about their extramarital sexual activities. Similarly, the mistress of former slave William Wells Brown attempted to match him with a slave woman of her choosing rather than his own.[21]

On farms, as in plantation households, intimacy at its worst led to the sexual abuse of slave women by their masters: the close living and working conditions increased the chances that they would attract the attention of male owners and their sons. A number of former Missouri slaves claimed that their fathers were members of the white family, and many others spoke of parents and grandparents who were the result of such unions. Ruth Allen recounted, "My mother was a slave, an' me daddy, ol' devil was her ol' white master. My mammy didin' have any more to say about what they did with her than the rest of the slaves in them days." Mary Estes Peters's

20. Stratton Collection; October 18, 1855, Priscilla Thomas Ingram Patton Diary, Patton-Scott Papers.

21. March 1857, September 14, 1862, and February 1863, Stratton Collection; William Wells Brown, *The Narrative of William Wells Brown* (Boston: Antislavery Office, 1847), 85–87.

mother experienced a horrific rape at the hands of her mistress's three teen-age sons: "While she was alone, the boys came in and threw her down on the floor and tied her down so she couldn't struggle, and one after the other used her as long as they wanted for the whole afternoon . . . that's the way I came to be here."[22]

Nothing changed the fact that slaves were the property of their owners. And if complete domination was not possible, slaveholders did control vital aspects of slaves' lives. A cruel master or mistress could inflict devastating results, and there were few, if any, checks on slaveholder abuses. Many slaveholders pushed slaves to their physical limits in order to extract the most work out of them, especially since each laborer was crucial to the economic well-being of Missouri's farms. James Monroe Abbot remembered of his mother: "Dey warn't never nuthin for her but work hard all de time[;] she neveh came in fum de feel' 'til dark, den had to feed wid a lantern." Life for women of childbearing years was extremely difficult. Although some slaveholders lightened the workload of pregnant slave women, many, like Cynthy Logan, gave birth after laboring in the fields all day. Paulina Stratton and Elvira Scott had their slave women back at light house-work within a fortnight of giving birth. And as in the plantation South, slaveholders often put new mothers back to work in the fields within a month of the births of their children. On farms with no female slaves available to watch the children, slave women took their babies with them to the fields in order to nurse them during breaks. Annie Bridges said, "Ma muthuh plow'd in de fiel' an' wud leave her baby layin' at one end ob de fiel', while she plow'd clear ta odder end an' kum back." Justina Woods wrote of the white woman she was boarding with while teaching school: "She makes old Darkey take her young babe out to the field and work, she says it wont pay to keep negroes and them not work."[23]

22. Paul Escott shows that throughout the South, 6 percent of former slaves interviewed by the Works Progress Administration (WPA) claimed that their fathers were white. Members of the slaveholding family accounted for 11.7 percent of the fathers of the former Missouri slaves interviewed. See Paul D. Escott, *Slavery Remembered: A Record of the Twentieth-Century Slave Narratives* (Chapel Hill: University of North Carolina Press, 1979); statistics are from the 102 WPA narratives of former Missouri slaves, located primarily in *AS* vol. 11 and supp., ser. 1, vol. 2. Ruth Allen interview, in *AS* supp., ser. 1, 2:101–4; Mary Estes Peters interview, in *AS* 10:328–29. See also Melton McLaurin, *Celia, a Slave* (Athens: University of Georgia Press, 1991).

23. James Monroe Abbot interview, in *AS* 11:1–5; Rachal Goings interview, in ibid., 11:121–24; Stratton Collection; March 1860, Elvira Ascenith Weir Scott Diary, 1860–1887, WHMC-C; Annie Bridges interview, in *AS* 11:44–51; Justina Woods to sister, April 18, 1856, Woods-Holman Family Papers, 1805–1906, WHMC-C.

In Missouri, as elsewhere, physical punishments were often unfairly and cruelly administered by slaveholding women. Mistresses may have held limited power in Missouri's slaveholding society, yet some slaveholding women used what little they had against their subordinates. As is often the case, greatest cruelty frequently comes from the least powerful. Most mistresses could not whip a grown slave man, but some routinely took out their frustrations on slave women and children. Some slaves claimed that their mistress was meaner than their master. Emma Knight remembered that her master treated the slaves better than her mistress, and Georgia Ann Dawson treated her slave girl, Margaret Nickens, so poorly that Nickens did not wish to meet her "in either hell or heaven." Slaves especially resented arbitrary or undeserved punishment. Former slave Louis Hill's mistress was nicknamed "Whip" because she "beat da ole folks mor'n tha kids. She used tha cowhide an we got a lickin' whether we did any thin' or not." Sarah Graves's mistress gave her the worst whipping of her life when she was unfairly accused by a white child of kicking dirt on a white bride's dress.[24]

Slave women were most devastated by mistresses who were sadistic. Mary Armstrong claimed that her cruel mistress whipped to death her nine-month-old baby sister when she tired of her persistent crying. Ellen Jackson Brown's mistress demanded that she keep her baby in a box so that she would not have to tend to him while she worked. The two-year-old boy was unable to walk for want of exercise and soon died. A number of slaves, such as Esther Easter, spoke of the whippings received from their mistresses. She remembered: "Master Jim's wife was a demon, just like her husband. Used the whip all the time, and every time Jim come home he whip me 'cause the Mistress say I been mean." While mistresses could be extremely cruel, the worst cases of physical abuse against both women and men were usually perpetrated by masters. Gus Smith spoke of the neighboring master as being "mean to his slaves. He whupped dem all de time. I've seen their clothes sticking to their backs, from blood and scabs, being cut up with de cowhide. He just whupped dem because he could." Hannah Allen remembered the punishment meted out to one slave woman: "De master took two boards and tied one to de feet and another to de hands and tied her back with ropes and whipped her with a cat-a-nine tails till she bled and den took salt and pepper and then put in de gashes." William

24. Emma Knight interview, in *AS* 11:218–21; Margaret Nickens interview, in ibid., 11:263–65; Louis Hill interview, in ibid., 11:184–85; Sarah Graves interview, in ibid., 11:126–38.

Wells Brown scoffed at the supposed mildness of Missouri slavery, relating an infamous St. Louis incident in which a man whipped a slave woman to death.[25]

The relationships between mistresses and their slave women were often the key to the quality of slave women's lives, but systemic factors were influential as well. Historians of plantation slavery have pointed to the slave family and the slave community as two important factors that worked to mitigate some of the harshest aspects of slavery. Due to the small size of most Missouri slaveholdings, many slave women were denied daily access to these crucial support systems. Nearly three-fifths of Missouri slave marriages were between couples living on different farms. The limited presence of abroad slave men made it understandably difficult for them to provide their wives and children with assistance, protection, and emotional support when they visited only once or twice a week. In addition, the economic circumstances of small-scale slavery resulted in temporary and sometimes permanent separations of families when slaves were hired out or sold, when owners migrated, or as estates were divided. Abroad slave families were even more susceptible to separations because their fates were dependent on the circumstances and wills of two different owners. There is ample evidence of viable abroad marriages and vital cross-farm slave communities, but unlike resident families and plantation slave communities, neither of these could be counted on for daily support.[26]

Despite evidence to the contrary, many Missouri slaveholders continued to believe that slavery in their state was more family oriented than that which prevailed in the plantation South. This domestic rhetoric was vital to the self-identity of small-slaveholding women, who interacted with slave women on such an intimate level. Mistresses like Paulina Stratton could never understand why their slaves did not respond to them with the same

25. Mary Armstrong interview, in ibid., 4:25–30; Jackson, *Story,* 12–13; Esther Easter interview, in *AS* 7:88–91; Gus Smith interview, in *AS* 11:321–32; Aunt Hannah Allen interview, in *AS* 11:8–17; Brown, *Narrative,* 27.

26. Abroad marriage statistics taken primarily from *AS* vol. 11 and supp., ser. 1, vol. 2; Benecke Family Papers, WHMC-C; and Civil War Pension Claims, 65th USCT, NA. For more on abroad slave marriages in Missouri, see Diane Mutti Burke, "'Mah Pappy Belong to a Neighbor': The Effects of Abroad Marriages on Missouri Slave Families," in Thomas H. Appleton Jr. and Angela Bosewell, eds., *Searching for Their Places: Women in the South across Four Centuries* (Columbia: University of Missouri Press, 2003), 57–78. For more on selling patterns and estate divisions in Missouri, see Hurt, *Agriculture and Slavery,* 230–38; and James W. McGettigan Jr., "Boone County Slaves: Sales, Estate Divisions, and Families, 1820–1865," *Missouri Historical Review* 72 (January 1978): 176–97, and 72 (April 1978): 271–95.

respect and affection found within families. On the other hand, slave women understood the limitations of this arrangement fully well, realizing that the existence of a more domestic slavery in Missouri was more rhetorical than otherwise. In Missouri, slave mistresses and their slaves were in a unique position to recognize the humanity of one another, but, more often than not, the more personal nature of small slaveholding fostered enmity rather than empathy. Slave women were better able to resist and negotiate, but positive effects notwithstanding, the circumstances of small slaveholding negatively impacted their lives as well. Most were afforded less individual autonomy, were more often separated from their husbands, had less community support, and were more likely to be sexually exploited by their masters. In the end, the quality of individual slave women's lives was profoundly affected by the treatment of their mistresses and masters. As former slave Sarah Graves summarized, "Some masters was good and some was bad." While this was true throughout the South, in a place like Missouri, where slavery consisted overwhelmingly of small holdings, her statement takes on increased significance.[27]

27. Sarah Graves interview, in *AS* 11:126–38.

City Sisters

The Sisters of St. Joseph in Missouri, 1836–1920

Carol K. Coburn and Martha Smith

The steamer *George Collier* docked safely in St. Louis on March 25, 1836, but not before a boiler had exploded, killing a crewman during the ten-day trip up the Mississippi River from New Orleans. Shaken by the experience but thankful to be alive and at their final destination, six young nuns, ages twenty-one to thirty-one, disembarked at the end of their long journey, having survived forty-nine days of rough seas and a nearly disastrous storm in the Gulf of Mexico before their sailing vessel, the *Natchez,* made port in New Orleans. Greeted in St. Louis by Bishop Joseph Rosati, who had invited them to establish a school for deaf children in Missouri, the young women, Sisters of St. Joseph from Lyons, France, stepped into a world whose people, language, and customs were foreign to them in every way.[1]

This inauspicious beginning is representative of the initial foundations of many Catholic religious communities of women in the United States. Most began with a small band of women—European, Canadian, or American-born—who began living and working together in spiritual, emotional, physical, and economic support networks that eventually spanned every region of the country. After the founding of the initial Ursuline order in New Orleans in 1727, Catholic nuns increased their number to 46,000 by 1900. By 1920, American Catholic sisters had created or were maintaining ap-

---

1. A full account of the Sisters of St. Joseph of Carondelet and their growth and influence nationally can be found in Carol K. Coburn and Martha Smith, *Spirited Lives: How Nuns Shaped Catholic Culture and American Life, 1836–1920* (Chapel Hill: University of North Carolina Press, 1999).

proximately five hundred hospitals, fifty women's colleges, and over six thousand parochial schools, serving 1.7 million schoolchildren in every region of the country, both urban and rural.[2] The Sisters of St. Joseph of Carondelet (CSJs) are rooted deep in Missouri soil, and their tenuous beginnings in St. Louis eventually spawned one of the largest and most geographically diverse Catholic religious orders in the United States. Between 1836 and 1900 in Missouri alone, the CSJs established or were staffing forty-five institutions, including parish schools, private academies, hospitals, schools for the deaf, and orphanages. Nationally, the CSJ community had created or staffed approximately two hundred institutions by the early twentieth century.[3]

The experiences of nineteenth-century nuns are critical to understanding the interaction of gender, ethnicity, religion, and class in the trans-Mississippi West. American sisters were some of the first white women brought in to "civilize" newly forming towns and other areas of settlement. Male clerics, who usually preceded the sisters' arrival and often had large territories to cover, frequently functioned as itinerant clergy, forced to travel vast distances to serve Catholic parishes and communities.[4] The sisters came in larger numbers and were important shapers of American Catholic urban culture and public life because they worked directly with the people on a daily basis, administering and staffing some of the first religious, educational, health, and social service institutions in isolated frontier settings that included both Protestants and Catholics. The scarcity of clergy meant that women religious often functioned as surrogate priests at baptisms, religious services and ceremonies, and at the deathbed. They trained the children, helped the poor, nursed the sick, and buried the dead.[5]

2. George C. Stewart Jr., *Marvels of Charity: History of American Sisters and Nuns* (Huntington, Ind.: Our Sunday Visitor, 1994); *The Official Catholic Directory* (New York: P. J. Kenedy, 1920), appendices C and D.

3. "Summary of Community Statistics," General Chapter Report, 1920 (Archives, Sisters of St. Joseph of Carondelet-Generalate, St. Louis [hereinafter cited as ACSJC-G]); Mary Lucida Savage, *The Congregation of St. Joseph of Carondelet: A Brief Account of Its Origin and Its Work in the United States, 1650–1922* (St. Louis: B. Herder Book, 1923), 319–23.

4. John Rothensteiner, *History of the Archdiocese of St. Louis* (St. Louis: Blackwell Wielandy, 1928), states that in the St. Louis diocese (which at one time included much of the territory in the Louisiana Purchase and beyond) in the late 1830s, one priest was responsible for two thousand Catholics who lived throughout the territories of Missouri, Illinois, and Wisconsin (1:581–85, 730–35).

5. Some sources that have attempted to integrate nuns in the history of the American West include Mary Ewens, "Catholic Sisterhoods in North Dakota," in *Day In, Day Out: Women's Lives in North Dakota,* ed. Elizabeth Hampsten (Grand Forks: University

The sisters' ability to accommodate and adapt to rugged and sometimes dangerous frontier conditions enabled them to provide much-needed
educational and social services to men, women, and children in a variety
of western settings, counteracting the often hostile, anti-Catholic attitudes prevalent in nineteenth-century America. In her study on American
sisters in the nineteenth century, historian Mary Ewens states, "it might
well be shown that sisters' efforts were far more effective than those of
bishops or priests in the Church's attempts to meet these challenges. It
was they who established schools in cities and remote settlements to in-
struct the young in the tenets of their faith, who succored the needy . . .
who changed public attitudes toward the church from hostility to respect."[6] Using their religious beliefs, convent training, and vows, the sisters—by their early presence in the trans-Mississippi West—were at the
forefront of the development and expansion of Catholic culture, particularly on the urban frontier.

Missouri as Religious Battleground

Although male religious orders, particularly the Jesuits and Franciscans,
had been in the trans-Mississippi West for centuries, the influx of white settlers, especially immigrants, created new opportunities and new demands
for services. Responding to the opening of lands for white settlement, Protestants and Catholics jockeyed for moral and cultural influence, hoping to
save the bodies and souls of Eastern transplants, European and Asian
immigrants, Hispanics, and native peoples who populated much of the trans-
Mississippi West. Lyman Beecher's *A Plea for the West* stirred many Protestants to "save the West from the Pope" and work toward fulfilling the
nation's manifest destiny through the spread of Anglo-Protestant influence
and culture. Calling the Catholic church "the most skillful, powerful, dread-
ful system of corruption . . . slavery and debasement to those who live under
it," he used fear to galvanize Protestants to fund "introducing the social
and religious principles of New England" to westerners. Hoping to pro-

---

of North Dakota, 1988); and Carol K. Coburn and Martha Smith, " 'Pray for Your
Wanderers': Women Religious on the Colorado Mining Frontier," *Frontiers: A Journal
of Women Studies* 15, no. 3 (1995): 27–52.

6. Mary Ewens, "The Leadership of Nuns in Immigrant Catholicism," in *Women and
Religion*, vol. 1, ed. Rosemary Radford Ruether and Rosemary Skinner Keller (New
York: Harper and Row, 1981), 101.

mote their own religious and cultural influence in the west, Catholics, with contributions from European philanthropic associations, aspired to support "the growth of the Roman Catholic Church in Protestant and heathen countries, and more specifically, . . . Catholic missions in the United States."[7] Both Protestant and Catholic women participated in this battle for the minds, hearts, and souls of the multiethnic peoples in Missouri and throughout the American West.

In the early nineteenth century, Catholic sisters coming from European convents rarely received a warm reception, or if they did, it was often short-lived. For many nativists, "American" meant not only white and Anglo-Saxon, but also Protestant. Except in a few eastern cities, American Catholics were a small minority in the United States until the mid-nineteenth century. However, during the three decades prior to the Civil War, when burgeoning numbers of Irish and German Catholics emigrated to America, many priests and male and female religious often found their patriotism questioned; during this time violence against clergy, churches, and religious was a fact of life. In 1830, the anti-Catholic weekly, *The Protestant,* began publication with the objective "to inculcate Gospel doctrines against Romish corruptions . . . to maintain the purity and sufficiency of the Holy Scriptures against Monkish Traditions," stating that no article would be printed unless it promoted this goal.[8]

Religious communities of women often took the brunt of anti-Catholic prejudice. As women who lived and worked in all-female environments, created and maintained schools and institutions in the public domain, wore "mysterious," distinctive clothing, and took vows of chastity and obedience while rejecting heterosexual marriage, nuns ran the gamut of Protestant fantasies. Alternatively seen either as captive, docile minions and concubines for male clergy or as uptight "abnormal" women, rejected by males

7. In 1834 and 1835, Lyman Beecher, a well-known New England minister and father of educator Catharine Beecher, minister Henry Ward Beecher, and author Harriet Beecher Stowe, made speeches to acquire donations for Lane Seminary in Cincinnati. These were published in *A Plea for the West* (Cincinnati, 1835); Bryan Le Beau, "'Saving the West from the Pope': Anti-Catholic Propaganda in the Settlement of the Mississippi Valley," *American Studies* 32 (spring 1991): 103.

8. Cited in Ray Allen Billington, *The Protestant Crusade 1800–1860: A Study of the Origins of American Nativism* (New York: Reinhart, 1938; reprint, Chicago: Quadrangle Books, 1964), 53. Catholic population data, particularly prior to the Civil War, is difficult to assess. The *Official Catholic Directory* for 1850 and 1860 stipulates 2 million and 3 million respectively. Gerald Shaughnessy, *Has the Immigrant Kept the Faith? A Study of Immigration and Catholic Growth in the United States* (New York: Macmillan, 1925), estimates 660,000 (1840), 1.6 million (1850), and 3.1 million (1860).

as unfit for marriage and motherhood and allowed to run amuck as "independent" women with masculine tendencies, American sisters had to cope with gender, religious, and ethnic bigotry in a patriarchal society that limited the power and aspirations of many people according to their sex, race, church affiliation, and native birthright. Prior to the Civil War, the CSJs and most women religious traveled in secular clothing to avoid potential insults and harassment that included death threats, convent burnings, and bodily assaults. Sister St. Protais DeBoille recalled that upon their arrival at the Ursuline Convent in New Orleans, the CSJs were advised to change into secular clothing before going out in public because "people would think that some nuns had escape[d] from the convent."[9]

In popular literature stories of "captive" or "escaped" nuns promised lucrative rewards for authors and publishers. Akin to the contemporary "tell-all exposé," sensationalized books about convent life provided lurid and fascinating reading for a Protestant population that found nuns and their presence on American soil frightening, if not "dangerous." The looting and burning of the Ursuline convent in Charlestown, Massachusetts, in 1834 proved that such books could and did provoke Protestant ire in a most virulent form.[10]

Another factor that seemed to place nuns at the flash point of anti-Catholic bigotry was related to Protestant perspectives on what was perceived to be the "feminization" of the Catholic Church. Ann Braude states that Protestant scorn of the "rich sensual environment . . . the cult of saints and especially the veneration of the Virgin . . . retains the anti-Catholic as well as the anti-woman bias of the standard narratives of American religion."[11] Viewed through a Protestant lens, religious statues, holy cards, incense, rosaries, priests in "skirts," and nuns in medieval religious habits symbolized this "feminization."

---

9. Memoirs of Sr. St. Protais Deboille, 11 (Archives, Sisters of St. Joseph of Carondelet, St. Louis Province, Mo. [hereinafter cited as ACSJC-SLP]).

10. For a description of this event, see Jeanne Hamilton, "The Nunnery as Menace: The Burning of the Charlestown Convent, 1834," *U.S. Catholic Historian* 14, no. 1 (winter 1996): 35–65; and Nancy Lusignan Schultz, *Fire and Roses: The Burning of the Charlestown Convent, 1834* (Philadelphia: Free Press, 2000). This was a shocking incident for many reasons. The sisters and student boarders barely escaped with their lives, and the mob spent hours defacing the structure, desecrating the cemetery, and opening sisters' coffins and pulling teeth from corpses. Local police and firefighters stood and watched while the convent was torched.

11. Ann Braude, "Women's History *Is* American Religious History," in *Retelling U.S. Religious History*, ed. Thomas A. Tweed (Berkeley: University of California Press, 1997), 105–6.

Antebellum St. Louis

Although prior to the 1830s relationships between Protestants and Catholics had been good in St. Louis, *The Protestant* and Eli P. Lovejoy's *St. Louis Observer* denounced the Catholic Church and inflamed passions that produced mobs and threats against the CSJs and other Catholic institutions prior to the Civil War. Beginning in antebellum America and continuing throughout the nineteenth century, groups such as the American Protestant Association, the Know-Nothing Party, the Ku Klux Klan, and the American Protective Association had many willing members anxious to stamp out "popery" in St. Louis and other urban centers across the nation.[12]

Although they arrived in 1836, the CSJs were not the first community of nuns to bring such visible symbols of Catholicism to the St. Louis area. The Society of the Sacred Heart (1818), the Sisters of Loretto (1823), the Sisters of Charity (1828), and the Visitandines (1833) preceded the CSJs, settling in and around St. Louis and across the Mississippi River in Illinois. Soon after disembarking in St. Louis, the six CSJs separated, and three sisters headed for Cahokia, Illinois, a French Canadian parish, while three stayed in St. Louis, lodging with the Sisters of Charity and taking English lessons at the Sacred Heart Academy until they could move into their log cabin convent in Carondelet, a village six miles south of the city.[13]

The sisters sent to Cahokia found a prosperous village and a Catholic population of several hundred highly devout parishioners who, with their priest, Father Peter Doutreluingne, had provided a set of buildings in the center of the village that the sisters could use for a convent and school. Affectionately, and to add dignity to the setting, the villagers dubbed the site "The Abbey," and the townspeople provided for all the sisters' needs both large and small. By contrast, the three sisters who opened the convent in Carondelet, south of St. Louis, rarely experienced such devotion and prosperity. Carondelet was originally named *Vide Poche*, or "Empty Pocket."

---

12. Nikola Baumgarten, "Education and Democracy in Frontier St. Louis: The Society of the Sacred Heart," *History of Education Quarterly* 34, no. 2 (summer 1994): 171–92; William B. Faherty, *Dream by the River: Two Centuries of Saint Louis Catholicism, 1766–1980*, rev. ed. (St. Louis: River City Publishers, 1981), 44–48, 76; Edwin Scott Gaustad, *Historical Atlas of Religion in America* (New York: Harper and Row, 1976), 108.

13. Savage, *Congregation of Saint Joseph*, 36–37; Rothensteiner, *History of the Archdiocese of St. Louis*, 1:300, 314, 447, 626, 634. St. Louis grew rapidly between 1830 and 1840 from 5,000 (whites) to 14,407, and Bishop Rosati sought additional sisters to support the growing Catholic population; see U.S. Bureau of Census, *Fifth and Sixth Census*, 1830 and 1840 (Washington, D.C., 1830, 1840).

The sisters understood immediately the significance of the name. Their log cabin convent, set high on a bluff overlooking the Mississippi River, had a beautiful view but—with the exception of a cot, a table, and two chairs—the two rooms and attic were destitute of furniture. Walking to the rectory to eat their first meal with the parish priest, Father Edmund Saulnier, they shared the priest's meager bread and cheese. After the sisters returned the next morning for breakfast, Father Saulnier informed them that he barely had enough to feed himself and they would have to fend for themselves and "beg" the parishioners for food. Unlike their Cahokia counterparts, the Creole parishioners at Carondelet were not only poor but also "had neither taste for religion or instruction." Although separated by the Mississippi River, the sisters in the two CSJ mission sites continued to see themselves as one community. Cahokia, Illinois, at first seemed to provide the financial and social advantages for success, but strangely enough, it was the poverty-stricken mission in Carondelet, Missouri, that became the "cradle of the institution" and birthplace of the American foundation.[14]

Located on a hill on the Missouri side of the river, Carondelet provided a healthier climate for the sisters; however, this mission site offered deprivations of a different sort. The sisters had to find an immediate means of financial support. In contrast to their experiences in France where church and state were ordinarily closely associated, the American CSJs could not depend on subsidies or contracts from local officials to help finance their institutions.[15] Financial problems were constant for transplanted European communities that had to learn to survive without wealthy benefactors or royal grants. Spinning, sewing, raising food, and farmwork were necessary to earn a livelihood in nineteenth-century America.[16] To obtain food, the Carondelet sisters tried to "grub their field but they were not strong enough" so they employed a hired man for the field and created their own industry by making "sacs for powder," selling them for a penny apiece. The school enrollment was small; the meager accommodations, primitive conditions, and knee-deep mud after rains limited the number of children

14. Memoirs of Sr. St. Protais Deboille, 13–23.

15. Although government payment for services was the exception rather than the rule, the CSJs and other religious communities did secure state monies for short periods of time. The CSJ school for the deaf in St. Louis received monies from the legislature between 1839 and 1847. See Dolorita Maria Dougherty, ed., *The Sisters of St. Joseph of Carondelet* (St. Louis: Herder Book, 1966), 67.

16. Ewens, *The Role of the Nun in Nineteenth-Century America* (New York: Arno Press, 1978), 65–69. Although the CSJs did not use slave labor, Ewens states that many religious communities did, and no communities that used slaves failed to survive in the American milieu.

who could attend. During the first winter, boarders brushed snow from their bedding, and an umbrella protected the cook stove from rain and snow. Students were encouraged to bring their own supplies or to bring firewood in lieu of tuition.[17]

As middle-class, educated French women, the sisters must have felt the stress and frustration of the harsh conditions, unfamiliar climate, poverty, and isolation thousands of miles from home in a foreign country that offered many threats to their personal survival as well as to their religious community. It was a welcome relief when, in 1837, they received two long-awaited reinforcements from Lyons. Chosen to be members of the original group to come to the United States, Sisters Celestine Pommerel and St. John Fournier had remained in France an extra year to learn sign language.[18] With two trained teachers, the community could now open its school for the deaf (the first in Missouri), which would provide the Carondelet sisters with additional income. Their numbers were bolstered even more with the entry of the first American-born postulant (candidate), Anne Eliza Dillon.

Early in 1839, the CSJs received monies from two unexpected sources— local and state government. St. Joseph's Institute for the Deaf, created by Mother Celestine Pommerel and Sister St. John Fournier, was gaining students and a statewide reputation. State leaders in Missouri wanted to establish a school for the deaf, but legislators could not agree on funding and location. Using his political connections, Bishop Rosati suggested that the sisters contract for state monies for deaf education until the legislature could build and fund a state institution. In February 1839, the state legislature agreed with this idea and later that year began sending the sisters annual stipends to board and teach Missouri children who needed services at the school for the deaf.[19] In April that same year, the local village of Carondelet, which had no public school, agreed to pay the CSJs "to educate in the ordinary branches of English and French languages the female children of the town of Carondelet, from six to eighteen years old." To alleviate hostility and out of kindness, the CSJs had wisely never turned away children from the school for lack of tuition and thus had made friends,

---

17. Memoirs of Sr. St. Protais Deboille, 25.

18. "Copy of a letter from Mother St. John Fournier to the Superior General of the Sisters of St. Joseph in Lyons, 1873," cited in Maria Kostka Logue, *Sisters of St. Joseph of Philadelphia: A Century of Growth and Development, 1847–1947* (Philadelphia: Newman Press, 1950), 327–52.

19. This bill was adopted February 8, 1839, Missouri Sessions Laws, 334, as cited in Savage, *Congregation of St. Joseph,* 52. It was not repealed until 1847 when the legislature finally provided money for a state institute.

both Protestant and Catholic, in local government.[20] With some financial stability assured, Mother Celestine then began her own projects to add further financial and material security to the American foundation.

A large contribution from a female benefactor, Mrs. John Mullanphy, allowed Mother Celestine to begin renovation of the convent and school to provide additional space for boarders and for a "select" school or academy.[21] Wisely promoting a "French" education to aspiring American parents, St. Joseph's Academy, or "Madame Celestine's School" as it was popularly called, attracted wealthy local girls and "daughters of Southern planters." Eliza McKenney Brouillet, daughter of a Virginian, recalled that her mother sent her to St. Joseph's Academy to acquire "a French education in all the purity of the language."[22] By spring 1841, a new three-story brick building welcomed seven boarders, and by the mid-1840s two additional wings had been added.

Boarding students, day students, deaf students, and orphans all interacted closely with the sisters in the 1840s, and their activities and experiences often intertwined in the multipurpose convent setting that housed an academy, orphanage, school for the deaf, parish school, and living accommodations for sisters, students, and orphans. In 1840, the sisters taught and cared for twelve boarders, seventy day pupils, four orphans, and nine deaf children. By the end of the decade, fifty boarders, eighty day pupils, and twenty-eight orphans and deaf students filled the premises. As one of the first students at St. Joseph's Academy, nine-year-old Eliza McKenney Brouillet spent six years with the sisters, and her memoirs provide interesting insights about everyday life in the convent and the physical and emotional strains of the early years of the CSJ foundation. Physical conditions for sisters and children were harsh, and the "cold winds had a high carnival in our dormitory, particularly during snow storms," when the nuns would have to come in the middle of the night to wake the children and

20. "Minutes of the Board of Trustees," April 23, 1839, cited in Savage, *Congregation of St. Joseph*, 53. See also "Copy of a Letter from St. John Fournier," 329. Fournier stated that although short on cash "the city paid us every year in land." The city hired a male teacher for the boys of the village.

21. The Mullanphy family were early donors to Catholic charities in St. Louis. A cotton merchant and realtor, John Mullanphy contributed land for a hospital for the poor, regardless of "color, country or religion," and gave a house to the Sacred Heart Sisters for the first girls' school in St. Louis. See Mary J. Oates, *The Catholic Philanthropic Tradition in America* (Bloomington: Indiana University Press, 1995), 10, 30.

22. Memoirs of Eliza McKenney Brouillet, 1890–1891, ACSJC-SLP. Written by one of the first students at the select academy, Brouillet's memoirs are particularly important to CSJ history since they are detailed but also lend a subjective understanding of life at the convent.

shake the snow from their beds. Winter mornings provided little relief and "sometimes we would have to wait until we got downstairs to bathe our faces as the water in the pails would be one solid cake of ice."[23]

As the CSJ numbers grew in the 1840s and 1850s, so did their outreach in St. Louis. The Carondelet convent and school continued to house a combination of boarders, day students, and orphans, and in 1845 the CSJs began teaching in an ethnically diverse parish school, St. Vincent de Paul, composed of German immigrants, English-speaking students, and, later, Irish immigrant children. However, their other outreach project, located in downtown St. Louis, caused a flare-up of anti-Catholic and racist sentiments. There, the CSJs opened a school for "colored" children in 1845. Children of free blacks were taught a general elementary curriculum, with French and ornamental needlework. After school hours and on Sundays, the children of slaves were prepared to receive the sacraments. The school appeared to be welcomed by the black population, as a hundred children (mostly girls) attended. One of the pupils wrote, "We felt at home and were happy, because the time and attention of the Sisters was all our own, and there was no one to tease us."[24]

This cross-cultural experience was short-lived, however. Within a year the sisters began to receive almost daily threatening demands to close the school. The director of the school, Sister St. John Fournier wrote, "Finally, one morning as I was leaving the [school], several people called out to me and told me that they were coming that night to put us out of the house. . . . At eleven o'clock [that night] the sisters awoke with a start when they heard a loud noise. Out in the street was a crowd of people crying out and cursing. . . . Suddenly the police patrol came and scattered those villains who were trying to break open the door. They returned three times that same night, but our good Mother protected us and they were not able to open the door from the outside or to break it down."[25] After the incident the mayor of St. Louis intervened, and upon his and Bishop Kenrick's advice the school was closed, although religious instruction continued. The CSJs had come to the United States to teach in antebellum St. Louis, but their "colored school" had to be abandoned if they were to survive in their new American home.

23. "Statistics of Carondelet School and St. Joseph's Academy," ACSJC-SLP; Memoirs of Eliza McKenney Brouillet.

24. This undated and unsigned quote is from a longer essay recorded in the *Community Annals*, 283–84, and cited in Savage, *Congregation of St. Joseph*, 64.

25. Memoirs of Sr. St. Protais Deboille, 29, and "Copy of a Letter of Mother St. John Fournier," 332–33; "Extract from the Records of St. Louis Diocese," Book 1:221, copy in ACSJC-SLP.

In 1846, the CSJs opened their first orphan home when they took over St. Joseph's Home for Boys. This was a significant decision on the part of Mother Celestine because it moved the American community beyond teaching into a second arena of service so vital to nineteenth-century American Catholic culture: the care of male and female orphans. Teaching boys and caring for male orphans made the CSJs especially popular with American bishops and with local secular authorities because although the need was great, some religious orders of women were forbidden by their European constitutions to work with male children.[26]

Besides this significant contribution in education and social service, the CSJs began a smaller but no less dramatic contribution that put St. Louis and the state of Missouri into the national arena involving deaf education. Two of the original eight Sisters of St. Joseph had received special training in sign language to prepare them to open a school for deaf children. This was Bishop Rosati's initial plan when he first invited the French sisters. The French were leaders in deaf education in the early nineteenth century, so the two nuns were probably some of the best-trained teachers in the United States when they arrived to begin the school in 1837.

Bishop Rosati wanted to provide the state of Missouri with its first educational institution that would serve all deaf children, regardless of religious affiliation—a politically savvy move that not only silenced some anti-Catholic sentiments but would potentially provide secular state funds for the CSJs when they opened St. Joseph's School for the Deaf. As early practitioners of deaf education, the CSJs began an institution that not only continues to the present day but also served as a teacher training site for CSJ institutions in Buffalo, Brooklyn, and Queens, New York; Oakland, California; Philadelphia; Boston; and Rutland, Vermont. This early institute also trained a large number of laypersons and male religious teachers who worked at a variety of public and private institutions in St. Louis in the nineteenth and early twentieth century. As some of the earliest trained teachers of the deaf in the United States, the CSJs taught classes for children and adults that included religious instruction, academic course work, and vocational education. Sister Mary Borgia Davis, superior of the institute from 1908 to 1928, traveled and lectured across the United States, participated in a professional network of deaf educators and institutions, and presented scholarly papers at national conferences.[27] By 1920, the

26. Patricia Byrne, "The Sisters of St. Joseph: The Americanization of a French Tradition," *U.S. Catholic Historian* 5 (summer/fall 1986): 254.

27. Dougherty, *The Sisters of St. Joseph*, 120–22, 344–47; and Alberta Ruth Ashton, "History of St. Joseph's Institute for the Deaf in St. Louis County, 1837–1944," MS in ACSJC-SLP.

CSJs had staffed forty-one institutions in the fast-growing city, including thirty-five parish schools and academies, two deaf institutes, three orphanages, and a home for working women.

Although relationships with male clergy (bishops or parish priests) could often be problematic, the CSJ success in St. Louis was certainly facilitated by the ongoing support of Bishops Joseph Rosati and Peter Richard Kenrick, who provided strong advocacy for the St. Louis CSJs during the early years and at critical times during the nineteenth-century expansion. Rosati played an important role with state and local politicians to secure monies for St. Joseph's Academy and St. Joseph's School for the Deaf, assuring the CSJs' subsequent financial survival in the United States. Kenrick's local support facilitated the CSJs' expansion into parish education and child care in St. Louis. At the national and international level, Kenrick intervened with other American bishops and with the Vatican to help the Sisters of St. Joseph of Carondelet receive "papal approbation," which established the St. Louis (Carondelet) Motherhouse as the center of governance for what was to become an international religious order in the twentieth century.

Kansas City

During the first thirty years in St. Louis, the Carondelet CSJs had also sent small groups of sisters to establish foundations as far north as Canada, as far east as New York, and as far south as Mississippi. In 1866, the community moved into western Missouri to anchor its presence across the state as white settlement continued to move west. For a three-year period (1856–1859), CSJs had staffed a school in Weston, Missouri, on the river northwest of Kansas City, but they did not return to the western part of the state until the conclusion of the Civil War. What they found in Kansas City in 1866 was similar to the earlier deprivations and primitive conditions they had experienced upon their arrival in St. Louis three decades earlier.

Kansas City, Missouri, began as a "glorified frontier camp" that, according to one historian, even prostitutes avoided in the 1850s. The town was best known as a jumping-off point for the Overland and Santa Fe trails and as a haven for pro-slavery renegades who made intermittent border raids into "Bleeding Kansas." In 1861, the town's four thousand inhabitants were joined by Union troops, who established a military outpost after the outbreak of the Civil War. Kansas City boomed after the war when the town won the rights to the economically strategic railroad bridge over the Missouri River that connected the city to Kansas and western markets; the town's future seemed assured. In the late nineteenth century, Kansas City grew as a transportation hub and as a center for social, commercial, and economic interests. The addition of the railroad stockyards in the 1880s established the city as a center for agricultural markets.[28]

Predicting economic prosperity and an influx of settlers, Father Bernard Donnelly called the CSJs to serve the fast-growing Catholic population. Donnelly, a local priest, proved to be a strong advocate for the early CSJs. He was a trained civil engineer whose skills were used by early town builders and developers and a savvy businessman whose vision and planning helped shape Catholic growth and influence in Kansas City. He invited the CSJs to become the first female religious order in the city and helped provide for their monetary needs, at times using his personal funds at the academy and later at the hospital and orphanage. For over two decades his shrewdness and foresight strengthened the Catholic community, and he helped it gain recognition in Kansas City and supported the CSJs and their institution building.[29]

However promising the future may have seemed, in 1866 when five CSJs arrived to begin a school, Kansas City was a cow town. Upon their arrival, the sisters found unpaved dusty or muddy streets, ugly wooden buildings, numerous saloons, open drunkenness, and frequent fights among a rough and transitory population, which included many thieves and gamblers. One of the women who led the CSJs to Kansas City was the forty-two-year-old Sister Francis Joseph Ivory, who had fifteen years earlier been a founder of the St. Paul, Minnesota, mission. Ivory, a native of Pennsylvania, was an important member of many "advance teams" to new mission sites because of her strong physical endurance, education, interpersonal skills, and English-speaking abilities.

Arriving by train in 1866, Sister Francis Joseph drew upon her years of

28. Lawrence H. Larsen, "Kansas City, Missouri," in *Encyclopedia of the American West,* eds. Charles Phillips and Alan Axelrod (New York: MacMillan, 1996), 2:803–4; A. Theodore Brown and Lyle W. Dorsett, *K.C.: A History of Kansas City, Missouri* (Boulder: Pruett Publishing, 1978), 9; Savage, *Congregation of St. Joseph,* 142–43.

29. Donnelly was a true entrepreneur. In the 1850s, he convinced civic planners that he could bring in crews (Irish Catholics) to lower the bluffs along the Missouri River to allow the city to spread south. A few years later, to facilitate building in the city, Donnelly had the soil surveyed on the church grounds and founded a brickyard that made large profits for the parish and other Catholic institutions in the city. Donnelly "propelled the Catholic church in Kansas City . . . and his shrewd management of real estate" provided monies for the CSJs and for other Catholic institutions in the city; see Dorothy Brandt Marra, "The Story," in *This Far by Faith: A Popular History of the Catholic People of West and Northwest Missouri* (Marceline, Mo.: Diocese of Kansas City and St. Joseph, 1992), 47–48, 71–73; Martha Smith, "Sisters of St. Joseph," in *This Far by Faith,* 611; and William J. Dalton, *Pioneer Priest: The Life of Father Bernard Donnelly* (Kansas City: Grimes-Joyce Printing, 1921), 139–43.

experience in fund-raising and establishing new missions. Within weeks she had acquired free railroad passes for the sisters and quickly raised funds for the convent and school. "We took possession of the walls as the house was not furnished. Our first possession was a cow—We got up an entertainment, and in one night cleared Thirteen Hundred Dollars thus we were able to furnish the house in necessaries. Providence came to our aid, that we had no difficulty in getting along on temporals." The sisters' school, St. Teresa's Academy, opened that fall with 150 pupils (girls and small boys), and for the next twenty-five years this was the only Catholic school providing more than an elementary education for girls in Kansas City. Unlike the anti-Catholic hostilities in antebellum St. Louis, the Kansas City reception to the CSJs was comparatively positive. Here, Catholicism was rarely visible or understood in the 1860s. Although other religious orders had institutions in western Missouri, nuns in habits were still a novelty in Kansas City, and Sister Francis Joseph humorously recalled that some excited local people stopped a group of sisters walking downtown because they "thought we were the Circus."[30]

CSJ institutions in Kansas City grew with the city's population and prominence. In 1874, the sisters opened St. Joseph's Hospital, the first private hospital in Kansas City and one of the earliest in the trans-Mississippi West. In the late nineteenth century, hospitals sponsored by ethnic and religious groups proliferated and formed a large segment of American hospitals. Kansas City, Missouri, provides a representative microcosm of late-nineteenth- and early-twentieth-century urban health care and the highly "segregated" character of urban hospitals. Although a municipal hospital began first in Kansas City, followed by St. Joseph's Hospital in 1874, other groups created institutions catering to particular patrons. At a locale dubbed "Hospital Hill," university and college hospitals were established, and other hospitals and clinics formed there, too, including those created by city funds as well as those founded by private interests such as the Wabash and Missouri Pacific Railroads, the Red Cross, Homeopaths, Osteopaths, African Americans, German Americans, Swedish Americans, the Christian Church, the Episcopal Church, the Lutheran Church, the Scaritt Bible School, and hospitals staffed by Catholic religious orders.[31]

30. See Marra, "The Story," 21–58; Gilbert J. Gerraghan, *Catholic Beginnings in Kansas City: An Historical Sketch* (Chicago: Loyola Press, 1920); and Savage, *Congregation of St. Joseph,* 142–43. See also Sr. Francis Joseph Ivory to Sr. Monica Corrigan, August 12 and September 10, 1890, ACSJC-SLP.

31. Caring for special groups usually in separate facilities or separate wings of the building, these Kansas City hospitals divided patients by religion, race, class, ethnicity, gender, age, and specific infirmities. This eclectic mix of hospitals also included the

With Father Donnelly's financial support, the CSJs opened St. Joseph's Girls Home in 1880. During this period, orphanages were sometimes used as temporary care facilities when a parent was ill, financially burdened, or simply unable to cope with child care. In light of the contemporary discussion on the "breakdown of the family" and nostalgia for the bygone days when families "took care of their own," CSJ orphanage records look amazingly current. Sometimes the children were brought to the orphanage because they were ill or handicapped and the parents would not or could not care for them. In 1910, two days after five-year-old twins and their seven-year-old sister were admitted to the sisters' care in Kansas City, they were rushed to St. Joseph's Hospital. Scarlet fever, smallpox, pneumonia, and measles were common illnesses of abandoned children. The records for the Kansas City Girls' Home listed the specific family situation for eighty-one children admitted during one year. Of the eighty-one girls, 16 percent had both parents living, 23 percent had both parents deceased, 26 percent had only a father living, and 35 percent had only a mother living. The fact that more children had a single mother probably said less about parenting commitment than the economic realities of working-class women trying to care for a family in a gender- and class-biased wage system. The sisters were no Pollyannas concerning their surroundings, and they peppered the ledger with additional comments about the girls' families, such as "parents divorced," "mother insane," "parents separated and worthless." In 1880, the addition of the orphan home completed the trilogy of the CSJ mission to Kansas City, so that within fifteen years of their arrival, the sisters had institutions in education, health care, and social service.[32]

In 1910, because of the growth and success of St. Teresa's Academy, it was moved from its downtown location in the Quality Hill neighborhood south to twenty acres near what was to become the exclusive Country Club Plaza area. The academy's new location, however, attracted the attention of a local "entrepreneur." Lamenting the fact that the acres north

---

"city pest-house boat" for smallpox patients, emergency hospitals, psychiatric hospitals, an eye and ear infirmary, and a tuberculosis hospital. See James L. Soward, *Hospital Hill: An Illustrated Account of Public Healthcare Institutions in Kansas City, Missouri* (Kansas City: Truman Medical Center Foundation, 1995), 20–21, 34–35, 52–53, 68.

32. Record Book of St. Joseph's Orphan Home for Girls, Kansas City, January 31, 1910, and 1880–1917. See also Martha Smith, "Sisters of St. Joseph of Carondelet," in *This Far by Faith,* vol. 2, ed. Michael Coleman (Marceline, Mo.: Diocese of Kansas City and St. Joseph, 1992), 607–13; and Coleman, "Saint Joseph Health Center," 572–75; "St. Joseph Orphan Home for Girls," 575–77; and "St. Teresa's Academy," 582–86.

of the new academy lacked trees, Mother Evelyn O'Neill readily agreed to purchase twenty trees from a "friendly" salesman who unexpectedly showed up at the academy gates wanting to sell the sisters large elms, offering to bring in two or three a day for a remarkable $12.50 per tree. Delighted with her good fortune and shrewd business acumen, Mother Evelyn was aghast when, a few weeks after the trees were purchased and planted, two local police officers came to her door inquiring about the trees. It seems the "friendly" salesman had stolen the trees from nearby Swope Park. After further discussion, the amused officers allowed the trees to stay at St. Teresa's, and Mother Evelyn and the thief both avoided jail for dealing in "hot" trees to beautify the academy.[33]

By the early twentieth century, the sisters had also expanded their teaching activities into a number of ethnically diverse parish schools, educating Irish, Germans, Hispanics, and a growing Italian population. In 1920, when Kansas City's population had grown to more than three hundred thousand, the CSJs had established or were staffing many successful institutions in Kansas City and western Missouri (St. Joseph, Sedalia, and Chillicothe). Serving thousands of women, men, and children, Protestant and Catholic, they conducted twelve parish schools, two academies, an orphanage for girls, a hospital, and a junior college for women.[34]

As the first female religious order in Kansas City, the CSJs were visible and active representatives of American Catholic culture. By establishing institutions in three important areas of service, education, health care, and social service (child care), the sisters became important players in nineteenth-century Missouri town building. Both Kansas City and St. Louis provide important milieus to better understand the significant role played by Catholic sisters in urban centers throughout the trans-Mississippi West.

It is hard to overstate the importance of the work done by the St. Louis and Kansas City CSJs in the trans-Mississippi West, as they established vital institutions that were among the first in many early cities. Like Protestant and secular women who formed organizations to promote schools, health care, and social services, sisters provided labor, time, and monies caring for children, the sick, and the poor. To raw frontier towns the sisters

33. Evelyn O'Neill, "St. Teresa's Academy in Kansas City, Mo.," MS in ACSJC-SLP.
34. Although Kansas City had fewer foreign-born inhabitants than many cities, the 1910 census registered 10.2 percent of the population as foreign born and 10 percent black, and for the first time it showed a larger proportion of females to males; see Brown and Dorsett, K.C., 183–86; and "Report to the General Chapter—St. Louis Province, 1920," ACSJC-G.

"brought higher education with its appreciation of culture and the arts, as well as practical science," particularly in the education of girls.[35] Many historians of the West have described the importance of eastern capital, government subsidies, and the migration of families in creating the urban West, thereby negating the myth of the rugged, lone male riding into the sunset, unencumbered by family and society, and "winning" the west. Clearly, institutions such as churches, schools, hospitals, and orphanages helped support frontier families by providing wanted and needed community services. Catholic and Protestant women's organizations were important builders and caregivers who helped these towns thrive and grow into urban centers in Missouri.[36]

Even with gender and religious ideology supporting women's active work, nuns, like their Protestant counterparts, often needed the support of influential males to make their institutions a reality in the gendered and patriarchal world of nineteenth-century America. Similar to Protestant women, who utilized the monetary and political connections of male relatives and friends, the sisters benefited from networking with clerics who had the political clout and influence to serve as "town boosters" in the secular realm and as advocates of the sisters' projects in promoting Catholic culture in their cities. In St. Louis and Kansas City, CSJs had the support of male clerics with the power and foresight to provide invaluable economic, political, and social support for their endeavors. However, the possibility of male interference was also a reality, providing hard and continuous lessons concerning the gendered politics both within and outside the church. Religious women always knew that a death or transfer of a supportive bishop or priest could bring a new cleric who utilized his patriarchal prerogatives to exploit the sisters or interfere with the sisters' lives and activities.

Religious and gender ideology and the support of influential males provided an effective combination for justifying and encouraging women's presence and work in the public domain. In fact, the religious rivalry between Catholics and Protestants may have aided the proliferation of female institution building, since these types of community services were often seen as a responsibility of the church as well as a continuation of nurturing activities that women performed in their families. Since religious affiliation

---

35. Marra, "The Story," 55.

36. John Mack Faragher, *Sugar Creek: Life on the Illinois Prairie* (New Haven: Yale University Press, 1986); Carol K. Coburn, *Life at Four Corners: Religion, Gender, and Education in a German-Lutheran Community, 1868–1945* (Lawrence: University Press of Kansas, 1992); William Loren Katz, *The Black West* (Seattle: Open Hand Publishing, 1987).

was such an important marker of nineteenth-century life, the animosity and suspicion between Catholics and Protestants made separate institutions desirable and often necessary as they "competed" for clients. Certainly Catharine Beecher and other Protestant educators utilized gender ideology and fear of Catholicism to raise funds for female seminaries to train Protestant teachers to "save the West" from teaching orders of nuns whose success they both respected and feared.[37]

Likewise, American Catholic clergy and sisters utilized the threat of Protestant proselytizing and bigotry to secure thousands of dollars from European and American philanthropic sources and to justify the need for sisters and their work. Hoping to acquire CSJs for a western school, one cleric wrote to Reverend Mother Agatha Guthrie, asking her to help him save the children from "our arch-enemy and his helpers . . . and accept that school and prevent it from dropping into Protestant control."[38] Such inflammatory rhetoric, as well as the real competition that existed between Protestants and Catholics, opened doors for nuns and Protestant women to help fund, staff, and administer educational and caregiving institutions in the West. From their initial journeys to St. Louis and to Kansas City in the mid-nineteenth century, the CSJs, with other Catholic sisters, contributed to the building of cities throughout the West. The CSJs shaped Catholic culture in locations such as St. Paul and Minneapolis, Minnesota; Fargo and Grand Forks, North Dakota; Denver, Colorado; Tucson, Prescott, and Yuma, Arizona; and San Diego, Oxnard, Los Angeles, Oakland, and San Francisco, California.[39]

By their presence and work in St. Louis and Kansas City, the CSJs helped to preserve, shape, and expand American Catholic culture in Missouri and the trans-Mississippi West, creating networks and institutions that provided important services to all kinds of people, young and old. Gender ideology, particularly "domestic ideology," supported the roles of both Protestant women and Catholic women religious. In discussing "domestic ideology" in the trans-Mississippi West, Robert Griswold defines it as "a shared set of ideas about women's place [that] also bound non-related

37. Kathryn Kish Sklar, *Catharine Beecher: A Study in American Domesticity* (New York: Norton, 1976), 122–25; Polly Welts Kaufman, *Women Teachers on the Frontier* (New Haven: Yale University Press, 1984), 1–49.

38. Fr. Zephyrin Engelhardt to Rev. Mother Agatha Guthrie, February 4, 1886, ACSJC-SLP.

39. This is not a complete list of CSJ institutions but highlights the larger urban settings in the trans-Mississippi West. A complete list can be found in Dougherty, "Chronological List of Establishments," in *The Congregation of St. Joseph*, 427–38.

women to each other . . . offering women a cultural system of social rules, conventions, and values—a moral vocabulary of discourse—that gave meaning to their daily behavior and to their friendship with other women."[40] Although Catholic and Protestant churchwomen defined their religious missions in different ways and at times competitively, both used gender ideology as an impetus and justification for expanding their influence and providing necessary social services in the trans-Mississippi West.

CSJs established women's support networks and institutions that educated the young and cared for the physically and spiritually needy. Gender ideology limited them even as it provided a justification for their educational and nurturing roles. Their vows of poverty, obedience, and chastity may have allowed more latitude in their behavior and provided ways to avoid male influence and unwanted attention. Present in larger numbers than male clerics, the CSJs and other women religious lived and worked daily with the people they served. Creating and staffing parish schools, private academies, colleges, hospitals, and orphanages, they expanded and shaped American Catholic culture and public life in the cities of Missouri and across the nation.

40. Robert L. Griswold, "Anglo Women and Domestic Ideology in the American West in the Nineteenth and Early Twentieth Century," in *Western Women: Their Land, Their Lives,* ed. Lillian Schlissel, Vicki L. Ruiz, and Janice Monk (Albuquerque: University of New Mexico Press, 1988), 15–33.

The Tale of Two Minors

Women's Rights on the Border

LeeAnn Whites

On August 14, 1894, Virginia Louisa Minor died in St. Louis, Missouri. With her passing, the women of the state lost one of the most dedicated advocates of their rights, especially of their right to the vote. In 1867, she helped organize the Missouri Suffrage Association, the first organization dedicated solely to the pursuit of the vote for women in the country, and for years she was its only president. In 1875, she was the plaintiff in a pivotal Supreme Court case, *Minor v. Happersett,* which determined that women were not entitled to vote based on their status as citizens, and that it would indeed require an amendment to the Constitution for them to do so. Undaunted, Virginia Minor redoubled her efforts, organizing, lobbying, and petitioning the state legislature for the vote for women until the end of her life some twenty years later. As her obituary in the *St. Louis Republican* put it, "She is best known to the public in this connection, having lived out her long life in the furtherance of the women's suffrage movement, being hand-in-hand with Miss Susan B. Anthony, Mrs. Lucretia Mott, Mrs. Julia Ward Howe and Mrs. Elizabeth Cady Stanton."[1]

Who was Virginia Louisa Minor? What motivated her to make the rights of women the centerpiece of her life? What opportunities of place, of time, of class, or of familial background empowered her to do what so many, indeed most, women could not? In 1845, when Virginia Minor first moved to Missouri with her husband, Francis Minor, she, like all other married

1. *St. Louis Republican,* August 16, 1894.

women in the state, was legally dead. She could not buy or sell property in her own name, make binding contracts, sue or be sued, have legal guardianship over any children she might have, or claim ownership of her own wages or personal effects. Legally, all these things were the province of her husband. The logic of this legal status on the part of married women was expressed succinctly by the great English common-law theorist, William Blackstone, when he stated, "By marriage the husband and wife are one person in law, that is the very being or legal existence of women is suspended during marriage, or at least is incorporated and consolidated in the husband." Writing some eighty years later in 1912, Mary Lawrence, a lawyer in Kansas City, described the status of a married woman in Missouri in 1845:

> The husband was her lord and master, whom she was compelled to obey. If she did not, he had a legal right to chastise her or put her in the stocks or on the dunking stool in order to compel obedience to him. Every cent she possessed became his absolutely at the time of the marriage. Her fortune was put in his hands. . . . And then it was his last will and testament that decided who would enjoy it after he was gone.[2]

With perhaps some understatement, Lawrence concluded, "This is not a pleasant picture." It was, however, a picture largely transformed by the time of her writing, in the early twentieth century, and it was arguably Virginia Minor more than any other single individual in the state who deserves the credit for this transformation. Of course, Virginia Minor could not know when she and her husband moved to St. Louis in 1845 that the city would become a hotbed of women's rights agitation some twenty years later, any more than she could know that she would find herself at the center of that agitation. Unlike the northeastern part of the country, St. Louis had no organized movement for women's rights in 1845. In the North, the first organized agitation for women's rights emerged in connection with efforts to abolish slavery. Thus it is not surprising that Missouri's organized movement for women's emancipation did not emerge until after the slaves were emancipated, in the midst of the Civil War, some twenty years after Virginia and Francis first moved to St. Louis.[3]

2. Mary D. Lawrence, *Laws of Missouri Particularly Applicable to Women and Children* (Kansas City: n.p., 1912), 49. See also John M. Krum, *Missouri Justice, Being a Compendium of the Laws* (St. Louis, 1845); and E. W. Decker, *The Legal Status of Women in Missouri: An Address before the Women's Suffrage Convention* (St. Louis, 1869).

3. Most of the literature on the Minors has focused on their activity in the women's rights movement after the Civil War and particularly upon their Supreme Court case,

What Virginia Minor was able to do then about her status as a married woman in St. Louis prior to the Civil War, she could do only as an individual within the context of her own household or community. While Elizabeth Cady Stanton and Susan B. Anthony were busy calling women's rights conventions and petitioning state legislatures for the reform of married women's property rights, Virginia Minor and her husband were quietly expressing their mutual commitment to gender equity within the frame of their own household. What the Minors did about the status of women in Missouri prior to the Civil War, they did in order to live their lives and to construct their household and their relationship to each other as they deemed appropriate. The arrangements they made in the early years of their married life became the groundwork of what would become, many years later, their public work for the reform of women's status in general.[4]

Although the author of Virginia Minor's obituary asserted that she had always been hand in hand with Elizabeth Cady Stanton and Susan B. Anthony in her struggle for women's rights, that was not an entirely accurate description. Virginia Minor was deeply attached to these two national leaders, and beginning with the organized struggle for the vote in Missouri after the Civil War, she militantly allied herself with their faction of the women's rights movement. In the longer scope of her efforts to achieve gender equity, however, she did not stand hand in hand with them. After all, Stanton and Anthony stood hand in hand with each other, creating one of the greatest political partnerships of the nineteenth century. In her own struggle to advance the status of women, Virginia Minor stood hand in

---

Minor v. Happersett, 1875. See Ellen Carol DuBois, "Taking the Law into Our Own Hands: Bardwell, Minor, and Suffrage Militancy in the 1870s," in Marjorie Spruill Wheeler, ed., *One Woman, One Vote: Rediscovering the Woman Suffrage Movement* (Troutdale, Oreg.: New Sage Press, 1995), 81–98; Monia Cook Morris, "The History of Woman Suffrage in Missouri, 1867–1901," *Missouri Historical Review* 25, no. 1 (October 1930): 67–82; Mary Semple Scott, ed., "History of Woman Suffrage in Missouri," *Missouri Historical Review* 14, nos. 3–4 (April–July 1920): 281–384; Laura Staley, "Suffrage Movement in St. Louis during the 1870s," *Gateway Heritage* 3, no. 4 (spring 1983): 34–41; and Loretta Mae Walter, "Woman Suffrage in Missouri, 1886–1880" (master's thesis, Washington University, 1963).

4. On the woman suffrage movement more generally during this period, see Ellen DuBois, *Feminism and Suffrage: The Emergence of an Independent Women's Movement in America, 1848–1869* (Ithaca: Cornell University Press, 1978); and Ellen DuBois, *Woman Suffrage and Women's Rights* (New York: New York University Press, 1998); Eleanor Flexner, *Century of Struggle: The Woman's Rights Movement in the United States* (Cambridge: Belknap Press, 1975); Nancy Isenberg, *Sex and Citizenship in the United States* (Chapel Hill: University of North Carolina Press, 1999); and Wheeler, *One Woman, One Vote.*

hand with her husband, Francis. Indeed, as Elizabeth Cady Stanton provided theories to fuel Susan B. Anthony's activism, so Francis Minor's
scholarship and legal theories fed Virginia Minor's public political agitation. Even after the women's movement emerged in Missouri in 1867, it
was Francis Minor's legal theory that underwrote Virginia Minor's attempt
to vote in the presidential election of 1872. His contributions were crucial
to their activism; Francis Minor and Virginia Minor filed their important
Supreme Court case jointly, and it was he who argued the case before the
U.S. Supreme Court. In the years that followed their defeat in *Minor v.
Happersett,* it was Francis Minor who continued to defend their case in
print.[5]

Despite the fact that the Minors clearly worked as a partnership in pursuit of the rights of women in Missouri, Francis Minor is rarely acknowledged for his contributions to their work. Indeed, even Susan B. Anthony
herself, who knew them both well, when asked to write an encyclopedia
entry for Virginia Minor, attributed their jointly conceived, filed, and argued legal case to Virginia Minor alone. While it is now a commonplace to
assume that behind every great man there is at least one great woman, we
are perhaps hesitant to recognize that behind every great woman there
might be a great man. Historians do discuss the rise of a more companionate relationship between husbands and wives, dating the emergence of
such relationships as far back as the American Revolution, but historians
document few instances of husbands choosing to put their wives' causes
first. While we might be able to understand why a slave owner would turn
his back on slavery, emancipate his slaves, and even embrace the abolition
of his race privilege, historians seem to find the idea that men might, at the
expense of their gender privilege, take a stand for the emancipation of
women, puzzling, if not inexplicable.[6]

It should come as no surprise, then, that historians of the nineteenth-
century women's rights movement have generally attributed the emergence
of the movement to the agency of women alone. While they acknowledge
that husbands sometimes acquiesced in their wives' women's rights ac-

5. Although most scholars simply collapse Francis Minor's contributions to the
women's rights movement into that of his wife, some are actively critical of that practice.
See, for example, Joan Hoff Wilson, *Law, Gender, and Injustice: A Legal History of
U.S. Women* (New York: New York University Press, 1991), 170–77, who suggests that
one of Francis Minor's important contributions was to masculinize the movement.

6. Susan B. Anthony Encyclopedia Entries, 1878, reel no. 20, Susan B. Anthony
and Elizabeth Cady Stanton Papers (microfilm, Olin Library, Washington University,
St. Louis).

tivism, the examples of men who actively worked for the emancipation of women are few and far between. Francis Minor was one such man, however, a "women's rights man." As we will see, it was the gender equality that the Minors practiced at home for more than twenty years as a married couple—not the inequality between them—that underwrote their eventual emergence as the leading advocates of women's suffrage in the state. Our exploration of this tale of two Minors begins with the early years of their marriage, and what we might term the "politics of companionability," before there was any organized women's movement in Missouri. It was this politics of companionability that formed the root of what would eventually propel Virginia Minor into formal public leadership of the women's rights movement in Missouri.

Before Francis and Virginia Minor were husband and wife, they were family. They were both Minors, distantly related as cousins. They grew up knowing each other as extended kin in north-central Virginia. Indeed, Francis and Virginia could trace their lineage back to Doodes Minor, a Dutchman who was admitted into full citizenship in the Virginia Commonwealth in 1673. Nonetheless, within a year of their marriage in 1843, Francis and Virginia chose to leave the state, never to reside there again. When the Minors arrived in St. Louis in 1845, it was a burgeoning commercial center. Migrants from the North and the South, as well as from overseas, streamed into the city. As the "Gateway to the West," it represented a stepping-off point to the opportunities of frontier settlement, and at the same time, as a slaveholding city in a slaveholding state, it represented the existence and probable expansion of slavery in the foreseeable future. The Minors appear to have participated ambivalently in this mixed legacy of the South and the West. On the one hand, their move to St. Louis constituted a move away from the southern slaveholding plantation social order. They brought no slaves with them and never purchased any in St. Louis. Indeed, the slave population in St. Louis was on the decline. By 1850, it would constitute only 3 percent of the total population, a percentage of the population that would continue to decrease as ever more new migrants to the state, like the Minors, declined to participate in the institution.[7]

While the Minors did not perpetuate their southern slaveholding background in St. Louis, they did carry on their landholding tradition. In

7. Helen R. Pinkney, "Minor, Virginia Louisa," in *Notable American Women*, 2:550–51. For a general discussion of St. Louis during this period, see James Neal Primm, *Lion of the Valley: St. Louis, Missouri* (Boulder, Colo.: Pruett Publishing, 1981), 155–238.

September 1845, almost immediately upon their arrival in St. Louis, Francis Minor acquired a city lot and house, valued at a fairly substantial six thousand dollars in the 1850 census. In 1853, the Minors sold their town property and acquired ten acres on what was then the outskirts of St. Louis, a land they named "Minoria." Perhaps Virginia and Francis Minor decided to move to what was then the outskirts of St. Louis in response to the birth of their first and only child, Francis Gilman Minor, in 1852. In 1849, 10 percent of the population of St. Louis died in an outbreak of cholera. The disease was particularly threatening to young children and the elderly. The Minors may have been prompted to move to the outskirts of the city in an attempt to insure the health of their only child after eight years of marriage. Francis Minor, in particular, had reason to fear the ravages of childhood disease. The youngest of twelve children, by the time he was eighteen only two of his siblings were still living. In any case, by the mid-1850s, with the notable exception of slaveholding, the Minors appear to have largely replicated their planter-class background. There was, in the first place, their cousin marriage, a practice deeply imbedded in the culture of the southern planter class. Then there was Francis Minor's successful career as a lawyer, a profession typical of the planters, and particularly of the Minor family. Finally, in the acquisition of their family estate, the Minors followed in the long tradition of their family, who for generations in Virginia had acquired such rural landholdings, naming them, for example, "Minor's Folly," "Briery Knowl," or "Woodlawn," the plantation on which Francis Minor grew up.[8]

If we look more closely, however, at the pattern of property acquisition by Francis Minor, especially the purchases of the Minors' homes in 1845 and 1853, we find that despite the outward appearances of class and gender normality, the Minors from early on in their married life together worked to subvert the patriarchal household order. Not only did the Minors decline to construct their household around African slavery, but also they did what they could to subvert the subordinated status of married women, the other cornerstone of the patriarchal household order. So although Francis Minor in September 1845 acquired his first piece of property in St. Louis in his name alone, as the law and social custom indicated, soon after, in May 1846, he put this same house and lot, together with all his "personal prop-

8. 1850 Manuscript Census, St. Louis County, p. 100; Surveyor General Records, Capitol Fire Volumes, Missouri State Archives, Jefferson City, Missouri, 52:82; 53:140–41; 55:183; *Laws of the State of Missouri, Passed at the Session of the 15th General Assembly* (Jefferson City, Mo., 1849), 67; John B. Minor, *The Minor Family of Virginia* (Charlottesville, Va., 1923), 97–102.

erty now owned . . . or that he may hereafter acquire," in trust for his wife, Virginia Minor. In this trust he gave a meticulous list of the young couple's personal effects, which gives a picture of their manner of living in St. Louis. The Minors owned

> six mahogany chairs, one mahogany rocking chair, one spring bottom sofa, three carpets and oil cloth, one hearth rug, one girondole [a type of phonograph], one card table, one writing desk, one wardrobe, one bedstead, one cooking stove and apparatus, one dining table, one bureau, one dozen common chairs, one wash stand, one feather bed, one bathtub, two ottomans, one set of silver tablespoons, one set of silver teaspoons, one set of silver forks, one pair of silver sugar tongs, one gold watch and the Library, according to the catalogue of Books.[9]

So why did Francis Minor, as a husband, move so quickly to put all his worldly goods, even the family phonograph and his own watch, into trust for his wife, Virginia? Historians have suggested that the volatile nature of the rapidly developing commercial economy of the antebellum period encouraged some men to agree to the establishment of what were termed "separate estates" for their wives' property at the time of their marriage. If the husband lost his property, at least the property in his wife's name would be protected from creditors and the household would not be entirely bankrupted. In the state of Missouri, separate estates were legal as early as 1821, but when the Minors arrived in St. Louis in 1845, and indeed until after the Civil War, these prenuptial agreements in no way modified the husband's power over property acquired during the marriage, even gifts given directly to the wife. All such property was entirely controlled by the husband. Even if the husband deserted the family and failed to support them, the wife could not access the "husband's" estate. Indeed the only circumstance under which a wife could sell even her own property or control her own wages was if her husband was sentenced to the penitentiary, and even then only so long as the husband was imprisoned. As Judge Krum noted in his 1845 legal commentary, *Missouri Justice,* "with regard to feme couvert [the "legally dead" status of women] the law of the state is very strict."[10]

Under such circumstances, what was someone committed to gender equity to do? Even the establishment of a prenuptial separate estate, as limited

9. Deed Book U3, September 17, 1845, 146, and Deed Book, Y3, May 18, 1846, 581, City Hall, St. Louis, Missouri.

10. Krum, *Missouri Justice,* 238.

as that was, was not a possibility for the Minors, an established couple at the time of their arrival in St. Louis. And while the women's rights movement was pushing for the reform of married women's legal status in the North, there was no such organized movement in the slaveholding state of Missouri. What was possible was the "creative" use of standing laws, that is, the use of a law that, while technically legal, subverted the law's general intent to render women legal nonentities. All that was required was a certain level of legal expertise on Francis Minor's part, along with his willingness to set aside his status as "lord and master" in order to endow his wife with legal personhood. We can see this strategy at work in May 1846, when Francis Minor bound his trustee in a way calculated to move Virginia Minor as close as possible to being a completely empowered individual in her own right. The trustee was instructed to hold the property in trust only until such time as Virginia Minor determined to "sell, mortgage, devise, bequeath or otherwise dispose of the same or any part thereof at her will and pleasure." Virginia Minor was further empowered to "at any time revoke the power of the old and appoint a new trustee." If the trustee should fail to carry out her will, she could change trustees until she found one that would do so to her satisfaction.[11]

Why would Francis Minor choose to empower his wife at what was both literally and figuratively his own expense? Unlike the case of a prenuptial agreement in which the future husband stands to gain financially, Francis Minor's legal activity neither acquired property for his household, nor did it protect the property he put in trust to Virginia from any debt he might incur, for it was not until 1849, three years after he drafted this initial trust, that the wife's separate property was exempted from the husband's debt in the state of Missouri. Francis Minor was not, therefore, attempting to trade his gender power in relation to his wife in order to protect his property from the vagaries of the St. Louis marketplace. Instead, the formal agreements between Francis and Virginia Minor would appear, at least in the formal legal ownership of their home and personal effects, to have the sole purpose of creating Virginia Minor as a legally empowered individual, with the power to buy, sell, and essentially to own property. Francis Minor undoubtedly expected to be able to "influence" Virginia Minor's decisions about their property. The power of influence, however, while not to be underestimated, was the power conventionally exercised by wives, not husbands. The husband "bought" the property, the wife "influenced" his decision to do so. In the case of the trust that Francis Minor drew up in the

11. Deed Book, Y3, May 18, 1846, 581.

spring of 1846, however, he essentially placed himself in the position of "wife," at least in regard to their property at law. He could influence Virginia, but she was the one legally empowered to act. She was the one who could buy, sell, rent, or give away her property, as it suited her—not him.[12]

In other states, most notably the state of New York, women's rights advocates were using the unstable nature of the economy to press for a general reform of the property rights of married women that would give all married women equal ownership of the property of their households. Indeed in 1848, just two years after Francis Minor drew up his trust, the state of New York passed a law that significantly advanced the status of married women in this regard. Married women were empowered to own property that was acquired during the life of the marriage itself. While married women shared ownership of this jointly acquired marital property, they still were not able to sell it. That right remained with the husband alone. The Minor trust went significantly beyond this pathbreaking legislation because Virginia Minor could both buy and sell the property of her household at will. Of course this trust only emancipated Virginia Minor with regard to her own household and did not affect women as a group. Only a public movement could transform the law itself, as in New York, and Missouri was sadly lacking in that regard.[13]

Although in the 1840s the Minors found no organized public movement in which they could agitate with others for a general structural change in the St. Louis legal system, they apparently discovered some like-minded individuals. For not only did Francis Minor use his legal expertise to subvert the law in his wife's case, but also he made possible the sale of property *between* married women, thus allowing married women to actually participate in the burgeoning St. Louis land market themselves. Thus on May 1, 1853, Virginia Minor bought the land that would become Minoria from another married woman, Elizabeth Goodfellow, and on May 6, 1853, only a few days later, she sold the Minors' town home to a different married woman, Rebecca Hapenney. In both cases the buying and selling of land was made possible through the use of trusts, where the husband's rights were given over to a male trustee, who was then instructed to act for the

12. It was not until 1849 that the Missouri state legislature amended the law so as to protect a married woman's property from her husband's debt. See *Laws of the State of Missouri, Passed at the Session of the 15th General Assembly* (Jefferson City, Mo., 1849), 67.

13. On married women's property law reform in the state of New York, see Norma Basch, *In the Eyes of the Law: Women, Marriage, and Property in Nineteenth-Century New York* (Ithaca: Cornell University Press, 1982).

wife. In the case of Rebecca Hapenney, who acquired land from Virginia Minor, the stripping of her husband's rights in relation to the property and giving them over to his wife was quite explicitly laid out. The property was put in trust to her "forever" and was to be "entirely free from all control restraint or interference whatever on the part of her said husband." Rebecca Hapenney was further empowered to dispose of the property "at her own will and pleasure and to receive to her own separate use and benefit the proceeds of such sale and all rents and profits arising."[14]

One can only imagine what the county recorder made of these legal arrangements, which, while clearly abiding by the letter of the law, were clear in their effort to subvert it. Indeed, the city recorder appears to have insisted upon having it both ways. For while the Minors' use of the law essentially made the married woman into the seller (one might say she is structurally the "husband"), while stripping the husband of his powers (thus making him into the "wife"), the standard law had certain practices designed to at least protect the wife in relation to the power of the husband, if not to empower her. The most important of these practices was the separate examination of wives at the time of the husband's sale of property by the city recorder. Thus at the Hapenney sale of the Minors' town home, the clerk not only dutifully recorded the transaction between Virginia Minor and Rebecca Hapenney but also dutifully took Virginia Minor aside and ascertained that "the said Virginia L. Being by me made acquainted with the contents of said instrument of writing and deed of trust, acknowledged, on an examination apart from her husband, that she executed the same freely and without compulsion or undue influence of her husband." In this transaction, then, Virginia Minor was placed as both the selling party (through her trustee) (that is, as the "husband") and as the more passive "wife" party, in that she was consulted as to her consent to what was, in fact, her own action![15]

And what of Francis Minor? Where did he figure in this transaction? If the letter of the trust were followed, he would have been the one taken aside by the clerk and examined separately to see if he, as the "dependent" partner in the marriage, consented to the legally empowered partner's decision to sell the property. For reasons perhaps unnecessary even to discuss, the clerk did not treat Francis Minor as the "wife"; instead, Francis was present in the transactions in two ways, as a sort of "shadow husband." First, he, along with Virginia Minor and Philip Mauro, the trustee, presented

14. Deed Book, Q6, 226–27, May 4, 1853; N6, 539, May 1, 1853.
15. Deed Book, N6, 541.

themselves as the selling parties to the recorder and to the recorder of deeds. He was also included in the transaction itself, although neither as the selling "husband" nor as the separately examined "wife" (both of those positions being occupied by Virginia Minor), but alongside the trustee. Both Francis and the trustee indicated their formal agreement to the transaction by the acceptance of a token dollar from the purchaser of the land. Thus, despite the legally binding trust that Francis Minor created many years earlier, giving his ownership of the land in question to the trustee, he was himself still included in each separate transaction, as a sort of shadow of his former legal self, repeatedly reavowing his assent to the blanket trust he had already made.[16]

While Virginia Minor's struggle to gain equal empowerment for herself and other women was arguably odd, there was a place for her, and women as property owners like her, in the social order. They wanted to be legally constructed as men were. In the case of the Minors, we can see this clearly, as Virginia Minor, through the somewhat convoluted vehicle of the trust, was made structurally into the "husband" and was thus legally empowered to buy and sell her property as she saw fit. However difficult the entire trust mechanism was, it was nonetheless possible to accommodate Virginia Minor as a "pseudo-husband." It was actually more difficult to accommodate Francis Minor as a sort of "shadow" of his former legal self. What we see in the structure of the law serves to echo the larger social problem, for while it may make sense to transform "wives" into "husbands," it makes little sense to reverse the process and to reduce Francis Minor to a position of "nonbeing," the passive party, the "wife." Francis Minor is therefore present in the only way he can be present, as the author of the trust, since he can be placed neither as the "husband," a position he has given over to Virginia, nor as the disempowered "wife."

As subversive to the gender order as the initial Minor trust of 1846 was as well as the transactions the couple made with it in the years following—especially the sale of property not only by a married woman (Virginia Minor) but *between* married women (Goodfellow and Hapenney and Minor)—one further detail of the 1853 transaction through which Virginia Minor acquired their Minoria estate was arguably *the* most telling in terms of the Minors' legal subversion of the patriarchal social order. It seems particularly fitting that it should be around the acquisition of this ten acres of land, the family estate, at the very moment that the Minors came closest to replicating the life that they had known as children in Virginia, that they

16. Ibid.

should strike the greatest blow at subverting the patriarchal underpinnings of it. Not only was the property held for Virginia Minor "free and clear from all management, control or interference on the part of her present or future husband," but also, turning traditional inheritance practices upside down, it was to be controlled by her heirs, and not to go automatically to Francis Minor, upon her death. Even if Virginia Minor left no will indicating how Minoria was to be passed down, the trust indicated that it would "descend to her child or children by the present marriage, if alive." Only if all of Virginia Minor's children were to die before the age of twenty-one would the property revert to Francis Minor and "his right heirs, if he be dead."[17]

It was one thing to be empowered to own property, and further, to be so empowered as to sell property. It was, however, even more empowering to be in the position to leave one's property to one's descendants. In constructing the Minoria land transaction as he did, Francis Minor gave Virginia Minor the power to will Minoria however she saw fit, and even if she died intestate, he bound himself to the descent of the property to their son, Francis Gilman Minor, and not to any children he might later have with any subsequent spouse. Here, arguably more definitively than in any of his other legal work to date, Francis Minor indicated the depth and the extent of his personal commitment to the obliteration of patriarchal power, not just in his lifetime, but as a matter of precedent for his descendants. He not only indicated his commitment to the abolition of patriarchal power, but also simultaneously indicated his commitment to his marriage, because regardless of what might transpire, the land they purchased together would descend to the children of their union alone, and even then, only if it was Virginia Minor's will to do so.

In acquiring this land and naming it Minoria, the Minors indicated the ways in which the landed and familial traditions of the planter class were still living traditions for them. But the way in which they constructed this household, never owning any slaves and never having a "wife," in terms of the ownership of the place, they indicated that their move to the west was for each of them a gateway to a more equitable social order. By way of comparison, we could look to the practices of other citizens of St. Louis in the 1850s, who would later, like the Minors, become prominent advocates of the women's suffrage movement after the Civil War. A survey of the property transactions of these couples indicates that none of them were engaging in such "creative" legal activities in the antebellum period. Many of

17. Deed Book, Q6, 226–27.

the men, such as John Krum, Arnold Kneckel, and Beverly Allen, were, like Francis Minor, lawyers, so they certainly had the legal expertise to construct similar trusts if they had so desired. Other St. Louis men—those whose names would come to be prominently associated with the suffrage movement after the war, such as Joseph Yeatman or William Greenleaf Eliot—may not have been lawyers themselves, but they certainly were active in the antebellum property market, yet they made no provisions for their wives as Francis Minor did.[18]

The will that Beverly Allen drew up in 1845, shortly before the first Minor trust, gives a clear picture of the gendered legal arrangements that were the norm among the propertied classes of St. Louis in the 1840s. The Allens are a useful foil to the Minors because they resemble them in so many other ways. While Virginia Minor would become president of the Missouri Suffrage Association upon its founding in 1867 and held that position for many years, Penelope Allen would for many years hold the position of vice president. Like Minor, she was a founding member of the organization; she also brought her three daughters with her into the post–Civil War St. Louis women's movement. Her husband, Beverly Allen, resembled Francis Minor in some key respects. He too had migrated to St. Louis from Virginia as a young man, and he also became a prominent St. Louis lawyer, arguably more prominent than Francis Minor. He too was from a distinguished slaveholding planter-class background. In 1845, he, like Francis Minor, also drew up a critical legal document, in this case his will. As with the Minor trust of 1846, Beverly Allen's will demonstrates the nature of the power relations between himself and his wife.[19]

In stark contrast to Francis Minor's trust, all the Allen property was held in Beverly Allen's name alone during his lifetime; in his will he agreed to relinquish control of some of the property to his wife, but only upon his death, and even then only for so long as she did not remarry. Out of Beverly Allen's considerable estate, Penelope Allen was given "for her use" what Beverly Allen referred to as "my household and kitchen furniture carriage and my house" as well as the use of "my servants during the same period (her widowhood), or until they respectively become free." The remainder of his property Beverly Allen then put in trust to one James Clements and instructed him in the way that the monies should (eventually) be distributed to his children and the manner in which his "servants" should

18. Oscar W. Collet, *Index to Instruments Affecting Real Estate Recorded in the Office of Deeds in the County of St. Louis,* vols. 1–3 (St. Louis, 1874).

19. "The Beverly Allen Home," TS, Missouri Historical Society, St. Louis, Missouri, 1–6.

be freed. He also indicated that his trustee should "Pay to my wife what may be necessary for her support in the comfortable manner during widowhood." Having instructed his trustee as to the distribution and management of the bulk of his estate, Beverly Allen did finally include his wife, appointing her along with the trustee as executors of his will, but he felt compelled to explain his wife's presence, noting, "it being my desire in associating my wife to give her a knowledge in the transaction of business."[20]

Apparently Penelope Allen never had the opportunity to gain such knowledge of Beverly Allen's estate during their married life together. Even after his death, she only acquired clear ownership and control of their residence and household effects and, even then, was given only an annual budget, the amount to be determined by the trustee, to run the household. At the time of Beverly Allen's death, Penelope Allen had lived her whole adult life with *his* servants, *his* horses and carriage, *his* household effects, and even *his* children. In a fundamental way, Virginia Minor lived in an entirely different world than Penelope Allen, a world in which she was sheltered by *her* house, which was decorated with *her* furniture, and in which she ate off *her* dining table using *her* teaspoons.[21]

The disparity between the Minor trust and Beverly Allen's will is striking and reveals just how unconventional were the Minors' opinions on gender. Even in appointing Penelope Allen co-executor of his estate along with the trustee, Beverly Allen only put her in the position of carrying out his will. Executors are required by law to take an inventory of the estate, oversee the sale of such property as was necessary to pay off the outstanding debts, and dispense the remaining assets as per the instructions of the will. By going through this process, Penelope Allen would acquire a good knowledge of exactly what the assets of the estate were, but she still had no power to manipulate those assets. The power to make actual decisions about the family property, even after the death of the husband, was instead conferred to the unrelated male trustee rather than to the life partner, a woman, the wife.[22]

Why were the Minors so singularly committed to gender equity in their personal lives? Perhaps their early childhood experiences influenced their attitudes concerning the powers that married women should have. When Virginia Minor was only six years old, her own father died suddenly, leaving her mother with his affairs "disordered," and with three young chil-

20. Deed Book, U3, 408, October 25, 1845.
21. Ibid.
22. Krum, *Missouri Justice*, 282–93.

dren—"orphans," as family correspondence described them. They were thrown upon the resources of their male relations, who took them in and did what they could for them. When Francis Minor was two, his mother was also widowed, and she was left with many children, a large plantation, and many slaves to manage. Even if she had experience within her own household with the demands of managing such a large operation, she was not empowered in the larger world to do so. Perhaps, rather than leave his wife yet another "man manqué," as his father had arguably left his mother, Francis Minor preferred to voluntarily take on the role of "shadow husband." After all, in the state of Virginia, Francis's and Virginia's mothers could (and did) look to the men of their extended family who were settled around them to cover for the loss of their husbands. The Minors, however, were thousands of miles removed from their place of birth and supportive kin connections. They were forced to rely upon their resources as a couple and, ultimately, upon their resources as individuals. Thus it was perhaps the combination of their devastating losses as children, their witnessing the struggles of their mothers in a slaveholding patriarchal landed economy, combined with their movement to the West and the mobile, volatile, individualizing experience of St. Louis, that can best explain the Minors' comparatively equitable property arrangements.[23]

It would, however, require more than a burgeoning economy and an occasional particularly committed companionate couple to fundamentally transform gender bias in the legal system, or even to lead a public movement organized to that end. In the case of St. Louis and the state of Missouri more generally, it would require the catalytic impact of the Civil War, a war that in four short years abolished the institution of slavery in the state and gave women the responsibility for acting like "deputy husbands," while the men were off at war. The Minors found themselves lifted up by this doubled breach of the patriarchal household order. What they had practiced privately suddenly emerged as the public order of the day. They both eagerly supported the Union cause in St. Louis, especially the Western Sanitary Commission, the organization most responsible for assisting the freed people and refugees who flooded into the city during the war. Virginia Minor found many new friends in the struggle for a more equitable status for women in the work with the Ladies' Union Aid Society, and

23. For discussion of how the Minor kin addressed the loss of both Virginia and Francis Minor's fathers, see Correspondence, 1830–1881, no. 3750, series 1, box 1, November 27, 1830; April 11, 1831; April 13, 1831; April 20, 1831; and May 30, 1831, all in Minor and Wilson Family Papers, Special Collections, Alderman Library, University of Virginia.

Francis Minor found an enlarged role for his legal talents as a U.S. claims agent representing the legal rights of soldiers' widows and orphans.[24]

In the war's aftermath, some of the men and women who had worked together for the Union cause in the Western Sanitary Commission went on to form the Missouri Suffrage Association. It seemed to them only fitting that women, who had shouldered so much of the burden of the war, both in running their households in their husbands' absence and in contributing to the public war-relief efforts, should now be equally empowered as citizens. The membership collected signatures on petitions for the enfranchisement of women and presented them formally to the state legislature beginning in 1867. In 1869, the National Women's Suffrage Association held its annual convention in St. Louis, a testament to the force and vitality the women's rights movement had gained in St. Louis after the war. It was at this meeting that the women's rights movement adopted Francis Minor's strategy for the acquisition of the vote, a strategy that echoed the Minors' earlier negotiation of women's property rights in Missouri. The way Francis Minor interpreted the Constitution (even if it was another "subversive" reading of the law), it in no way denied women the right to vote. He argued that as citizens of a democracy, participants in fact at the very founding of the nation, women *already* had the right to vote. They simply needed to exercise that right.[25]

In the presidential election of 1872, advocates of women's rights across the country attempted to put this direct action strategy into effect. In St. Louis, Virginia Minor and several other women attempted to register to vote and were denied. The Minors were prepared for this outcome, and in October 1872, they jointly filed a suit against the registrar, Reese Happersett, who had denied Virginia Minor the right to register to vote in the state. The case, *Minor v. Happersett,* was taken up by the U.S Supreme Court in 1875. Had the Supreme Court agreed with the Minors' reading of the law, the road to political rights for women would have been much shorter. Instead, the Court decided unanimously against the Minors, stating that the state of Missouri had the right to determine the qualifications of voters, including qualification based on sex.

After the flurry of organizational activity and legal reform generated by

24. On Virginia Minor's participation in women's wartime voluntary activity, see Paula Coalier, "Beyond Sympathy: The St. Louis Ladies' Union Aid Society and the Civil War," *Gateway Heritage* 11, no. 1 (summer 1990): 38–51; and William E. Parrish, "The Western Sanitary Commission," *Civil War History* 36, no. 1 (1990). On Francis Minor's legal representation of soldier's dependents, see Francis Minor, Civil War Claims Book, vol. 6, clipping, Missouri Historical Society, St. Louis, Missouri.

25. *Minor v. Happersett,* State Archives, Jefferson City, Missouri.

the Civil War and its aftermath in the state, the women's rights movement gradually lost public support. Nonetheless, having entered the public arena in the name of women's rights, the Minors maintained their support of the cause, pressing for a public reflection of the equity they had established personally. In the 1870s and 1880s, Virginia Minor continued to present petitions to the state legislature in favor of the vote for women, and Francis Minor continued to advocate in print for their legal interpretation of women's rights.[26]

In February 1892, Francis Minor died suddenly at the age of seventy-one. In his will, he left his entire estate to his wife, Virginia. He made only one request, and that was that only his immediate family should ever be buried in the family plot in Bellefontaine Cemetery. He not only had made Virginia Minor his sole beneficiary, but also had made her his executor. Resigning her current position as vice president of the National Women's Suffrage Association, she carried out the role of executor of her husband's estate meticulously, carefully listing all the assets of the estate and paying off all the outstanding debts. On June 4, 1894, she filed the final paperwork on the estate, and shortly thereafter, on August 14, 1894, Virginia Minor herself passed away.[27]

Virginia Minor's will received much more public attention than that of Francis Minor. It was published in the daily press because of its unusual bequests. In the first place, Virginia Minor left half of her estate to her two single nieces, with the proviso that if either of them should ever marry, the married niece should give her half of the inheritance to the niece who remained single. As she had struggled to advance women's economic and political autonomy in life, so Virginia Minor gave what she had at the end of her life to assist the most independent women in her family, the single women. Virginia Minor left the other half of her estate to the nineteenth century's best-known single woman and advocate of women's autonomy, Susan B. Anthony, as Virginia Minor explained, "in gratitude for the many thousands she has expended for woman."[28]

On August 17, 1894, the funeral ceremony was held for Virginia Minor at Bellefontaine Cemetery, without the benefit of clergy. She declined the services of the ministry because, as she explained, so many of the clergy had opposed the struggle for women's rights, the cause to which she had

26. Francis Minor, "Woman's Legal Right to the Ballot," *Forum,* December 1886; Francis Minor, "Citizenship and Suffrage, the Yarborough Decision," *Arena,* 1889.

27. Final Settlement of the Estate of Francis Minor, June 4, 1894, City Recorder's Office, City Hall, St. Louis, Missouri.

28. Clipping, Virginia Minor Necrology File, Missouri Historical Society, St. Louis, Missouri.

dedicated her life. She was buried in the family plot alongside her husband and her son, as Francis Minor had willed. In her obituary, the press attempted to minimize the seriousness of her commitment to the women's movement by emphasizing the ways in which she put her marriage first. According to the press, she was always the dedicated wife and mother and only belatedly was an advocate of women's rights. Those citizens of St. Louis who knew the Minors, however, knew better. Virginia Minor was not a public advocate for women's rights only insofar as it did not detract from her role as wife to Francis Minor. In fact, her marriage and her husband stood at the center of her advocacy of rights for women. It was, after all, Francis Minor's will that made it possible for Virginia Minor to leave what was actually *their* entire estate to single women. And while Virginia Minor turned her back on those men, like the clergy, who opposed her struggle for women's autonomy, she had every reason to know that gender was no bar to the advocacy of women's rights. Indeed, it was the very companionability of the Minors' marriage that stood at the center of their commitment both to the integrity of their household and to the individual rights of women. In 1894, conventional gender norms still could not encompass both. The politics of companionability remained a challenge for the twentieth century, despite the very real private and public accomplishment of pioneering couples like the Minors, advocates of women's rights on the border.

The Changing Role of Protection on the Border

Gender and the Civil War in Saline County

Rebekah Weber Bowen

The onset of the American Civil War and the heated political debates over slavery and states' rights that preceded it can easily give way to an overly simplistic regional division between the "North" and the "South." Within this traditional regional interpretation, Northern men joined the Federal army to fight to preserve the Union, Southern men joined the Confederate army to protect the institution of slavery, and women on both sides remained in the background of the home front. These strict divisions, however, become complicated in areas such as Missouri. Before, during, and after the Civil War, Missouri walked a political tightrope, for as a border state it was a place where political divisions often became personal divisions and where traditional gender roles temporarily became one of the casualties of war.

The gender roles and power ascribed to men and women blurred amidst the hostilities and terrors of war. Nowhere was this more evident than in the issue of protection, the deeply entrenched social norms that men should be protectors of home and family, while women, by the nature of their sex, should be dependent upon male protection. Challenges to societal gender rules are clearly visible in the state of Missouri because of its special position as a slaveholding state on the border. As violence increased among the different political and military factions in the state, the protection of life and property grew in importance, as did the issue of who held the power of protection. When war on the border upset the balance of everyday life, the hierarchy of gender roles proved unstable.

The battle over slavery and states' rights is a central foundation of Missouri's history and contributed to the instability that plagued the region. The 1820 Missouri Compromise, which allowed Missouri to join the Union as a slave state and Maine as a free state, set the stage for later battles. After the Kansas-Nebraska Act of 1854, which allowed popular sovereignty to determine slave or free status for states, Missouri and Kansas had their own personal border war. The 1850s brought constant battles and acts of retaliation between Missouri slaveholders and Kansas Free-Soilers. Missouri's placement on the political tightrope of the border during the Civil War, therefore, was not a new position.

The tightrope of the border also revealed itself in the definition of "enemy." Although Missouri officially remained a part of the Union, it cannot be assumed that most residents of any particular area strongly identified with the North. Similarly, even in highly concentrated areas of slaveholding, one cannot assume that all citizens would take up arms in defense of the South. In Missouri, the war was fought on home turf where men, women, and children lived their everyday lives and the enemy was not a nameless figure in uniform—he was more likely a friend or a neighbor. In 1863, Ruth Knox described the ambiguity of the battlefield in Saline County, Missouri, when she wrote from Ohio to her cousin Dr. Glen Hardeman in Saline County: "It must be terrible living in Missouri now[,] for that state of insecurity must be worse in reality than having actual battles around you. I think poor Missouri is to be really pitied."[1]

While all of Missouri existed in a state of heightened tension, Saline County faced a particularly intense wartime experience. Nestled within central Missouri and bordered on the north by the Missouri River, this one county contained all the elements that proved so dangerous throughout the rest of the state. First and foremost, Saline County was a prominent slaveholding county. The rich soils along the Missouri River made the county an attractive agricultural area, so it became a magnet for slavery. In 1860, Saline County was home to 9,800 whites and 4,876 African American slaves; slaves made up a third of the county's population, thus providing a huge portion of the county's labor. Saline County's percentage of slaves relative to the entire county population was the second highest in the state.[2] Free

1. Ruth Knox to Glen Hardeman, October 4, 1863, Glen Hardeman Collection, Western Historical Manuscript Collection–Columbia, University of Missouri–Columbia (hereinafter cited as WHMC-C).

2. R. Douglas Hurt, *Agriculture and Slavery in Missouri's Little Dixie* (Columbia: University of Missouri Press, 1992), 220.

residents in Saline County also hailed from differing backgrounds. In 1860, 30 percent of the settlers in Saline County came from the Upper South slave-holding states of Virginia, Kentucky, and Tennessee. The county's largest foreign-born group, Germans, traditionally opposed slaveholding. When men began enlisting in the war effort, the only township in Saline County that showed a significant percentage of Union enlistments over Confederate was in the southwest corner, which was dominated by German-settled communities. Saline County, therefore, was populated with residents who both supported and opposed slavery.[3]

When the Civil War ultimately reached Missouri, 109,000 men in Missouri enlisted to fight for the Union, while only 30,000 enlisted to fight for the Confederacy.[4] Loyalties were clearly divided, yet these divisions were not evenly spread throughout the state. In Saline County, white men joined the fight for the South in a rate of almost two to one over men who joined the Union.[5] In 1862, the rebellious nature of the county would prompt Federal forces to occupy the county to maintain order. Conflicts over slavery and political ideology between opposing factions led to guerrilla warfare. The split over personal and political loyalties fueled aggression and violence. In Saline County the battlefield proved to be the home, and enemies could not be easily ascertained. As white men struggled to identify threats, they faced constant and legitimate fears of potential death at the hands of every man they encountered. Within this environment of fear and violence, white men lost their power to protect home and family and ultimately were unable to effectively protect themselves. While men lost this power, white women took on the role of protector and revealed new expressions of female power not visible in normal conditions.

The "normative" view of gender in war appeared as celebrations erupted on May 13, 1861, when the first company of troops was officially raised in Saline County. The Saline Jackson Guards, a Confederate company named after Saline County resident and pro-secession governor Claiborne Fox

3. Compiled Service Records of the Union and Confederacy, State Historical Society of Missouri, University of Missouri–Columbia (hereinafter cited as SHS); 1860 Manuscript Census, Saline County, Missouri; *History of Saline County, Missouri* (St. Louis: Missouri Historical Company, 1881); *History of Saline County* (1881; reprint, Marshall, Mo.: Marshall Commemorative Sesquicentennial Book Committee, 1967); *History of Saline County, Missouri* (Marshall, Mo.: Marshall Publishing, 1983); *Marshall, Missouri: 1839–1989* (Marshall, Mo.: Green Printers, 1989).

4. Lorenzo J. Greene, Gary R. Kremer, and Antonio F. Holland, *Missouri's Black Heritage,* rev. ed. (Columbia: University of Missouri Press, 1993), 76.

5. Compiled Service Records, SHS.

Jackson, were honored by a parade in Marshall, the county seat. After participating in the parade, local resident Sue Isaacs presented Captain John Sappington Marmaduke with a flag made by the white women of Marshall. The flag was promptly handed over to the company bearer, Sergeant R. Gaines, who gave a short speech to the crowd:

> We are called to repeal the invasion of our territory and of our liberties as a state; and until that be effected this banner shall float over our contending hosts. *It is for you that we fight. The weakness of woman is no defense against the violence of fanaticism.* It is to avenge the slaughter of women and children that we take our arms, and our grasps shall not be relaxed, nor our energy abated until the barbarian emissaries of a ruthless tyrant shall be driven beyond our borders.[6]

While Gaines formally referred to the struggles of wartime and to the threat of enemy aggression in Missouri, his words have meaning on different levels. Gaines addressed expectations of white manhood during the trials of war. It was the duty of men to fight to defend the state from invasion in order to protect their freedom and liberties as white men. White manhood necessitated political freedom, independence from outside control, and the willingness to fight for these goals.

His remarks reveal ideas about white womanhood in war, as well. White men also fought to protect the weakness of women. In his speech, Gaines envisions that these helpless and weak women would fold immediately during the conflict, unable to face their uncertain futures. His words imply that women required the support and protection of men during the threat of warfare, reflecting established gender roles. Womanhood required women to be protected, and manhood required men to be protectors.

Gaines, however, was not the only person to speak on that May day. When Sue Isaacs presented a flag made by the white women of Marshall, she also addressed the men preparing to leave for war:

> Gentlemen of the Saline Jackson Guards: I have the honor of presenting you, in behalf of the ladies of Marshall, with this banner, the emblem of your state, hoping you will receive it as a slight token of the high regard which is entertained by them toward you, for the valor and patriotism you have displayed in the ready willingness to go where your country calls; and while we feel confident that its honor will ever by you be gallantly protected and sustained, we hope that it

---

6. *History of Saline County, Missouri* (1881), 276 (emphasis added).

may be to you in the hour of trial and of battle, an evidence of the interest that will ever be manifested by the ladies of your county in the glorious cause you have so nobly espoused.[7]

Isaacs's words display the patriotism and confidence that the white women of Marshall had for the men who were heading off to protect their institutions and way of life. Her words echo Gaines's remarks; it is clear that, prior to the war, the popular gender norm dictated that white men had a duty to protect their homes, their state, their political beliefs, and their women. Even in times of peace, such norms required men to protect and provide for their families and women to be obedient, submissive, and grateful to the men in their families.

Yet Isaacs's references to the flag also speak on a deeper and more subtle level, revealing a glimpse of the future changes in gender roles that the war would bring. Isaacs told the men to remember that the flag was more than a flag. It was also a representation of the white ladies' interest in the men and would be there, like a woman, to support them in times of need. Thus the flag became a symbol of the women of Saline County. Through this flag, the women of Saline County would accompany the soldiers to the battlefield. In May 1861, Isaacs implied that women would symbolically protect men. But as the battlefield became the home in the guerrilla war, men would need the real protection of women.

White women living within the patriarchal order were expected to remain passive and to remain within the private sphere of the home. Because they were not considered real citizens, they were expected to remain outside the bounds of political controversy and were not obligated to take up arms to fight for their political beliefs. With the arrival of the Civil War, white men felt compelled to enter the armed forces in order to fulfill their duty as citizens, while white women were perceived as innocent bystanders without rights, without duties, and without a threatening position. However, as Victoria Bynum, who has studied the changing roles of North Carolina women, explained, women became the "visible partner" of the household, exposed, while men fought at war or remained hidden as deserters.[8] While men upheld their rights as men and as citizens in fighting, women were left behind in the vulnerable position of having to deal with the immediate repercussions of war at home.

These repercussions could be severe. Most bands of civilian guerrillas

7. Ibid.

8. Victoria E. Bynum, *Unruly Women: The Politics of Social and Sexual Control in the Old South* (Chapel Hill: University of North Carolina Press, 1992), 144.

and companies of soldiers, considering themselves men, vowed not to physically harm any women. Women, after all, were not citizens and were not soldiers, therefore, in most male minds, they could not possibly be threats. Although guerrillas and soldiers alike vowed not to kill white women, they had few moral qualms about robbing women and children of their earthly possessions, burning their homes to the ground, or killing any male family members who might have remained at home. As the "visible partner," women dealt firsthand with these terrors. Since women were accepted as individuals with no rights, they were inadvertently empowered to serve as intermediaries and protectors. In this time of crisis, women became the few residents of Saline County who could effectively protect both the hearth and the hearts of their families. As women became recognized protectors, men became the protected—a significant shift in gender roles.

Female protection in Saline County took different forms. First, women often sought to protect their homes and personal property from guerrilla and army looting. The turbulence of the Civil War put many families in financial straits, making the preservation of belongings crucial to the survival of the family. Second, white women became the physical protectors of their families in general and of men in particular. In these instances, women went to great lengths to save the lives of their husbands or male kin. Third, female protection took on alternative forms that did not involve women physically protecting the men of their families. In cases where women were separated by great distances from their husbands, sons, and fathers, they had to find other ways to serve as protectors, embracing strategies with political or legal leanings.

Female protection has gone unrecognized because historians have often equated victimhood with being female, viewing white women as weak bystanders acted upon by powerful men. For example, in his analysis of an infantryman's letters home to his wife, describing the looting of a woman's home, the historian Michael Fellman summarizes: "The defenselessness of the women, their benumbed silence when being plundered, and their poverty and potential starvation made them seem pitiable victims to Stevens" (the infantryman).[9] Women in this analysis are not only victims because of the horrors of war, but also victims because they were women: weak, passive, and submissive. However, all people were victimized by the events of the Civil War. Men and women alike were placed in circumstances during the war where they were at the mercies of others. It is crucial to understand that "victim" should not be gendered female.

9. Michael Fellman, *Inside War: The Guerrilla Conflict in Missouri during the American Civil War* (New York: Oxford University Press, 1989), 193, 203.

In particular, the issue of attacks on the home can be interpreted in a different way when "victim" is not assumed to be either weak or female. Surviving evidence in Saline County reveals that women whose homes were under attack had to make immediate decisions that had a long-ranging impact upon themselves and their families. Elvira Scott, an avid supporter of the South, lived with her merchant husband, John, and two daughters, Pet and Hebe, in Miami, Missouri.[10] Scott was one of many women who faced bands of guerrillas throughout the war. Her journal provides a clear example of a woman facing guerrillas not as a passive subject, but rather as a decisive individual forced to make difficult and immediate decisions. A journal entry dated Thursday, July 23, 1863, described a group of men dressed in Federal uniforms who entered the village of Miami. The Scott family soon learned these men were bushwhackers in disguise by their rousing cheers in support of Confederate president Jefferson Davis. These troops still represented a threat to the Southern-sympathizing Scott family because Federal forces occupied Saline County. When some of the men approached the Scott home demanding breakfast, Elvira recorded the events as follows:

> I told them that I could not do what they asked, that they must know that when the Federals came in town they would punish me if I did, perhaps burn my house. One of them, Dr. Graves, that I had seen the day Bob Myers was killed[,] said, "Well, Madam, if you don't do it[,] *we* will burn the house. *You can make your choice.*" I could say nothing more, but told them to go in.[11]

Dr. Graves's words are a poignant reminder of the trials faced by women in Saline County. Elvira Scott was indeed given an unpleasant choice: She was allowed to choose between the possible destruction of her home by Federal soldiers at a later date if she complied with the guerrillas' demand, or the definite, swift, and immediate destruction of her home if she did not. Although Elvira Scott did not have to feed and harbor this band of guerrillas, she recognized the imminent consequences of not complying. Women in Saline County often chose the course that provided the most immediate sense of security. They did this not because they were weak victims, but because the protection of their families and homes was their priority.

The great lengths to which white women went to protect family property can be seen in the story of Martha Horne. Martha and Richard Horne

10. 1860 Manuscript Census, Saline County, Missouri.
11. Elvira Scott Diary, WHMC-C, 212a–213 (emphasis added).

spent the majority of their married lives in Cass County, about fifteen miles from the Kansas border. Union forces along the Kansas border were convinced that guerrillas were thriving because they had supporters and families who provided them with food, shelter, and information, enabling them to continue in the constant and vicious border warfare. Federal forces hoped to stop these guerrillas with Order Number 11, issued by General Thomas, which became effective on August 25, 1863. Order Number 11 called for the forced removal within fifteen days of all persons living between the Missouri and Osage Rivers. This included people in Jackson, Bates, and Cass counties and parts of Vernon County.[12]

Order Number 11 had forced the Hornes from their home, land, and property, making them refugees. In the spring of 1864, the Hornes moved to the Arrow Rock area of Saline County. One day shortly after their arrival, a group of Federal soldiers from the state militia ventured around the residence of the Hornes, preparing to help themselves to the corn that Mr. Horne had just brought back from town. It is unclear where Mr. Horne was at this point. Whether he was home or not, Martha Horne saw the impending threat of robbery and proceeded to stand in front of the corncrib, refusing to unlock the door. The officer present announced that he would have the corn and took up a large rock to break open the lock. At this moment, confronted with the loss of the valuable corn, Martha Horne took on the traditionally male role of protector. She described what happened next:

> I took a step toward him, drew back the ax over my shoulder and told him if he struck that lock I would brain him. He gave me one full look in the eyes, his hands mechanically parted and the rock fell at his feet. The whole party then left, and I could hear them laughing for several blocks. And I, of course, womanlike, went home all of a tremble and had a good cry. But I know that if that officer had hit that lock I would have hit him, whatever might come of it.[13]

Although she had stepped out of her woman's role temporarily, Martha Horne quickly returned to it, for she described herself as crying and trembling.

---

12. Thomas Goodrich, *Bloody Dawn: The Story of the Lawrence Massacre* (Kent, Ohio: Kent State University Press, 1991), 152–53; William E. Parrish, Charles T. Jones Jr., and Lawrence Christensen, *Missouri, the Heart of the Nation,* 2d ed. (Arlington Heights, Ill.: Harlan Davidson, 1992), 178–79.

13. *Reminiscences of the Women of Missouri during the Sixties* (Jefferson City, Mo.: Hugh Stephens, 1913), 42–44.

Yet she followed her description of "feminine" emotions with an acknowledgment that she would have indeed taken aggressive action to protect the corn, if she had to—an expression of threatening emotion traditionally considered male. Horne's strength under fire and her open anger in such a hostile situation were far from weak and "trembling." When faced with the loss of her family's personal property, Martha stood up and defended it.

The second and most dramatic form of female protection reveals that women faced down adversaries in order to save the lives of the men in their families. While many men enlisted, leaving women at home to protect their families, not all men left home to serve. Even when men remained at home, male protection often proved ineffective. Saline County, like many other areas of Missouri, was a daily battleground. Each day brought potential confrontations with opposing bands of roaming troops or guerrillas, and each day, therefore, brought the possibility of mortality. During these turbulent times, white men legitimately feared for their lives when facing guerrillas and depended on female protection. Elvira Scott found herself in such a situation when Kansas guerrillas known as Redlegs arrived at the Scott family home. Elvira did not refuse the men when they asked for food. In fact, she wrote that she tried to give them her best so as not to provoke them. Elvira provided the men with food and eased a sigh of relief when they left without looting or destroying her home.

Shortly after they left, Elvira discovered that one of the soldiers had her husband, John, at gunpoint. Elvira recalled, "In an instant I was between them, holding both of them apart as well as I could. . . . I kept between them until we got around to the dining room door, when the man thrust me out from between them. But I got back. As I did so, I felt the gun come up against my back, but I maintained my position."[14] John's capture by this Kansas Redleg is a perfect example of the vengeful retaliation found in guerrilla warfare throughout Saline County and the state. John Scott was being taken prisoner in retaliation for the murder of two Federal soldiers, who had been murdered in retaliation for the murder of a Southern sympathizer. Elvira was able to talk the soldier into lowering his weapon. Her husband was still taken prisoner, but she had been able to protect his life. If a man had taken a similar stand, both easily could have been shot in the struggle. The protection afforded to Elvira as a woman allowed her, in turn, to protect others.

Perhaps even more significant is the case of Jenny Flannery, who also strove to protect men; she even chose to place herself in danger for men

14. Elvira Scott Diary, WHMC-C, 199.

who were not members of her own family. In the middle of July 1864, a skirmish between the Missouri state militia and a band of bushwhackers occurred near the village of Arrow Rock. The battle resulted in the wounding of the guerrilla captain, a man named Yager. Captain Yager was removed to a bushwhacker camp in nearby Cambridge Township. It is at this point where Jenny Flannery enters the picture. Jenny's age is unknown, but she is referred to in the 1881 *History of Saline County* as "Miss Flannery" and as a "young lady."[15] Jenny apparently lived near the camp, which was located in a cornfield on a farm owned by a man named Gilliam. Jenny visited the captain on a daily basis and gently cared for his needs as she nursed him back to health.

After the captain had recuperated, Federal forces arrested Mr. Gilliam for harboring the bushwhackers. When Jenny heard of Gilliam's arrest, she promptly rode to Marshall and informed the Federal forces that she alone had nursed Yager and that Gilliam should be released. Strikingly, the Federal forces complied. Gilliam was released, and Flannery was arrested in his place. Jenny's actions arguably saved two lives, Yager's and Gilliam's. Although Flannery was imprisoned for her crime, she was released within a few weeks.[16] Had he remained in captivity, Mr. Gilliam might not have been as lucky. Jenny was able to take sole responsibility for the crime yet live to tell about it because she was a woman. The role of female protector even extended beyond the bonds of family.

Female protection took alternative forms when women were not able to physically protect their men. Partilla Bell, although separated from her husband, David, by a great distance, nevertheless sought to save his life after he had been arrested and sentenced to death. Her strategy for preventing his death, therefore, had to accommodate the distance. She chose to apply political pressure by launching a letter-writing campaign. Bell also exploited prewar gender norms about manhood and womanhood to advance her cause. The 1860 census records David and Partilla Bell as being residents of Salt Pond Township, an area on the southwest corner of the county. David was a twenty-nine-year-old blacksmith from New York state; Partilla was twenty-five and born in Missouri. The Bells had no children, no slaves, no real estate, and only one hundred dollars' worth of personal property. David Bell joined the Union army and served as a sergeant in Company B of the 7th Regiment of the Missouri state militia.[17] Partilla Bell's role as protector began in May 1863 with the arrest of her husband for murder. That spring, David Bell and his company were in the commu-

15. *History of Saline County* (1881), 315.
16. Ibid., 315–16.
17. Federal Manuscript Census, 1860, Saline County, Missouri; Compiled Service Records, SHS.

nity of Longwood, Missouri, located in northern Pettis County about five or six miles south of the Saline County border and very close to the recorded location of the Bells' Saline County residence.

On May 2, 1863, David Bell was playing cards in a Longwood saloon. A ranking officer, referred to only as McGuire, approached Bell and asked him if he knew where a local man named William Majors lived. Bell, being from the area and a neighbor and former employee of Majors, knew the exact location. McGuire claimed that Majors had been harboring rebel soldiers and needed to be arrested. Bell and an undisclosed number of men rode along with McGuire to the home of William Majors. The men approached the Majors residence and inquired about William's whereabouts. Mrs. Majors, who was home at the time, directed the men to her husband, who was working in a nearby field. Details of what happened next remain sketchy. The only thing that is certain is that William Majors was shot in the head at close range and died. No one present, however, claimed responsibility or knowledge about who the shooter was. David Bell was arrested for the murder and sent to Gratiot Military Prison in St. Louis, sentenced to die.

Mrs. Majors was not successful in protecting her husband from death, but Partilla Bell would be. David Bell had been placed in Gratiot until he could be transferred to the greatly feared military prison in Alton, Illinois. Partilla, also highly literate, began a letter-writing campaign to protect her incarcerated husband by preventing his transfer to Alton. Her first attempt at protection, aimed at her husband's jailors in St. Louis, failed, for David Bell was transferred to Alton Prison to await his death sentence. Partilla Bell did not quit, however. Her new goal was her husband's release.

Partilla's second attempt to save her husband from afar used more formal methods than those used by other white women in Saline County. She chose to enter the military legal system to save David. Partilla wrote a two-page letter informing David's jailers that she had collected a petition with over three hundred names of Pettis County citizens and had sent this petition to the president, requesting her husband's release. Partilla focused on the honorable manhood of her husband, noting that he had strong moral character and was known as a gentleman. Such a man, she argued, did not belong in prison. Even more important was Partilla's use of the language of womanhood, strategically emphasizing her weakness as a woman. She wrote specifically of her inability to support herself, noting, "My health being so bad that I am not able to make my support. I have to depend on the Mercy of our friends."[18]

18. Letter from Partilla Bell [n.d.], Compiled Service Records, SHS.

The strength of Partilla's case depended upon her ability to prove she was weak. She knew that in order to protect her husband she had to convince other men that she was entirely dependent on him for support. Partilla's hard work was fulfilled on July 5, 1865, when a presidential pardon remitted David Bell's sentence and he was released. Although it is impossible to know how much or how little her words had to do with David's release, it is significant that Partilla recognized her power as a source of protection. Rather than waiting to see how events would unfold on their own, Mrs. Bell took up the pen and fought as best she could to save her husband's life.

Finally, it is important to recognize that female protection was not always successful. In these instances, the shock and grief of loss were usually compounded by intense guilt. Martha McReynolds, for example, lived with her husband, Allen, their eight children, ranging in age from twenty to three months, and seven slaves in Grand Pass Township. On the afternoon of December 24, 1864, Mrs. McReynolds went to town to go shopping with three of her children, probably in preparation for the Christmas holidays. Her husband, Allen, and the rest of her family, including their eldest daughter, Lizzie, remained at their family home. Accounts of what transpired differ according to their source. What appears certain is that a group of Federal troops arrived at the home of Allen McReynolds posing as bushwhackers and demanding information about the whereabouts of Federal troops. McReynolds walked right into their trap and provided them with the information, even leading them outside to give them directions. At that point, these Federal troops shot Allen McReynolds three times in the head and five or six times elsewhere in his body.[19]

McReynolds's daughters Angeline and Lizzie wrote to their brother William who was away at school in Illinois. Angeline described the events of the day:

> I seat myself with tears in my eyes to relate to you the sad and dreadful news of our *beloved Father's death;* Saturday evening Christmas eve, he was taken out of the house, by a company of federal soldiers unbeknown to any of the family, save Lizzie who was here all alone, she had the little ones busy putting up the dishes after they had eat their dinner, knew not that Pa had gone with them until they had gotten almost to the church; then she started after them, they I spose

19. Federal Manuscript Census, 1860, Saline County, Missouri; *Saline County History* (1881), 323.

saw her, hurried him around the orchard fence down there in the road and shot him eight times, then kicked him in the face.[20]

Lizzie clearly recognized the danger posed by the unwelcome houseguests that evening, evidently more than her father did. It is striking that the instant Lizzie realized that her father had left the home with the masquerading troops that she ran out after them. She feared for her father and believed that she might have the power to protect him.

The letter written to William by his sisters is wrought with emotion over the recent death of their father. No letters remain from Martha, but the girls' description of their mother's plight shows a woman consumed by guilt. Angeline continued her letter to William:

> Mother, Sam, Gustie and myself had gone up to town that evening, or morning rather, it was almost 12 o'clock when we left home . . . on our return home Calvin met us up the road and told us the *sad* and *awful* news. Oh what a dreadful shock it was to us all, and especially to our dear mother. *She will never forgive herself for leaving home,* second time she had been off the place since Pa had come back.[21]

Lizzie then added in her own letter: "Mother don't sleep any";[22] Martha McReynolds was deeply in grief at the loss of her husband and at the same time racked with guilt that she was away from home at the time of her husband's death. Even if she had been home, Allen McReynolds still could have been murdered. Yet Martha believed that she might have been able to protect him if she had been home—that her presence might have made the difference between life and death for her husband.

This should not imply that all white women in Saline County during the Civil War embraced a role as protector or that any lived through the war years feeling secure and fearless. Some clearly longed for protection and male guidance in their lives. For example, while her husband was away with the Missouri militia, Mrs. Jim McRoberts refused to spend the night in her home by herself, preferring instead to stay with nearby neighbors.[23] Martha McReynolds relied from the instant of her husband's murder on her son William. William even wrote irritated letters to his mother that she

20. Letter from Angeline McReynolds, December 26, 1864, McReynolds Family Papers, collection 3605, WHMC-C.
21. Letter of December 26, 1864, ibid.
22. Letter from Lizzie McReynolds, December 26, 1864, ibid.
23. Lizzie Renick to Mary McRoberts, August 14, 1862, McRoberts Collection, collection 375, WHMC-C.

relied on the advice of too many men to settle her affairs. He desired that his mother find one knowledgeable man to listen to and then make her decisions concerning the business future of her family.[24]

Another woman, Mollie McRoberts, was most pronounced in her desire for protection. During the early years of the war, Mollie and her young daughter, Nannie, fled the violence of Saline County for the safety of her home state, Ohio. Her husband, A. J., remained behind on their Saline County farm. When A. J. suggested that she and Nannie return to Missouri, her response was not positive. She wrote, "I can come if you want me to, but what will I do when I get there, I could not live there on the plains alone and you in camp and to live together in constant fear as I have done, I would rather be dead." A year later, in September 1863, she wrote, "I have been deprived of your society and protection so long that my fortitude is nearly exhausted. . . . I am tired of being dependant on the charities of other people."[25] Mollie's more direct calls for protection are most likely influenced by her relative safety in Ohio. Mollie's daily life was not directly or physically impacted by the anxiety that guerrilla war brought upon other women living in Saline County.

Females taking protective roles in Saline County accepted great risks and by no means acquired complete control of their chaotic lives. Women emerged as protectors only amidst the heightened chaos and turbulence of the guerrilla warfare that flourished throughout the state. White men saw other white men as imminent dangers to their personal safety, yet they perceived white women as nonthreatening subjects. Guerrillas and soldiers alike promised not to physically harm women because they were considered first and foremost helpless noncombatants. By perceiving women as helpless, white men inadvertently empowered white women, enabling them to emerge as protectors. At a time in Saline County when war raged, order was scarce, and revenge flourished, white men were unable to maintain the traditional boundaries of the social order. Only within this chaos, where war left the majority of white men relatively helpless, did women acquire the power to protect.

The introduction of the female protector is evidence of the major transformation of gender that took place during the Civil War. In 1861 women were told they needed male protection, yet by 1865 women were protectors of property, children, and even men. This shift from protected to protector

24. William McReynolds to Martha McReynolds, June 5, 1865, McReynolds Family Papers.

25. Mollie McRoberts to A. J. McRoberts, September 23, 1862, and September 27, 1863, McRoberts Collection.

is a direct consequence of the intensified nature of war in mid-Missouri and Saline County. In a border state infused with hostility, anxiety, and political strife, guerrilla warfare controlled everyday life. The traditional battlefield was not the prominent site of aggression within Saline County or the state at large. No man, woman, or child was safe from the constant threat of violence along city streets, along rural roads, or even within their own homes. When friends, family, and neighbors chose sides and men enlisted to fight and fulfill their duties as men, white women were left behind to fill the void.

The shift of female gender roles from protected to protector created an almost dual image of white women. Many Saline County women, such as Elvira Scott, Partilla Bell, and Jenny Flannery, acted aggressively in their attempts to save property and lives. Their actions were forward, bold, and sometimes threatening. In Saline County, women were referred to as rebellious, treasonable, or worse, but they would never be physically threatened by male troops or fear for their lives in the same ways as men *because* they were women. Martha Horne might have raised an ax, but this act of traditionally male aggression and protection could never be fully removed from the image of the helpless and feminine Sue Isaacs, graciously presenting a flag to the first company of troops. The aggressive and "manly" acts committed by women were done so in defense of their families and homes, an extension of commonly accepted feminine virtues. Regardless of how many times women committed treason, they were still women. Men could never forget that these women were still not soldiers, still at the bottom of the patriarchal order, and still not citizens. White women in Saline County, positioned on the tightrope of the border, lived their lives in a delicate and often precarious balance amidst the horrors of the war-torn Missouri countryside.

Her Will against Theirs

Eda Hickam and the Ambiguity of Freedom in Postbellum Missouri

Kimberly Schreck

In 1890, some twenty-five years after the institution of slavery had been officially abolished, a forty-two-year-old African American woman living in Cooper County, Missouri, filed suit against the white family with whom she had lived since childhood. Eda Hickam had been a slave in the Hickam household since the age of seven, and she said that, despite the abolition of slavery in the United States, she had continued to live and work as a slave from 1865 to 1889. It was not until her slaveholder, Joseph Hickam, died in 1889, that she was informed of her freedom. In her suit, she claimed that she deserved back wages for the twenty-five years the Hickam family had kept her in ignorance of her freedom. She would spend the next four years trying to gain compensation from Joseph Hickam's estate. This peculiar scenario—that a slave never heard about emancipation and that a white family concealed an event of such magnitude from her—was the story that arose in Eda Hickam's court trials. Her attorneys sought to prove that she had been fraudulently led to believe she was still a slave, while the attorneys for the white Hickam family argued she had been informed of her freedom and had knowingly

This article was published in slightly different form in *Beyond Image and Convention: Explorations in Southern Women's History,* ed. Janet L. Coryell, Martha H. Swain, Sandra Gioia Treadway, and Elizabeth Hayes Turner (Columbia: University of Missouri Press, 1998), 99–118.

thrown herself at their mercy, asking to be allowed to stay with them and to continue to receive their support.[1]

The records cannot reveal whether Eda Hickam was indeed informed of her freedom in 1865 or whether Joseph Hickam and his family intentionally concealed her freed status from her. Court records do, however, show that Eda Hickam and the white Hickam family had greatly differing notions of the meaning of *freedom*. For Eda, there was a discrepancy between her legal status as a freed person and her ability to experience a heightened sense of independence from the family that had owned her as a slave. For many slaves, especially women and children, the change in their legal status from slaves to freed people did not immediately translate into more independence in or control over their lives. Eda Hickam is one example of a woman who found herself in a vulnerable position at the time slaves were emancipated; her new legal status in 1865 did not alter her dependent status within the household in which she had long been a member. Because of her youth and gender she was deeply subordinated within a household that had been charged with meeting her basic survival needs. The white family members expected reciprocity in the form of Eda's unpaid labor as compensation for their part of the deal. With the death of the household patriarch came the demise of the structures of dependence that suspended Eda Hickam between slavery and a true departure from it. The conflicting perspectives held within the Hickam household—one as exploitative and the other as benevolent—when examined within the context of postbellum race and gender relations, reveal a need for a more careful consideration of the word *freedom* and its relationship to household composition.[2]

As a small child, Eda lived with the Hickam family on their farm in Moniteau County. She would have been sixteen when slavery ended in 1865. In 1876, she moved with the Hickams twelve miles north of their farm in Moniteau County to Cooper County. Upon Joseph Hickam's death in the summer of 1889, as Joseph's children were dividing up his estate, they turned Eda away to fend for herself, and did so without offering her

1. *Hickam v. Hickam,* Cooper County Records, case no. 4003. Kimberly Schreck, "Their Place in Freedom: African American Women in Transition from Slavery to Freedom, Cooper County, Missouri, 1865–1900" (master's thesis, University of Missouri–Columbia, 1993).

2. For a discussion of the precariousness of slave families immediately following emancipation and of freed people's difficulty in attaining a sense of freedom without a strong network of real or fictive kin, see Leon Litwack, *Been in the Storm So Long: The Aftermath of Slavery* (New York: Knopf, 1979), 292–342.

any portion of Joseph Hickam's ample estate, the total of which amounted to more than seven thousand dollars.[3]

Eda Hickam's awakening came as Joseph's surviving kin both literally and figuratively alienated her from their family. As they were in the process of selling and dividing up Joseph's assets, Eda stood before a judge in the Cooper County Probate Court arguing that between 1865 and 1889, the entire Hickam family had purposefully kept from her information about the emancipation of slaves. When she finally learned of her freedom after Joseph's death, she sued in Probate Court for $1,440 in wages for her twenty-five years of unpaid service, which amounted to five dollars per month plus interest.[4]

As Eda sought remuneration for the years she had worked without payment for the Hickams after emancipation, James Hickam, the youngest son and administrator of Joseph Hickam's estate, aggressively maintained that Eda Hickam willfully stayed with the family while knowing full well she had been freed in 1865. Eda challenged her former owners' power to define as "freedom" what was a subordinate, if not legally enslaved, experience. If she had been free, Eda argued, then the white Hickams should have to pay her back wages.

James Hickam, however, held tight to the family inheritance. He argued that Eda Hickam had been "fully informed" of the Emancipation Proclamation and had, in 1865, been offered the choice of "remaining at her old homestead or leaving." He further argued that Eda had desired to remain with her master, and did so "of her own free will and accord." According to existing records, no one questioned how James knew what Eda had been told, even though he was only three years old in 1865. Nor did anyone point out the contradictions that arose when he referred to the Hickam household as Eda's "old home" or when he implied she had a "free" choice to remain or leave. Apparently James Hickam believed it was Eda's "home" so long as she lived there under the terms set by the white members, which meant living there as an unpaid, subordinate worker. The fact that James Hickam paid to the local newspaper a fee of eighteen dollars to publicize his arguments reveals the lengths to which he sought affirmation from the white populace during his trials with Eda Hickam. The *Boonville Weekly Advertiser* furnished James a means to portray himself and his deceased father as benevolent and generous patriarchs. But on January 9, 1890, the Cooper County probate judge, who perhaps was cog-

---

3. Cooper County Probate Records, estate no. 2567.A.
4. *Hamilton–News Graphic,* January 3, 1890.

nizant of the discrepancy between the Hickam men's actions and their words, awarded Eda Hickam $785, about half of what she had requested.[5]

In order to untangle the roots of Eda and James Hickam's disparate understandings of Eda's inclusion in the Hickam family, their relationship must be understood within the context of institutionalized slavery. Eda Hickam's perception of her relationship to the white Hickams was certainly informed by her slave experience. She was raised in the "Little Dixie" region of Missouri, which comprised the fertile counties in the middle of the state, bordering on the Missouri River, where slaves accounted for more than 25 percent of the total population. The 1850 census shows that the largest slave owner in Cooper County owned seventy slaves; the second largest owned thirty-two. There were, of course, a great many white households that owned only one or two slaves. Farmers in this region usually owned only a small number of slaves who assisted them in the cultivation of commercial crops and in various other tasks necessary for the homestead to run efficiently. Slaves from this region, historians have argued, were less likely to work in gangs, as did slaves in other parts of the South, and they frequently performed a wide variety of tasks for their owners, including agricultural and domestic work. Depositions from Eda's suits against the Hickam family suggest that her work within the Hickam household resembled that which might have been performed by a family slave, even after slavery should long have ended. As Joseph Hickam's only slave, Eda was probably closely supervised, and she lacked the support of a slave community that would have afforded her reprieves from the company of her white owners. She would have had difficulty developing a sense of dependence, emotional or otherwise, on any people except those who owned her.[6]

It is not difficult to imagine why Eda might have perceived herself as a member of the Hickam household, even if only as a subordinate member. After all, southerners often used their slaves' supposed status as family members in defense of the institution of slavery. Joseph Hickam's son Squire revealed in his court deposition that his father had inherited Eda and a slave boy when they were young children, and except for the short

5. *Boonville Weekly Advertiser*, December 27, 1889; *Hamilton–News Graphic*, January 3, 1890; *Hickam v. Hickam*. James Hickam's age in 1865 is determined from the Tenth U.S. Census, Cooper County, Missouri, Saline Township, roll 683, 1880.

6. On "Little Dixie," see R. Douglas Hurt, *Agriculture and Slavery in Missouri's Little Dixie* (Columbia: University of Missouri Press, 1992), 215–16; and Harrison A. Trexler, *Slavery in Missouri, 1804–1865* (Baltimore: Johns Hopkins University Press, 1914), 100, 106–8.

time Hickam kept the boy, Eda was their only slave. The only black kin mentioned in any of the depositions was Eda's stepfather, Sam Davis, with whom, the records indicate, she was not closely associated. There is also no evidence to suggest that Eda interacted with other African Americans living in the region. In fact, court records and newspaper articles about the case imply that Eda claimed that the white Hickams prevented her from doing so. Isolated from the comforts that could be cultivated in a separate slave culture, Eda grew increasingly dependent on the family that owned her, and her dependence on them no doubt influenced her perception of her relationship to them.[7]

If Eda had in fact considered herself a member of the family, she quickly realized that she was not to enjoy such status permanently. She was forced to reevaluate her relationship to the family in whose household she had long resided. Eda decided that if she were not going to receive any money or material possessions as a member of the family, she would seek compensation for labor she had performed within the Hickam household as their employee. She argued that the white Hickams had exploited her unpaid labor by withholding from her the information that slaves had been freed in 1865, an idea no doubt stemming from the fact that each member of the Hickam family except for her was awarded money and property from Joseph Hickam's estate. Thus, it was after her expulsion from the Hickam household that Eda Hickam began to understand her relationship to the family in market terms.

As a slave, Eda was fundamentally bound via a market relationship to her owner, Joseph, yet her understanding of her relationship to the Hickam family seems to have remained a nonmarket one so long as the family did not sever their familial ties to her. When they did, however, Eda argued before a judge that if she had not been "bound" to the Hickams as a family member, as was proved by their abrupt adieu to her without any offer from the estate, then she had been illegally bound to them as a slave. As she actually was not their slave after 1865, Eda Hickam wanted their acknowledgment of her transformation from slave to employee. Her demand challenged the Hickams' right as white patriarchs in the South to define household dependents—both white and black—as family, when the family bond was extended to Eda only so long as the family patriarch, who benefited from this arrangement, lived. The probate judge, who awarded Eda

---

7. Squire Hickam, deposition, July 17, 1890, Cooper County Court Records, case no. 4003; U.S. Census, 1860 Slave Schedule, Moniteau County, Missouri; *Hamilton–News Graphic,* January 3, 1890; Mr. Cosgrove, deposition, May 5, 1890; Sam Davis, deposition, May 4, 1890; Litwack, *Been in the Storm,* 226–27.

Hickam half of the back wages for which she sued—perhaps in recognition of the different ways that the plaintiff and the defendant viewed Eda's relationship to the Hickam family—compromised rather than completely validated either argument.

Dissatisfied with the award, Eda appealed the probate court's decision in the Cooper County circuit court. This was the second of Eda's four efforts to recover back wages. A jury of the Hickams' peers considered the depositions of at least fifteen people, taken during the six months that followed the probate court ruling, before deciding she was not deserving of more than $785 in back wages. During this trial, white acquaintances of the Hickam family testified that it seemed unlikely Eda could have lived with them for twenty-five years and never have been informed of her freedom. Others who had known the Hickams in both Moniteau and Cooper counties, however, admitted under oath that in all the years they had been in the Hickams' acquaintance, they had never known Eda to correspond with other members of her race who might have informed her of her freedom in the event that her white family failed to do so. Whether Eda interacted with other members of her race was specifically asked of almost every person called upon to testify. While no one could confirm that she had interacted with other freed people outside the close supervision of white family members, nearly everyone doubted the probability of the white family members successfully preventing Eda from speaking confidentially to other freed people during the twenty-five year period in question.[8]

Attorneys for Eda sought to prove she had in fact been fraudulently led to believe she was still a slave, had been treated no differently since 1865 than she had before, and had deliberately been prevented from interacting with other freed people who might have revealed her freed status to her. To that end, Eda's attorneys gathered witnesses who testified that her freedoms had been restricted. In one deposition, a Mr. Cosgrove, an African American man, testified that once, while passing the Hickam farm in Cooper County, he greeted Eda out by a woodpile. When Eda replied, "Good morning," James Hickam reportedly struck her in the face with a stick and told her she was not allowed to talk to "no dam free negro." Similarly, Sam Davis, Eda's stepfather, remembered a conversation he had with Joseph Hickam about a year prior to his death in 1889. When, after many years had passed since he had seen her, Sam Davis asked to visit his stepdaughter at the Hickam farm in Cooper County, Joseph allegedly told him she was "getting along fine" and that he did not want Sam to "disturb her."

8. Depositions for Circuit Court trial, *Hickam v. Hickam.*

According to Sam Davis, Joseph Hickam then said, "I don't want no dam free niggars to come around me there, no how."[9]

It seems the Hickam men were aware of the limits they placed on Eda's freedom, even if they did not regard her as a slave. Or perhaps these testimonies indicate their awareness of the different way in which the black population calculated freedom and slavery. Perhaps Joseph Hickam saw a need to isolate Eda from people who might have posed a threat to the dependent relationship that allowed the Hickams to keep Eda in a slavelike position without considering her part of their family, an argument that is supported both by the physical punishment they meted upon her and by their omission of Eda's name from the Hickam family household in the 1880 census. Only the white Hickam family members and the black hired fieldworkers were listed, suggesting that Eda was correct in arguing that she fell into neither category. The fact that the Hickams employed black men to work their fields might weaken Eda's argument that she had been excluded from interacting with other African Americans, but whether or not they had been able to inform her she was free, it is clear that she had a different understanding of freedom than the whites for whom she worked.[10]

The presence of other African American workers endangers Eda's argument that the Hickams secluded her from contact with other freed people, though this point was not raised by the defense in the trial depositions. This seems to suggest either that census data do not necessarily reveal an accurate picture of mixed-race household structure, or that it was a common understanding that rural households completely separated fieldworkers from household servants. Whatever the case, it seems that the presence of other black workers nearby was not an issue, which underscores the importance of analyzing Eda Hickam's relationship to the Hickam family without centering on whether or not there is evidence to confirm or refute her knowledge of the emancipation of slaves in 1865.

When Eda Hickam appealed the probate judge's decision, James Hickam's defense attorney argued that she had been fully informed of her freedom and had knowingly rejected her right to leave. The defense further contended that both parties knew Eda had chosen to remain with the Hickam family, who were kind enough to permit her to stay because she had no other options for survival. The defense's case was constructed on testimonies that supported this contention. Squire Hickam, for instance, recalled a conversation between himself and his father wherein Joseph

9. Mr. Cosgrove, deposition, May 5, 1890; Sam Davis deposition, May 4, 1890.
10. Tenth U.S. Census, Cooper County, Missouri, Saline Township, roll 683, 1880.

asked Squire, "What am I to do with my niggers? Lincoln has freed my niggers." Squire then reminded his father, "Pa, you haven't got but one," and told him he should "Notify her, Pa, of her freedom." Upon allegedly taking his son's advice, Joseph told her, "Ede, you are free, . . . and I want you to go and do for yourself; I have nursed you long enough, and took care of you." According to Squire's testimony, Eda then pleaded, "Master, I don't want to go; I want to stay with you as long as you and mistiss lives; I am not able to make a living for myself." According to Squire's recollection of the conversation, both slave and master recognized that if Eda Hickam could not succeed in the market, she could not be "free."[11]

Squire Hickam portrayed his father as a benevolent slave owner who, after 1865, maintained a sense of obligation to care for his erstwhile property even though he was under no legal or moral compunction to do so. In his depositions Squire recalled that Joseph had tried to encourage Eda to leave at the time of emancipation, "Now Ede . . . you had better get out and do for yourself, I am not able to hire you." After this, according to his story, Eda had begun to crying and expressed her desire to stay, at which point Joseph Hickam allegedly struck the deal that doomed the teenaged Eda to twenty-five more years of unpaid servitude. "Well Ede," he said, "if you will be a good nigger, and mind me as you have heretofore, just that long you will stay with us; but when you get too big to mind us, you have got to go and hunt a new home." Eda's response, according to Squire, was to implore, "Master, I am getting all the wages I ever expect to get, I don't want to go, I want to be one of the family."[12]

Squire's testimony demonstrates his anticipation of the crux of the plaintiff's accusations, particularly his argument that Eda was granted permission to remain a member of the Hickam family, even after the law no longer upheld their right to extract labor from her even though they provided her food and shelter. He testified, "She was treated just like one of the family. She had the same kind of grub, and the same kind of clothing." Yet he betrayed the family's sense that she stood apart from them by also referring to her as "a very intelligent, good common sense nigger." By arguing that Eda was included in the Hickam family, Squire tried to deflect her accusations that she had been kept as a slave. Yet his evaluation of her reflects a race consciousness indicating she was neither perceived as an equal. Squire Hickam's definition of slavery as a familial category supports

11. Squire Hickam, deposition; Litwack, *Been in the Storm*, 292–342; Jacqueline Jones, *Labor of Love, Labor of Sorrow: Black Women, Work, and the Family, from Slavery to the Present* (New York: Vintage Books, 1985), 44–78.

12. Squire Hickam, deposition.

his argument that she was treated like "one of the family," yet it simultaneously renders the white family's expulsion of Eda from their household and exclusion from the elder Hickam's estate in 1889 an abridgement of traditional family bonds.[13]

The Hickams, perhaps without realizing the contradiction of their own argument, modified their definition of *family* in order to serve their purposes. They argued for Eda's inclusion in their family until it came time for the family heirs to divide the deceased patriarch's estate; then, they no longer wanted to claim her. This reflects the difficulties white Southerners had in letting go of the assumptions developed during antebellum slave system; there was a period of readjustment while they learned to interact with blacks under the labor conditions of the New South. Joseph Hickam's white family reaped the benefits of their father's use of an old system that defined a black woman as part of the family, yet when her inclusion in the family would have meant sharing their father's estate with her, they embraced the newer ideology that, lacking the ownership of Eda's body, they could also repudiate their claim to her as a family dependent. This ambiguous definition of *family* persisted in the white press's reporting of the Hickam affair. The *Hamilton–News Graphic,* a newspaper from a neighboring county, for example, illustrates the tendency of whites to regard Eda Hickam as the lowest-status dependent within the Hickam household. While Eda was described as being "apparently as intelligent as any of her race," the writer of the article also sympathized with the embarrassment that the Hickam family, being "one of the wealthiest and most influential in that part of the county," experienced as a result of what they described as Eda's unwillingness to leave the Hickam household twenty-five years previously.[14]

Other members of the community appeared ambivalent when testifying about Eda's relationship to the Hickams in the postbellum years, alternately supporting and rejecting her claim. Mrs. Lucy D. Moore, a longtime acquaintance and frequent visitor to the Hickam farm, testified that she could neither confirm that Eda had known of her freedom nor deny she had been fraudulently induced to continue living with the Hickams under the pretense she was still their slave. Although Moore thought she recalled Eda's interaction with other persons of color, it was possible, she admitted, that she was remembering interactions that had taken place prior to 1865. Moore, who had been acquainted with the Hickam family between 1863

13. Ibid.
14. *Hamilton–News Graphic,* January 3, 1890.

and 1873, also recalled that Eda had spent a great deal of time sick in bed, needing her white "family" to care for her.[15]

Eda's poor health increased her dependence on the Hickam family, as evinced by the testimony of the Hickam family physician, a Dr. Christian. He testified for the defense that Eda had suffered from "catalepsy" for most of her life. The "falling fits" from which she suffered caused her to lose consciousness for entire days at a time, according to Dr. Christian, and were due to obstructions to her monthly cycles resulting from overwork and undue stress. Dr. Christian testified that he had been present when Joseph Hickam first informed Eda of her freedom in 1865. Joseph Hickam allegedly had declared in Eda's presence, "I don't want her here; I have told her that she was freed by Abe Lincoln and that she could go." According to the doctor, Eda then queried, "Where will I go? I've got no place to go to and who would take care of me?" It is impossible to know whether Eda's workload in the years after 1865 was overly strenuous, or whether her daily work schedule resembled conditions under which she had worked as a slave; however, there can be little doubt that Eda's dependence on the Hickams was intensified by her need for nursing and medication and her lack of other kin or friends to take her in.[16]

Another contributing factor to Eda Hickam's continued dependence on her white family was her youth at the time of emancipation. In the years immediately following the war, it was not uncommon for former slaves who were younger than eighteen to be detained by their former owners under apprenticeship laws. These young people were not necessarily protected even if they had kin. White authority could override the wishes of freedmen and freedwomen with nothing more than a testimony that the parents were unable to adequately provide for their children. This phenomenon, which pervaded the South, did not bypass Cooper County. Children who were under the age of eighteen at the time of emancipation who lacked kin networks were especially vulnerable to getting caught in nebulous relationships with their former owners that precariously suspended them somewhere between the exploitative aspects of slavery and the actualization of a departure from it. Lacking kin and being somewhere between fifteen and seventeen years of age in 1865, Eda Hickam would have fallen into this crack.[17]

15. Lucy D. Moore, deposition, February 12, 1890.
16. Dr. Christian, deposition, February 14, 1890.
17. On the exploitation of freed children, see Ira Berlin, Steven F. Miller, and Leslie S. Rowland, "Afro-American Families from Slavery to Freedom," in Darlene Clark Hine, ed., *Black Women in American History: From Colonial Times to the Nineteenth Century* (New York: Carlson Publishing, 1990), 84–117.

Census data from Cooper County indicate that, around 1870, between 10 and 14 percent of the households in rural Cooper County townships were composed of both white and black members, with the latter group composed almost entirely of women and children. Apparently, most of the African American children living in white households in Cooper County after emancipation were living with their former owners. The most compelling evidence for this conclusion was that they, like Eda, shared the same surname as the whites living in the home. Often single freedwomen with children lived in white households, presumably because they, too, were bound by a relationship of dependence on their former owners. Without kin, single women and children probably had little prospect of gaining autonomy from the white families upon whom they had depended for food and shelter prior to emancipation.[18]

Even if Eda's ability to realize her freedom had not been limited by poor health and youth, freedwomen had few employment options outside of domestic service. Between 1870 and 1920, opportunities for gainful income in Little Dixie counties changed very little. In fact, they changed only in that black women's jobs in domestic service became increasingly specialized and black domestic workers became increasingly likely to live away from the white families who employed them. Those freedwomen who successfully escaped working in conditions that recapitulated the slave relationship of antebellum households tended to be those who were able to pool their resources with other kin and move away from isolated rural areas. Freedwomen who lacked this alternative often continued to toil in white households as they had in slavery.[19]

Eda Hickam made a third attempt to recover what she believed the Hickams owed her. This time the case was argued before the court of appeals in Kansas City, Missouri. This trial turned not on who was telling the truth but on Eda's understanding of her relationship to the rest of the Hickam family. Eda's attorney argued she had fraudulently been detained as a slave, and that if "by fraud, deceit, or duress she was kept in ignorance of her rights" and was induced to render Joseph Hickam services, then she should be entitled to payment, whether or not he intended to pay her or she intended to charge him. James Hickam's defense, conversely, centered on Eda's responsibility to know of her free status, as well as to know her

18. Ninth and Tenth U.S. Censuses, population manuscript, 1870–1880; Schreck, "Their Place in Freedom," 47–53, 76, 77–84, 90–97; Jones, *Labor of Love*, 58–77.
19. Schreck, "Their Place in Freedom," 47–53, 76–84, 90–97; Jones, *Labor of Love*, 71–72.

place within the Hickam family, arguing that there was no evidence to support her charges. Consequently, the defense argued, the white heirs were under no obligation to pay for her services. They should not be penalized for presuming that Eda knew that "under the law of the land she was a free woman," and that "ignorance of the law, which every man is presumed to know, does not afford an excuse." Finally, defense attorneys cited cases affirming that according to Missouri law, there should be no compensation for labor done within the context of a family unless there was at the time an expectation of the one member to give, and the other to receive, pay for such services. Thus James Hickam's case was bolstered by a claim that Eda had indeed been considered a family member, even as he and his siblings had turned her out of their household to fend for herself.[20]

The court of appeals judge was persuaded that Eda's case had been too quickly dismissed in the Cooper County circuit court judgment, and that sufficient evidence existed to prove she had been "fraudulently induced, by the conduct of Joseph Hickam, to render services for him under the belief that she . . . owed him such labor as his slave." Believing it possible that the Hickams had purposefully kept Eda as their slave, the judge reversed the judgment for $785.00 and remanded the case for retrial.[21]

Eda Hickam did not benefit from the appeals court's decision. When the case was returned to the Cooper County circuit court for a second trial, almost four years after Eda's first attempt to gain back wages, the jury declined to grant her anything, despite the judge's instructing them to vote that the Hickam estate owed her back wages "if they believe valuable services were rendered by Eda for Joseph, regardless of a contractual agreement to pay for such services." Nonetheless, on May 4, 1893, Eda's suits against the Hickam estate ended. Not only had she lost the $785 she was originally awarded, she had also exhausted her opportunities for appeal.[22]

Throughout the four trials in the *Hickam v. Hickam* dispute, neither side could prove that Eda either had or had not ever been informed of her freedom, nor could they prove whether Joseph Hickam and his family had intentionally deceived her. The lack of evidence in Eda Hickam's initial suit led the jurors in the first circuit court trial to maintain the probate judge's split decision over Eda's place within the white Hickam household by upholding his decision to award her half of the back wages for which she sued. By the fourth and final trial, the jury sided completely with the defendant

20. *Missouri Appeals Reports*, 501.
21. Ibid., 498–99, 505, 508.
22. *Hickam v. Hickam*, May 3, 1893, Cooper County Court Records, case no. 4003.

and deemed Eda Hickam undeserving of any back wages. Perhaps Eda's tenacity stripped the white jury of whatever sympathy they may have had for her four years earlier when they supported the probate judge's decision to award her $785 in back wages. Possibly the jurors also resented Eda's assertion that a respectable white family had behaved in a criminal manner. Perhaps they feared that her victory in this case might put ideas into their own servants' heads, potentially threatening their ability to employ domestic help cheaply. Eda's persistence in seeking compensation from whites, who she claimed had exploited her labor, may have been regarded by whites as impudence. Early in her trials it seems that at least some whites were willing to consider the possibility that Eda's slavelike living conditions since 1865 were the result of exigencies beyond her control. Yet by her fourth trial, whites seem to have resented Eda for her agency more than they pitied her for her victimization. Indeed, the longer Eda Hickam pursued her legal quest for back wages, the more she compelled the white Hickams and other community members to regard her as an assertive and potentially threatening, rather than as a submissive, "safe," member of the black populace.

The context of the trial further affected its outcome. Cooper County was in the midst of a period of virulent racism, strengthened no doubt by the fact that the African American population was becoming more self-sufficient and economically empowered with each passing year. Many whites believed that African American men had regressed toward bestiality and unrestrained sexuality even as they continued to employ African American women as domestic servants in their households, regarding the women as passive, safe, and domestic. As one article in a Cooper County newspaper explained, African American women were regarded as "negroes" because they were industrious, respectful, and "amenable to authority" in the racial caste system whites tried to maintain. African American men, on the other hand, were often deemed to be "niggers" because they were "idol, brutal drunkards" and a "perpetual menace to public order." This bipolar view of former slaves reflects contradictory understandings among whites of freedom's meaning in the postbellum period. Prior to emancipation there was little ambiguity over what it meant to be a slave. Even though conditions varied widely among slaves, one constant was slaves' legal status as property of their owners, which subsequently limited slaves' ability to control the course of their own lives. They were not free, despite the successful efforts of many slaves to carve some degree of autonomy for themselves. Historians of slave culture have argued that the same kinship networks that enabled slaves to achieve control and autonomy within the slave community were also utilized by freedpersons in their quests to gain independence from their former owners. But if slaves lacked both a slave community and kinship ties, they would find it more difficult to enjoy or experience their legal freedom, whether or not they were informed of their emancipation.[23]

The historiography of late-nineteenth-century race relations generally equates the virulent racism whites held toward blacks with the assertive behavior of black men. White attitudes toward African Americans were highly gendered in the 1890s and first decade of the twentieth century, and African American men's access to legal, political, sexual, and economic power posed the greatest threat to the race-based social order to which whites so desperately clung. Evidence for this can be found in the plentiful suggestions in Democratic newspapers that African American men were "increasing in criminality" and "deteriorating morally" with "frightful rapidity" in the absence of the slave system's strictures to keep them in line.[24]

Such attitudes, which prompted the codification of racial segregation throughout the South in the 1890s, had implications for Eda Hickam. In her efforts to distance herself from the antiquated and restricting system of slavery and actualize a sense of freedom, Eda Hickam altered somewhat the way she was perceived by whites. But the gendered nature of racism during this period meant her image remained unfettered by the brutal castigations that were directed toward assertive black men in the county, despite the possibility that her persistence through three appellate court trials against her former owners exhibited to whites an unacceptable degree of assertiveness.

Since emancipation, both white and black residents of Cooper County were compelled to negotiate many difficult changes in the ways they interacted with one another. By the late 1880s and 1890s, a new generation of whites, most of whom had not been alive during slavery but who had been raised in a society that promoted white supremacy, began to launch aggressive attacks on the black populace. They felt increasingly threatened by the new generation of African American men, many of whom refused to submit to white rules regarding racial hierarchy. White men in Cooper County were particularly vexed by black men's political power. To justify

23. *Boonville Weekly Advertiser,* January 9, 1903; Patricia Morton, *Disfigured Images: The Historical Assault on African-American Women* (New York: Greenwood Press, 1991), 18–37.

24. *Boonville Weekly Advertiser,* January 29, 1904; see also Schreck, "Their Place in Freedom," 102–51; Joel Williamson, *The Crucible of Race: Black/White Relations in the American South since Emancipation* (New York: Oxford University Press, 1984); and C. Vann Woodward, *The Strange Career of Jim Crow* (New York: Oxford University Press, 1955).

opposition to political activity among black men in the 1890s, whites dredged up arguments that African Americans were biologically inferior to whites. These arguments were generally directed at black men and, consequently, chastising references to black women virtually disappeared from newspaper articles, leaving black men as the recipients of racial slurs.[25]

In 1889, the *Boonville Weekly Advertiser* featured a diatribe penned by a Mississippi Delta newspaper editor, James K. Vardaman, flagrantly asserting the inferiority of black men. The speech, entitled "A Southern View of the Negro," declared, "Southern people will not have negro rule. The negro is not a white man with black skin. His is a different race. He is a barbarian, and barbarians cannot rule civilized people." By the 1890s, whites in Cooper County were making distinctions between different degrees of racial inferiority. Vardaman's demagoguery reflects a transition in white attitudes toward black men. Whites saw them as having changed from compliant, obedient, and trustworthy "Sambos" into impertinent, unintimidated, and brutish "niggers."[26]

The distinction made between a compliant, deferential "negro" and a impudent and dangerous "nigger" depended on the degree of social and sexual threat a black person could pose to white power. "Niggers" were defined in the *Boonville Weekly Advertiser* as "idle, brutal drunkards, with complete disregard for the 'decencies of society.'" They tended toward "vice and vagrancy" and were "a perpetual menace to public order" and a "curse to the community." Those described as "Negroes," however, were "good citizens . . . staunch Americans" who were respectful of laws, amenable to authority, good family providers, useful to their community, and showed "proper respect for appearances." However, "negroes" were not spared all condemnation. Instead, the "negro" in Cooper County was held "responsible to a regrettable degree for the 'nigger,' " and, it was said, as "decent" black people, they owed it to themselves "to cast out the vagabonds and criminals . . . who bring reproach on [them] and who keep alive the prejudice against the race." According to this definition, African American women fell almost exclusively into the category of "negroes," a necessary characterization, given that domestic servants with whom whites interacted on a daily basis were only acceptable to whites if they could be perceived as docile.[27]

25. *Boonville Weekly Advertiser,* January 29, 1904; Williamson, *Crucible of Race,* 78–86.

26. *Boonville Weekly Advertiser,* October 4, 1889; Williamson, *Crucible of Race,* 70–86, 147–51.

27. *Boonville Weekly Advertiser,* October 4, 1889.

Eda Hickam's resistance against her white family took place in this gendered context; she was never characterized in newspaper articles or depositions as menacing or threatening. As a woman, she could not pose the degree of threat to white male preeminence, even within the Hickam family, that a black man could if he dared to cast a vote or have sexual relations with a white woman. After all, black women working as domestics in private white households occupied the most directly integrated sector of southern society, just as white people were taking actions in the 1890s to segregate the races in the public sector.[28] Because she was a woman, Eda Hickam was excluded from the primary objective of white supporters of Jim Crow legislation, disenfranchisement. Because she was a woman, she was able to challenge her white family's decision to sever her connection to them via a legal system from which black men were being excluded.

The Hickams, their attorneys, and their white peers in the county judged Eda's resistance quite differently than they would have judged a black man who dared to challenge his racially defined place in their society. For example, approximately five years after Eda Hickam's suits ended and five miles from the Hickam farm, in neighboring Howard County, a black man named Frank Embree was lynched in the presence of more than one thousand whites from the Little Dixie region for the alleged rape of a fourteen-year-old white girl. Described in local newspapers as a "black fiend," a "devil," and a "brute," Embree was relentlessly tracked until caught and then locked in an Audrain County jail, some twenty miles from the alleged crime scene. A "better organized or more orderly mob was never seen," the *Fayette Democratic-Leader* reported, when they carted Embree back to the area where the alleged crime had been committed. After one hundred and three "fearful lashes" to his nude body, the noose was thrown around his neck, and his body was pulled into midair. All concurred, the "negro rapist . . . was given no more than he deserved."[29]

This horrific event relates indirectly to this essay's question of defining a "family." In justifying their actions on the basis of protecting white women, white mobs sought to protect their own gender identities as paternal protectors and providers of their families. But they espoused the alleged threat of rape as causal in their actions when in fact it was the actual threat of race mixing that moved them to violent extremes. Gender thus made a structural difference in racism since it was men who could make and name families and who could become patriarchs in their own right; thus in a

28. Woodward, *Strange Career*, 82, 67–109.
29. *Fayette Democratic-Leader*, June 22, 1899.

racist and patriarchal structure, black men had power. Women, on the other hand, continued to be perceived as familial dependents. Black women, whether they were living in mixed-race or African American households, could not threaten the patriarchal social order—not even Eda Hickam, who challenged the way whites defined her position in their household. What Eda Hickam really called into question in her trials was not racial identity so much as the bounds, responsibilities, and benefits of patriarchy.[30]

Certainly the battle Eda waged was taken quite seriously and fought quite aggressively by Joseph Hickam's white descendants. James Hickam, in fact, spent no less than $544.20 of his father's $7,000 estate in legal fees in his campaign to deny Eda the $1,440 for which she sued. Yet throughout the ordeal, Eda was regarded as being childlike and intellectually inferior by whites rather than as being calculating. Perhaps because she had lived under conditions that closely resembled those she had known for so long in slavery, people in the county harkened back to an outmoded racial conceptualization of her attempts to challenge white power over black freedoms. Although she was mocked, Eda Hickam was not accused of criminal behavior nor upheld as evidence that the black population was retrogressing into a less civilized state outside of slavery. Eda Hickam, in fact, accused whites of criminal and indecent behavior, and she called into question their reliance on an old social order—the paternalistic relationship of a master to his slaves—to justify their exploitation of her labor.[31]

It is impossible to know whether or not the Hickams intended to conceal Eda's free status from her. It is however clear that in working without wages for the family that had previously owned her, Eda Hickam's life did not significantly change after 1865. She continued to have her freedoms restricted by rules set by whites whose watchful eyes, oppressive demands, and physical punishments she was unable to escape. It is also evident that Eda did not regard being turned away from the Hickam household in 1889 as a liberating experience, as her long-awaited acquisition of "freedom." The reality was that Eda was "free" only to starve by herself in a world that no longer had a place for her and was not interested in developing one. And if she was held as a "slave" between 1865 and 1889, then it is also true that to the extent she ever had family, she had it under her years of uninformed "freedom." Because Eda lacked a kin network that would have enabled her to escape dependence on the white family that had owned her, she was left with no choice but to define her relationship to the white

30. Jones, *Labor of Love*, 58–62.
31. Cooper County Probate Records, estate number 2567.A.

Hickams as familial. They, on the other hand, had the luxury of altering their definition of *family* as it suited them. The Hickams' perception of their relationship to Eda was rooted in the antebellum ideal of a paternalistic slaveholder. This image was extended into the postbellum period only insofar as it reinforced the white Hickams' claim to the deceased patriarch's estate.

Eda Hickam's suits against the only people she had ever considered her family reveal the complicated meanings of *slavery* and *freedom* during the postbellum period. For Eda Hickam, *slavery* was defined as labor performed for a family that neither claimed her nor paid for her services. Yet for the white family to deny she was illegally held as a slave, they had to argue she was a free member of their family. Ironically, they offered this argument for the purpose of keeping a family member out of the will. They could do this because they were defending a definition of *family* that only white family members perceived. For the white Hickams, the "family" was composed of white and black members, where only the white members were truly free, and where the persistence of a black, servile worker enabled them to operate for many years under the charade that slavery had not been legally abolished.

Sedalia's Ladies of the Evening

Prostitution and Class in a Nineteenth-Century Railroad Town

Rhonda Chalfant

Sedalia, Missouri, was founded in 1860 by General George R. Smith as a railroad center along the Pacific Railroad. Its prominence as a railroad town led to its being used as a Federal military post during the Civil War and, in 1867 and 1868, its becoming the terminus for cattle drives from Texas. The existence of the military installation and cattle-shipping industry suggests a disproportionately high number of single men, giving Sedalia a short-lived boomtown atmosphere. The forces of civility began to encroach on the frontier town by the mid-1860s when churches, public schools for both white and black children, and shops featuring luxury items such as jewelry and millinery appeared. By 1874, the cattle drives had moved and Sedalia marked the intersection of the Pacific and the Missouri, Kansas & Texas railroads. Both railroads had built shops for the repair of engines and railcars. In addition to hosting a "large transient population" of commercial travelers and workers brought in by the railroads, Sedalia maintained an almost equal balance of men and women, with married couples outnumbering single adults. By 1900, Sedalia had become, according to Sedalia boosters, "the commercial, industrial and educational metropolis of Central Missouri . . . a desirable place of residence as well as a manufacturing and distributing center," with a population of just over fifteen thousand.[1]

---

1. At this time Sedalia was the fifth-largest city in the state. C. Robert Haywood, *Victorian West: Class and Culture in Kansas Cattle Towns* (Lawrence: University Press of

As Sedalia grew, a middle class developed and grew to dominate the city. The historian Michael Cassity, in his study of Sedalia's working class and the labor movement, describes the growth of Sedalia's "ruling class" and shows that it was "made up not simply of well-placed individuals but of men sharing certain values and ambitions that separated them from the rest of society." This group also included ambitious small businessmen, entrepreneurs, and factory owners, who were described in 1882 by one of their own—local business booster I. MacDonald Demuth—as "Missionaries of the New Business Gospel," a phrase conflating the acquisition of wealth with a tone of religious fervor. In his 1898 pamphlet *A Feast of Cold Facts*, Demuth again lauded the spirit that fostered Sedalia's growth. His descriptions of the city—of not only the businesses, factories, and banks, but also the schools, homes, and churches—show an overwhelming interest in visible wealth and social status. His preoccupation with wealth and status reflected the beliefs of popular lecturer Russell Conwell, whose "Acres of Diamonds" speech postulated that a man had "a Christian duty to become rich," and the Reverend Henry Ward Beecher, who believed that in America poverty was "presumptive evidence of sinfulness." These related ideas were accepted by Sedalia's middle class, which believed itself not only better off financially, but by virtue of its wealth also better socially and spiritually.[2]

Sedalia's middle class, Cassity points out, segregated its neighborhoods from those of the working class and African Americans. Additionally, this separation "pervaded all realms of social relationships." The "ruling class" described by Cassity functioned as a social elite, grouping themselves together "to reinforce their own values, flaunt their respectability and discipline themselves." They followed a set of capitalist economic attitudes that

Kansas, 1991); Marion S. Goldman, *Gold Diggers and Silver Miners: Prostitution and Social Life on the Comstock Lode* (Ann Arbor: University of Michigan Press, 1981); Jacqueline Baker Barnhart, *The Fair but Frail: Prostitution in San Francisco, 1849–1900* (Reno: University of Nevada Press, 1986); George Scrutton, ed., *Sedalia, Missouri* (Sedalia: Sedalia Evening Sentinel, 1904), quotation on title page; I. MacD[onald] Demuth, *The History of Pettis County, Missouri* (1882; reprint, Clinton, Mo.: The Printery, n.d.); U.S. Census Summaries, 1860, 1870, 1880, 1890, 1900.

2. Michael Cassity, *Defending a Way of Life: An American Community in the Nineteenth Century* (New York: State University of New York Press, 1989), 60; Demuth, *History*, 460; I. MacD[onald] Demuth, *A Feast of Cold Facts*, rev. ed. (Sedalia, Mo.: n.p. 1898), passim; Russell Conwell, *"Acres of Diamonds": The Story of a Four Million Dollar Speech* (New York: Harper, 1915), 20; Beecher cited by John A. Garraty, *The New Commonwealth, 1877–1890*, New American Nation Series (New York: Harper and Row, 1968), 311.

encouraged entrepreneurial activity and produced a set of behaviors that made up middle-class culture, including adherence to appropriate gender roles, concern for proper public appearance, conspicuous consumption, genteel deportment, and involvement with church and charity.[3]

In addition to being a center of entrepreneurial bourgeois culture, Sedalia had also been, since its founding, a center of vice. In 1877, the *St. Louis Post-Dispatch* called Sedalia the "Sodom and Gomorrah of the nineteenth century," a comment reprinted in the *Sedalia Democrat* without rebuttal. Prostitution, though illegal, had become an integral and visible part of Sedalia's public life. A survey of manuscript censuses, circuit court records, and newspaper accounts of police court sessions identifies over five hundred women working as prostitutes during the years between 1867 and 1900; in most of those years, twenty to thirty women plied their trade on Sedalia's streets and brothels. During this time, Sedalia's prostitutes adopted capitalist attitudes and behaviors and attempted to adopt middle-class culture. They participated in many of the economic activities encouraged by the middle class: they managed businesses, made and banked money, paid taxes, borrowed money and received credit from merchants, owned or rented business and personal property, shopped in local stores, and patronized local medical and legal professionals. Although the city enacted laws against the existence of "bawdy houses and other disorderly houses" and against "being found in bawdy house," or "being found in company with lewd women or prostitutes," enforcement of these laws was largely unsuccessful.[4]

The question of why prostitution continued so openly is linked to the development of Sedalia's "ruling class." Although illegal and unrespectable, prostitution was profitable to many middle-class individuals. Sedalia's business spirit contributed greatly to the growth of prostitution in the city. The city's position as a railroad hub, a position the ruling class actively sought and encouraged, brought a large number of transient men—railroad employees and commercial travelers—to the city. In addition, other factors, related to the amount of money generated by prostitution, further contributed to its increase. During the 1870s, a system of real estate made prosti-

---

3. Cassity, *Defending a Way,* 60–73.
4. *Sedalia Democrat,* August 12, 1877; Sedalia City Charter, Sedalia City Statutes; *Sedalia Democrat,* 1868–1900, passim; *Sedalia Bazoo,* 1869–1900, passim; *Sedalia Sentinel,* 1895–1900, passim; *Sedalia Capital,* 1899, passim; 1870, 1880, and 1900 manuscript censuses; Pettis County Circuit Court Records, 1868–1900, passim. Newspaper accounts of police court sessions are used because the original records have been destroyed.

tution profitable to both building owners and lessees: speculators erected buildings and then leased the entire buildings to businessmen who operated shops on the ground floor and rented individual rooms upstairs to prostitutes. Bankers and businessmen profited from the interest paid by the prostitutes on loans and consumer debt. Although voters disapproved of prostitution, they were so reluctant to approve taxes for even the most basic city services they demanded that they preferred to rely on monies generated by fines paid by prostitutes in special monthly court appearances to pay for those services. A significant part of the city's economy came to be grounded in prostitution, which, although not respectable, was certainly profitable.[5]

Prostitution was also profitable to some of the prostitutes themselves, who attempted to use their wealth in ways approved of by the middle class. In order to achieve the status accorded the middle class in Sedalia, it was necessary to be both capitalist and cultured. Some of their attempts at participation in a middle-class capitalist economy, such as their ownership of real estate or their challenges to the legal system, were perceived as a threat by male businessmen. In addition, prostitution was thought to pose a threat to the business community by reducing property values near areas where prostitution was openly practiced. The prostitutes themselves were seen as an intangible threat as well. When they participated in a middle-class economy by functioning as entrepreneurs, as borrowers, or as accumulators of wealth, they were scorned for violating the gender boundaries that underscored middle-class culture. They were further rebuffed in their attempts to adopt the middle-class culture's behaviors of giving to charity, attending church, or dressing well. Despite their participation in middle-class capitalism and culture, they were denied the status of middle class for reasons that included not only the illegal nature of their occupation but also their willingness to violate the established class and gender roles that underwrote middle-class culture. When they attempted middle-class behaviors, they were rebuffed by the middle class they were imitating. Prostitutes came to be seen as a separate class that could threaten the middle-class way of life and its status, and which thus needed to be separated physically and psychologically from the middle class. Ultimately, the prostitutes' attempts to imitate the middle class became more a threat to the

5. Rhonda Chalfant, "The Building at 217 West Main, Sedalia, Pettis County, Mo.," National Register of Historic Places Nomination, 1996; "The Girls Must Pay," *Sedalia Capital*, May 6, 1899; throughout the late nineteenth century, prostitutes were referred to by Sedalia newspapers as a "class," a term that connotes both an economic level as well as a status level.

middle class than any economic threat they might pose. However, the middle class found that it could not let go of the profits created by prostitution, so their profession was allowed to continue, despite the threat it posed to middle-class status.

The deconstructionist argument of binomial pairs suggests that in order to define *respectable* behavior, a definition of *unrespectable* must be present. The respectable define themselves by noting that they are different from the unrespectable, who become the "other" to whom the respectable attribute a host of negative qualities. The more fragile a group's sense of identity, the more it needs to emphasize its separation from that "other." Sedalia's middle class saw its adherence to its culture as a way to further separate its members from those identified as "others." The behavior of Sedalia's ruling elites was typical of the middle class, which, according to Peter Stallybrass and Allon White's *The Politics and Poetics of Transgression,* "consolidated itself as a respectable and conventional body by withdrawing itself from the popular, [and] . . . by constructing the popular as grotesque otherness." Shannon Bell, in *Reading, Writing, and Rewriting the Prostitute Body,* elaborates on Stallybrass and White's concept of exclusion and class, noting that the middle class "defined itself through the exclusion of what it marked out as low—as dirty, repulsive, noisy, contaminating. The act of exclusion was constitutive of its own identity. The low was externalized under the sign of negation and disgust."[6]

One means by which the middle class separated itself from what it viewed as contaminating is described by Richard Symanski as the "geopolitical sink," which he explains is a geographical space that defines and reflects social norms. Transgressors of those norms, whether they violate racial, economic, or moral standards, must live, either by law or by custom, in a space apart, on the fringe of the settlement or contained in a ghetto or slum. By the late 1870s, Sedalia had isolated its poor, idle whites in Stringtown, on the west edge of town, its blacks in Lincolnville, on the north boundary, and its lower-income working-class whites in East Sedalia, while its middle class concentrated itself in neighborhoods west of Ohio Avenue and along Broadway Boulevard, the city's most exclusive residential street.[7]

6. Peter Stallybrass and Allon White, *The Politics and Poetics of Transgression,* cited in Shannon Bell, *Reading, Writing, and Rewriting the Prostitute Body* (Bloomington: Indiana University Press, 1994), 43.

7. Richard Symanski, *The Immoral Landscape: Female Prostitution in Western Societies* (Toronto: Butterworths, 1981), 3; *Sedalia Bazoo,* November 2, 1881, and July 21, 1885; *Sedalia City Directory,* 1886; and Chalfant, "Building."

Cassity suggests that the rapidity of Sedalia's move into the industrial age resulted in an unplanned sprawl of factories, businesses, brothels, and homes for both black and white residents. While people living near brothels complained frequently, the continued resistance of Sedalians to zoning regulations exacerbated the mixture within the neighborhoods. In Sedalia during the 1870s, bawdy houses existed in residential neighborhoods throughout the city—on Washington Street near the iron bridge, on the west side of town near the pond, north of the railroad tracks near Kentucky Avenue, near the fairgrounds (now Liberty Park), just west of Harter's Mills at Vermont and Main, and on Brown Avenue between Sixth and Seventh streets. During the 1880s, bawdy houses were established in an as-yet-unidentified area known then as Happy Hollow, in a neighborhood south of the city limits near Eighteenth Street and Hancock Avenue, at a site west of Laupheimer's Wool and Hide Market on West Main Street, and near the gasworks at Moniteau and Benton. Again, these houses were in residential neighborhoods. During these decades, a few prostitutes occupied apartments in rooms above businesses on the downtown streets, including the Cooperative Store on East Fifth, the Stanley, Lowman Company at 217 West Main Street, and at 310 West Main Street, in the city's business district.[8]

During the 1890s, however, Sedalia's bawdy houses came to be concentrated in a more specific area, which had become notorious as a center of prostitution. Most of Sedalia's brothels were then located above businesses on West Main Street, causing local newspapers repeatedly to bemoan the miscegenation and immorality occurring in the "dives" there. A red-light district, such as El Paso's "tolerated zone" or New Orleans's Storyville, is also a geopolitical sink. The changes in location of Sedalia's many brothels were paralleled by brothels in Kansas cattle towns, which somewhat confirms Symanski's theory of the geopolitical sink. In the cattle towns of Kansas—Dodge City, Caldwell, and Abilene—houses of prostitution appeared throughout the cities in both residential and business districts during the town's early years, but these gradually came to be grouped into a specific area. However, the location of Sedalia's brothels—they were just a block from the police station and in the heart of the city's business and commercial district—provides something of a contradiction to Symanski's theory in that the prostitution district was neither concealed nor isolated by geographical space. It was, however, separated by time of day and isolated

8. Cassity, *Defending a Way,* 55–56; *Sedalia Bazoo,* November 9, 1870, July 24, 1871, July 29, 1879; *Sedalia Democrat,* August 6, 1877, July 1, 1879, October 20, 1879; *Sedalia Bazoo,* November 29, 1883, May 18, 1885, June 23, 1885; *Sedalia Democrat,* August 8, 1884, February 16, 1878.

by darkness; local custom held that "a respectable woman was not seen north of Second Street after sun-down." The location further suggests that prostitution was tied to middle-class business activity but shunned as less than respectable.[9]

Sedalia's middle class psychologically separated itself from prostitutes by defining them as a threat to middle-class status, which in Sedalia had come to mean the possession of visible wealth. Bell points out that "in the hegemonic discourse of the Victorian period, the medical-legal-moral discourse . . . produced two master images of the prostitute, both profane: one a ruined, destroyed, victimized body; the other a destroying body, a disease that spreads and rots the body politic." Sedalia's newspaper editors, who saw themselves as spokesmen for the middle class, reflected these images in much of their rhetoric, frequently printing articles that described the descent of a "ruined" or "fallen woman." Comments warning citizens of the dangers of the "social evil" and "loathsome disease" were present, but they were less frequent than denigration of prostitutes themselves; generally comments about a diseased prostitute served as part of a description of the woman rather than as a warning against contracting a venereal disease. In 1892, Sedalia women presented Mayor Stevens with petitions begging that the houses be closed in order to protect their husbands, brothers, and sons. Residents wrote letters to the editors of newspapers and to the city council begging that the "social evil" be abated. Mayor Stevens denied any knowledge of prostitution, claiming it did not exist in Sedalia. Other mayors and city councils did little to eliminate prostitution.[10]

Despite middle-class fears that prostitutes could cause harm, Sedalia's prostitutes did not pose as great a threat to the middle-class family as believed. True, many prostitutes did have venereal diseases that could be spread to the wives and children of their male patrons, and local tradition suggests that venereal disease was common in Sedalia. However, the fear of

9. *Sedalia Bazoo*, August 27, 1885, March 8, 1887, July 23, 1890, August 3, 1890; Pettis County Circuit Court Records, 1893–1894, passim; H. Gordon Frost, *The Gentlemen's Club: The Story of Prostitution in El Paso* (El Paso: Mangan Books, 1983), 12; Al Rose, *Storyville, New Orleans, being an authentic, illustrated account of the Notorious Red-Light District* (University, Ala.: University of Alabama Press, 1974), 1; Haywood, *Victorian West*, 78–79; B. B. Ihrig et al., eds., *Sedalia, Missouri: The First One Hundred Years* (Sedalia: Hurlburt, 1960), 61.

10. Bell, *Reading*, 44–45; *Sedalia Democrat*, January 15, 1899; *Sedalia Capital*, November 29, 1898; *Sedalia Bazoo*, August 7, 1874. *Sedalia Gazette*, February 18, 1892; *Sedalia Bazoo*, January 7, 1892; *Sedalia Democrat*, November 21, 1873, August 9, 1879, October 9, 10, 1884, December 3, 1893, December 8, 1893, December 17, 1893, November 16, 1894.

infection was limited to the families of men who patronized prostitutes; the truly upright man, one who genuinely practiced the moral values advocated by the middle class and who avoided prostitutes, would not contaminate his wife or children. While some men did spend money on prostitutes that might have been better spent on the support of their families, as an editorial in the *Bazoo* pointed out, this loss of support affected only those families whose men used the services of the prostitutes.[11]

However, certain aspects of the prostitutes' presence in the marketplace were viewed as threats to the middle-class economy. One of the major fears involved property. The middle-class feared that property values near the brothels would decline. This, however, did not happen. During the 1870s and 1880s, property values throughout the city continued to rise, even in those areas where brothels were located. In addition, property values on West Main Street, the center of prostitution, remained high and allowed other members of the middle class—those who owned the buildings occupied by prostitutes—to prosper from rent monies.[12]

The prostitute who owned property provided another sort of challenge. For example, Lizzie Cook, who owned the properties in which she conducted her businesses, lessened the amount of money a male property owner could collect in rent. Cook, who worked in Sedalia from 1870 through 1879, is the city's best example of a prostitute-entrepreneur; she owned a number of parcels of property, including two bawdy houses and several pieces of investment property. When in 1879 the police closed the Junction House, her brothel within the city limits, Cook was forced to continue her business at the "Farm," outside the city limits; she wrote to the mayor asking for "honest competition," complaining that "less respectable bawds" were being allowed to work in Sedalia.[13] Her claim, while appropriate for a businessperson in a free-market system, was ignored to the degree that a poor woman who prostituted herself was seen as more acceptable than a woman who dared to imitate men's behavior by managing a business, handling money, supervising employees, and dealing with the law, and who, in addition, purchased property from a male property owner.

Yet another way in which the prostitutes challenged the middle class was by their presence in the legal system, which potentially could cost the city and county money spent in fruitless prosecution. In addition, their presence in the legal system provided a challenge to middle-class standards of

11. *Sedalia Bazoo*, July 24, 1871.
12. Chalfant, "Building"; Pettis County Deed Records, 1875–1900, passim.
13. *Sedalia Democrat*, March 14, 1877.

law and order, which provided that lawbreakers be punished. Sedalia's prostitutes were especially familiar with the law, as they appeared monthly in police court to pay their fines. As a result of their payment of these fines, which functioned as a type of license fee, prostitutes were seldom brought into criminal court. When they did appear in circuit court, they were represented by attorneys who often used the system against itself by delaying court dates and by repeatedly filing motions requesting that charges be dropped. Although the grand jury reported in 1908 that it approved prosecution of crimes against "public morals and decency," that same body had complained in 1893, 1894, and 1907 that it could very seldom find witnesses willing to testify against either prostitutes or landlords.[14]

Although prostitutes were clearly outside the law, they demanded the same protection under the law provided to the more respectable, a situation which again offended the middle-class standards of law and order. They appeared in criminal court as victims of assault and demanded that their attackers be prosecuted and punished. Rowdy men, their inhibitions lowered by alcohol, frequently attacked the women and trashed the brothels. During her nine-year career in Sedalia, Lizzie Cook was shot twice. In 1890, Minnie Stephens was attacked by James Brown and W. A. Stogells: the men threw bottles at her and even beat her dog. In 1896, Chicago House proprietor Josie Jackson was beaten and kicked by a gambler who shot out the electric lightbulbs. These men seemed to feel justified in their actions because the prostitutes, having forgone the protection and courtesy accorded respectable women, could be accused of having brought the violence upon themselves. When the courts attempted to prosecute those who assaulted the prostitutes, generally the cases resulted in dismissal or acquittal, a situation which confirmed the middle-class notions of the law and which reminded prostitutes of their status.[15]

The prostitutes also sought redress in the courts for violence perpetrated against them by the police. In 1873, Cook filed charges of excessive force against a marshal named Inch after he broke down the door to her room and tore her clothing; she asked for $2,500 in damages. The case dragged on for over a year before Cook dropped the charges at cost to her. In 1900, Josie Jackson was shot by police officer Bart Jackson, and although several city councilmen and the editor of the *Sedalia Sentinel* called for Jackson to be punished for this and other unprofessional behavior, charges against

14. *Sedalia Capital*, May 6, 1899; Criminal Court Records, 1867–1910, passim.
15. *Sedalia Bazoo*, September 3, 1890; *Sedalia Daily Capital*, January 23, 1896; Criminal Court Records, 1865–1900, passim.

him were dropped and he retained his job.[16] The message sent by the courts suggests that one outside the law and middle-class economy and culture could not expect protection from a system ruled by the middle class.

The fears that prostitutes' presence in the legal system would increase the costs of maintaining the system were groundless. Those found guilty of prostitution were required to pay court costs in addition to their fines. Costs incurred in maintaining the courts and jails were offset by the periodic "fines" or "license fees" the prostitutes paid at regularly scheduled special court sessions, which occurred monthly from 1873 through 1900. In fact, the city realized the extent of its dependence on prostitution in 1899, when it discovered that it could not pay its police force without the regular "contributions" by the prostitutes to the city treasury.[17]

The actual threat the prostitutes posed to the community was subtle but nevertheless potent, for it involved a psychological threat to status. The city's reputation was tarnished by the presence of prostitutes. The 1877 description by the *St. Louis Post-Dispatch* of Sedalia as resembling Sodom and Gomorrah reflected badly on the morality of the community. Sedalia's reputation as "wide open," commented on frequently during the mayoral election campaign of 1892, further emphasized the negative view others had of Sedalia. Despite Demuth's 1898 assertion that Sedalia was an upright, moral community, its reputation for vice could, after all, hurt the chances of business and industrial growth, and affect the middle-class's chances of further economic success, which would in turn lessen its claim to middle-class status.[18]

Despite concerns about status, a businessman who dealt with prostitutes was not, as a rule, condemned. The store owners who extended credit to prostitutes were looked upon as good businessmen, as were those who arranged mortgages on brothel properties. For example, Clute Brothers Hardware, Bixby and Houx Hardware, and Richard Ritter Lumber Company, from whom Cook purchased supplies when she rebuilt the Junction House after a fire in 1873, were praised for their acumen by the 1882 *History of Pettis County*. James Thompson, an officer of the First National Bank during the 1870s and 1880s, who arranged several mortgages on the Junction House and the Farm, was considered one of Sedalia's most promising young

16. *Sedalia Democrat,* March 28, 1873; Criminal Court Records, 1873–1874; *Sedalia Sentinel,* April 1, 2, 6, 1900.

17. *Sedalia Bazoo,* August 10, 1873; *Sedalia Democrat,* 1873–1900, passim; "The Girls Must Pay," *Sedalia Capital,* May 6, 1899.

18. *Sedalia Democrat,* August 12, 1877; *Sedalia Gazette,* February 18, 1892, March 20, 1892; Demuth, *Feast,* 28, 67–68.

men. The lawyers who represented the prostitutes in court retained their reputation as upstanding professionals; in fact, William Snoddy gained recognition as an attorney when he represented Cook in a case presented to the Missouri State Supreme Court and won a decision concerning the rules of evidence.[19]

Another businessman, William Riley, purchased the Farm from Cook when she left Sedalia in 1879. He sold the building to madam Sallie Hicks, but he reclaimed it when she left the business. He then leased the place to Stella Seymore, who continued to run the establishment as a brothel. Riley's reputation as a businessman and owner of his Riley Hotel remained, for the most part, intact. When he ran for city council in the early 1880s, only the *Sedalia Bazoo* called his brothel ownership into question, but even the *Bazoo* was more concerned about his penchant for buying African American votes with free beer. Alford Hawkes remained a deacon at the First Baptist Church after he bought the Junction House from Cook in 1879 and rented the building to madam Sallie Hicks and later to madam Edith Thompson.[20]

Throughout 1890, the *Sedalia Bazoo* railed against the Main Street businessmen who charged that the presence of prostitutes hurt their businesses but who refused to sign formal complaints against their colleagues. Their reluctance to sign complaints suggests a tacit agreement that prostitution was acceptable. Several years later, in 1907, Henry Laupheimer, a prominent businessman and owner of several West Main Street properties, was prosecuted and fined for leasing a building to be used as a bawdy house. Twenty-two of Sedalia's businessmen petitioned the courts to reduce his fine, which was then cut from $240 to $100. That same year, two other Sedalia businessmen, Charley Williams and James Parmerlee, were also prosecuted for leasing buildings for prostitution. Williams was granted a change of venue to neighboring Johnson County; Parmerlee was found guilty but appealed for a new trial, and the charges were later dropped.[21]

The aspect of the prostitutes' behavior that seemed most threatening to Sedalia's middle class was their imitation of middle-class culture, for a suc-

19. Demuth, *History,* 615, 631, 670, 720–22; William B. Claycomb, *A History of Northeast Pettis County* (Dayton, Ohio: Morningside Press, 1996), 109; Truman A. Post, *Reports of Cases Argued in the Supreme Court of the State of Missouri* (St. Louis: W. J. Gilbert, 1877), 64:260–62.

20. *Sedalia Bazoo,* March 1882, passim; Demuth, *History,* 664; *Sedalia Bazoo,* August 12, 1880, October 24, 1881, March 7, 1882, June 12, 1883.

21. *Sedalia Bazoo,* July 8, 1890, July 23, 1890, August 3, 1890; Criminal Court Records, Pettis County, I.

cessful imitation of middle-class behaviors made it impossible to know
who really had such status and who did not. The scholar Quentin Bell
noted that "emulation occurs where status can be challenged, where social
groups become strong enough to challenge the traditional pattern of society . . . [when] a strong proletariat emerges to compete with the middle
class."[22] While Sedalia's prostitutes did not constitute a true proletariat, in
that for the most part they were independent businesswomen, they did
constitute a group able to compete with the middle class for status. While
the sale of their sexual services horrified middle-class moralizers, much of
their other behavior seemed to imitate middle-class culture, and thus they
offended those they imitated.

The prostitutes' presence in the marketplace and the courtroom violated
the ideas of appropriate behavior for middle-class women. The concept of
"separate spheres" popular during the middle nineteenth century placed
women in the home, where they were to create a refuge for the husband
away from the stresses of the business world. The few jobs available for
women in the 1870s—teaching school, waiting on tables, working as a
household servant—seemed appropriate for women but reiterated their
position as domestic and servile. While those women who had no male to
support them might go into business sewing, making hats, or doing laundry, none of these enterprises was lucrative.

Bazoo editor J. West Goodwin lamented the poor job opportunities and
low wages paid women during the late 1870s. He expanded the possibility
of gainful employment by hiring women as typesetters. During the 1880s,
the Working Women's Home, a charity providing shelter for unemployed,
single women, tried to find positions for women in need of employment,
but most jobs available in Sedalia paid badly. By the 1890s, women had
moved into positions as store clerks, typists, and factory workers at Lamy's
Clothing Company, and the majority of teachers were female, but the prevailing wages were still barely enough to support a person.[23] In addition,
job opportunities still followed rigid gender lines.

The position of women had changed by the end of the century as groups
like the Woman's Christian Temperance Union and suffrage organizations
campaigned for moral purity and voting rights. Women's clubs and church
groups provided women the opportunity to learn organizational and fund-

22. Bell cited in Joan L. Severa, *Dressed for the Photographer: Ordinary Americans
and Fashion, 1840–1900* (Kent, Ohio: Kent State University Press, 1995), xv.

23. *Sedalia Bazoo,* April 10, 1877, October 17, 1877, March 9, 1883, April 5, 1883,
April 11, 1883; Demuth, *History,* 578–83; Demuth, *Feast,* 9–13; *Sedalia Capital,*
March 9, 1897.

raising skills. Women's roles had expanded beyond the separate spheres ideology, but gender expectations still discouraged a woman, especially a middle-class woman, from competing in the marketplace or the courtroom against men. The middle-class woman was still to be involved in socially approved activities such as educational clubs, church socials, and charitable work, where her activities might reflect well on her husband or father, by whose name she would be identified in the press. When prostitutes attempted to practice some of the behaviors—charity, churchgoing, and dressing well—that in respectable middle-class women would have met with approval, they were generally rebuffed. The middle class seemed to view prostitutes' practice of these behaviors as a challenge, in part because charity, churchgoing, and dressing well were what helped the middle class to define itself.

Charitable giving was essential in Sedalia, for poverty was a constant problem. Each winter between 1870 and 1900, the churches and community mounted collections of food, clothing, fuel, and cash for the benefit of the "worthy" poor. Cassity sees an ulterior motive behind the contributions of the middle class: "the patronizing donation to the poor in the winter months ironically added a social buttress to an economic distance" between the middle class and those less well-off, and, in the minds of many Sedalians, less respectable. That charity was extended to the *worthy* poor (those attempting to live by middle-class standards or those suitably groveling) further intensified the distance the donors established. In the *Sedalia Bazoo,* Goodwin condemned donors who gave moldy meat and tattered clothing to the poor, which might have enabled them to feel superior for having contributed but also allowed them to express their negative beliefs about the poor by treating them badly.[24]

When the prostitutes attempted to be charitable, their behavior, while sometimes noted and praised by the *Democrat,* was scorned by the power structure to the extent that the prostitutes were sometimes denied the right to practice charity by the middle-class power structure. Throughout the 1870s, 1880s, and 1890s, Sedalia's prostitutes provided numerous charitable acts, caring for the sick, taking in abandoned infants, and giving shelter to the homeless. The *Sedalia Bazoo* recorded instances when prostitutes extended kindness to others, for example, making special reference to two "scarlet sisters" who cared for an impoverished sick woman and her children. Minnie Stephens, alias Babe Hunt, was praised for the "quiet and unostentatious" way in which she helped the poor, as was Mrs. Meyer. However, city government sometimes took a dim view of prostitutes' char-

24. Cassity, *Defending a Way,* 61; *Sedalia Bazoo,* December 5, 1882.

ity. In 1892, Mayor Stevens refused a donation of six bags of flour to the annual charity drive by prostitute Dora Dewitt. Although the city's poor were in need, they were allowed to do without in order that Mayor Stevens, who had earlier that year denied any knowledge of prostitution in Sedalia, could appear righteously indignant about the existence of prostitution.[25]

Another behavior the middle class looked upon favorably, church attendance, was also denied prostitutes. Prostitutes were refused the opportunity to worship, not only in the elite churches but also in less formal situations. In an 1871 interview with a local minister, a Sedalia madam bitterly complained: "If I wanted to go to your church, hoping that I might worship God, and that Christ would cast a pitying look upon me, is there any pew that would be open to me? Is there a lady in your congregation who would not shrink from contact with the folds of my dress, much less take me by the hand? Dare you take me to your house and introduce me to your wife and friends as a rescued whore?" Her view of the church was confirmed by the actions of at least one minister; in 1874, the Reverend Hollenbech refused to perform a funeral service for Fanny Drury, claiming that his doing so would cause people to question his Christianity. In 1876, a group of Cook's prostitutes were denied entrance to a Methodist camp meeting. One of them, Dorah, complained in a poem entitled "A Magdalene's Complaint," published in the *Bazoo,* that Sedalia's Methodists did not follow the example of Christ when they excluded her. William Mugford, the city editor of the *Bazoo,* concurred, writing a poem denouncing the "sanctimonious whine" of Christians who thought themselves superior to sinners. Evidence of the middle class's hold on Sedalia society is seen in the scorn given the *Bazoo* itself, because of the outspoken nature of its editorials, which attacked smugness and hypocrisy.[26]

Meanwhile, those denominations specifically targeted to the poor and to the more flagrant sinners were condemned by the middle class. The *Sedalia Democrat* mounted an irrational battle against the Salvation Army, complaining about its raucous parades and presence on Main Street. The *Democrat,* when noting that prostitutes attended Salvation Army rallies, went so far as to call the Salvation Army an assignation house, suggesting that any meeting that had a number of prostitutes among its congregation was obviously for sexual purposes and that prostitutes were beyond spiritual redemption.[27]

25. *Sedalia Democrat,* May 10, 12, 1895; *Sedalia Bazoo,* January 5, 1892.
26. *Sedalia Bazoo,* July 24, 1871; August 7, 1874; August 29, 30, 1876.
27. *Sedalia Democrat,* January 7, 1887, April 22, 1887, April 24, 1887; *Sedalia Bazoo,* September 8, 1889, September 10, 1889, September 17, 1889.

Perhaps the most visible and successful way in which the prostitutes challenged the middle class was by dressing well. Social position was thought to be equivalent to respectability; such thinking led to the conclusion that those who dressed well must be good people. To the middle-class sensibility, however, prostitutes, who often dressed well in order to be more attractive to potential customers, clearly were neither respectable nor good. The social critic and economist Thorstein Veblen noted that the visibility of one's clothing makes it one of the best ways by which one's "pecuniary standing" may be seen.[28] Clothing also formed one of the most outward and obvious signs of respectability. Style, fabric, decoration, and accessories were evaluated, as were cleanliness, modesty, and neatness, when making conclusions about a woman's social position and morality on the basis of her clothing. Women's clothing was frequently described in newspaper articles about weddings and parties, giving the middle-class woman the extra status of being praised publicly for her taste and style. The woman's dress, in turn, reflected on her husband's abilities as a provider and thus enhanced his social position. That some of Sedalia's prostitutes dressed well was an affront of the worst sort to the middle-class woman. That the prostitutes may have earned the money used to purchase fine clothing from middle-class husbands who used prostitutes made their dressing well especially unpleasant.

The *Bazoo* described the women from the Junction House as "dressed in all the bright colors of the market, hatted, booted, feathered, and veiled in the latest style." Georgia Thompson, a slender, attractive redhead, was "elegantly dressed." At her trial for prostitution, Mary Ming appeared in court "neatly dressed in dark brocaded silk, fashionably made. She wore a heavy gold neck chain to which was attached a gold watch." And thirty-year-old Maggie Hill was described as a "portly good-looking woman dressed in genteel style." Local newspapers carefully pointed out that these women were neither "gaudy" nor "chromatic," indicating that prostitutes understood the standards of taste as well as Veblen's conviction that "loud dress becomes offensive to people of taste, as evincing an undue desire to reach and impress the untrained sensibilities of the vulgar."[29]

The middle class expected prostitutes to dress badly—to be shabby and dirty, or to be flashy and to dress in cheap imitations of fine clothing. For

28. Thorstein Veblen, *The Theory of the Leisure Class: An Economic Study of Institutions* (1899; reprint, New York: Dover, 1994), 104–5.

29. *Sedalia Bazoo,* March 2, 1875; *Sedalia Weekly Bazoo,* November 8, 1881; *Sedalia Bazoo,* August 26, 1885; August 10, 1873; June 16, 1879; Veblen, *Theory of the Leisure Class,* 114.

example, "Otterville Ann" Smith was usually described as "filthy and slov-enly." The frugal use of flour-sack fabric for clothing that might be praised in the "worthy poor" was ridiculed in prostitutes; Flora Brown was mocked for wearing a "smart red jacket and a couple of dirty flour sacks sewed together." The use of the word *cheap* to describe things either inexpensive or shoddy was sometimes applied to prostitutes and their clothing. For example, Lilly Allen, who wore "cheap lace," was herself essentially condemned, as Veblen suggests, as "cheap and nasty"—in the sense that her lace was of inferior quality and in the sense that she herself was cheap and nasty, morally. Once again, the prostitutes were held to middle-class standards of taste and cleanliness while they were simultaneously denounced for doing so.[30]

Sedalia's middle class held on to its sense of status and superiority tenaciously and desperately, fearing that the slightest deviation from its own rules could cause any one of them to slip from the position of superiority. The lack of self-control that prompted some men to purchase sex, and the middle-class loss of social control evidenced by the continued presence of prostitution would lead, the middle class was certain, to total chaos, especially if the separations between classes were dissolved. Sedalia's prostitutes, by imitating the middle-class capitalist economy and behaviors, spurred that fear to intense extremes.

30. *Sedalia Bazoo*, December 13, 1875; February 19, 1877; July 18, 1871; Veblen, *Theory of the Leisure Class*, 104.

Domestic Drudges to Dazzling Divas

The Origins of African American Beauty Culture in St. Louis, 1900–1930

De Anna J. Reese

Our ideas of manhood and masculinity have traditionally involved power, physical strength, and the ability to provide economic security; similarly, our perceptions about womanhood and femininity have come to center around themes such as beauty. For black women, these notions took on new importance in the first decades of the twentieth century, when many relied on hairstyles and clothes to demonstrate their move out of the field and into the urban marketplace. Although unburdened by the distortions of modern-day commercials and music videos, black women of that time were not spared the mixed messages or trauma associated with a society at times unwilling and unable to accept the range and depth of their natural beauty. In fact, most found it increasingly difficult to gain acceptance in a world where anything "black" was considered far from ideal.

In the early twentieth century, the growing public presence of women and the social, political, and economic changes that accompanied their lives increased the value placed on women's physical appearance. This was especially the case for black women, many of whom bought and tested new products designed to enhance their beauty while increasing their chances for social mobility. The first major center of black beauty culture, St. Louis was home to the development of an industry that created two of the nation's most successful black women entrepreneurs. Helping launch the careers of both Madam C. J. Walker and Annie Turnbo Malone, St. Louis offered hundreds of black women the opportunity to increase their earnings, showcase their femininity, and redefine the image of black woman-hood.

In the early years of the twentieth century, contradictory messages were sent by black advertisers, who encouraged black women to both emulate and refute a mainstream beauty aesthetic that devalued their African features. Nevertheless, St. Louis's beauty culture created a variety of social and economic options for black women, and this is evident in the early careers of Madam C. J. Walker and Annie Malone. At that time, St. Louis had one of the largest black populations of any American city, and its strategic location at the confluence of the Mississippi and Missouri rivers made it a magnet for black migrants and European immigrants alike.

A city often splintered over issues of race, St. Louis's pattern of segregation and discrimination did not completely prohibit some blacks from taking advantage of the city's thriving business and commercial environment. Ranked as one of the nation's largest manufacturing and distribution centers, the city's ample railroad lines, breweries, and tobacco, shoe, and lead factories offered steady employment. And though most blacks were relegated to unskilled, temporary, and seasonal work, a sizeable middle class developed among those able to secure jobs as porters, barbers, teachers, seamstresses, and businessmen. By 1900, its thirty-five thousand residents supported three weekly newspapers, over a hundred businesses, and several prosperous, self-contained communities along the riverfront downtown, in the Mill Creek Valley west of Union Station, and in "the Ville," home to many of the city's black institutions.[1]

However, the most dramatic increase in St. Louis's black professional class to which Walker and Malone would soon belong came during the 1904 World's Fair. Attracting approximately a hundred thousand black visitors, the fair's large number of exhibits and inventions served as incentive to a host of aspiring black entrepreneurs. Witnessing the success of her brothers, three of whom were local barbers, Madam Walker's visits to the fair introduced her to other prominent blacks, many of them church and club women. Their poise and confidence strongly influenced her aspirations for a more attractive appearance while underscoring the benefits of respectability and financial independence. For Walker, both were extremely important, for she had toiled for years as a laundress to support both her

1. For background information on St. Louis, see Katharine T. Corbett and Mary E. Seematter, "Black St. Louis at the Turn of the Century," *Gateway Heritage* 7, no. 1 (summer 1986): 41; Katharine T. Corbett, "Missouri's Black Heritage," *Gateway Heritage* 4, no. 1 (summer 1983): 21–22; and A'Lelia Bundles, *On Her Own Ground: The Life and Times of Madam C. J. Walker* (New York: Scribner, 2001), 45–59.

and her daughter, A'Lelia. Denied employment within St. Louis's manufacturing and meatpacking plants, most black women had few economic options outside domestic service. For those that did find work in the city's
nutcracking and tobacco factories, poor wages and a lack of mobility
dashed hopes for economic security.[2]

Undeterred by obstacles of race or sex, Annie Malone, from Illinois,
who had launched a hair-care business for African Americans and was
looking to expand her market, also saw the opportunities presented by the
World's Fair. Her arrival in St. Louis two years before the fair clearly put
her in a position to build one of the city's most successful black businesses
of the period. Malone harnessed the town's economic expansion to widen
her clientele and her business contacts, and she used both the "fair" and
"black" newspapers to launch an extensive advertising campaign, in 1906
adopting and copyrighting the trade name Poro.

The early decades of the twentieth century were marked by severe racial
and ethnic intolerance, and African Americans found themselves the tar-
gets of virulent racism, expressed through political and legal disenfranchisement, the humiliations of a racist popular culture, and the horrors of
lynching. Aimed at stripping African Americans of their rights and dignity,
these acts of discrimination worked alongside stereotypes that dehuman-
ized and devalued the hair and features of African Americans. In the midst
of such images, black women sought to affirm their femininity by taking
advantage of the wide variety of services, products, and economic opportunities available through beauty culture. In turn, many gained the skills
and respectability long denied them as black women and consumers.

In the early twentieth century, two of several new consumer industries,
beauty aids and cosmetics, helped redefine and commodify images of beauty
among American women as a whole. Once viewed as symbols of immorality and self-indulgence, beauty products became acceptable and
even necessary for a woman's success and accomplishment. While economic constraints mediated the purchases of most black consumers, those
who could afford the beauty aids manufactured by black and white companies consistently found images that idealized European features.

Unable to escape these standards of beauty, black women found numerous ads offering advice on how to improve one's figure, skin color, facial
features, and hair, all symbols for achieving "feminine perfection." Sug-

2. Bundles, *On Her Own Ground,* 70, 44; William Crossland, *Industrial Conditions
among Negroes in St. Louis* (St. Louis: Washington University School of Social Economy, 1914), 94–95.

gesting new ways to reduce or correct personal features, the "Household Column" of the *St. Louis Palladium* instructed women on how to build hollow cheeks, lighten the complexion, cultivate a graceful posture, and sculpt the body weight. A May 1903 article described the ideal body type with the following measurements: Height 5 feet, 5 inches; weight 138 pounds; waist 27 inches, bust 34 inches; arm at shoulder 13 inches; wrist 6 inches; ankle 8 inches; and thigh 25 inches. While such measurements by today's standards may not seem extreme, the diet, health and workload of most black women during this period made these goals less than realistic. Nevertheless, this did not lessen their popularity. Other newspaper ads made bold claims associating a healthy complexion with fair skin and keen features. According to one 1919 *Argus* ad, beautiful skin that was "fair and smooth—bright, lustrous and wholesome looking could only be maintained by bathing with Dr. Fred Palmer's Skin Whitener Soap."[3]

Another article explained how the nose should be given special attention—squeezed and molded in early childhood so as to prevent it from standing out and spoiling the symmetry of the face. In one instance, black women were told, "The straight Grecian nose is the pretty nose of today. And the woman whose [nose] turns up or down, or lies flat, is the woman who needs to put in a little time massaging her nose." At the same time such ads deprecated African features, others emphasized pride in one's African heritage. In April 1920, beauty entrepreneur Madam Murray Stewart urged black customers, "Be proud of your race. You can't be white and don't want to be, but golden Brown Ointment will lighten and brighten your skin better than any other preparation."[4] Such ads clearly reminded black women that the lighter their complexion, the better. According to beauty scholars A'Lelia Bundles, Kathy Peiss, and Noliwe Rooks, the use of such products has for years been the source of ongoing debate within black communities.[5] While there is little doubt that African Americans were encouraged to adopt mainstream trends, it is unclear to what extent these ads affected the self-perceptions and buying habits of black women over time.

3. *St. Louis Palladium,* May 30, 1903, 3; *St. Louis Argus,* March 7, 1919, 3.

4. *St. Louis Argus,* March 7, 1919, 3; April 2, 1920, 4.

5. For an in-depth look at the politics of cosmetics and hair-care products in the black community, see Bundles, *On Her Own Ground;* Kathy Peiss, *Hope in a Jar: The Making of America's Beauty Culture* (New York: Metropolitan Books, 1998); Noliwe Rooks, *Hair Raising: Beauty, Culture, and African American Women* (New Brunswick, N.J.: Rutgers University Press, 1996); and Julie Willett, *Permanent Waves: The Making of the American Beauty Shop* (New York: New York University Press, 2000).

Urging black women to alter their natural features in favor of those more closely European, such ads were a classic example of more popular stereotypical images that either blatantly demeaned African features or set standards that for most were impossible to achieve. Thus, both black- and white-owned companies were known to exploit these fears by using ads featuring young women whose appearance was radically different than those of its primary consumers.[6] This was especially the case with hair-care advertisements in St. Louis's black newspapers.

Like skin tone, hair texture has long been a divisive issue within black communities. During the early twentieth century, the issue of how to grow healthy tresses took precedence. In the absence of products specifically for the task, some African Americans attempted to straighten their hair, for example, by wrapping and twisting it. Such processes often were not only painful but also damaging. While some product ads offered advice on hair maintenance, few were sensitive to the reasons black women suffered hair loss. Stressful working conditions, poor diet, and scalp problems such as dandruff, ringworm, tetter, and eczema involved treatments with chemicals so harsh they often stripped hair of essential oils. Searching for ways to stimulate hair growth, black women tried washing their hair with baking soda, borax, ammonia, goose fat, alcohol, and other homemade concoctions.[7] Such methods not only were unsafe but also contributed to early baldness.

Many advice columns were insensitive to the beauty issues of black women, and offered poor advice on handling black beauty concerns, especially on hair. All the time, they upheld the notion that European looks were desirable. According to one 1903 beauty article, "Next in importance to the complexion in effect upon a woman's looks is her hair. . . . If it is curly they [the African American women] rejoice; if it is straight and stiff they deplore." As for "the women of sparse locks," they were said to "mourn over the stinginess of nature in this regard, but it does not occur to many of them to take simple measures for improving the quantity of their hair." Like Madam Walker, many black women found such measures far from simple, as few could escape the reality, and associated stigma, of having what some pejoratively termed "kinky, unruly hair." Thus, advertisements like Plough's Black and White Hair Dressing in November 1919 were appealing, even if unbelievable. The ad promised hair that was "Long, soft, glossy, easy to brush and comb, and dress to become your style of

6. Bundles, *On Her Own Ground,* 66.
7. Ibid., 66–68.

beauty."[8] Eager to achieve freedom and flexibility in their hairstyling procedures, black women painstakingly worked to gain control over their
hair, hoping to enhance their physical appeal as well as to become likely
candidates for greater acceptance in middle-class circles. In fact, many believed that a polished, well-groomed appearance would earn them a place
among the city's social elite.

During a time in which black women were presented with increased social activity, greater spending power, and a wider array of available products, smooth and healthy hair became a symbol of femininity, modernity,
and class status. And with the rise of black women entrepreneurs Madam
C. J. Walker and Annie Turnbo Malone, black women found new options
for enhancing both their self-image and their perception by society. Beauty
culture not only responded to these issues of appearance and health but
also served as a resource for the larger community. An icon among American businesswomen, Madam C. J. Walker's career classically illustrates
both. Before leaving St. Louis in 1905, Madam Walker, then known as Sarah
Breedlove McWilliams, briefly worked as a sales agent for Annie Turnbo
Malone. Having had the chance to familiarize herself with industry operations, Walker's dream-inspired remedy for hair growth would compel her
to market her own version of a "Wonderful Hair Grower."

Intrigued by St. Louis's diversity of residents, Madam Walker found a
bustling city filled with ragtime music and a tight-knit black community.
Even under the heavy toil of work as a laundress and scrubwoman, Walker
became actively involved in the St. Louis community, joining St. Paul AME,
the city's first black church, and later its Mite Missionary Society, an organization dedicated to assisting low-income members of the community.

Terribly self-conscious about her own hair, Walker sought to develop a
product that would help black women grow healthy, abundant locks. Under
the tutelage of her then-employer and later rival Annie Malone, Walker
worked for a short time as an agent for Poro products. Eager to launch her
own line of products, Walker developed her version of a product known as
"Wonderful Hair Grower," a medicated pomade used to combat dandruff
and other scalp conditions related to hair loss. The early success of Poro,
however, left Walker with no room to develop either her product or her
business. In turn, Walker headed for Denver, but not before establishing a
lasting friendship with Charles Joseph Walker, her soon-to-be third husband. Although Walker's new business venture would later adversely affect
her relationship with Malone, both found inspiration among the city's

8. *St. Louis Palladium,* May 30, 1903, 3; *Argus,* November 9, 1919, 2.

well-cultured and educated elite, many of whom came to St. Louis to witness the excitement, exhibits, and opportunities associated with the 1904 World's Fair.

Inspired by the range of class distinctions among black St. Louisans, Walker observed black women whose mannerisms and elegant dress styles distinguished them from their peers. Equally impressive was their ability to organize and speak out on issues of race and gender equality. With the right clothes and hairstyle, Walker believed that not only could she, too, exude the same confidence and poise of these middle-class women, but that in doing so, she could also represent the struggles and dignity of working-class women.[9]

Although her phenomenal success as a businesswoman and entrepreneur occurred *after* leaving St. Louis in 1905, Madam Walker's experience in Missouri was critical to her later success. Inspired by the creativity and innovation of her surroundings, Walker formed networks across class lines that not only gained her lifelong acquaintances and friendships, but also sharpened her insight into the beauty needs of black women. Having learned to sell and market products from Annie Malone, Walker took with her the skill and determination that would carry her from agent to entrepreneur. Furthermore, her exposure to the manufacture and distribution of Poro beauty products provided her with the experience and expertise she would soon need in both the marketing and factory operation of her multi-million-dollar company. Preaching the gospel of self-help and economic independence for black women, Walker's development of black hair-care products and commitment to racial progress readily expressed itself in her philanthropic contributions to the St. Louis community.

A celebrated figure among African Americans, Walker recognized the power of self-determination; her own life was a living testimony to the benefits of hard work and discipline. Using pictures to illustrate her results, Madam Walker lectured across the country offering the secrets to her success, as reported in a contemporary newspaper: "Faith in God, faith in her fellow men, and faith in herself, combined with pluck, grit and tenacity."[10] Like many black women of the period, Madam Walker became increasingly vocal on political issues, committing her name and pocketbook to the fight against lynching and discrimination. When she died in 1919, the *St. Louis Argus* announced her will, reporting that Madam Walker donated a total of six thousand dollars to the St. Louis Colored Orphans and Old Folks Homes, the Pine Street YMCA, and the People's Hospital.[11] Issuing

9. Peiss, *Hope in a Jar,* 81.
10. *Argus,* June 13, 1919, 1.
11. Ibid., May 19, 1919, 1.

smaller sums to friends, Walker's frequent visits and close contact with friends and business acquaintances in the Gateway City made St. Louis one of the places she regarded as "home."

With an accumulated fortune of more than one million dollars, Madam Walker influenced hundreds of black women to pursue careers as entrepreneurs. Inspired by Walker's success, many trained at the Walker School of Beauty before becoming agents and shop owners. Ambitious and self-supporting, these women were part of what some might term the period's "New Negro Woman," embodying the ideals of self-help and race progress while publicly representing herself through middle-class-inspired hairstyles, dress, and beauty ideals.

Cast in the shadow of her former student and competitor, Annie Turnbo Malone's legacy to black beauty culture has far too often gone unnoticed. A pioneer in the development of black hair care, Malone's contributions remain relatively obscure compared to those of her former student. One of the most successful black women of her time, Malone's shrewd business skills and ingenuity enabled her to establish one of the nation's premier black beauty institutions. Although St. Louis would also become her home, Malone's fascination with enhancing the appearance of black women took shape years before, in her hometown of Metropolis, Illinois.

Having grown up styling the hair of her sisters, Malone's chemical experiments proved successful with the development of her first product, the "Wonderful Hair Grower." Moving from Peoria to Lovejoy, Illinois, Malone began her business in a small two-story building in 1900. Enjoying rave reviews from satisfied customers, Malone gained recognition among black women across the Mississippi who heard of her treatments and were eager to try them. The national publicity surrounding the upcoming World's Fair prompted her to move to St. Louis in 1902. A four-room flat at 2223 Market Street was the base of operations from which Malone launched an extensive advertising campaign, including press conferences and a tour of the South where she trained women, such as Madam Walker, to sell her products. With increasing product demands from across the country, Malone dedicated her efforts to building a multidimensional facility large enough to train and mentor future stylists while continuing to serve and pamper her customers.

Offering one of few avenues of economic opportunity open to black women, Poro College provided a unique economic and educational experience to the 250 men and women involved in manufacturing, shipping, and supervising the administration of Poro products. A training center for those desiring to learn the Poro system of hair-care management, Poro College offered black women dignified work and the confidence for achieving their own means of economic independence. By teaching women the art of looking better and feeling better about themselves, and placing economic and social success within reach, Poro College opened new possibilities for black women in St. Louis.

Praised for its services both within and outside the classroom, Poro College was known for its contributions to the community. In 1918, Malone's vision of a large, modern facility that would both enhance the business and serve her community became reality. Located at the corner of St. Ferdinand and Billups avenues, in the historic suburb of Elleardsville, the college held a five-hundred-seat auditorium, dormitory, emergency first-aid rooms, committee rooms, cafeteria, elegant dining room, and roof garden apartment. It also became home to the city's first African American–operated post office in 1929.[12] A popular social and cultural center among the black middle-class, Poro College stood next in line to churches as the preferred site for conferences, meetings, art displays, banquets, and weddings.

The fact that so many black St. Louisans took advantage of Poro College as a gathering place perhaps had as much to do with the feel of the space as it did with the spirit of its owner. The institution's warm, inviting policy toward its employees and the community earned Annie Malone and her husband, Aaron, the respect of honorary "parents," to whom some employees turned for material and emotional support. In addition to the space she set aside for future business expansion, Annie Malone owned blocks of property; some of these were used to build homes for her employees.[13] In January 1920, the Malones designated the second Thursday of the month as "Parents' Day" where all the students were asked to bring either their parents or a stand-in to be recognized by a ceremony and dinner. "From now on all of the PORO Family will turn to Mr. and Mrs. Malone not alone as their employers but as their parents for advice—for help—for strength to bear bravely the burdens of this life." According to the *Argus,* one of the city's most popular black newspapers, the occasion not only celebrated the Malones' recognition of their employees' families, but also demonstrated the reverence felt by many for their place in the community.[14] In an effort to continue the family-like atmosphere that had helped make the college an overwhelming success, Malone expanded the five-acre campus with the purchase of additional space.

12. Ibid.; February 15, 1929, 1.
13. "'Poro' in Pictures: With a Short History of Its Development by Poro College," Missouri Historical Society, St. Louis, 1926, 7.
14. *Argus,* January 2, 1920, 1.

Attracting students and workers alike, the college's amazing growth during its first two years called for increased space in what later became the Poro Annex. Equipped with a laundry, bakery, and refrigerating plant, the annex's opening in November 1920 was cause for celebration. A boon to the neighborhood and its owners, the twenty-thousand-square-foot annex adjoined the college, increased production efficiency, and raised the college's building investments to five hundred thousand dollars.[15] It also drew a favorable response from the city's "outstanding members," giving rise to what the Malones believed would promote a greater racial consciousness.

An institution of considerable size and worth, the importance of Poro College was further dramatized by its personal and collective meaning in the lives of black women. Guided under the mentorship of its founder and president Annie Malone, black women gained a new sense of identity and self-worth that encouraged their professional development and increased their expectations of the possibilities denied them by race and sex. A poem written in Malone's honor and published in the *Argus* summarized these possibilities.

> . . . But it shall be my object
> Just to state it as it is,
> And let the world know truly
> All about the Poro bis.
> I do not mean to tell it all,
> (For half I do not know),
> But every word I tell you
> You will truly find it so.
> Instead, I've taken washing sir,
> And ironing, to be sure;
> I have served as cook and housemaid,
> And have done some nursing, too.
> The reason why I did it
> Was because I didn't know
> The higher possibilities
> For agents of Poro.
>
> I found out what the cost would be
> To enter in the work,
> I paid the stipulated price
> With not a moment's shirk
> And now today, I'm glad to say

15. Ibid., December 3, 1920, 1.

> With all my soul and main,
> I count the cost as nothing lost,
> But everything to gain.[16]

Moving black women away from the drudgery of domestic work, Poro College offered them an opportunity for economic advancement and self-improvement. It also helped to build an economic base from which the community could sustain its needs and accumulate greater material resources. Employing thousands of women through its agencies and supply stations, Poro College achieved international acclaim in Africa, the Philippines, North, Central, and South America, and the Caribbean.[17]

Despite her reputation as an extraordinary businesswoman and benefactor, Annie Malone enjoyed far less success in her personal affairs. By 1927, her growing estrangement from her husband of thirteen years and Poro copresident Aaron Malone resulted in a temporary receivership for the college and later divorce. After settling the receivership suit out of court, Aaron Malone received thirty-five thousand dollars in cash and property estimated of the same value. But while Annie Malone had triumphed in maintaining ownership of Poro College, there is evidence revealing a host of financial problems that would eventually undermine the stability of her business, including a string of lawsuits that forced her to sell two of the college's main buildings.

Although poverty and plenty were part and parcel of life in most American cities by the turn of the century, segregation, financial hardship, and discrimination were daily realities for most African Americans—yet these conditions reveal only part of the story. The growth of manufacturing, the advent of new consumer products, and increased leisure time profoundly impacted the lives of black women in St. Louis, who, despite limited resources, made the most of every opportunity to indulge and entertain themselves with new services, products, and clothing. These items were given greater appeal with the help of beauty pioneers Madam C. J. Walker and Annie Turnbo Malone. Both recognized the problems black women faced in caring for their hair and found St. Louis's steady stream of visitors and thriving business community an appropriate place from which to begin their beauty empires. Committed to the ideals of self-help and race progress, Walker and Malone revolutionized the way black women cared for and viewed themselves. They also made generous donations to St.

16. Ibid., June 18, 1915, 1.
17. Bettye Collier Thomas, "Annie Turnbo Malone, 1869–1957," in *Notable Black American Women,* ed. Jessie Carney Smith (Detroit: Gail Research, 1992), 725.

Louis charities, earning them the admiration and respect of the community, which praised them for their talent and philanthropy.

Enticed by the remarkable display and greater access to manufactured goods and materials, black women were not merely concerned with hairstyles and beauty rituals as a means of differentiating themselves from their less-privileged sisters. Only a couple of generations removed from slavery, their appearance served as an outward symbol of their status as free and independent women. Although an American beauty aesthetic may have informed their choices, it by no means limited their creativity. Instead, black women grew their hair, purchased makeup, and wore fashionable attire as an expression of their individuality and desire to look and feel good in a society where blackness was rarely associated with beauty. With the assistance of black cosmetology schools like Poro College, many gained the skills, earnings, and opportunity to begin professional careers in beauty culture.

The greater emphasis on beauty and cosmetics by black women in St. Louis reflected a need to counter demeaning images of African Americans while responding to a burgeoning consumer culture that linked beauty and femininity to a growing materialism and social status. Although the twenty-first century has brought with it a broader spectrum of beauty images, it too has yet to fully celebrate the diversity of "the natural woman." In their attempt to address these issues, black women in St. Louis developed their own standards and meanings for appreciating beauty, enjoying the freedom to choose but unwilling to compromise their dignity or their self-respect.

"We Are Practicable, Sensible Women"

The Missouri Women Farmers' Club and the Professionalization of Agriculture

Rebecca S. Montgomery

In July of 1910, Progressive journalist Ida M. Tarbell of *American Magazine* wrote the governor of Missouri "asking for the names of two or three women who are doing things which are deserving of public notice and approach." Governor Herbert Hadley found it difficult to narrow his selection of prominent female leaders to such a small number. He, in turn, contacted the president of the Missouri General Federation of Women's Clubs for advice in the matter. One name on the list that Hadley subsequently drew up was that of Frances Pearle Mitchell of Rocheport, Missouri, whom he described as "a successful farmer" in his reply to Tarbell. In this instance, as in so many others, Mitchell was recognized primarily for her work in agriculture rather than for her numerous organizational activities in women's clubs and the church. This recognition stemmed from the simple fact that the main difference separating her from most other middle-class clubwomen was her public assumption of the identity of "farmer." Although she, as a woman farmer, was considered an oddity, Mitchell was not alone in making a claim for the legitimacy of agriculture as a profession for women. She represented educated women of means who, like many of their prosperous fathers and brothers, desired to perpetuate the family farming tradition even when other sources of self-support were available. Five months after Governor Hadley responded to Tarbell's inquiry, Mitchell helped to found the Missouri Women Farmers' Club

(MWFC), an organization dedicated to establishing commercial agriculture as a viable option for all rural women.[1]

When Mitchell and eight other women met to form the MWFC in January 1911, it was the only organization of its kind in the country. There was the International Congress of Farm Women with its affiliated national branch, the American Congress of Farm Women, but there was no formal state or regional group of women farmers in the United States. The small group of Missouri women who established the MWFC were acutely aware of the pathbreaking nature of their collective activities, which they hoped would smooth the way for the young women who came after them. However, within a mere five years of the club's founding, its members found that the obstacles to their success were even greater than they imagined. Their enthusiastic support for scientific agriculture should have found a sympathetic audience among experts in the field, but opposition and disagreement over the role of women in agriculture limited their ability to form alliances with male-dominated institutions. Gathering support from their "natural allies" proved difficult as well, as conflicting notions of "woman farmer" and "farm woman" interfered with their attempts to organize rural women and expand MWFC membership. Discouragement set in as the women farmers became increasingly aware of their own isolation, and as it began to appear more unlikely that they would be able to effect large-scale organization.

The MWFC emerged during a critical stage in the development of agriculture and the professions. In the decades after the Civil War, large landowners and local elites who stood to gain from higher property values began a sustained push to expand railroads and establish links to new markets. Throughout the remainder of the nineteenth century, as mile after mile of new track was laid, railroad companies became some of the most vocal proponents of agricultural reform. Railroad officials knew that increased agricultural production would bring them a profit bonanza through increased freight volume and higher values for property holdings. They joined with land speculators and agriculture-related businesses in calling for farmers to embrace large-scale commercial production, urging them to increase productivity and efficiency by adopting more scientific and businesslike methods. The State Horticultural Society, the State Board of Agriculture, and the University of Missouri College of Agriculture joined

1. Herbert S. Hadley to Ida M. Tarbell, July 6, 1910, Herbert S. Hadley Papers, Letterbooks, 15:228, Western Historical Manuscript Collection–Columbia, University of Missouri–Columbia (hereinafter cited as WHMC-C); 1905 obituary for Ernest L. Mitchell, North Todd Gentry Papers, folder 185, WHMC-C.

forces to provide institutional support for these goals. The task at hand was about more than just profit from economic growth; it also involved the transfer of authority from farmer to expert. Industrialization had produced such tremendous advancements in science and technology, reformers argued, that the informal apprenticeship of sons to fathers must be replaced with formal training under the direction of professional agriculturalists. A similar process occurred in other occupations—education, law, and medicine, for example—as professional organizations and the state began to regulate training and to control access to occupational legitimacy.[2]

Unfortunately for MWFC members, part of the process of professionalization involved limiting access for women. The importance of gender has been greatly neglected in the history of professionalization, and no studies of the development of the professions consider women farmers. However, historians and sociologists who study the relationship between gender, knowledge, and power have shown how patriarchy was maintained during the professionalization of occupations in the late nineteenth and early twentieth centuries through men's use of political and institutional authority to control access to material resources and formal knowledge. Men used two related strategies, exclusion and segregation, to deny women full professional status. In agriculture, these strategies were manifested in the refusal of male experts in agricultural colleges and governmental agencies to accept women as farmers and in their attempts to deny professional women careers equivalent to their own by channeling them into the related but subordinate field of domestic science. Segregation was formalized when the Smith-Lever Act provided federal matching funds for agricultural education in 1914, and the U.S. Department of Agriculture divided extension work into two categories, farmwork and housework. This construction of gender-specific knowledge through an artificial division between men's work and women's work obscured the nature of farming as a collective process that involved both sexes, and it institutionalized a hierarchy that placed greater value on men's productive labor.[3]

2. David Thelen, *Paths of Resistance: Tradition and Democracy in Industrializing Missouri* (New York: Oxford University Press, 1986; reprint, Columbia: University of Missouri Press, 1991), 28–40, 185–89.

3. Joan Jacobs Brumberg and Nancy Tomes, "Women in the Professions: A Research Agenda for American Historians," *Reviews in American History* 10 (June 1982): 275–96; Katherine Jellison, *Entitled to Power: Farm Women and Technology, 1913–1963* (Chapel Hill: University of North Carolina Press, 1993), 16–17; Mary Neth, *Preserving the Family Farm: Women, Community, and the Foundations of Agribusiness in the Midwest, 1900–1940* (Baltimore: Johns Hopkins University Press, 1995), 214–43; Sally

Although women faced considerable opposition to their presence in virtually all professions, the members of the MWFC faced particular difficulties unique to agriculture. Farming arguably was the most rigidly male of all occupations. Whether contained within the image of the rugged frontiersman or the virtuous yeoman farmer, the concept of "farmer" was attached to physical strength and masculinity. Some professions that emerged later, such as engineering, also came to be labeled masculine, but they lacked farming's direct connection to male property ownership and political rights that was rooted in the nineteenth century. Historically, property ownership served as a basis for the franchise, because it gave citizens a direct stake in public policy. The farmer maintained both economic independence and the right to political participation through the ownership and control of property, and the custom of male inheritance enabled him to bestow this status upon his sons as well. "Farmer" was synonymous with "head of household." The rural woman was the farmer's wife or the farmer's daughter, a farm woman rather than a woman farmer. In the case of the wife, she paradoxically was a partner who also was a subordinate. Thus women who wanted public recognition as farmers in their own right were going against a set of social beliefs and practices through which men constructed both their private and public identity.[4]

For women farmers to organize in the face of such formidable obstacles required an optimism that can be explained, in part, by the resounding successes of female social and political reformers during the Progressive Era. Even though women were connected firmly to the realm of the home in the minds of most nineteenth-century Americans, by the 1890s middle-class women openly disputed the definition of domesticity as a purely private sphere of feminine influence. They were convinced that the problems caused by industrialization and urbanization threatened the health and well-being of all households and necessitated their involvement in public affairs. Many female social and literary clubs were transformed into study groups dedicated to self-education on issues such as juvenile delinquency, child

Shortall, *Women and Farming: Property and Power* (New York: St. Martin's Press, 1999), 118–20; for a summary of theoretical approaches from the sociological perspective, see Anne Witz, *Professions and Patriarchy* (London: Routledge, 1992).

4. Deborah Fink, *Agrarian Women: Wives and Mothers in Rural Nebraska, 1880–1940* (Chapel Hill: University of North Carolina Press, 1992), 11–24; Carolyn E. Sachs, *The Invisible Farmers: Women in Agricultural Production* (Totowa, N.J.: Rowman and Allanheld, 1983), 64–65; Shortall, *Women and Farming*, 2, 31–36; Samuel Haber, *The Quest for Authority and Honor in the American Professions, 1750–1900* (Chicago: University of Chicago Press, 1991).

labor, communicable disease, and the adulteration of foods and medications. A wave of female organizational activity swept the nation as middle-class women strove to fulfill their sense of collective social responsibility through community improvement projects and municipal reform. Many activists used their new civic visibility as the basis of demands for the full rights of citizenship, including equal access to higher education and professional training. Professional careers offered educated women an opportunity to combine the need for intellectual development with the desire to be socially useful, while also providing a means of self-support. In spite of persistent opposition from male professionals and their organizations, women made small but significant inroads into both old and new occupational fields between 1890 and 1910.[5]

The members of the MWFC were themselves products of these changes; they were educated middle-class clubwomen who participated in a myriad of organizations that were both social and political in nature. Two of the founding members, Frances Pearle Mitchell and Rosa Russell Ingels, described themselves as "club woman farmers" to emphasis their commitment to organizational activities and community-based reform. Mitchell was state vice president of the United Daughters of the Confederacy, president of her church guild, secretary of the board of managers for the Missouri Colony for the Feeble Minded and Epileptics, secretary of the Missouri Home Makers' Conference, and a member of the Governor's Commission on Tuberculosis. Ingels, a suffragist who joined the peace movement during the First World War, was president of the Fourth District of the Missouri Federation of Women's Clubs, past president of the Tuesday Club of Columbia, and a member of both the Public Library Board and the Christian Women's Board of Missions. Other women farmers held offices in the State and General Federations of Women's Clubs, the state chapter of the Mothers' Congress, the Missouri Pure Food and Drug Commission, woman suffrage organizations, and later, the League of Women Voters. Clearly, MWFC members were seasoned community activists with great confidence in their ability to scrutinize, analyze, and surmount obstacles in their paths.

The founding members of the MWFC met by chance in 1911 at the annual Farmers' Week convention at the University of Missouri College of Agriculture. The women had traveled to Columbia "to hear the lectures on

5. Karen J. Blair, *The Clubwoman as Feminist: True Womanhood Redefined, 1868–1914* (New York: Holmes and Meier, 1980); Anne Firor Scott, *Natural Allies: Women's Associations in American History* (Urbana: University of Illinois Press, 1992), chapters 6 and 7.

corn raising and farm management," and to attend the annual meeting of the Missouri Home Makers' Conference that was held concurrently. Their attendance at both events was odd in itself—no doubt the basis of their mutual attraction—and was illustrative of the peculiar position of female farmers. The College of Agriculture and State Board of Agriculture began collaborating in 1909 to stage educational sessions for farmers that would introduce them to new methods and techniques. Farmers' Week was held in early January, at a time when there would be little work for men to do on the farm, and mostly consisted of four-day short courses on subjects such as animal husbandry, horticulture, dairying, and poultry. The Missouri Home Makers' Conference, established in 1908 by middle-class women concerned about the quality of rural home life, assisted in offering the domestic science sessions that were held separately in the Department of Household Economics. The organizational structure of Farmers' Week served to separate farmers from farm women, segregating the business of the farm from domestic concerns. There was no defined place, no acknowledged identity for women farmers—rural women who supervised the work in the fields as well as the work in the home.[6]

Not surprisingly, the women farmers immediately felt drawn together by a sense of common purpose. They sought assistance in improving their farming methods but were frustrated because Farmers' Week agricultural lectures lacked what Frances Pearle Mitchell called "the woman's view of this farm management problem, the feminine solution." The founders of the MWFC believed that women needed a particular kind of instruction in farm management because they lacked the firsthand experience of male farmers who had grown up performing all phases of the work themselves. Some women had taken full responsibility for farm management only after the deaths of their fathers, and they were concerned that their previous training had failed to provide a level of knowledge adequate to the task. They had never baled hay or dug fence-post holes, for example, and they feared that they would not know if hired hands or tenants were performing work improperly. They worried also that they might be defrauded in the purchase of goods and services because of the limitations of their experience.[7]

---

6. Frances Pearle Mitchell, "The Women Farmers' Club," from the minutes and proceedings of the Missouri Women Farmers' Club, *Forty-Third Annual Report of the Missouri State Board of Agriculture* (Jefferson City, Mo.: Hugh Stephens, 1911), 195–96.

7. Mitchell, "Women Farmers' Club"; Mitchell, "President's Address," *Forty-Fourth Annual Report of the Missouri State Board of Agriculture* (Jefferson City, Mo.: Hugh Stephens, 1912), 292–93.

The club members' concerns illustrate how the sexual division of labor on family farms hindered the ability of female heirs to farm their properties efficiently and profitably, thus diminishing their chances of keeping the land in the family. This was particularly true in cases in which the heir was single, widowed, or married to a man who was engaged in a profession other than farming. As one club member noted, the ability to manage property successfully was a matter of survival for women with dependents whose only asset was land. Even a male lecturer at one of the group's annual meetings who refused to endorse the idea of encouraging women to become farmers had to admit to clubwomen that the options of female heirs were problematic at best. The institute lecturer, J. Kelly Wright of the State Board of Agriculture, told the women farmers that when a woman found herself left with the family farm after the death of a husband or father she had the choices of "getting married and turning the farm over to her husband, renting it out, selling it, or running it herself." He labeled the first choice "risky," presumably because there would be no guarantee that the new husband would safeguard the property interests of the wife. Similarly, tenants could not be counted upon to take a long-term view of land and building maintenance when there were short-term profits to be made. Since, according to Wright, the third choice was "out of the question," the only real answer to the unmarried female landowner's dilemma was for her to educate herself on all aspects of agricultural production.[8]

The backgrounds of the members of the MWFC illustrate the varieties of instances in which a woman either single or married might come into possession of the family farm. In many cases there were no living male heirs, or at least none interested in taking up farming. Frances Pearle Mitchell had one living brother, Ernest L. Mitchell, a merchant and editor of the *Columbia Daily Tribune,* and he showed little interest in farming before his early death in 1905. Although she also had a surviving stepbrother from her father's first marriage, his banking career and political ambitions (including a term as state bank commissioner) left little time for farming. Frances Pearle was born in 1864 to Newman Tompkins Mitchell Sr., a pioneer of Boone County, and to his second wife, Katherine Wells (Slack) Mitchell. Her father was a successful farmer who went into banking, and her mother was the daughter of another prominent Boone County farmer, who served on the first board of curators and later became vice president of the University of Missouri. Mitchell grew up on her parents' farm and

8. Adella Blew, "Why Women Farm," *Forty-Fourth Annual Report,* 296–97; J. Kelly Wright, "Extracts from Address before Women Farmers' Club," *Forty-Fifth Annual Report of the Missouri State Board of Agriculture* (Jefferson City, Mo.: Hugh Stephens, 1913), 581–83.

attended college in Columbia, which was only about eight miles east of her home, graduating with honors from Stephens Female College in 1880. She began assisting her mother in the management of their 320-acre farm near Rocheport after the death of her father, and as her mother's health deteriorated Mitchell assumed more and more responsibility. After her mother's death, Mitchell continued to manage the farm because of her "attachment to the old home" and her "desire for occupation as a definite outlet for my latent energy."[9]

Another founding member of the MWFC, Secretary-Treasurer Alice E. Kinney, also was motivated by family obligations and personal inclination to accept responsibility for the family estate. She was one of eleven children, but she had only two surviving sisters when she assumed control of Rivercene, a four-hundred-acre farm of rich Missouri river-bottom land in Howard County. Her father, Joseph Kinney, was a riverboat captain and owner of a fleet of steamboats who amassed a fortune in the mid-1800s ferrying settlers westward. After purchasing the property at Rivercene in 1869, he tried his hand at growing vegetables, fruit, and pecans. When Joseph died in 1892, Alice and brother Noble expanded farming operations and hired as many as fifty men to assist in maintaining the orchards and fields. Alice followed the example of her brother, who had attended the University of Missouri College of Agriculture, and dedicated herself to learning the methods of scientific agriculture and livestock raising through independent study. Tragedy struck in 1895 when Noble died at the age of twenty-six, leaving Alice in sole charge of the extensive farming operation. She somehow continued to manage the property while also remaining active in church and club work and in the "good roads" campaign for rural improvement. Alice became famous in surrounding counties for her "hot house hogs" after using greenhouses to shelter livestock during a severe winter storm. The experiment worked so well that she persisted in the practice despite receiving a good deal of ribbing about it in the local press.[10]

9. Howard L. Conard, *Encyclopedia of the History of Missouri* (New York: Southern History Company, 1901), 4:439; John C. Crighton, *A History of Columbia and Boone County* (Columbia, Mo.: Boone County Historical Society, 1987), 284–85; William F. Switzler, *History of Boone County, Missouri* (St. Louis: Western Historical Company, 1882), 1044–46; "Women Farmers and Their Farms," *Forty-Third Annual Report*, 196–98.

10. Clipping, Ethelda Henry Collection, folder 1048, WHMC-C; Lilburn A. Kingsbury Collection, folder 229, WHMC-C; Alice Kinney to Elizabeth B. Gentry, August 23, 1911, Arrow Rock Tavern Board Papers, folder 4, WHMC-C; *Kansas City Star*, March 5, 1933; T. Berry Smith and Pearl Sims Gehrig, *History of Chariton and Howard Counties, Missouri* (Topeka, Kans.: Historical Publishing Company, 1923), 344–45; "Women Farmers and Their Farms," 198–99.

Maude M. Griffith, who succeeded Kinney as secretary-treasurer of the MWFC, was one of eight daughters. As with Mitchell, her father was a successful farmer and stockman who went into banking and other business enterprises. After moving to Missouri in the 1870s, Wesley Griffith accumulated around sixteen hundred acres of land in St. Clair County and also owned considerable property in Illinois inherited from his parents. In the absence of any male heirs, Maude became his "son" for all practical purposes. He began grooming her as a child to eventually assume control of farming operations. He took her with him when making the rounds of his property and discussed with her business matters and all aspects of agricultural work in order to educate her on the general management of the farm. As she grew older, he placed her in charge of overseeing work and making decisions whenever he was away. Maude went on to earn a bachelor's degree from Columbia Christian College and then attended the University of Missouri for three years. She had a great deal of freedom before her father's death, working first as a teacher in Missouri and Colorado before opening her own mercantile business in Kansas. However, she dutifully returned home to assume full responsibility for running the estate when he died, and from that time onward agriculture became her central interest. Like other members of the MWFC, she was known for her constant efforts to stay abreast of modern farming methods and wrote numerous articles for farm journals.[11]

While Mitchell, Kinney, and Griffith were single when they shouldered the responsibilities of farm management (and Mitchell and Kinney remained so), some club members were married women whose husbands were engaged in other occupations. All three members of the club's executive committee—Cora F. Shewell, Mrs. R. A. Cook, and Emma E. (Cortelyou) Simonson—were married women who owned and operated their own farms. Shewell, whose husband owned a business in St. Louis, was a serious livestock breeder who spent the winters in the city and had a tenant look after her farm and livestock while she was away. Cook lived on a farm year-round and had sole responsibility for its management while her husband worked as a merchant in a nearby town. Simonson was married to the Jefferson City school superintendent, who was himself from a farming background. She chose farming as her profession in 1901, when she sold a farm in Illinois and used the money to purchase a 160-acre farm in Scotland County, in northeast Missouri. She lived on the property for most

11. Maude M. Griffith, "Managing a Big Farm and Raising English Blue Grass," *Forty-Fourth Annual Report,* 297–302; Allen Glenn, *History of Cass County, Missouri* (Topeka, Kans.: Historical Publishing Company, 1917), 738–50.

of the year, returning to Jefferson City only during the winter months. After taking full advantage of government assistance to farmers, Simonson ensured that the family farming tradition would be passed down to the next generation by including her son, Clarence, in the planning and execution of demonstration work.[12]

Other members of the MWFC more closely fit the stereotype of the woman farmer as a widow who assumed control of farm property after the death of her husband. According to the stereotype, such women only entered farming because they had no choice, and thus they were considered objects of pity rather than respect. The proverbial "widow woman's farm" was a farm that showed signs of mismanagement and neglect, proof of the inevitable decline of the family farm that accompanied the death of the male head of household. In contrast to this "common wisdom," the MWFC widows were neither completely ignorant of farming methods nor reluctant to assume responsibility for property management. Virginia E. Mitchell married Richard P. Bland, a lawyer and son of a farmer, in 1872. Five years later, they purchased a 160-acre farm near Lebanon in Laclede County, where Richard conducted a law practice. Since he was elected to the U.S. Congress that same year and spent much of the next twenty years in Washington, it seems likely that Virginia already had a basic knowledge of farming when he died in 1899. Luna Patterson, the daughter of a St. Joseph wholesale shoe dealer, married one of the largest landowners in central Missouri when she exchanged vows with Turner S. McBaine Jr. in 1881. The McBaine farming operation produced 25,000 bushels of wheat, 1,000 head of cattle, and 1,500 hogs for the market annually. When her husband died in 1908, Luna was left with the responsibility of managing this huge enterprise, and she also had the duty of supervising the numerous tenant farmers that resided on the property. Bland and McBaine provide two examples of how grieving women frequently rose to the challenge of running a farm, choosing to educate themselves further instead of hiring men to make decisions and supervise work on a day-to-day basis.[13]

12. "Women Farmers and Their Farms," 199–200; "Some Members of the Women Farmers' Club," *Forty-Fourth Annual Report*, 305–6; Thomas H. Bacon et al., *Mirror of Hannibal* (1905; reprint, Hannibal, Mo.: Hannibal Free Public Library, 1990), 275; *Portrait and Biographical Record of Marion, Ralls, and Pike Counties* (1895; reprint, New London, Mo.: Ralls County Book Company, 1982), 227–28; Emma Simonson, "Experimental Farming," *Forty-Fourth Annual Report*, 294–95; "Women Farmers and Their Farms," 199.

13. *A Reminiscent History of the Ozark Region* (1894; reprint, Cape Girardeau, Mo.: Ramfre Press, 1966), 69–70; Leo Nyberg, *A History of Laclede County, Missouri, 1820–1926* (Lebanon, Mo.: Rustic Printers, 1926), 84–85; Floyd Calvin Shoemaker and Walter Williams, *Missouri: Mother of the West* (Chicago: American Historical

As these brief descriptions illustrate, MWFC members were women from relatively privileged backgrounds. They were not the products of small subsistence farms, but rather of substantial market-oriented enterprises in which mechanization had greatly reduced the need for family labor. In many cases, their fathers were pioneer farmers who had been in a position to benefit from early industrialization and postbellum economic development, using the proceeds from farming and property sales to start second careers in business and finance. It was their reduced need for family labor that afforded their daughters the opportunity for a college education and encouraged them to see farming as a managerial profession rather than as strictly a family enterprise. In Missouri in the late nineteenth century, many such rural women went away to college, sometimes married into the growing professional and merchant class, yet retained their strong ties to the countryside. Women such as Frances Pearle Mitchell and Emma Simonson did not want to lose the ties to the past that farm ownership represented, and they saw in agriculture an opportunity for independent, rewarding careers. If middle-class men could be banker-farmers and lawyer-farmers, why could not their wives and daughters be clubwomen-farmers? Women farmers could manage the labor of others and still have time to serve as officers and volunteers in women's clubs, political and civic organizations, and state-run charity and social services boards (as most did). And by maintaining the family farm in good order, women could uphold family tradition as well as prove their competence in a profession historically reserved for men.

Organization was a necessary first step for the Missouri women, since there were no local groups that met their personal and professional needs. The agricultural organizations that met in Columbia during Farmers' Week were sexually segregated, reflecting the structure of state and federal services. MWFC members felt comfortable at the meetings of the Missouri Home Makers' Conference, since it was a women's organization that acted as an advocate for the rural home and family and lobbied for greater funding of home extension services. The women farmers felt more out of place, however, when they crossed the gender barrier and attended agricultural lectures aimed at men. Mitchell described the future members of the MWFC as being "timid" and hesitant to identify themselves as true farmers when she first met them at Farmers' Week activities. She believed that having their own organization would provide them with a critical source of moral and

---

Society, 1930), 76–77; Conard, *History of Missouri*, 239–40; *Columbia Missouri Herald,* Historical Edition, April 1895.

technical support, allowing them to learn from each others' farming experiences and convincing them that they were indeed "real" farmers. Furthermore, it was only through association that they could become visible. So
long as they remained scattered throughout the countryside, showing up
only in scarce numbers for farmers' institutes and conventions, it would be
easy for others to continue ignoring their needs and concerns.[14]

Education had to accompany organization if the women farmers were
to prove their competence, but obtaining knowledge from the obvious
sources was difficult. Experts in the university's College of Agriculture and
the Department of Agriculture tended not to take them seriously. Farmers'
Week officials relegated MWFC meetings to the overcrowded home economics department, forcing club members to form a committee to push for
the transfer of their group to the agricultural building after repeatedly finding themselves without a vacant auditorium. No professors gave technical
talks at their meetings, and the dean of the College of Agriculture and one
member of the State Board of Agriculture were the only men to speak encouraging words to the group. This behavior on the part of agricultural experts is especially revealing when contrasted with their willingness to give
talks to the Home Makers' Conference on poultry raising, butter making,
and other topics deemed appropriate for farm women. Male agriculturalists could relate to rural women's productive labor only as secondary to the
"real" work of the farm, the work of the (male) farmer, even when female
labor was aimed at market sales. To compensate for institutional discrimination, MWFC members adopted a course of study involving the reading
of agricultural journals and the sharing of their individual knowledge
through formal paper presentations and discussions at annual meetings.
Much as they had educated themselves on social problems as clubwomen,
they pursued self-study as the answer to their professional needs.[15]

At the heart of the tension between women farmers and male agricultural experts was a struggle for control of formal knowledge and economic
resources. If the central purpose of scientific agriculture was to promote
economic development, then maintaining neat divisions between men/farm/
business and women/home/domesticity could justify channeling most state

14. Ibid.; "Object of the Association," *Forty-Fourth Annual Report,* 290; A. J. Meyer,
"Extracts from Address before the Women Farmers' Club," *Forty-Fifth Annual Report,*
578–80.

15. Minutes of Proceedings, *Forty-Fifth Annual Report,* 576–77, *Forty-Sixth Annual
Report of the Missouri State Board of Agriculture* (Jefferson City, Mo.: Hugh Stephens,
1914), 449–50, and *Forty-Seventh Annual Report of the Missouri State Board of Agriculture* (Jefferson City, Mo.: Hugh Stephens, 1915), 305–10.

and federal resources into educational services for farmers—namely, rural men. And programs for men did, in fact, receive the lion's share of public funds. As a consequence, the work of male agriculturalists appeared more valuable, more "technical," and more professionally important than that of female domestic science experts, even though the latter often had advanced degrees in science. Career opportunities for women professionals in educational institutions and governmental agencies conducting agricultural work were confined to low-ranking assistant positions in research science, or to teaching and administrative posts with considerably lower pay and prestige than equivalent jobs open to men. The construction of discrete categories of knowledge facilitated the survival of the patriarchal structure of agriculture in a new era, in which the application of business methods and technology had, at least in the eyes of MWFC members, the potential to make the profession of farming into an even playing field for men and women.[16]

This is not to say that all rural reformers who sought to impose the ideology of separate spheres on the rural household intended to subordinate women in the process. Members of the Missouri Home Makers' Conference believed that transforming "farm wives" into housewives would elevate their status by removing the drudgery of manual labor and allowing more time for self-fulfillment and self-improvement. MWFC members regarded the goals of the Home Makers' Conference as entirely compatible with their own, and Mitchell and Kinney served as officers for both groups. Like middle-class female reformers across the United States, they had taken their cue from farm women themselves. When Theodore Roosevelt's Country Life Commission conducted a survey of rural households in 1908–1909, it received numerous complaints from farm women regarding poor living conditions and a general lack of mechanical conveniences to lighten their burden of work. The respondents were not so much expressing discontentment with rural life as they were protesting male control of farm capital and men's tendency to invest it in technological improvements for the fields rather than the homes. This opposition to patriarchy represented a common ground for women farmers and farm women, but the identity of "clubwoman-farmer" confounded the categories. To be recognized as farmers, the members had to distinguish themselves as separate from farm women, to emphasize their independent agency and authority as property owners. To combat gender discrimination, they needed to cast a wider net and link their cause to other rural women, but most farm women—despite their

16. Neth, *Preserving the Family Farm,* 214–17.

complaints—tended to view farming as a collective family enterprise rather than as an individual one.[17]

In their efforts to present farming as a "gender neutral" profession, club members very cleverly drew upon male agricultural reformers' own rhetoric. Mitchell described the emergence of women farmers as the natural product of social and technological advancements that had removed "brawn and muscle" as requisites for success and paved the way for the woman farmer, who "directs, superintends, buys and sells." Agricultural scientists and business leaders who wanted to persuade stubborn farmers to abandon traditional methods often argued that "brains rather than brawn" was the key to modern farming. They intended this argument to convince farmers that the growing importance of formal knowledge was a natural result of evolutionary change—as society became more complex, the authority and necessity of the expert increased. Mitchell linked this process of change to gender equality. If trained intelligence had replaced physical strength as the requisite for farming, there no longer was any reason to consider farming a male occupation. If scientific knowledge, management skills, and bookkeeping proficiency were the keys to success in agriculture, then women farmers could become as competent as any man through the acquisition of formal knowledge. From this perspective, technological advancement could turn the farm woman (or housewife) into a farmer.[18]

The women who founded the MWFC carefully distinguished themselves from farm women as a way to establish their professional identity. From the beginning of the group's existence, the single most important requirement for membership was that women manage their own property. Members took this requirement seriously, as evidenced by the resignation of the acting secretary, Maude M. Griffith Wood, in 1915. Wood had a difficult task in managing her parents' extensive farm operations after her father's death, yet she did it successfully before and after her marriage in 1913. At the time she resigned her post, she had recently moved into a large antebellum home on a new farm, had a one-year-old son, and was pregnant with another child. The minutes of the MWFC annual meeting emphasize that her resignation was the result of "Mrs. Wood having retrograded by giving over the management of her affairs into the hands of a

17. Jellison, *Entitled to Power,* 1–32; Jane B. Knowles, "'It's Our Turn Now': Rural American Women Speak Out, 1900–1920," in *Women and Farming: Changing Roles, Changing Structures,* ed. Wava G. Haney and Jane B. Knowles (Boulder, Colo.: Westview Press, 1988), 303–18.
18. Mitchell, "Women Farmers' Club."

husband—from a woman farmer and a charter member of this club into a mere farm woman." The judgmental tone of this statement suggests why Wood did not attend the meeting but sent word of her resignation instead. Mitchell took the opportunity to provide "a short history and explanation of the meaning and aims of the Missouri Women Farmers' Club, making it clear that eligibility to the club depended entirely upon a woman's managing her own farm." It appears that club members considered their professional position to be so tenuous that exceptions to the rule could not be made even for someone like Wood, who was an obvious supporter of the cause.[19]

Perhaps the women farmers held such a firm line against retrogradation, as they put it, because they felt so much was at stake. In many ways, their struggle for recognition as farmers represented an attempt to fully realize the privileges of property ownership. Possession of real property was a concrete, enduring form of economic independence, and although not failsafe, it was one that was arguably more secure than skilled wage labor and most professional occupations. For single and widowed women, management of commercial farming concerns represented a lucrative and liberating source of support, and for married women it represented both a career and insurance in the event of divorce or widowhood. One club member, Adella Blew, gave a simple but forthright explanation of the women farmers' position when she declared that "we are sensible, practicable women, seeking to learn how to manage our farms and land interests in an intelligent and profitable way, in order that we may realize the largest possible returns from them." If they were to be successful, they had to persist in their efforts to exercise the basic rights enjoyed by the men of their class. Women farmers who handed control of their property over to their husbands were, by default, accepting patriarchal tradition and abdicating the right to act as independent economic agents. The public would have little reason to distinguish between someone like Griffith Wood, who made a conscious choice to allow her husband to assume responsibility for property management, and women who did not question male authority in such matters.[20]

Despite their efforts to distinguish themselves from the "mere farm woman," Missouri women farmers ultimately had to recognize the ways in which the interests of all women were interconnected. They quickly moved

19. Minutes of Proceedings, *Forty-Seventh Annual Report*, 305–6; Glenn, *History of Cass County.*
20. Adella Blew, "Why Women Farm," *Forty-Fourth Annual Report*, 296–97.

beyond the desire for self-help that had been the immediate impetus for forming their association and soon were attempting to apply their strategies of organization and education to the wider community of rural women. As a district president of the Missouri Federation of Women's Clubs, Rosa Russell Ingels drew upon a ten-county network of contacts in organizing rural women's clubs. At the national level, the MWFC sent delegates to meetings of the International Congress of Farm Women and reported back to rural women at the Home Makers' Conference. Club members also encouraged public recognition of the importance of farm women's work, both "domestic" and "productive." In her four years as president of the Home Makers' Conference, Alice Kinney appeared at numerous conferences and fairs to emphasize the importance of solving the problems of the farm home as well as the "outside problems" of the farm. MWFC members never abandoned their distinction between the woman farmer and the farm woman, but as their own privileges of property ownership were constricted by gender conventions, they understood the necessity of improving the status of both groups.[21]

The MWFC tried to widen its pool of potential members by encouraging rural girls and women to think of farming as a female profession. They explicitly stated that one object of their association was to "encourage young women to enter agricultural schools, fitting themselves to follow the natural life." Club members funded the first female agricultural scholarship in 1912 and established a corn-growing contest shortly thereafter to attract interest among rural girls. The competition had the same rules as the boys' corn-growing contest sponsored by the State Board of Agriculture, with the exception that the girls could supervise rather than perform some of the manual labor, such as plowing. In addition to the usual premiums, the top-placing girl received a scholarship from the women farmers to study agriculture at the University of Missouri. The girls' contest was a great success and attracted the attention of numerous local newspapers and farm journals, which carried stories about the winners and the competent work performed by female contestants. The MWFC enjoyed an unusual level of support from governmental agencies and institutions in creating the contest and scholarship because its support for vocational and industrial training in public schools fit well with the educational reform

21. Alice Kinney, presidential reports, Proceedings of the Missouri Home Makers' Conference, *Forty-Fourth Annual Report,* 139–42, *Forty-Fifth Annual Report,* 159–62, *Forty-Sixth Annual Report,* 545–48; Rosa Russell Ingels, "Women's Clubs for Farm Women," *Forty-Fourth Annual Report,* 303–4; Maude M. Griffith, "An International Movement for the Betterment of Rural Homes," *Forty-Fifth Annual Report,* 272–75.

efforts of a diverse group of social reformers in the country life and domestic science movements. Similar to advocates of domestic science, club members argued that agricultural education was appropriate for both the homemaker and the professional, as it left girls well prepared to begin adult life as either women farmers or farm women.[22]

Even though the girls' contest brought favorable publicity to their cause, club members' efforts to recruit rural women made little progress, and MWFC membership growth stalled. In 1915, Frances Pearle Mitchell reproached women attending the annual meeting for "not showing the proper zeal" and for failing to reach the "hundreds of women farmers in our State who should be allied with our club." Little progress had been made in another of Mitchell's pet projects, the Women Farm Managers' Association. When the International Congress of Farm Women met in Tulsa, Oklahoma, in October 1913, representatives from nine states came together to form this new group. Mitchell, who was elected secretary, reported back to her club that it had been the creation of the MWFC that sparked interest in the organization of women farmers and thus inspired the delegates to form a national association. Members were prominent farmers from the states of Oklahoma, Illinois, North Dakota, Michigan, Colorado, California, Idaho, and Arkansas, in addition to Missouri. All MWFC members were urged to attend the next meeting of the association at the following year's International Congress of Farm Women, but only one woman went. Even the Missouri Home Makers' Conference had difficulty attracting large numbers of rural women. Despite their successes in promoting educational opportunity for rural women, women farmers found it difficult to expand their influence beyond a core group of committed women. Throughout the 1910s, membership remained steady at about twenty-five women.[23]

Like many other pioneers of women in the professions, MWFC members failed to secure a place in their chosen career for succeeding generations of women. "Farmer" continued to be defined as male, despite Frances Pearle Mitchell's expressed hope that her club would forge a pathway for "young women who are educated, trained farmers, and [who] will not have the hardships of pioneering, such as most of ours have experienced." One reason her hopes were not realized was that rural women were hesi-

22. Mitchell, "President's Address," and Meyer, "Extracts," *Forty-Fifth Annual Report*, 577–80; "Girls Will Make Boys Hustle," *Blackwater News*, May 2, 1913, 3; "This Girl Grows Corn," *Missouri Ruralist*, May 5, 1914, 7.

23. Frances Pearle Mitchell, "President's Address," *Forty-Sixth Annual Report*, 451–52; Maude M. Griffith Wood, "Report of Women Farm Managers' Association," *Forty-Sixth Annual Report*, 454–55; Minutes of proceedings of annual meeting, *Forty-Seventh Annual Report*, 309.

tant to endorse the MWFC vision of farming as a career choice for women. A female student from the College of Agriculture told club members that the women's course of study did not focus on farm management because "there are comparatively few women who voluntarily choose this work." The agricultural component of female degree programs was tailored to enable women to manage the farm "if the occasion demands it," or in other words, if no man was available to take charge. Since most rural women lacked access to land and credit, female students' educational choices are understandable—if they farmed it would be as farmers' wives, who had full responsibility for domestic work, and not as independent farm managers. Even those who stood to inherit land had reasons to reject the MWFC model of farmer, because its emphasis on individual agency contradicted most rural women's concept of farming as a collective family enterprise. The female agricultural student alluded to this perspective when she asserted that women needed enough knowledge to be able "to counsel wisely," as it was "impossible to separate the management of a farm from the management of the home."[24]

The attempt of MWFC members to separate the concept of farmer from physical labor also may have diminished their appeal to rural women. In statements aimed at the public, women farmers often insisted that they were "womanly women," that they did not "follow the plow or pitch the hay," and that they certainly did not neglect their household and familial duties. Although this was a highly political move intended to divorce the concept of farmer from masculine strength, its appeal to rural women is questionable. In the Missouri rural press, it was common for farm women as well as women farmers to express pride in their ability to perform all necessary tasks on the farm. They were proud that they could do the same work as a man. Furthermore, studies of rural women suggest that many farm women found more enjoyment and fulfillment in outdoor labor than in housework, and so actually preferred to work in the fields whenever possible. This represented an essential class difference between MWFC members—college-educated women who were free to engage in an independent career and volunteer activism—and less-wealthy rural women whose physical labor was needed on the farm.[25]

24. Penina Migdal Glazer and Miriam Slater, *Unequal Colleagues: The Entrance of Women into the Professions, 1890–1940* (London: Rutgers University Press, 1987), 22–23; Shortall, *Women and Farming,* 115; Frances Pearle Mitchell, "President's Address," *Forty-Fifth Annual Report,* 578; Georgia E. Cantrell, "The Agricultural Course for Women," *Forty-Fifth Annual Report,* 584–85.

25. "Missouri Women Farmers," *Kansas City Star,* February 28, 1912; Mary B. Kreutz, "Did She Need a Partner?" *Missouri Ruralist,* February 5, 1914, 22.

A final obstacle to the goals of the MWFC was that women who sought to farm independently, especially those who were unmarried, lacked the flexibility afforded by access to family labor. This problem is particularly evident in the tragic decline in the Kinney family fortunes. In the 1920s Alice and her widowed sisters, Margaret Ravenel and Cora Hurt, were the only remaining heirs to the family estate. They lived together at Rivercene until the last surviving sister died in 1948, and provide a classic example of women whose only resource was land. Kinney attempted to support the household through farming, but sole responsibility for farm management and the expense of hired labor apparently were too heavy a burden to bear for an elderly woman without children or financial resources. By the mid-1920s she and her sisters had to sell portions of land and sign oil-drilling leases merely to meet living expenses, a pattern that continued until their deaths. Farming as a family enterprise persisted well into the twentieth century because it was a flexible arrangement in which various family members could contribute their labor when it was needed and hire themselves out for wages when it was not. Single or childless women were in a less favorable position to ride out changes in the agricultural economy. Mechanization may have reduced the need for family labor, but it also encouraged the trend toward large-scale farming and increased dependency on credit, thus still leaving women at a distinct disadvantage due to gender discrimination in banking practices.[26]

The successes and failures of the Missouri Women Farmers' Club speak to the many difficulties facing women in agriculture who wanted to professionalize their work on the farm. The MWFC came into existence at a time when increasing numbers of women were gaining admittance to business and science careers that previously had been reserved for men. The Missouri women had reason to believe that they might lower the barriers in agriculture, too, thus giving rural women a way to become independent while still remaining on the farm. As technology changed the face of farming, they hoped that it might also change the face of the farmer. During the early stages of the development of commercial agriculture, it was not entirely clear what technological advancement would mean for rural society and whom it would benefit. Their attempts to spread the benefits more widely fell victim not just to rural class differences and the old patriarchy

26. Clipping from *Columbia Missourian,* August 7, 1977, Ethelda Henry Collection; Lilburn A. Kingsbury Collection; Alice Kinney farm demonstration records, University of Missouri Agricultural Economics Department Papers, folders 1835, 1851, 1872, 1946, WHMC-C.

of the family farm, but also to the new patriarchy of male professionals who were in the process of consolidating their power through control of knowledge and resources. It was this latter obstacle to success that MWFC members shared with other women in Missouri who sought entrance to male-dominated professions.

Euphemia B. Koller and the Politics of Insanity in Ralls County, 1921–1927

Gregg Andrews

On February 24, 1930, Euphemia B. Koller, age sixty-eight, died while confined in Missouri's State Hospital for the Insane in Fulton. In an obituary, the *Hannibal Courier-Post* noted that she and her sister, Mary Alice Heinbach, formerly co-owned the unincorporated town site of Ilasco, a largely Slavic community of about two thousand residents, just across the Marion/Ralls county line near the Mark Twain Cave, about three miles south of Hannibal. According to the obituary, the Atlas Portland Cement Company had purchased the Ilasco tract from them about twenty-five years earlier when it built a plant next to their property. A Ralls County probate judge had ordered Koller's confinement as a private patient in August 1927. To underscore the special tragedy of her fate in the asylum, a New London newspaper recalled that "many years ago she was a brilliant woman, being well-educated, refined, and a fluent talker."[1]

The *Hannibal Courier-Post,* although well aware of the connections between Koller's fate and a bitter, protracted legal battle over the twenty-six-acre tract on which much of Ilasco was located, used her death to promote an official "booster" version of Ilasco's history that concealed an important secret and glorified Atlas's paternalistic role in the community. In a complex case that went to the state supreme court several times, Koller and

---

1. *Hannibal Courier-Post,* February 26, 1930; Euphemia B. Koller, Certificate of Death, February 24, 1930, Missouri State Board of Health, Bureau of Vital Statistics, Jefferson City; *Ralls County Record,* February 28, 1930.

her sister had battled to hold onto the tract in the face of relentless efforts by local officials, attorneys, and other intermediaries who hoped to turn Ilasco over to the cement company. At times the sisters also fought each other, but the establishment of a guardianship over Heinbach in the Ralls County probate court in 1921 paved the way for a court-ordered sheriff's sale of the tract in December 1921. After Atlas scooped up the tract, Koller contested the sale for years and tried to expose the political machinations that led to the final conversion of Ilasco into a company town.[2]

Why was this tract so important to Atlas, the nation's top cement producer? The Ilasco plant—Atlas's first west of the Mississippi River—was crucial to the company's efforts to challenge its main rival in the markets of the Mississippi River valley, but the community on the perimeter of the plant had posed serious problems for company officials since its inception in 1903. Ongoing labor unrest crested in 1910 when the Missouri National Guard occupied the town to quell a violent strike at a time when Atlas was experiencing financial difficulties and a shakeup at the top. Continued disruptions at the Ilasco plant threatened production and dramatized how important it was for Atlas to acquire greater control over the community. In addition, nativist hatreds and sensationalized, inflammatory area newspaper accounts of crime and alcohol stirred considerable opposition toward the company's "foreign colony," thus contributing to Atlas's growing determination to stabilize Ilasco.[3]

As an autonomous, divorced woman with substantial financial resources, gender consciousness, and a deep-seated contempt for the male-dominated legal profession, Koller often acted as her own attorney in a lonely battle to hang onto the Ilasco tract. Charging corruption and complaining of a "confederated conspiracy" by Atlas officials and key area lawyers and politicians, she sued several prominent elites and tried to oversee her own state court appeal of the sale of the tract to the cement company. Until her confinement to a mental hospital, she also resisted a campaign by county authorities to place a guardianship over her. The prosecuting attorney—one of the defendants named in Koller's lawsuit and frustrated by her determination to fight the case out to the bitter end—insisted that she was afflicted with "monomania." Resurrecting a labeling long used against reformers and critical thinkers, particularly if

2. For a fuller development of this case, see Gregg Andrews, *Insane Sisters: Or, the Price Paid for Challenging a Company Town* (Columbia: University of Missouri Press, 1999).

3. Gregg Andrews, *City of Dust: A Cement Company Town in the Land of Tom Sawyer* (Columbia: University of Missouri Press, 1996), 112–14.

they were women, he argued that she was gripped by a single-minded obsession to file lawsuits.[4]

This fascinating case raises several important questions. When the county sheriff finally whisked Koller away to the state hospital at her own expense in 1927, was it a clear matter of wrongful confinement and abuse of power by tightly interlocked elites in a small agricultural county that was thoroughly dominated by the Atlas Portland Cement Company? Or did the case itself break Koller down mentally? To what extent was her alleged insanity based on the complex interactions of class, gender, and law in the history of this property dispute? Or was this an ambiguous case based on concepts of insanity that prevailed at the time but that would fall short of meeting our standards today? Drawing heavily from state and local court records, this essay explores the final phase of the legal war between Koller and area officials that led to her confinement. It raises questions about the use of guardianships and insanity as methods of social control against women who dared to trespass on legal and entrepreneurial terrain dominated by men at a time of rapidly changing roles for women in the public arena.[5]

Before examining the conflicts that led to Koller's confinement, it will be useful to explore the sources of empowerment that gave her the self-confidence and consciousness to tangle with lawyers, corporate officials, and county politicians and other elites over the fate of Ilasco. Born in Pennsylvania in 1861, she was the daughter of Edwin H. and Sarah J. Sykes, who brought their family to Ralls County and set up a mill there shortly after the Civil War. The evidence is sketchy on Euphemia Sykes's teenage years, but she apparently returned to the East for marriage and perhaps education. By 1880, she had married John A. J. Koller, a clerk, and moved to Baltimore, but she divorced him in 1893 and began a new life of indepen-

---

4. *Euphemia B. Koller v. Mary Alice Heinbach and her Guardian, J. E. Megown, et al.*, case no. 11606, January 24, 1923, Ralls County, Office of the Circuit Clerk and Recorder, New London; Estate of Euphemia B. Koller, case no. 4713, Samuel Elzea, guardian, appointment made January 5, 1925, Ralls County, Office of the Probate Clerk, New London; E. S. Holt, informant, "In the Matter of the Alleged Insanity of Euphemia B. Koller," case no. 13217, April 7, 1925, Office of the Clerk, Hannibal Court of Common Pleas, Hannibal.

5. For recent discussions of the literature on American mental institutions and the mentally ill, see, for example, Peter McCandless, *Moonlight, Magnolias, and Madness: Insanity in South Carolina from the Colonial Period to the Progressive Era* (Chapel Hill: University of North Carolina Press, 1996), 1–11; and John S. Hughes, ed., *The Letters of a Victorian Madwoman* (Columbia: University of South Carolina Press, 1993), 1–12.

dence, autonomy, travel, self-directed studies, and self-indulgence. She moved to Manhattan and worked as a writer, although it is not clear what kind of writing she did, or for whom. She often returned to Hannibal, where she owned property, but spent most of her time over the next decade rotating between Baltimore, New York City, Washington, D.C., and St. Louis. She also traveled extensively into New Mexico and Oklahoma, where she owned a boardinghouse in Shawnee. The freedom and autonomy of her post-divorce life thrilled her, for, as she explained, she did not like to be tied down: "I am a writer, and I spend most of my time wherever I please. I don't spend any specified time in any place."[6]

In many ways, Koller did not conform to traditional images and expectations in regard to women at the time. In a more conservative rural area such as Ralls County, her unrestricted freedom of mobility and her failure to live up to the caregiver responsibilities assigned to women particularly encouraged resentments of her. For example, when the wife of her brother—Tom Sykes—died and left six children in his care, the family expected Koller to take care of them. She had the wherewithal and the time, and she was divorced. According to Jane Hemeyer, her great-niece, Koller's refusal to do so strained family relations. In the view of many, Koller had selfishly neglected her motherless nieces and nephews.[7]

One of the sources of public empowerment for Koller was the spiritualist movement that had attracted many freethinkers and reformers in the nineteenth century. For numerous women attracted to spiritualism, the movement encouraged a broader critique of women's subordinate position in marriage, the home, politics, and society. By the turn of the twentieth century, spiritualism as an organized movement was in sharp decline,

6. U.S. Federal Manuscript Census, 1870, Saverton township, Ralls County, Mo.; U.S. Federal Manuscript Census, 1900, Mason township, city of Hannibal, Marion County, Mo.; U.S. Federal Manuscript Census, 1880, city of Baltimore, eighth precinct, seventh ward, Baltimore County, Maryland; *Euphemia B. Koller v. John A. J. Koller,* August 5, 1893, book 33–B, 116, Baltimore City Circuit Court, Equity Papers A, Miscellaneous, Maryland State Archives, Annapolis; Charles D. Eby to Euphemia B. Koller, November 19, 1900, and "Sheriff's Deed under Trust Deed Sale," Miscellaneous Deed Record, book 162, 78–81, Marion County, Office of the Circuit Clerk and Recorder, Palmyra, Mo.; Marion M. Kerfoot and Ida M. Kerfoot to Mrs. E. B. Koller, April 30, 1902, Warranty Deed Record, book 22, 210, Pottawatomie County, Officer of the Court Clerk, Shawnee, Okla.; *Euphemia B. Koller, Plaintiff, v. John H. Woodbury Dermatological Institute and Frederick S. Kolle, Defendants,* April term, 1907, Cases and Exceptions, 1896–1911, book 2316, 34, Supreme Court of the State of New York, Appellate Division—First Department, New York State Library, Albany.

7. Jane Hemeyer, telephone conversation with author, October 30, 1994; Jane Hemeyer to author, October 29, 1994, and February 10, 1995.

but many individuals, Koller among them, continued to be drawn to seances, astrology, mesmerism, and spirit phenomena. Koller was especially interested in the mystical aspects of physical and emotional healing, including the power of hypnosis, magnetic healing, and clairvoyance. In fact, she learned (and at times demonstrated) the art of hypnotism after enrolling in a course at Sidney Weltmer's unconventional but popular American School of Magnetic Healing in 1902 in Nevada, Missouri.[8]

Koller was also likely influenced by nineteenth-century health and women's reform advocates who endorsed hydropathy—the application of cold-water therapeutics—to cure many physical and nervous ailments that plagued women at that time. When her niece, Mabel Sykes, contracted tuberculosis around the turn of the century, she took her to New Mexico for alternative health treatments, probably at one of the territory's mineral springs that had become fashionable for people with money at that time. Although the popularity of spas and mineral springs retreats had contributed to the demise of cold-water cures during the Gilded Age, they still retained certain common features. Those in charge of water-cure establishments stressed not only the miraculous curative powers of water, but also the importance of fresh air, relaxation, exercise, and dietary and other lifestyle changes. In many cases, such retreats also offered a female-centered culture and community that helped to nurture gender consciousness.[9]

Koller sought alternative health treatments for herself, too, sometimes staying in New Mexico for months at a time. A bundle of energy on occasions, while prone to excessive fatigue and exhaustion on others, she periodically sought prolonged treatments at a center in New Mexico to recover from nervous and physical exhaustion. Like so many middle-class women at the turn of the century, she at times displayed symptoms of irritability, physical weakness, nervous ailments, and other so-called fashionable diseases. She may have suffered from what is today called bipolar disorder, or manic depression, and like many others, she perhaps tried homeopathic and water-cure remedies out of frustration with more conventional medical practices and orthodox physicians.[10]

8. Maxine Harris to author, January 11, 1998; *Koller v. Woodbury Dermatological Institute*, 35.

9. Jane Hemeyer, telephone conversation with author, October 30, 1994.

10. Statement and Brief on Behalf of Defendant Euphemia B. Koller, 3–4, in *Molly Heinbach et al. v. Euphemia B. Koller et al.*, October term, 1919, box 222, reel 72 (no. 21), Pike County, Office of the Circuit Clerk, Bowling Green, Mo.; Ann Douglas Wood, "'The Fashionable Diseases': Women's Complaints and Their Treatment in Nineteenth-Century America," *Journal of Interdisciplinary History* 4 (summer 1973): 25–52.

As more and more college-educated and other independent women sought careers, personal autonomy, and productive outlets for their talents and creative energies, a confining Victorian ideology around the turn of the century had condemned them for channeling energies into higher education, social activism, or social independence instead of marriage and traditional domestic pursuits. According to this view, such women were disruptive to harmonious social and gender relations. Countless male doctors, educators, politicians, psychiatrists, and asylum directors warned that chasing intellectual stimulation and independence would damage women's emotional and physical health and only bring hysteria and insanity. For such "experts," the underlying cause of nervous ailments among such women was rooted in their rejection of traditional women's sphere. In other words, a heavy dose of submissiveness, domesticity, and male authority would provide the perfect antidote for what ailed them.[11]

Little wonder that Koller and many others rejected such remedies and became increasingly angry and insistent that less, not more, dependency on men was the answer to their problems. An increasingly suspicious, angry Koller was anything but deferential to men who were in a position to take advantage of women. Hannibal's Josh Brashears discovered this on May 5, 1909, when he went to her house to collect a bill for carpentry work that he had done for her. Either because she disputed the bill or because of the poor quality of his work, she gave him a sharp tongue-lashing at the door. He was so outraged by the "unladylike" boldness with which she attacked him that he filed a complaint against her for allegedly disturbing his peace. The police arrested her, but in a trial she was acquitted and released. As a local newspaper observed, "Brashears evidently doesn't like to have women talk to him in anything but a moderate feminine tone."[12]

The law was another source of empowerment for Koller, who had acquired considerable legal expertise, apparently through self-study, and at least in part because she did not trust lawyers. This gave her the confidence to act with the power of attorney on behalf of her sister's interests in a will dispute in Bowling Green in 1909, and it was this expertise that her sister soon enlisted in the legal battle that began in 1910 over the Ilasco tract. In Ilasco, Koller became known for her powerful intellect and knowledge of the law, as well as her eccentricities. Many regarded her as the community's

11. Carroll Smith-Rosenberg, *Disorderly Conduct: Visions of Gender in Victorian America* (New York: Knopf, 1985), 258; Braude, *Radical Spirits*, 157–61; John S. Haller Jr. and Robin M. Haller, *The Physician and Sexuality in Victorian America* (Urbana: University of Illinois Press, 1974), 24–43.
12. *Hannibal Courier-Post*, May 6, 1909.

resident legal expert and at times asked her for legal advice. Her contempt for lawyers was well-known. As one of her attorneys pointed out, both she and her sister believed "that moral delinquencies among lawyers are the rule instead of exceptions." In fact, he conceded, "They are excusable if not justified in assuming the law is a kind of puzzle to be worked out by craft and intrigue. From their standpoint it may absolutely seem so."[13]

Although the law represented an important outlet for Koller's intellectual passion, this was an area that provided few professional opportunities for women at the time, despite important breakthroughs. Most law schools accepted female students and most states admitted women to the bar by the early twentieth century, but the law remained a thoroughly male-dominated profession with formidable structural barriers for women. Institutionalized masculinity remained a central feature of the American legal system. Courtrooms, judges' chambers, bar association meetings, and informal and formal professional codes were filled with masculine discourse, rituals, and assumptions. In St. Louis, for example, the exclusion of women attorneys from the area bar association prompted Victoria Conkling-Whitney to found the Women's Bar Association of St. Louis in 1912. When feminists mounted a challenge to the barriers against women's participation in the legal profession, many male lawyers in the late nineteenth century resisted, insisting that women inherently lacked the intellectual and physical attributes necessary for the tough business of lawyering.[14]

By 1921, the year in which the Atlas Portland Cement Company bought the Ilasco tract at a sheriff's sale, Koller's contempt for the legal system and for Ralls County politicians had deepened considerably. Between 1910 and 1918, she had played an important role in financing and winning her sister's suit to probate her dead husband's will and inherit the tract—a suit made necessary because of interference by J. O. Allison, a former Democratic state representative, lawyer, and political boss of Ilasco who instigated an unsuccessful will dispute to smother the tract in litigation. Koller defended Heinbach, her nearly deaf sister, against allegations and gossip that she was crazy, pointing out that "the term crazy or insane was never applied to her so far as I can learn until she became possessed of valuable

13. Statement and Brief on Behalf of Defendant Euphemia B. Koller, 7, in *Heinbach et al. v. Koller et al.*, October term, 1919, box 222, reel 72 (no. 21); *J. E. Scott et al. v. Perry Tinsley et al.*, February term, 1909, box 168, reel 67 (no. 20); both in Pike County, Office of the Circuit Clerk, Bowling Green; Angelo Venditti, interview by author, July 9, 1993.

14. Lucile Wiley Ring, *Breaking the Barriers: The St. Louis Legacy of Women in Law, 1869–1969: The St. Louis Legacy of Women in Law, 1869–1969* (Manchester, Mo.: Independent Publishing, 1996), 39–47.

real estate." Koller also denied allegations that she intended to place a guardianship over Heinbach. "I shall never seek to make myself her guardian, nor aid any one who so seeks to be such," she pledged. "My belief is that if justly and fairly treated by men [with] whom it becomes necessary for her to transact business in the course of life, that she is competent to do so—and that this condition applies to mostly all women alone in the world unprotected by father or husband or brother."[15]

To repay Koller for her help in the will suit, Heinbach drew up a deed of joint tenancy with a survivorship clause, but this complicated things for the latter's attorney, Charles E. Rendlen Sr., a Hannibal Republican in the early stages of an ambitious political career. In 1918, taking advantage of tensions between the sisters over strategy during the long tenure of the case, Rendlen tempted Heinbach with a deal to sell the entire tract without consulting Koller. There was a catch, however, for Heinbach would receive only about half of the tract's value; the other half would go to the buyer. The plan required litigation to break the joint deed, but Rendlen already had lined up a buyer who allegedly offered to finance a suit against Koller. The buyer was Petru Sirbu, a Romanian labor agent for Atlas and incorporator of the Ilasco Supply Company, an Atlas subsidiary. Rendlen would prosecute the case on the premise that Koller had threatened physical coercion to force her sister to make her a co-owner of the tract. In the meantime, Heinbach must disappear and remain in hiding, allegedly out of fear that Koller planned to kill her and assume sole ownership of the Ilasco property.[16]

15. Euphemia B. Koller, "Affidavit," April 14, 1911, Miscellaneous Record, book 93, 214, Ralls County, Office of the Circuit Clerk and Recorder, New London. For a synopsis of Heinbach's case, see *Mary Alice Heinbach, Appellant, v. Jesse Heinbach et al.,* November 24, 1914, *Missouri Reports: Reports of Cases Determined by the Supreme Court of the State of Missouri* (Columbia, Mo.: E. W. Stephens Publishing Company, 1915), 262:69–91, and *Molly Heinbach v. Jesse Heinbach et al.,* April 26, 1918, *Missouri Reports: Reports of Cases Determined by the Supreme Court of the State of Missouri* (Columbia, Mo.: E. W. Stephens Publishing Company, 1919), 274:301–26. On the role and career of Allison, see *Portrait and Biographical Record of Marion, Ralls, Pike Counties Missouri 1895* (1895; reprint, New London, Mo.: Ralls County Book, 1982), 700–701; and Andrews, *City of Dust,* 45, 110, 111, 112, 213.

16. "Suggestions in Opposition to Motion to Reinstate Appeal," March 10, 1921, *Molly Heinbach v. Euphemia B. Koller,* case no. 21498, Missouri Supreme Court Files, Missouri State Archives, Jefferson City (hereinafter cited as MSCF-MSA). On Sirbu, see *Molly Heinbach v. Jesse Heinbach et al.,* April term, 1918, case no. 20303, trial transcript, 682–97, MSCF-MSA; and Andrews, *City of Dust,* 32–33, 51, 52–53, 110. For a brief biographical sketch of Rendlen, see David D. March, *The History of Missouri* (New York: Lewis Historical Publishing Company, 1967), 4:1104–5.

Between 1918 and 1921, Koller legally thwarted this equity suit to cut her out as co-owner of the tract, but during that time she and Rendlen developed a bitter hatred for each other, and she endured a systematic campaign of harassment aimed at driving her from the community. When Sirbu allegedly bought the tract in 1918, he immediately rented out the orchard tract surrounding the house in which Koller lived, and then he moved to Youngstown, Ohio. John Lendak, a Slovak immigrant who rented the pasture from Sirbu, quickly cut down a few fruit trees and pastured his cattle in the orchard, causing damage to the fruit. Koller petitioned for an injunction to keep him off the premises until the court decided who owned the land. She also feared for her personal safety, complaining that Lendak, who was also Rendlen's client, had often "assaulted her and used profane language in addressing her." She expressed fear of him "and the class of men" who came with him onto her property.[17]

When the Pike County circuit court ruled in late 1920 that Koller was a legal co-owner of the Ilasco tract, Heinbach returned from hiding and patched things up with her sister, only to have a guardianship placed over her by Benton B. Megown, the Ralls County probate judge. John E. Megown, a banker and brother of the probate judge, became her guardian, and cooperated in the execution of the sheriff's sale of the tract on December 16, 1921. Atlas plant superintendent Ray Hoffman took the land for only ten thousand dollars, less than half of what it was worth. Even the supportive *Ralls County Record* expressed a bit of sarcasm at how little money the land brought at the sale: "The price paid was cheap enough and the Atlas company has a bargain."[18]

This was the context in which Koller launched a legal battle that would end with the doors to the state mental hospital slamming shut behind her. First, she filed a motion to set aside the order of sale. On March 7, 1922, the circuit court denied her request for a new hearing but granted an appeal to the Missouri Supreme Court. To complicate matters for her, however, the

17. "Injunction Restraining the Renting of the Heinbach Orchard Tract for the Purpose of Pasturing Stock and the Damaging Thereby of Fruit-bearing Trees," in *Euphemia Belle Koller v. John Lendak*, May 9, 1919, case no. 11255, Ralls County, Office of the Circuit Clerk and Recorder, New London. On the hatred between Koller and Rendlen, see "Statement and Brief on Behalf of Defendant Euphemia B. Koller," 7–8, in *Heinbach et al. v. Koller et. al.*, October term, 1919, box 222 (no. 21), Pike County, Office of the Circuit Clerk, Bowling Green.

18. *Ralls County Record*, December 23, 1921. On the Megowns, see Floyd Calvin Shoemaker, *Missouri and Missourians: Land of Contrasts and People of Achievement* (Chicago: Lewis, 1943), 5:266–68; and Portrait and Biographical Record, 439–40, 453–54.

circuit court withheld her share of the proceeds of the sale—$2,520.16— thus making it even more difficult to finance her appeal to the state court.[19]

Acting as her own attorney, and with her appeal filed in the state supreme court, Koller initiated a damages suit against several county officials and her sister's guardian and lawyer, as well as against the Atlas Portland Cement Company. She insisted that her sister had been "lured by the interferance [sic] and criminal designs of others to throw the Heinbach estate into litigation, and so cover it with judgements, liens, and deeds of trust, thereby to enforce its sale." She complained, in fact, that her sister's sanity had been " 'Bargained away' for the sole purpose of money graft," and charged that probate judge Megown had "appropriated to his own use and profit" unspecified but significant sums of money.[20]

As Koller understood the case, certain lawyers and county officials may have played a sleazy role in what she regarded as "an open case of Grand Larceny & Embezzlement," but they were merely pawns on the chessboard of corporate politics. In her view, they were nothing more than instruments of the Atlas Portland Cement Company, which she charged had "incited the havoc." She sued the company for twenty-five thousand dollars as the "instigator," including a claim for punitive damages. In perhaps tragic recognition of the devastating toll that the case had taken on her, she described herself as a "talented and gifted writer" whose "mental vitality has been for 14 years, consumed in the struggle to live, and to keep her realty intact—But now, she is homeless—because all she owned is gone."[21]

From Koller's vantage point, it was crucial to remove the case from Ralls County, where tightly interlocked elites had maintained power since the Civil War era. To make matters worse, A. G. Croll, general superintendent of the Atlas Company, had married into a prominent New London family with close kinship ties to county officials, including the Megowns and circuit judge Charles T. Hays. In addition to the power that Atlas wielded by virtue of its economic importance in the county, this gave the company even greater leverage in county politics.[22]

19. "Motion for a New Trial," in *Mary Alice Heinbach v. Euphemia B. Koller et al.,* May 7, 1921, case no. 11429; Circuit Court Record, Book S, 334–35, 375–76, 383–86, 393, 401, 404; all in Ralls County, Office of the Circuit Clerk and Recorder, New London.

20. *Euphemia B. Koller v. Mary Alice Heinbach and her Guardian John E. Megown et al.,* case no. 11606, January 24, 1923, Ralls County, Office of the Circuit Clerk and Recorder, New London.

21. Ibid.

22. Andrews, *City of Dust,* 118–19.

Trying to handle this case, as well as the appeal to the state supreme court, by herself, and with limited resources, put Koller at a clear disadvantage. She requested and received from the state court a continuance on December 29, 1923, and another on April 7, 1924. She emphasized in her requests that she did not have the money to pay for the transcribing of evidence, the printing of the Bill of Exceptions, and her abstract and legal brief. Therefore, she needed a continuance in order to prosecute the damages suit against Atlas and the others; then, she argued, she would devote her full attention to the appeal before the state court.[23]

The Missouri Supreme Court sustained Koller's motion for a continuation of her appeal until the October term, 1924, but she quickly found herself facing a new threat. Benton Megown, a target of her suit, who had since left the probate court bench to become prosecuting attorney, went after her in his new position of authority. On June 14, 1924, just a week after Koller requested a change of venue in her damages suit, he and Sheriff E. S. Holt filed a petition of inquiry into her mental condition, urging the appointment of a guardian to protect her and her "considerable amount of property."[24]

The petition came at a critical time for Koller. The impending insanity hearing absorbed her energy and resources at a time when she needed to devote full attention to the appeal in the state supreme court and her damages suit in the circuit court. At stake now was the loss of her very legal identity and financial independence. If Megown succeeded in having her declared mentally incompetent, she would no longer be allowed to sue him or anyone else under the law without the consent of a court-appointed guardian.[25]

In the damages suit, Koller managed to file an amended petition on August 2, 1924, but time was running out on her appeal to the Missouri Supreme Court. On November 6, the state court threw out her appeal on grounds that she had failed to comply with the rules of the court. This upheld the Atlas Portland Cement Company's clear title to the Ilasco tract, including that part on which Koller and Heinbach were still living.[26]

23. *Mary Alice Heinbach, by her guardian J. E. Megown, respondent, v. Euphemia B. Kohler* [sic], *appellant,* April term, 1924, case no. 23970, MSCF-MSA.

24. E. S. Holt, informant, "In the Matter of the Alleged Insanity of Euphemia B. Koller," April 7, 1925, case no. 13217, Office of the Clerk, Hannibal Court of Common Pleas, Hannibal; Circuit Court Record, Book T, 9, 11, 70, and *Koller v. Heinbach and her guardian John E. Megown et al.,* January 24, 1923, case no. 11606, Ralls County, Office of the Circuit Clerk and Recorder, New London.

25. William R. Dittmar, *Insanity Laws* (New York: Oceana Publications, 1952), 42–43.

26. *Heinbach, respondent, v. Kohler* [sic], *appellant,* April term, 1924, case no. 23970, MSCF-MSA; Circuit Court Record, Book T, 116, Ralls County, Office of the Circuit Clerk and Recorder, New London.

It was clear from the probate court's procedure for selecting jurors for Koller's insanity hearing that she would face an uphill battle. Many of Missouri's county courts at that time used methods of obtaining jurors that gave added leverage to the officials who had filed the petition for an insanity hearing. In some cases, courts left the selection up to the sheriff, while in others the court "selected" jurors rather than drawing names from a box. Although the Missouri Supreme Court had invalidated a method in which prosecuting attorneys picked jurors, an appellate court had subsequently upheld a jury selected as the result of discussions between a county court and prosecuting attorney. In Koller's case, probate judge Harry G. Weaver empowered the constable of New London's Spencer township to summon twelve prospective jurors for the hearing. As a result, her jury would come from the New London area, not from Ilasco.[27]

At the insanity hearing on December 29, 1924, Koller faced ten hostile witnesses, including two doctors who offered an opinion that she was incompetent, and an assembled jury of six men. One of the hostile witnesses was a defendant in her damages suit, and others were county officials or otherwise closely tied to Atlas through business connections. The jurors were tightly connected to New London officials and bankers through kinship, marriage, and social ties. They were from families who had been among the county's leading settlers long before the Civil War.[28]

After the jury determined that Koller was of unsound mind, Judge Weaver appointed Samuel Elzea as her guardian. The well-connected Elzea, assistant cashier at the Bank of New London, formerly held positions with the Hannibal Trust Company and the Federal Reserve Bank in St. Louis. The *Ralls County Record* praised the court's actions, blaming Koller alone for all of the money spent to date on litigation over the Ilasco tract: "She has squandered thousands of dollars that belonged to her and her sister . . . and the verdict of the jury was a just one, both to Mrs. Koller and those with whom she has been associated."[29]

---

27. William Leonard Bradshaw, *The Missouri County Court: A Study of the Organization and Functions of the County Board of Supervisors in Missouri* (Columbia: University of Missouri Studies, 1931), 65–68; Estate of Euphemia B. Koller, Samuel Elzea, guardian, appointment made January 5, 1925, case no. 4713, Ralls County, Office of the Probate Clerk, New London.

28. Estate of Euphemia B. Koller, Samuel Elzea, guardian, appointment made January 5, 1925, case no. 4713, Ralls County, Office of the Probate Clerk, New London; E. S. Holt, informant, "In the Matter of the Alleged Insanity of Euphemia B. Koller," April 7, 1925, case no. 13217, Office of the Clerk, Hannibal Court of Common Pleas, Hannibal; Andrews, *Insane Sisters*, 175–76.

29. *Ralls County Record*, January 2, 1925. On Elzea's banking career, see *Ralls County Record*, July 12, 1918, January 16, 1920, September 7, 1923, and November 16, 1923.

With the guardianship established, the circuit court ordered Koller's damages suit stricken from the docket, but she geared up for an appeal of the verdict at her insanity trial. Thanks to a 1921 statute in Missouri's probate law that clarified the right of an alleged incompetent to appeal a probate court decision to the circuit court, she obtained an appeal to the circuit court and then a change of venue to the Hannibal Court of Common Pleas.[30]

When Koller's second insanity hearing opened in the Hannibal Court of Common Pleas on April 27, 1925, the Ralls County prosecuting attorney opened by insisting that she was afflicted with monomania, that she was obsessed with money and filing lawsuits. According to the law at that time, there were two general classes of mania: intellectual and moral. Monomania was a form of intellectual mania that often "grows out of a perversion of the intelligence, or reasoning powers." In effect, monomania amounted to partial insanity, either permanent or temporary. The prevailing legal view was that monomania usually led to delusions and paranoia. As one legal expert explained it, monomania "affects the mind of the subject as to one subject, or a limited number of subjects. . . . The person so affected may be perfectly rational, and even unusually bright, as to all other subjects; and be insane as to the particular subject which incites the mania."[31]

According to the legal definition of monomania-related delusions at the time, such alleged delusions could not be related to more abstract subjects such as legal and political theories. Neither could they be related to a person's unorthodox religious beliefs such as spiritualism, but Koller's prosecutor apparently disregarded this and made some of her unorthodox views an issue at this hearing. Unfortunately, a transcript does not appear in the records, but a newspaper reported that a witness asserted during testimony that Koller had "peculiar ways." It is not clear whether the witness was referring perhaps to Koller's spiritualist beliefs or other unorthodox views, but whatever the case, Koller felt compelled to interrupt the proceedings at

30. Circuit Court Record, Book T, 165, Ralls County, Office of the Circuit Clerk and Recorder, New London; Almon H. Maus, *Missouri Practice,* vol. 3, *Probate Law and Practice* (Kansas City: Vernon Law Book Company, 1960), 538–39; Charles U. Becker, comp., *Laws of Missouri* (Jefferson City, Mo.: Hugh Stephens Press, 1921), 124; Estate of Euphemia B. Koller, Samuel Elzea, guardian, appointment made January 5, 1925, case no. 4713, Ralls County, Office of the Probate Clerk, New London.

31. George A. Smoot, *The Laws of Insanity* (Kansas City: Vernon Law Book Company, 1929), 20–21; E. S. Holt, informant, "In the Matter of the Alleged Insanity of Euphemia B. Koller," April 7, 1925, case no. 13217, and Record 43, 459, 508–9, 515, 587, both in Office of the Clerk, Hannibal Court of Common Pleas, Hannibal.

that point. According to the reporter covering the hearing, she "demanded to be heard, and made a short talk on the subject upon which the witness was giving testimony."[32]

This time, Koller's attorney presented a much stronger case, due in part to the testimony of Dr. Robert Heavenridge, of Hannibal, and several Hannibal businessmen who had conducted financial transactions with Koller and apparently enjoyed less antagonistic relations with her. Perhaps even more importantly, many of her eighteen witnesses were Ilasco neighbors and supporters—farmers, workers, or both.[33]

Getting the case out of Ralls County paid off for Koller. It took the Hannibal jury less than twenty-five minutes to conclude that she was of sound mind, thus reversing the earlier verdict. Ralls County officials refused to concede, however, and filed a motion for a new trial on grounds that a doctor who was out of state during the hearing would have testified that Koller was "really an old nut" obsessed with filing lawsuits. The Hannibal court denied the motion but granted an appeal.[34]

With the appeal pending for the next year and a half, Koller continued to live in Ilasco but without direct access to her own money. Her guardian continued to control her money, and at times she was reduced to begging him, probate judge Weaver, and others at the Bank of New London to release payments or to honor checks that she had written to creditors so that she could continue to buy food and other necessities on credit in Ilasco. On November 5, 1926, for example, she desperately requested that Elzea pay a bill in the amount of $14.39 that she owed to C. E. Miller, an Ilasco merchant and justice of the peace. "Mr. Elzea," she pleaded, "please honor this request. It means my bread and butter. I want credit of Mr. Miller."[35]

Elzea's record of transactions and final settlement indicates that Koller had anything but a luxurious existence during this period in Ilasco. In fact, the evidence suggests that the guardianship further marginalized her. During the first year of the guardianship, the balance of her estate only dropped from $2,490.04 to $2,219.67. According to these figures, she spent only $270.37 for the entire year, including a guardian's commission of $30.00

32. Smoot, *Laws of Insanity,* 21–23; *Ralls County Record,* May 1, 1925.

33. Estate of Euphemia B. Koller, Samuel Elzea, guardian, appointment made January 5, 1925, case no. 4713, Ralls County, Office of the Probate Clerk, New London.

34. *Hannibal Courier-Post,* April 28, 1925; Record 43, 515, 587, and E. S. Holt, "In the Matter of the Alleged Insanity of Euphemia B. Koller," April 7, 1925, case no. 13217; both in Office of the Clerk, Hannibal Court of Common Pleas, Hannibal.

35. Estate of Euphemia B. Koller, Samuel Elzea, guardian, appointment made January 5, 1925, case no. 4713, Ralls County, Office of the Probate Clerk, New London.

and probate fees of $8.15. There is no indication in her probate file that Elzea or the Bank of New London credited any payments of interest to her estate.[36]

Squeezed by the guardianship, Koller's mode of dress and spartan living conditions reflected her descent into broken health and spirits. If her guardian or any Ralls County officials were concerned about her physical and mental health, they apparently did nothing to ensure that she had access to medical care. Elzea's record does not show a single payment to a doctor for the entire period of her guardianship. The collective memory of Ilasco residents and relatives who remember her reveals vivid images of the impoverished living conditions that she endured during the final phase of her life in the community. Melvin Sanders and Angelo Venditti recalled that she wore ankle-length dresses made of gunnysacks, and Anna Sunderlik Venditti remembered that she often went about the town dirty, accompanied by several dogs that lived with her. Fay Scheiner, one of her great-nieces, recalled that she, in fact, often traveled between Ilasco and Hannibal looking like a "rag picker."[37]

It is not clear when county officials first considered involuntary commitment of Koller as an option. As a result of state politics and changes in the governance of Missouri's mental institutions, Hannibal and New London interests had gained influence in the management and oversight of those institutions in the early 1920s. In 1921, the legislature had created a governor-appointed State Eleemosynary Board with authority to appoint superintendents and stewards. Arthur M. Hyde, the newly elected Republican governor, named Hannibal Republican attorney Charles E. Rendlen Sr., Koller's bitter enemy, to the bipartisan board. Perhaps at Rendlen's request, he also appointed Joseph W. Elliott, a former postmaster and one of New London's leading, if rare, Republicans, as the steward of State Hospital No. 1 for the Insane in Fulton. Elliott had once been in the mercantile business and was a farmer from whom the Atlas Portland Cement Company bought hay for its horses and mules at the Ilasco plant. Elliott, too, had close ties to the Bank of New London.[38]

Elliott may have served as an important conduit of information between Ralls County officials and Fulton state hospital authorities, but Republican

36. Ibid.

37. Ibid.; Melvin Sanders, interview by author, July 17, 1993; Angelo Venditti, interview by author, July 9, 1993; Anna Sunderlik Venditti, interview by author, July 27, 1993; Fay Scheiner, interview by author, July 13, 1996.

38. First Biennial Report of the Board of Managers of the State Eleemosynary Institutions of the State of Missouri, 1921–1922, 6–8.

intraparty squabbles led to his removal as steward of the Fulton hospital, and to Rendlen's subsequent resignation from the state board. Soon after the Hannibal jury found Koller to be of sound mind, the new Republican governor, Sam A. Baker, replaced Elliott. Rendlen, whose term on the eleemosynary board did not expire until June 19, 1926, then resigned in protest, complaining that Governor Baker, a fellow Republican, was playing patronage politics with the board. When Elliott returned to New London, he accepted a position on the Board of Directors of the Bank of New London—the repository of Koller's money.[39]

What, if anything, precipitated the county's final action against Koller in 1927 is not clear. On February 13, 1926, the county sheriff had filed the final settlement of the partition case that led to Atlas's purchase of the Ilasco tract. Perhaps for public relations purposes, Atlas allowed Koller to live on land to which it now held clear title, particularly since the house in which she lived did not stand in the way of company quarrying or manufacturing operations. In fact, plant officials could have continued to tolerate this arrangement, simply ignoring her and allowing her to live out her remaining years on Atlas property in Ilasco. This would not have hurt Atlas financially, since the company charged other town residents only a nominal fee of one dollar per month in ground rent.

At stake in this case, however, was much more than mere ground rent. Koller had become consumed with passionate, perhaps obsessive hatred for those who had handed the Ilasco tract over to the cement company. To local officials, she had become more than a mere nuisance; she stood in the way of the company's paternalistic plan to promote schools and churches on land that once belonged to her and her sister. In a community now dominated by Atlas paternalism, Koller was a symbol of defiance against the methods by which a corporation wielded power in a county that it thoroughly dominated. From the perspective of county officials, they had run out of options in regard to removing her from Ilasco. In most cases, it was at the request of a relative or guardian that private patients were involuntarily committed to mental institutions, but if her brother, New London's Tom Sykes, would not call for confinement proceedings, county officials would have to take the initiative. If no male would step forward to assert patriarchal authority over her, the state then would have to assume that function.[40]

39. *Ralls County Record*, April 24, 1925, January 15, 1926; Missouri Secretary of State, *Official Manual, 1923–1924* (Jefferson City, Mo.: Hugh Stephens Press, 1923), 649; *Hannibal Courier-Post*, May 8, 1925.

40. Bradshaw, *The Missouri County Court*, 187.

In many cases of alleged insanity around the nation, state hospitals often screened potential patients in advance. In Alabama, for example, statutes required judges, physicians, or families to respond first to a list of interrogatories about the individual in question before a hearing could be scheduled. The state hospital put forth the interrogatories to learn as much as possible about the behavior of the individual beforehand. This meant that insanity hearings usually took place only after the hospital superintendent had already agreed to admit the patient. In this context, the very fact that a hearing took place at all predisposed the judge and others involved in the case to conclude even before the hearing that the person at the center of the inquiry was insane. Doctors were more likely than not to endorse commitment if the individual in question exhibited any behavior that might be construed as strange, particularly if that person seemed disrespectful or antagonistic. Given this presumption of insanity, such hearings were often mere formalities; even if hospital physicians questioned the commitment, they at times used broad criteria to justify certifying the patient anyway.[41]

Of course, such procedures were costly, and this is perhaps what deterred Ralls County officials from pushing forward their appeal of the verdict in which a Hannibal jury had vindicated Koller in 1925. On April 5, 1927, however, the Missouri General Assembly amended a statute to allow county officials to recover money from the estate of insane persons to compensate for their maintenance, support, or confinement. This opened the door to new proceedings against Koller without the county's having to bear any of the expenses. County officials then acted quickly, first by closing the books on the appeal of the Hannibal verdict. On August 6, 1927, Koller's guardian handed over to her the balance of her estate—$1280.94— but four days later, the authorities went after her again. Sheriff J. A. Palmer and new prosecuting attorney Oney Newlon petitioned for yet another inquiry into her alleged insanity. Probate Judge Weaver hurriedly scheduled a hearing for August 18, giving Koller only one week to prepare her defense. Koller apparently did not have the time or inclination to get an attorney, and, as a result, six male jurors heard only the testimony of prosecution witnesses. After a quick finding of insanity, judge Weaver reappointed Elzea as her guardian and ordered the sheriff to haul her as a private patient to the State Hospital for the Insane at Fulton as soon as possible. The county would bear none of the financial responsibility. To add insult to in-

41. John S. Hughes, "Alabama's Families and Involuntary Commitment of the Insane, 1861–1900: New Solutions to Old Problems" (Institute for Legal Studies, University of Wisconsin–Madison, Working Papers, ser. 2, May 1987), 19–20; McCandless, *Moonlight, Magnolias, and Madness,* 265–69.

jury, the court required Koller to pay the expenses of her own confinement.[42]

Koller's case raises intriguing questions. Was she, in fact, clinically insane? Six male jurors who were laypersons had decided her fate, influenced by a handful of lay witnesses and a single doctor. Most doctors, themselves, could hardly qualify as "expert" witnesses in such matters at the time, for even they at best had only a limited, superficial understanding of insanity.[43] Most Ralls County officials, lawyers, and Atlas officials probably had no trouble believing that Koller was crazy, indeed, for continuing to protest the sale of the Ilasco tract. From this perspective, what else could explain her rebellious, eccentric, and defiant behavior?

Of course, there were plenty of "old nuts" in Ilasco and other communities, but most did not end up in institutions for the insane. Why Koller? In many cases of women's insanity around the turn of the century, doctors often attributed insanity to their forceful personalities and willful resistance to male authority and socially proscribed roles. If Koller was a "monomaniac" obsessed with litigation, the same could be said about some of the male lawyers who seemed equally obsessed with initiating and continuing litigation against both Koller and her sister. Such lawyers, of course, earned a good living through manipulation of litigation, and they acquired status and built political careers in the courts. Not so with Koller: The law was still a man's game, and for defending herself and counterattacking in response to litigation against her and her sister, she in contrast became an "old nut" allegedly obsessed with filing lawsuits.

Would Koller have been confined to the state hospital if she had not defied the Atlas Portland Cement Company? Would she have experienced a different fate if she had simply taken her share of the proceeds from the sale of the Ilasco tract and left town in 1921? Or, what if she had then melted into the community, asking with appropriate deference and gratitude to remain in her former house and pay rent to Atlas, like so many other Ilasco residents? Would her peculiar ways have then disturbed county officials enough to take her off to Fulton?

In 1946, sociologist Edwin M. Lemert pointed out that rural communities such as Ilasco generally found more flexible ways to absorb and take care of eccentric residents, even if they were clinically insane. Why, then,

42. Estate of Euphemia B. Koller, Samuel Elzea, guardian, appointment made August 22, 1927, case no. 4858, and Estate of Euphemia B. Koller, deceased, Henry T. Sykes, administrator, appointment made March 10, 1930, case no. 4998; both in Ralls County, Office of the Probate Clerk, New London.

43. Hughes, "Alabama's Families and Involuntary Commitment of the Insane," 8–9.

could a community such as Ilasco, a popular place for folk superstitions, ghost stories, hypnotists, traveling medicine shows, and other peddlers of unorthodox remedies, no longer make room for Koller? What was the source of opposition to her continued presence in the community?[44]

As a company-dominated town, Ilasco was far from representative of rural communities, however, and Koller's broad-based defiance of male authority and corporate class prerogatives tested the paternalism of county authorities and Atlas officials beyond endurance. In the view of many doctors at that time, female insanity typically resulted when forceful, deviant women rejected male authority or deviated from conventional roles. Koller's combativeness and persistent attacks on the New London courthouse as a den of thieves in the service of Atlas vividly exposed the "iron fist" inside the "velvet glove" that dispensed company paternalism. From the standpoint of county authorities, only a show of state-delivered force in the form of hospital confinement could silence her and put an end to the turmoil that had lasted for seventeen years.[45]

44. Edwin M. Lemert, "Legal Commitment and Social Control," *Sociology and Social Research* 30 (May–June 1946): 371, 373. On the culture of Ilasco, see Andrews, *City of Dust*, 228–54.

45. Elaine Showalter, "Victorian Women and Insanity," in Andrew Scull, ed., *Madhouses, Mad-Doctors, and Madmen: The Social History of Psychiatry in the Victorian Era* (Philadelphia: University of Pennsylvania Press, 1981), 324.

Breaking into Politics

Emily Newell Blair and the Democratic Party in the 1920s

Virginia Laas

In the first decade after women gained the vote, Emily Newell Blair was a familiar name to anyone interested in the progress of women in partisan politics. Vice chairman of the Democratic National Committee from 1922 to 1928, she worked to integrate women into party politics and sought to gain positions of leadership for them within party organization. As one of only a few female politicians visible on the national scene, she demonstrated that women could be capable political activists. Although she did not gain equality for women, her own career demonstrated that a woman could lead and could be accepted by men. At the same time, she wrote regularly in national magazines and journals, explaining her approach to and justification for women's active participation in party leadership. Through her articles and interviews, Blair wrestled with the problems women faced in striving for equality in the public arena. While she was never able to solve the problem of power sharing, her intelligent discussions, shaped by her own practical experience in breaking into politics, explored a variety of approaches to thinking about men and women and political power in the first years after suffrage.[1]

1. Among the many works dealing with women in the years after suffrage was won are Kristi Andersen, *After Suffrage: Women in Partisan and Electoral Politics before the New Deal* (Chicago: University of Chicago Press, 1996); Dorothy M. Brown, *Setting a Course: American Women in the 1920s* (Boston: Twayne Publishers, 1987); J. Stanley Lemons, *The Woman Citizen: Social Feminism in the 1920s* (Urbana: University of Illinois

Born in Joplin, Missouri, in 1877, Emily Newell grew up in nearby Carthage. After one year of college and two years of schoolteaching, she married her high school classmate, Harry Blair. Hers was a typical, conventional, small-town, middle-class life, filled with children, friends, club work, civic projects, and extended families. In many ways, it was an idyllic life: she loved her husband, took pride in her children, enjoyed her friends, and was devoted to her mother, brother, and sisters. She had all that small-town life could offer. There were hints, however, that it was not enough. In August 1905, she wrote in her diary: "I wish I could find the gang as interesting as they find each other. We seem to have such different ideals & ideas on all subjects. With them it is all have, have have & not at all be or *do*. I wonder if they have any aspirations other than for money. Do any of them long to improve, to have culture, to know, to be gentle—or perhaps they do & fail just as utterly as I. But they seem so much happier & better satisfied with life than I & is it not because I do aspire & fail & know it."[2]

By 1909, Blair had begun to involve herself in projects that gave notice that her life was not to be commonplace. She was an original organizer and promoter of the Carthage Co-Operative Kitchen, an innovative plan to lessen the burden of food production on nearly twenty middle-class families. For more than two years, these friends shared three meals a day. She even published an article about it in the *Woman's Home Companion*. She also began to publish articles and short stories in popular magazines such as *Cosmopolitan, Outlook, Woman's Home Companion, Lippincott,*

Press, 1973); Felice D. Gordon, *After Winning: The Legacy of the New Jersey Suffragists, 1920–1947* (New Brunswick, N.J.: Rutgers University Press, 1986); Nancy Cott, "Across the Great Divide: Women in Politics before and after 1920," in Louise A. Tilly and Patricia Gurin, eds., *Women, Politics, and Change* (New York: Russell Sage Foundation, 1990); and Paul Taylor, "The Entrance of Women into Party Politics: The 1920s" (Ph.D. diss., Harvard University, 1966).

2. Emily Newell Blair Diary, August 27, 1905, folder 50, Emily Newell Blair Papers, Western Reserve Historical Society Library, Cleveland, Ohio (hereinafter cited as ENB Papers). Biographical sketches of Blair include those by Estelle B. Freedman, *Dictionary of American Biography,* supp. 5, 61–63; and by Margot Jerrard in *Notable American Women: The Modern Period: A Biographical Dictionary,* ed. Barbara Sicherman et al. (Cambridge: Harvard University Press, Belknap Press, 1980), 82–83. Useful contemporary profiles are Ernestine Evans, "Women in the Washington Scene," *Century Magazine,* August 1923, 507–17; and Anne Hard, "Emily Newell Blair, 'Politician,'" *Woman Citizen,* April 1926, 15–16. For a current evaluation of Blair, see Kathryn Anderson, "Practicing Feminist Politics: Emily Newell Blair and U.S. Women's Political Choices in the Early Twentieth Century," *Journal of Women's History* 9 (autumn 1997): 50–72.

and *Harper's Bazaar,* establishing her reputation as a professional writer.[3] Through the regular publication of her short stories and articles, Blair became a familiar and respected figure to women and men not only in Missouri but also throughout the country. As her writing career developed, Blair found that she had other talents that further expanded her horizons and contacts. Her active participation in the 1914 countywide campaign to pass a tax for building a new almshouse had a profound effect on her: "Never afterwards was I to be content to limit my social intercourse to my own small social circle. I felt suddenly part of a larger whole."[4]

Blair's experience in the suffrage movement gives proof to historian William Chafe's contention that, for many middle-class women, suffrage "became the final link between the private culture of women's separate sphere and the public culture of traditional politics." As editor of *Missouri Woman,* the state suffragists' monthly magazine, she became a familiar figure to women across the state. In 1916, Blair came to the attention of national suffrage leaders when she attended a planning session for the suffrage demonstration to be held at the Democratic National Convention in St. Louis. It was she who suggested to Carrie Chapman Catt the famous Golden Lane—the walkless, talkless demonstration at the 1916 Democratic Convention in St. Louis. Conventions, conferences, and association with national leaders gave Blair a sense of direction and a taste of new possibilities. She later thought of her suffrage days as "a step out." It was during this period, she wrote in her autobiography, "there came to me the thought, ambition, or temptation, whatever it was, that my life need not be bounded by the four walls of a home. Another way to put it would be that the cocoon of Victorianism was beginning to crack."[5]

Special domestic conditions made it possible for Blair to participate in public life. Her mother lived in her home for extended periods, and she had four younger sisters who were willing and able to help with her children. Equally important, her husband, Harry, content in his small-town law practice, supported her efforts. It was not altogether easy; she often felt guilty and on occasion drew back to her family responsibilities. Carthage

3. The experiment lasted from September 1909 to January 1912. *Carthage Evening Press,* September 17, 1909, December 19, 1911; "Our Cooperative Kitchen," *Woman's Home Companion,* October 1910, 50.

4. Blair, *Bridging Two Eras,* 158; *Carthage Evening Press,* February 11, 1914.

5. William Chafe, "Women's History and Political History: Some Thoughts on Progressivism and the New Deal," in Nancy A. Hewitt and Suzanne Lebsock, eds., *Visible Women: New Essays on American Activism* (Urbana: University of Illinois Press, 1993), 105; Blair, *Bridging Two Eras,* 162.

was provincial and conservative; her activities did not fit the traditional mold. In these early years, she faced a constant struggle to balance personal fulfillment and conventional expectations.[6] In 1916 Catt had urged her to come to New York and work for suffrage at the national level. That was too big a step, and Blair had declined.

Her opportunity to move to a wider stage came during World War I, when Harry volunteered to go overseas for the YMCA. Emily moved to Washington to work for Anna Howard Shaw and Ida Tarbell on the Woman's Committee of the Council of National Defense. In Washington, she increased her knowledge of publicity tactics, learned about organization and administration, and, more importantly, associated with "women of dominant personalities, brilliant, full of ideas, the leaders of women in the country. And they took their jobs seriously." Her mother and son went with her, while her daughter attended boarding school in Wisconsin. Those seven months in Washington during the war were, she wrote, her "Rubicon." It allowed her to think of life outside small-town Missouri: "thereafter, it was taken for granted by myself and everyone else that I should pursue extra home activities to any extent I wished, even if they took me away from home for weeks."[7]

While she was in Washington, Blair tangled for the first time with Missouri senator James A. Reed and earned his lasting animosity. It was an enmity that followed her for her entire political career. With the backing of the Pendergast political machine in Kansas City, Reed had been elected to the U.S. Senate in 1910. On the Senate floor, Reed made what suffragists thought were disparaging remarks about them. Intimating that their lobbying effort was "a disgraceful proceeding," and "obnoxious," he characterized suffragists as "a petticoat brigade" with a "female general" and referred to "some fair damsel of uncertain age." When Illinois senator J. Hamilton Lewis defended the women, Reed replied: "when a man comes at you with doubled-up fists and with the glare of battle in his eyes, you know what to do; but when you catch a flutter of lace, and your nostrils

6. Glenna Matthews has vividly captured the dilemma faced by women in politics during the 1920s: "There was no cultural expectation that a woman should be able to 'have it all.' If she chose serious engagement with politics, for example, she was unlikely to combine this with a husband, let alone raising children. In the event she was brave enough to attempt to combine public life with marriage and children, she was expected to bear the entire responsibility for the maintenance of private life herself. Small wonder that so few women entered into this terrain." See Matthews, *The Rise of Public Woman: Woman's Power and Woman's Place in the United States, 1630–1970* (New York: Oxford University Press, 1992), 178–79.

7. Blair, *Bridging Two Eras*, 185–86, 208.

are intoxicated with a delicate perfume, you do not know whether you ought to resort to blows or embraces." Reed maintained that he was referring to Lewis, who had a penchant for elegant, rather foppish dress, but suffragists, including Blair, as she later explained, thought his remarks "revealed a contempt for women, an insult which should not, I believed, go unchallenged."[8] And so she wrote Helen Miller, the president of the Missouri Equal Suffrage Association. Her views were published. Reed's remarks, known as his "Kisses or Kicks" speech, rallied Missouri suffragists, and Blair gained notoriety as an opponent of James Reed.

Reed caused further rupture in the Missouri Democratic Party as the leading Democratic "irreconcilable" to the League of Nations, and his strident opposition embroiled Missouri Democrats in a bitter fight. The remarkable result was that St. Louis Wilsonians allied with outstate Democrats to deny Reed, the senior senator from Missouri, a place in the state's delegation to the National Convention in 1920. As Franklin Mitchell has pointed out, "in no state did the League question provoke so much bitterness and dissension as it did in Missouri."[9] The very divisiveness of Missouri Democratic politics provided the opportunity for Blair to move into national politics and broadened her base of support beyond suffragists. Believing that the Democratic Party was the best vehicle in the struggle for social justice, liberalism, internationalism, and feminism, Blair took strong stands on the very issues that inflamed Missouri Democrats. As a veteran of the suffrage campaign, a fervent supporter of Woodrow Wilson's League of Nations, and an implacable foe of bossism, she rose to power on the strength of her support from clubwomen, suffragists, and internationalist male Democrats from outstate Missouri.[10]

Blair attended that 1920 Democratic state convention on a Carthage proxy. It was her first convention, and she was impressed by the role played by Katherine Martin from Cape Girardeau. Representing the type of woman who would soon follow Blair's lead, Martin had been active in

8. *Congressional Record*, 65th Cong., 2d sess., September 27, 1918, 11774–77; Blair, *Bridging Two Eras*, 191.

9. Mitchell, *Embattled Democracy*, 16; Jan Hults, "The Senatorial Career of James Alexander Reed" (Ph.D. diss., University of Kansas, 1987).

10. As Robin Muncy has pointed out, "the battles of partisan women for representation in party hierarchies and on ballots succeeded best when intense electoral competition sent parties scurrying for every vote they could muster." See Muncy, "'Women Demand Recognition': Women Candidates in Colorado's Election of 1912," in *We Have Come to Stay: American Women and Political Parties, 1880–1960*, ed. Melanie Gustafson, Kristie Miller, and Elisabeth I. Perry (Albuquerque: University of New Mexico Press, 1999), 45.

the suffrage movement and the Women's Christian Temperance Union. The president of the Missouri Federation of Women's clubs, she was a member of the first Women's Democratic State Committee, effectively participating in state politics. Opposed to Reed as a delegate to the national convention, Martin took the platform, pointedly reminding the unruly assembly that women voters outnumbered Kansas City votes. Blair later recalled her reaction to Martin's speech: "Why she was talking politics. Not a word of sentiment—just common sense. When she finished, the whole audience stood and cheered."[11]

In the midst of this controversy over Senator Reed came Emily Newell Blair's bid for party office. When Missouri's first national committeewoman, Mattie (Mrs. Burris) Jenkins of Kansas City, resigned in February 1921, Blair was the overwhelming choice of women for the position. They remembered her rebuttal of the nationally known Reed in his attack on suffragists in 1918. As she later recalled: "this incident dramatized me as an opponent. Those who opposed him on other grounds put me forward as their spokesman; and those who agreed with him opposed me. Thus I gained a following and notoriety I would probably never otherwise have had."[12]

Letters sent to Missouri's national committeeman, Edward Goltra, demonstrate that support and illustrate the overlapping network of women's organizations and alliances. Laura Brown of Joplin, an old suffrage friend who served as treasurer of the Women's Democratic State Committee of Missouri, wrote Goltra: "I have a number of pledges from the State committee men and women, and have not heard of anyone who objected to Mrs. Blair or suggested any one else." State committeewoman Rachel Tingle of Butler, pointing out Blair's opposition to Reed, asserted to her friend Mary Semple Scott: "I firmly believe that if the committee doesn't see fit to put such a woman as Mrs. Blair and what she stands for, on the committee—that our best workers will quit. I have found this the sentiment everywhere." Scott's support for Blair was unequivocal: "Mrs. Blair could lead the women as few others could." Her analysis was pointed: "given the kind of high-standard, big gauge leaders the women themselves want, they will stay in the Party and help bring it to victory and great deeds—while if

11. On Martin, see clipping in box 23, folder 21, Edward Goltra Papers, Missouri Historical Society, St. Louis; *Missouri Manual, 1923–1924,* "Biographical and Genealogical Sketches of Members attending the Missouri Constitutional Convention, 1922–23," TS, State Historical Society of Missouri, University of Missouri–Columbia; Blair, *Bridging Two Eras,* 200–201.

12. Blair, *Bridging Two Eras,* 193.

they are not organized by a leader they trust, they will either drift to the other party or eventually, form a separate independent party." She also connected Blair's election to opposition to Reed: "If Reed is to be defeated the movement should be started *at once* by appointing such a woman as Mrs. Blair."[13]

In addition to an official endorsement from the executive committee of the Women's Democratic Central Committee and a personal letter from Anna McKnight of King City, the chairman of the Women's Democratic State Committee, men and women from across the state supported her nomination. Although Goltra had no vote in the matter, he was convinced that Blair was the "choice of the Democrats" and that "there is no question in my mind but that Mrs. Blair is equipped to thoroughly and efficiently fill the position."[14]

It was not until the last day of October, just the day before the National Committee meeting, that the Missouri Democratic Committee elected Blair. Her selection became intertwined with the attempt to replace George White as chairman of the national committee. There was a movement to name St. Louis attorney Breckinridge Long as successor to White, who had presided over the disastrous 1920 presidential campaign. Long, an opponent of the Reed faction (Long ran against Reed in the 1922 senatorial primary), agreed to back Blair in the state committee in exchange for support of his chairmanship candidacy on the national committee. Reed and his supporters did not, of course, support Blair; only when they realized that Blair had enough votes for election did they decide not to offer a competing candidate. Although she became an important national figure, her relationship to Missouri Democrats was always strained. She was not a woman who could be docilely led; she had political support (from club and suffrage women) that was independent of the male power structure; and she belonged to a faction of men and women who opposed bossism and Reed and supported the League of Nations. Reed and Tom Pendergast, however, wielded sufficient power to keep her continually on the defensive within

13. Laura Brown to Edward Goltra, September 5, 1921; Rachel Tingle to Mary Semple Scott, October 13, 1921; Mary Semple Scott to Goltra, October 14, 1921, all in box 20, folder 20, Goltra Papers.

14. Goltra to Frank L. Gass, October 21, 1921, Ellis Meredith to Goltra, October 20, 1921, W. W. Fray Jr. to Goltra, October 22, 1921, and Goltra to Mrs. Ellis Meredith, October 24, 1921, box 16, folder 6, Goltra Papers. See also Mary E. Parsons to Goltra, April 23 [1921]; Anna McKnight to Goltra, May 28, 1921; Laura Brown to Goltra, June 4, 1921; Goltra to Mrs. J. W. McKnight, June 9, 1921; Mrs. J. Arthur Daugherty to Goltra, June 20, 1921; and Haywood Scott to Goltra, October 18, 1921, all in box 20, folder 20, Goltra Papers.

the state. As she later admitted, "never while I was National Committee-woman was I cordially welcomed at any Missouri Caucus or Convention."[15]

When she joined the Democratic National Committee, she surprised many of the men. No strident harridan, she was a short, forty-three-year-old matron who was very much a lady. Coming from southwest Missouri, she appeared to be a congenial combination of southern and western woman. One reporter described "that gentle exterior and feminine beauty of hers which masks an analytical mind and a steel will."[16] Comfortable working with men, she enjoyed an easy camaraderie with them. Still, it became well known that one Missouri politician had early on nicknamed her after a popular bourbon, "Southern Comfort"—she went down smooth but had a powerful kick.

Because many men were suspicious of women in politics, Blair began her tenure by modestly soliciting the advice of her male counterpart. Confessing "I am such a beginner in politics," she plied Goltra with questions on procedures and protocol, asking, "Will you not take pity on my ignorance and tell me." Blair's tactics give proof to historian Anne Firor Scott's observation that "maintaining the ladylike image was still considered to be good politics."[17]

She quickly, however, set forth her agenda, writing to the new national chairman, Cordell Hull, on November 28, setting out her ideas for bringing women voters to the Democratic Party, "tiding us over this period when women have outgrown 'Women's Aid Societies' and yet still need some 'Special Organization.'" To bring women to equality within the party, such an organization should be, she thought, a "collaboration not segregation." Suggesting that the placement of a woman at national headquarters to serve as "a connecting link between the women democrats and the National Committee," she emphasized that the appointee should be given appropriate standing by making her a vice chairman and placing her on the executive committee. While never mentioning her own name to Hull, she pointed out that someone "who has already gained the confidence of women" must

15. While Long supported Blair, he was not elected chairman of the DNC. Robert E. Woolley to Mrs. Brooks Peters Church, September 20, 1950, box 12, folder 84, ENB Papers. Newspaper clipping, dated St. Louis, December 29, in possession of Newell Blair. Edward Goltra to George White, telegram, February 17, 1921, box 16, folder 2, Goltra Papers. *Joplin News Herald,* November 1, 1921. Blair, *Bridging Two Eras,* 217.

16. Hard, "Emily Newell Blair, 'Politician,'" 16.

17. ENB to Goltra, November 17, 1921, box 18, folder 10, Goltra Papers; Anne Firor Scott, "After Suffrage: Southern Women in the Twenties," *Journal of Southern History* 30 (August 1964): 301.

fill the position. She did, however, tell Goltra that "women in different parts of the country" were asking her to organize the women and that she felt the job was "a great opportunity." The women of Missouri took matters into their own hands, sending a petition to Hull urging the appointment of Blair to head the organization of women.[18]

After obtaining Goltra's approval, Chairman Hull called Blair to Washington to be his assistant representing women in the party. With the title of "Resident Headquarters National Committeewoman," she and her assistant, Marion Banister (Senator Carter Glass's sister), began planning a program of action. It was not easy. All the records from the 1920 campaign of the previous chairman of the Democratic Woman's Bureau, Elizabeth Bass, had been destroyed, and the men at national headquarters were not overjoyed with Blair's presence. In Blair's view, "it was woman leadership the men instinctively feared."[19] It was a problem that Carrie Catt had anticipated. At the 1920 League of Women Voters convention, Catt had warned that men would accept women voters but, she claimed, "when it comes to administrative work within the party, that is still the exclusive man's business." Historian Kristi Andersen points out that Catt was not alone in recognizing the difficulties women faced in exercising real power, retelling a favorite anecdote of Cornelia Bryce Pinchot. When one man worried about woman suffrage, the other, while allowing that voting women were acceptable, concluded, "Just don't let them get into politics."[20]

On the brink of the passage of the Nineteenth Amendment, Blair had begun to define her vision of women's role in politics. Never did she think that women would clean up politics or make it more moral. Never assuming that women would vote as a bloc, she thought they would act just as males did: their political goals would be determined by their economic and social status, their emotions and ideals. Proclaiming that "the brain is not a sex organism," Blair anticipated women making decisions "as human beings, irrespective of sex." From the beginning, however, she understood the fundamental conundrum that had always faced the woman's movement:

18. ENB to Cordell Hull, November 28, 1921, box 16, folder 7; ENB to Goltra, December 1, 1921, box 18, folder 10; Petition of Missouri Democratic women, enclosed with letter, Mrs. Thornton Brown to Goltra, January 24, 1922, box 16, folder 8, in Goltra Papers.

19. Blair, *Bridging Two Eras,* 222. Cordell Hull to Goltra, February 4, 1922; Goltra to Mrs. Thornton Brown, February 7, 1922, box 16, folder 9; ENB to Goltra, March 7, 1922, box 18, folder 10, Goltra Papers; Undated press release, folder 48, ENB Papers.

20. Cited in Andersen, *After Suffrage,* 80.

the desire for equality coupled with the recognition of difference. While she had personally associated with many women who were intelligent and sophisticated leaders, she recognized that the mass of women voters needed special encouragement to overcome their reluctance to play a part on the public stage. She was sure that women should participate in politics equally with men, but Blair knew that inexperienced women needed a "transition period" of education and special consideration before they could compete on a basis of equality. In addition, there were some issues, she recognized, "which custom has made into women's special interests." However much she wanted sex not to be an issue for politicians, she knew that on topics such as child labor, education, health, marriage, and divorce laws, "women stand apart as women."[21]

In 1922, after her appointment as "Resident Headquarters National Democratic Committeewoman," Blair was quite optimistic that women could make special contributions to politics. They brought to the forum, she claimed, "the idealism of the untried, the zeal of youth, the devotion of the long denied." She envisioned women leading the reform of party organization by offering their unpaid, disinterested labor, by putting principles before self-advancement, and by replacing the male inclination to work only at campaign time with women's habits of year-round organization.[22]

Despite a cool reception from the office workers in the Washington headquarters, Blair went to work with a will. By April 1, she had sent letters to all national committeemen explaining her plan of organization. In the same month Blair held a special conference of Democratic national committeewomen, state chairwomen, members of the Democratic Congressional Committee, and the National Finance Committee to present her "Club Plan." She devised a complete plan of organization for women from national to local levels. Dividing the states into seven regions, she called for a regional director to be elected by national committeewomen and state vice chairmen. These state officials then oversaw the organization of women's Democratic clubs at the county and precinct level. At the national level, Blair, as the woman in charge of women, provided plans for organization, literature, and study programs. Her office also sent a field secretary to work with state and local groups. Blair's plan called for clubs to have monthly meetings to discuss various specific political issues, such as civil service, conservation, the tariff, or farm policy. In addition, Blair's office

21. ENB, "Platforms for Women," *Green Book*, July 1920, 23–24, 98.
22. ENB, "What Women May Do with the Ballot: An Address before the Democratic Women's Luncheon Club of Philadelphia," n.p., August 28, 1922.

sponsored "Schools of Democracy" in each region. The goal of Blair's organization was clearly stated: "that Democratic women may be able to speak through their party for the things in which they believe and in order that they may make a direct contribution as Democratic women to the policies of government." She envisioned that the women's clubs would present planks for the party platform and work with other women's organizations, such as the Federation of Women's Clubs, the League of Women Voters, the Consumers' League, and the Women's National Trade Union, to influence Democratic Party policy.[23]

Blair set for herself an ambitious schedule to visit as many state organizations as possible. In May and June, for example, she appeared in the New England states, Ohio, Indiana, Missouri, Kansas, Tennessee, Virginia, New York, Delaware, Pennsylvania, Michigan, and Illinois. Money was a perennial problem. When in New York, Blair met with Bernard Baruch, armed with a letter from Carter Glass. Praising Blair's work in organizing women, Glass wrote Baruch that she was "making brick without straw," and urged him to assist the women: "the inescapable fact is that unless splendid women of Mrs. Blair's type, who are devoting their intelligence and strength and enthusiasm to the Democratic cause, are immediately given assistance, we had as well disband the party organization and let matters go by default." When Blair asked Baruch for ten thousand dollars, he refused, saying he was "through with the big end of it." He was, however, she wrote in her diary, "sympathetic with my ideals and wondered at my having the courage to undertake the work." Two days later he sent Cordell Hull a check for one thousand dollars for Blair's work, admonishing the chairman that this money should not reduce whatever the committee had already allocated but was "to be in addition to what she receives, and is given specifically for her purposes. I believe she should be encouraged."[24]

Despite her grinding pace, Blair found time to take stock of her purpose. She had gone to Washington thinking her position would open a way for her to earn a living. After "a period of mental & emotional travail," she told Harry, she realized that she could not "see myself degenerating into a

23. See, for example, her letter to Carter Glass, April 1, 1922, Carter Glass Papers, box 169, University of Virginia (hereinafter cited as Glass Papers); ENB, "General Plan of Organization"; and ENB to Goltra, April 1, 1922, and November 10, 1923; box 18, folder 10, Goltra Papers.

24. Glass to Baruch, May 25, 1922, Baruch Correspondence, box 1, Glass Papers; ENB diary, May 26, 1922, folder 51, ENB Papers; Baruch to Hull, May 27, 1922, box 169, Glass Papers.

politician selling myself for place or victory." She found an idealistic goal: "to organize & mobilize the liberals of this country . . . to prevent our becoming the most despotic plutocracy of history." The Democratic Party, she thought, "is almost defunct," and Hull's only goal was to "harmonize" all factions. Her objective was "the reinvigoration & rehabilitation of the Democratic Party by the women." If she could make "fundamental democrats out of the women" and adapt "their habit of year-round intensive organization," to the entire party, then the Democrats would attract both men and women, leading to victory at the polls. "I don't doubt that I'll go thro much hell-fire before I'm thro—& I don't expect any rewards but there it is! My vision & my job, as I see it."[25]

Blair did go through "much hell-fire," especially from Democrats in her own state. Reed backers accused her of using the women's clubs to bolster opposition to the reelection of the senator.[26] Indeed, Reed had reason to be suspicious. Blair wanted to use her own state as a model for others, and knowing the territory and strong women leaders, she placed considerable emphasis on organization in Missouri. At the same time that Blair began organizing independent Democratic women's clubs, the League of Loyal Democrats formed to oppose the reelection of Missouri's senior senator. Particularly telling in the case against Blair was the female membership of anti-Reed organizations. The St. Louis League of Women Voters and the Missouri WCTU both urged their memberships to vote against Reed. Blair's old suffrage friend Mary Semple Scott was chairman of the Women's Division of the League of Loyal Democrats, and Florence Reid, an ardent supporter of her DNC bid, was instrumental in forming the Missouri Women Opposed to Senator James A. Reed, popularly known as the "Rid-Us-Of Reed" club. Even within the regular party organization there was strong female opposition to Reed. Moreover, after the general election, Florence Reid gave the membership lists of the Loyal League and the Rid-Us-Of Reed to Edith Bradley for the continuing project of organizing women's Democratic clubs in Missouri.[27] Technically, Blair could truthfully assert her impartiality during the primary, but there is no doubt of the close connection between her and the anti-Reed forces.

Reed himself spoke out publicly against separate women's political organizations. Both Hull and Blair repeatedly reiterated the neutrality of the

25. ENB to Harry, May 7 [1922], folder 32, ENB Papers.

26. See, for example, A. W. Thurman to Cordell Hull, May 30, 1922; and Bennett Clark to Cordell Hull [May 1922], folder 25, ENB Papers.

27. *St. Louis Post-Dispatch*, August 8, 1922; Florence Reid to ENB, November 12, 1922, folder 15, ENB papers.

women's clubs in primary elections, but Reed's friends were never satisfied. Although Blair publicly asserted her neutrality, her private correspondence shows something less than impartiality. She wrote her husband that when Carter Glass "said some of the men would not understand my failure to accept the primaries—the 'rules of the game,' I said we women did not make the rules, they were made before we were in politics and they did not bind us."[28]

Ultimately, at Carter Glass's suggestion, Hull backed Blair by arranging her election as a vice chairman in August 1922. Explaining that "no one seems to understand her status" as resident committeewoman, Hull concluded: "Our experience and my judgment is that it would add to her prestige in connection with her work, and in other important respects strengthen and clarify her situation to the benefit of the party." It was an important victory for Blair. She understood full well that women wanted strong leadership, that "they were not going to be delivered as so many bobheads by an agent of the men." Being a vice chairman gave her the opportunity to establish "a place for myself" as the recognized and strong leader of women.[29]

Despite grumbling from Missouri, Blair established a remarkable record of organization of Democratic women. There was good reason that the *St. Louis Post-Dispatch* said that she was called "the little Napoleon" and claimed that "generalship is her strong point." She oversaw the creation of seven hundred Democratic women's clubs by September 1922, and she placed Marion Banister in charge of a newsletter, the *Fortnightly*. Field organizer Laura Brown and Blair both traveled extensively, spreading the word of opportunity for women within the Democratic Party. Blair's office prepared and distributed all manner of pamphlets and literature, sent speakers and organizers into the field, and thereby increased women's participation in the party and educated them on many issues. To further that goal, Blair and Mrs. Halsey Wilson, director of education, had, by January

28. No women's advocate, Reed expressed his opposition to the Sheppard-Towner legislation, asserting that the Children's Bureau "was composed of unmarried women who seemed to be possessed of a desire to take charge of the babies other women might bear." Manuscript of speech given at St. Louis Coliseum, July 29 [1922], folder: Misc., MSS 1921–22, box 42, James A. Reed Papers, Western Historical Manuscript Collection–Kansas City, University of Missouri–Kansas City. Cordell Hull to Bennett Clark, May 30, 1922, and ENB to Clark, June 1, 1922, folder 25; Hull to Reed, June 5, 1922, folder 97; ENB to Harry, August 16, 1922, folder 32; ENB Papers.

29. Her election was accomplished by letter vote of the committee. For samples of the letter, see Hull to Glass, August 2, 1922, and Glass to Hull, August 3, 1922, box 169, Glass Papers; Hull to Goltra, August 2, 1922, and Goltra to Hull, August 4, 1922, box 16, folder 12, Goltra Papers. See also Blair, *Bridging Two Eras,* 231.

1924, organized twenty-four Schools of Democracy in seventeen states and developed a correspondence course on democracy.[30]

The Club Plan, according to Blair, was a means to empower women. By using a technique with which women were familiar—club organization— the Democrats could bring women into the party; equally important, those clubs could then become "a proving ground for the development of woman leadership . . . that women themselves would follow." And women ap- plauded her efforts. Sue White appreciated the inclusion that women had found only in the Democratic Party, writing: "They are sincerely trying to be true to women, inside the party. This is constructive work which is not being lost upon the observing women."[31]

The manner in which Blair envisioned her club plan working is illustrated in her letter to congressional candidate Ralph Lozier of Carrollton. While admitting that women were new to politics and "utterly untrained" in the particular methods of political organization, she assured Lozier that there were many who had "long experience" in organizing women. She urged him to contact the established women leaders in his district: "Experience has proven that it takes women to organize women. They understand each other, and they have different reactions and work habits from men." Moreover, it was essential to choose a recognized leader, "a woman whom the women will follow." She also pointed out to the candidate the differences in appeal- ing to women. Because women "do not meet in the same places as men," supporters must contact women in their homes. Moreover, "women will re- quire and desire information about candidates and education and training in the matter of issues and voting that men do not." Ideally, she suggested, there should be a woman in every precinct, working with the precinct com- mitteeman. She emphasized the importance of united action by emphatically stating: "good results can only be obtained by *closest cooperation between these two,—cooperation in the planning as well as the execution of the plans.*" Urging Lozier to take advantage of her club plan, Blair warned him: "Do not make the mistake of thinking that women vote like their husbands and depend on the men to get out the woman vote. Experience has shown that the women are better organized when they are recognized as a special problem and are approached accordingly."[32]

30. ENB to Carter Glass, March 1, 1924; Report of Vice Chairman Democratic Na- tional Committee, February 1922–January 1923 [1924], folder: Democratic National Committee 1923, box 238/239, Glass Papers.

31. Blair, *Bridging Two Eras*, 224; Sue S. White to Cordell Hull, November 18, 1922, reel 2, Cordell Hull Papers, Library of Congress.

32. Blair to Ralph Lozier, October 5, 1922, folder 4153, Ralph Lozier Collection, Western Historical Manuscript Collection–Columbia, University of Missouri–Columbia.

In 1922 Emily Newell Blair had one other vision to revitalize the Democratic Party. She wanted to establish a national Democratic women's clubhouse in Washington. As the party out of power, the Democrats had no meeting place in the capital to exchange ideas or entertain dignitaries. Together with Daisy (Mrs. J.) Harriman, Blair was responsible for the creation of the Woman's National Democratic Club, which opened its doors in January 1924. While it did rent a few rooms to visiting Democratic women, the main purpose of the clubhouse was to provide space for Democratic social gatherings, sponsor educational programs for women, present outstanding speakers, and cultivate publicity for the party. Although the club experienced serious financial difficulties in the early years, it became an institution of note in Washington.[33]

By 1925, after three years as the first vice president of the national committee, Blair was still modestly optimistic. Women had made "not a bad showing for five years of woman suffrage." She saw two avenues for becoming an effective politician. First, a woman could gain the confidence of established politicians so that they trusted and relied on her. That took time, more than five years. Or women could form a distinct voting bloc (as advocated by Alice Paul's National Women's Party), a method she discounted, calling it a "hallucination." Blair clung to the belief that women could succeed in politics by "boring from within," by garnering support of "a 'deliverable' following," by fighting and earning authority and position within the party.[34]

After she had retired from the National Committee at the close of the 1928 convention, Blair was less optimistic. Her practical experience in the political world, coupled with her current distance from it, gave her some perspective. Or perhaps, being out of politics, she simply felt freer to be more honest. Whatever the reasons, Blair showed some impatience. Women had been brought into the political parties but had yet to attain significant power. She placed some of the blame for this circumstance on women themselves. Claiming that men would not share power with anyone without good reason, she asserted that women had not been "willing to do the necessary hard work and take the blows." Between women giving up and men favoring more docile women, Blair saw that the early strong leaders

33. Scrapbook, Club Letters and Minutes, 1922–1926, the Woman's National Democratic Club Archives, Washington, D.C. Minutes of the Organization Committee of the Woman's National Democratic Club, December 29, 1922, the Woman's National Democratic Club Archives.

34. ENB, "Are Women a Failure in Politics?" *Harper's Magazine* 151 (October 1925): 522, 521; Emily Newell Blair, " 'Boring from Within': An Answer to 'The Lady and the Tiger,' " *Woman Citizen*, July 1927, 49–50.

had been replaced by women who were more inclined to follow the lead of men or who were simply the wives of male politicians. Having achieved their unified goal of suffrage, women no longer had a strong power base and had lost the leverage necessary to attain power. The result had been that the women on the political committees had come to "represent the choice of women far less than their predecessors did."[35]

By 1930, Blair had embraced a new approach to politics: a feminist solidarity aimed at gaining power for women. In an interview, she acknowledged that she had been wrong to think that she could gain lasting power for women by acquiring influence for herself. She called for women not to form a separate party but to "organize as women, work as women and stand behind women." In two articles in the *Woman's Journal* the next year, she analyzed women's progress after ten years of voting. In the immediate years after the suffrage amendment, men had appointed strong women who were proven leaders. As it became evident that women were not going to vote or act as a bloc, men turned to women whom they could control. As a result, many of the women in the political parties were beholden to men for their positions and therefore felt no obligation to feminist issues: "They participate in politics by ignoring other women." Moreover, Blair stated, the strategy "to drop the sex line in politics" had been wrong. She herself had accepted that approach, assuming that if she convinced men to trust and accept her, then more women could assimilate into the existing political structure. But that approach had not worked. In an address to the National Education Association annual convention in 1931, she stated flatly, "I think women exercise very little influence in politics today." Ideally, she had hoped that both men and women could gain power strictly on their merits, but practically, the obstacles for women had been too great. Feminism offered an answer. Women should form a bloc within the party, working together to support and elect women to positions of power. Only in this way could they expect to advance to equality with men.[36]

Blair's evolving ideas on women in politics had mirrored her own experience. As vice chairman of the DNC, she had worked hard to give women a political education and to accustom men to accepting women in politics. Although she had personally become well known in political circles, she

35. Emily Newell Blair, "Women in the Political Parties," *Annals of the American Academy of Political and Social Science* 143 (May 1929): 225, 222, 220.

36. Her definition of a feminist was fairly simple: "the woman who, whether she calls herself a feminist or not, wants to make it easier for women to contend with men in politics without disability because they are women." See Emily Newell Blair, "Putting Women into Politics," *Woman's Journal*, March 1931, 14.

had never shared equally in power; more disappointing to her was the fact that she had not been able to translate her elevation to national office into lasting progress for other women. When she left the DNC in 1928, she was frustrated. As she watched from the sidelines, knowing that women were moving no closer to equality, she became discouraged. It was then that she began to reevaluate her strategy to empower women, advocating feminist solidarity.

Blair's optimism revived with the increasing probability of a Democratic victory in 1932, and she returned to national politics to play an important role in Franklin Roosevelt's election. Because of the efforts of Eleanor Roosevelt and Molly Dewson, there was the promise of opportunity for women in the new administration. Blair was among the foremost women who deserved reward for her service to the party. Ironically, she turned down the chance to take a job in the Roosevelt administration; instead, she asked for a position for her husband. Thus the woman who had worked hardest to find a place for women in the party gave up her chance for higher office. Although Blair was eventually appointed to the Consumers' Advisory Board of the National Recovery Administration, she did not become the central figure she could have been in the network of women active in the New Deal.

Like other female leaders of the 1920s, Blair had emphasized the integration of women into the existing political system. Always a politician, Blair had focused not on radical demands or theoretical purity but on what she had thought were realistic and attainable goals. Yet that request for access to power was more than the political and cultural climate would allow. The acceptance of women as equals would have required, as Lois Scharf has written, "revolutionary change" that challenged "cultural ideology and social institutions."[37] As a practical politician, Blair had confronted determined resistance to cultural change and had modified her approach to securing power and responsibility for women. Although her career was not the ultimate breakthrough for women that she had hoped, Emily Newell Blair had played a significant role in advancing the cause of women during the first decade after suffrage.

37. Lois Scharf, "ER and Feminism," in *Without Precedent: The Life and Career of Eleanor Roosevelt,* ed. Joan Hoff-Wilson and Marjorie Lightman (Bloomington: Indiana University Press, 1984), 246.

The Doctor's Wife

Fannie Cook and Social Protest in Missouri, 1938–1949

Bonnie Stepenoff

Why should skin color, gender, or ethnic identity limit any person's hope for fulfillment? Why must poverty kill, injustice persist, and the fight for equality end in apathy or defeat? In the 1930s and 1940s, novelist and activist Fannie Cook boldly and explicitly asked these questions. Through her fictional characters, she spoke with many voices, including that of a college-educated middle-class woman, an African American household worker, a Jewish shoe salesman, and an altruistic physician in the Missouri Bootheel. In the pages of her novels, some characters found answers or partial answers to these questions, some gave up, and some found ways to continue the search. Others, like the Bootheel doctor's wife, accepted injustice as the way of the world, asking only for privacy and protection in the limited space they called home.

"I have taken an active part in the life of my own city and State but always as two persons: one partaking, and one watching and reporting to the writer-self," Fannie Cook said of herself.[1] As an author, Cook valiantly tried but ultimately failed to develop a coherent ideology of racial justice and gender equality. As a social activist, she spent most of her adult life participating in movements aimed at addressing social issues in the city of St. Louis and in the state of Missouri. Her involvement in causes made her aware of the painful complexities inherent in attempting to improve the

1. *Current Biography* (New York: H. W. Wilson, 1946), 129–30.

human condition. Cook saw herself as two people, the participant and the writer, and these two parts of herself may not always have been in harmony.

The daughter of Julius Frank, a German Jewish immigrant, and his wife, Jennie Michael Frank, she was born October 4, 1893, in St. Charles, Missouri. Her father was a partner in Fishlowitz and Frank, a large company that manufactured neckwear. She received a bachelor of arts degree in English from the University of Missouri in Columbia in 1914 and a master's degree from Washington University in 1917. In 1915, she married Dr. Jerome S. Cook, a practicing physician, who became director of medicine and chief of staff at Jewish Hospital. While teaching at Washington University, she raised two sons, Robert and Howard. By continuing to work after marriage, Cook defied middle-class conventions as well as the traditions of the European Jewish immigrant community.[2]

Although she supported suffrage and actively participated in the St. Louis League of Women Voters, Cook opposed the Equal Rights Amendment (first proposed in the 1920s). In an unpublished manuscript, "Equal Rights Amendment—Prohibitive Legislation," she argued that the ERA would invalidate special laws protecting women's health and safety. Because of their physical role as mothers, she believed women should not be allowed to work in hazardous or overly strenuous occupations. To her, issues of health and economic well-being outweighed issues of political equality. In another unpublished essay, she wrote that "the struggle for sex rights is but a by-play in the vast economic battle."[3]

During the Great Depression of the 1930s, she focused her attention on the problems of poverty and racial injustice. Missourians suffered greatly from the economic collapse in both manufacturing and agriculture. By 1933, the state's unemployment rate topped 38 percent, well above the national average. In St. Louis, thousands of jobless people took refuge in tents and other makeshift shelters in a gigantic "Hooverville" on the west bank of the Mississippi River. Among black workers in the city, unemployment rose as high as 60 percent.

2. Helen Frances Levin Goldman, "Parallel Portraits: An Exploration of Racial Issues in the Art and Activism of Fannie Frank Cook" (Ph.D. diss., St. Louis University, 1992), 2; Jean Douglas Streeter, "Fannie Cook Papers: Register" (directory to collection, Missouri Historical Society, St. Louis, 1988), 3; Susan A. Glenn, *Daughters of the Shtetl: Life and Labor in the Immigrant Generation* (Ithaca: Cornell University Press, 1990), 238–41.

3. "Equal Rights Amendment—Prohibitive Legislation," box 26, folder 14; and "Are the Ladies Inconsistent?" box 26, folder 4; both in Fannie Cook Papers, Missouri Historical Society, St. Louis (hereinafter cited as Cook Papers).

Many black women and girls who had worked in domestic service lost their jobs as middle-class families cut back on their expenses. The Depression was equally severe in rural areas.[4] In southeastern Missouri, drought, flood, and falling cotton prices bankrupted landowners and threw many white and black tenant croppers and sharecroppers out of work.

Under President Franklin D. Roosevelt, the federal government created New Deal programs that addressed the economic hardships of the Depression, but these did not challenge existing social divisions. Agricultural programs boosted prices by encouraging farm owners to take land out of production. This brought even greater distress to tenants and sharecroppers. Programs such as the Civilian Conservation Corps (CCC) offered government employment to men only. Although black men could join the CCC, they lived and worked in segregated camps. Works Progress Administration programs employed mostly men, offering gender-specific programs, such as sewing circles, to unemployed women. Women employed in New Deal arts and theater projects accepted conventional portrayals of manliness and womanliness, placing male images in the foreground as workers and females in minor roles as nurturers.[5]

Cook joined other middle-class women in efforts to combat the worst effects of the Depression. From 1930 to 1934, she chaired the Department of Race Relations of the Community Council of St. Louis. She also supported the right of workers, including domestic workers, to organize under federal policies established by the New Deal. Her friend Edna Gellhorn served as a member of the St. Louis National Recovery Administration Mediation Board. In 1939, Cook and another St. Louis writer, Josephine Johnson, organized the St. Louis Committee for the Rehabilitation of the Sharecroppers, a group that supported the roadside demonstrations of tenant farmers and farm laborers in southeastern Missouri. As chair of this committee, she supported the creation and maintenance of Cropperville, a haven for displaced sharecroppers in Butler County, Missouri, from 1939 to 1949.[6]

Despite a heart condition, she continued her involvement in civic orga-

4. Richard S. Kirkendall, *A History of Missouri,* vol. 5, *1919 to 1953* (Columbia: University of Missouri Press, 1986), 132–35.

5. David Eugene Conrad, *The Forgotten Farmers: The Story of Sharecroppers in the New Deal* (Urbana: University of Illinois Press, 1965), 52; Bonnie Stepenoff, "The Tree Soldiers," *Missouri Resource Review,* fall 1993, 3; Nancy Ellen Rose, *Put to Work: Relief Programs in the Great Depression* (New York: Monthly Review Press, 1994), 108; Barbara Melosh, *Engendering Culture: Manhood and Womanhood in New Deal Public Art and Theater* (Washington, D.C.: Smithsonian Institution Press, 1991), 215.

6. Box 4, folder 1, Cook Papers; see also Jean Douglas Cadle, "Cropperville, from Refuge to Community: A Study of Missouri Sharecroppers Who Found an Alternative to the Sharecropper System" (master's thesis, University of Missouri–St. Louis, 1993).

nizations and political movements in the 1940s. From 1942 until her death, she was a founder and board member of the St. Louis People's Art Center, an interracial organization that provided art classes for children and adults. She served on the St. Louis Mayor's Race Relations Commission from 1943 to 1946. In 1948 she supported the formation of the Progressive Party of Missouri, serving on the Missouri Citizens for [Henry A.] Wallace committee and the national Wallace for President committee. During that same year, she testified in the *Schelley v. Kraemer* case that struck down covenants aimed at maintaining racial segregation in St. Louis neighborhoods. She died on August 25, 1949.[7]

Her literary career began in the mid-1930s, when she started selling articles, stories, and novels through a New York agent.[8] In her fiction, she returned again and again to the matter of human equality, although she framed the issue in different terms as events of the 1930s and 1940s shifted the ground under her feet. Cook's identity as an American Jew shaped her views on social justice. Of all the voices in her novels, it was a Jewish voice that articulated the issue most dramatically and succinctly. In Cook's novel *Storm against the Wall,* the character Marcus Kleinman, an American Jew, the son of a St. Louis shoe salesman, sums up her ideas on human rights: "Hitler called the Jews an inferior people. The Jew knows that's a lie. He knows it is also a lie when negroes are called an inferior people. A man must not live by a lie."[9] The fictional character did not add the corollary, that neither must any woman live by a lie, but the author—by her words and actions—certainly implied its truth.

Her first novel, *The Hill Grows Steeper,* opens with a vignette that casts the issue of gender equity in very simple terms. A young twin brother and sister, Harry and Harriet Andrews, are equal in every way—intelligent, healthy, good-natured, and rambunctious—differing only in gender. On their birthday, their grandfather marks this difference by giving Harry a present of five dollars and Harriet one of fifty cents. In protest, Harriet takes her money and pays the local barber to shave off her pretty, feminine curls. Harriet's act of childish defiance exposes the fallacy that allowed a grandfather to rate a short-haired boy at ten times the worth of a female child in curls.[10]

7. Cadle, "Cropperville," 58. For biographical information on Fannie Cook, see Annora K. Koetting, "Four St. Louis Women: Precursors of Reform" (master's thesis, St. Louis University, 1973); and Mary K. Dains, ed., *Show Me Missouri Women: Selected Biographies* (Kirksville, Mo.: Thomas Jefferson University Press, 1989), 227–28.

8. Goldman, *Parallel Portraits,* 150.

9. Fannie Cook, *Storm against the Wall* (Garden City, N.Y.: Doubleday, 1948), 254.

10. Fannie Cook, *The Hill Grows Steeper* (New York: G. P. Putnam's Sons, 1938), 11–16.

Of all the characters in Cook's novels, only Harriet squarely addresses the issue of gender inequality. As a growing girl in the fictional town of Springdale, Missouri, Harriet reads Horatio Alger's rags-to-riches stories and identifies with their young male heroes. When she disapproves of people or disrespects them, she calls them "sissies"—a gendered slur. Her father sees to it that both she and Harry go to the university in Columbia, where she glides easily through her studies. Her only poor grade is for a paper on women's rights, glorifying Jane Addams and Florence Kelley.[11] These middle-class reformers, who placed feminism in the larger context of social welfare, were role models both for Cook and for the fictional Harriet.

Like Addams and Kelley, the middle-class Harriet expresses great empathy for working-class women. In a fit of youthful defiance, and as a way to avoid early marriage, she runs off to St. Louis and goes to work in a shirt factory. Although she quickly enrolls in a stenography course and finds a white-collar job, she feels a continuing attraction to her factory friend Rebecca Cohen. Harriet admires Rebecca's commitment to unionism and feels uneasy about her own progress up the career ladder. She does not go back to the factory, following instead in the footsteps of Addams and Kelley, going to work for a philanthropic organization that pushes for labor reform.[12]

In her portrait of Harriet, Cook elucidated the class consciousness that sometimes undercut middle-class women's reform efforts. Harriet sometimes treats Rebecca, the factory worker, to dinner, taking her to an out-of-the-way place where middle-class associates would not see them. The well-groomed Harriet was continually aware of the contrast between her own appearance and "the dumpy Semitic poverty that was Rebecca."[13] The implied anti-Semitism in this remark separated the author, a Jewish woman, from her fictional character, a gentile. Unintentionally, perhaps, Harriet's distaste for the Semitic Rebecca revealed Cook's own ambivalence about her ethnic identity. At this point in her career, she was unwilling to express her Jewishness explicitly in her fiction.

By exploring Harriet's inner life, Cook was able to examine issues of race, class, and gender as they played out, intimately, in kitchens and bedrooms. Harriet feels an adolescent attraction to Moberly, the Andrews's African American housekeeper. The middle-class girl is thrilled to learn

11. Ibid., 8, 29, 66–67.
12. Ibid., 115, 127–29, 130–38.
13. Ibid., 129.

that Moberly defied sexual norms by having had four husbands and two or three lovers. Secretly, the young Harriet longs to emulate the black woman but feels compelled to seek a conventional marriage. Her fears about taking this step come to the surface when Miss Amy Mattucks, a white seamstress, expresses a working-class cynicism about married life. It is the seamstress's banter that inspires Harriet to take the drastic action of leaving her intended at the altar.[14]

Issues of love and sex complicate Harriet's life and ultimately restrict her choices. In addition to running away from her first intended groom, she also draws away prissily from a friend who was a lesbian. Although she seems to be steering a course toward independence and a career, she reluctantly changes directions when she finds love. Her intense attraction to Paul Kramer, a high-minded reporter, affects her profoundly, and Cook writes about it in conventional romantic terms: "Harriet's pulses leaped. He had justified her whole existence!" Harriet continues to pursue her career, and she defies middle-class morality by becoming pregnant before marriage. But in the end she marries Paul and, in accordance with the standards of the 1930s, gives up her job. This is a hard sacrifice, though and she grieves for it "as for a child that was dying."[15]

Unlike the fictional Harriet, Cook did not sacrifice her career or her personal ambition. But in some respects, their choices were the same. Near the end of the novel, Harriet tells her husband that she will no longer strive for gender equality. Instead, she will devote her efforts to solving the more pressing problems of poverty, violence, and injustice. Her speech to Paul sounds more like a lecture to herself: "I should be out trying to change the world, trying to make it warless and maternal, a world willing to feed its children and wanting to mother the weak. That's what I ought to be doing—instead of trying to obtain rights for women."[16] Harriet's downplaying of women's rights reflects the author's long-standing belief, articulated in her rejection of the ERA, that issues of health and economic welfare took precedence over gender equity. In this belief, Cook remained well within the mainstream of American fiction writers in the Depression era.

According to historian Laura Hapke, American novelists of the 1930s, whether radical or conservative in their politics, almost unanimously "reinforced a disturbingly regressive perception of the feminine role."[17] John

14. Ibid., 33, 76–81.
15. Ibid., 68, 113, 147, 275.
16. Ibid., 146.
17. Laura Hapke, *Daughters of the Great Depression: Women, Work, and Fiction in the American 1930s* (Athens: University of Georgia Press, 1995), 3, 221.

Steinbeck's Ma Joad became the archetypal female; she was strong and admirable but relegated to a dreary domesticity. During the Depression, both male and female authors extolled the virtues of maternal, home-loving women who wanted to "mother the weak" as Harriet Andrews does.

In her second novel, *Boot-heel Doctor,* Cook created a character who conformed to the stereotype of the long-suffering wife. The novel focuses on two strong male heroes, one white and one black. Joel Gregory, the title character, devotes his life to healing the sharecroppers who are his neighbors in the cotton country of southeastern Missouri. Although he is a good man and not an overt racist, he clearly feels superior to his poor white and black patients, treating them in a fatherly way, talking to them as though they were children, and feeling frustrated by their refusal to consistently follow his advice. At the climax of the novel, however, he clearly recognizes the strength and dignity of the poor white and black sharecroppers and especially of the black labor leader, Reuben Fielding. When Fielding and the sharecroppers go out on strike against the big planters, Gregory admits that, "By God, they're about to do the bravest thing's ever been done in the boot-heel."[18]

The doctor's wife, Hester, never emerges as a hero in the novel; she instead remains in the background as the doctor's emotionally deprived helpmate. Joel never abuses her, but he never recognizes her true humanity. Day after day, he fails to notice the effort she puts into keeping house, doing charity work, and sewing quilts. Without realizing it, he treats her in the way he treats his sharecropper patients, as someone who needs his advice and counsel—although she would probably be too stubborn to heed it. In Cook's words, Joel perceives her "as if she were not a middle-aged woman, but a pretty child."[19]

Although his wife lionizes him, Joel possesses a true humility about his profession. He expresses this in highly gendered language, comparing the service he performs to work that is traditionally assigned to women: "Reckon it's nothing much but bonesetting and baby bringing, being kinda neighborly, something for an old woman not know anything much about science to do."[20] It is, in fact, just the kind of work Hester does, when she volunteers to distribute clothes for the Red Cross and to provide other social services to farmworkers made homeless by a flood. But she does not regard these activities as "work" in the sense of her husband's professional endeavors.

18. Fannie Cook, *Boot-heel Doctor* (New York: Dodd, Mead, 1941), 235.
19. Ibid., 3.
20. Ibid., 95.

She makes her husband the center of her world. The troubles of the sharecroppers affect her mainly as a threat to the health and well-being of her husband. Her mission in life is to care for him. She attaches importance to her role because "Joel's little finger was worth more in a minute than the bodies and souls, too, of all those folks he slaved for were worth in a year."[21] She shelters an orphaned child, and she has real sympathy for displaced farm laborers, but her true concern is for her husband and her home.

To a great extent Hester shares the feelings of her friend Belle, who takes "croppers" into her home but soon grows impatient with their lack of manners. Hester reports the situation from Belle's point of view: "Belle says her croppers went in the corners before she could stop them. Now she'll have to repaper. Her place smells right bad." For Hester, the sanctity of the home takes precedence over questions of economic and social justice. She is shocked, for instance, when her husband allows the black Reuben to exit through her front door.[22]

Among all Cook's characters, Reuben Fielding most clearly represents an actual historical figure. His real-life counterpart, Owen Whitfield, won fame as the leader of the 1939 Bootheel sharecroppers' roadside demonstrations in southeastern Missouri. In 1936, Whitfield was a sharecropper, a preacher, and a friend of Thad Snow, who owned a cotton plantation near Charleston, Missouri. During that summer, Snow defied convention by inviting the Southern Tenant Farmers' Union to organize workers on his land. Whitfield joined the union in 1937. The following year he moved with his wife, Zella, and their children to the Farm Security Administration's La Forge housing project near New Madrid. Snow called Whitfield "the smartest organizer in Missouri."[23] In 1939, Whitfield used his eloquence and charisma to lead black and white sharecroppers and tenant farmers, displaced by the Depression, in a massive demonstration along Highways 60 and 61 in southeastern Missouri. Threats against his life caused him to flee to St. Louis.

When news of the roadside demonstrations appeared in the national papers, friends called Cook and asked her to take some action. She went to the offices of the St. Louis Urban League and there met Whitfield. Quickly she formed a coalition with the Pulitzer Prize–winning novelist Josephine

21. Ibid., 14.

22. Ibid., 98–99, 177–78.

23. Cadle, "Cropperville," 14–16; note from Snow to Ralph Coghlan of the *St. Louis Post-Dispatch,* folder 32, Thad Snow Papers, Western Historical Manuscript Collection–St. Louis, University of Missouri–St. Louis.

Johnson and representatives from the Urban League, Eden Theological Seminary, the Fellowship of Reconciliation, and the United Cannery, Agricultural, Packing and Allied Workers of America. This group coalesced into the St. Louis Committee for Rehabilitation of the Sharecroppers. On January 22, the group sponsored a mass meeting, attended by six hundred people, at the Amalgamated Clothing Workers Union Hall in St. Louis, to raise awareness of the sharecroppers' plight and also to raise money for relief.[24] For the next ten years, the committee sponsored the Cropperville community.

Anxious to study conditions in the Bootheel, Cook wrote to Snow in March 1939, asking him to arrange for her to stay with a local family. He suggested she contact E. G. Gilmore of East Prairie, who could "get you in touch with everything and everybody better than any one I know."[25] On April 17, 1939, she wrote a long letter to her friend Edna Gellhorn, reporting on a three-day visit to "the sharecropper country." The only bright spot in the picture, as she saw it, was that many middle-class people sympathized with the croppers. The rest, she wrote, was a nightmare:

> I saw hungry women with scrawny babies gnawing at their breasts. I saw families where no child had a change of clothing. I saw families living under torn tents on ditch dumps—fine-looking people keeping alive on $3 a MONTH for the three or four of them. These were NOT sharecroppers who had taken part in the roadside demonstrations, but exfarmers, white people.[26]

Reporting on the plight of the demonstrators, whom she called "Whitfieldians," she said they had been "dumped" by state police, who cleared their tents from the roadside. In Charleston, they lived in stalls made of cardboard boxes, propped up against bare walls. Women gave birth without medical care. "Sick, bilious people [lay] on the bed in another camp half-conscious with no one to find out whether they have the flue or smallpox!"[27]

Cook befriended Whitfield's wife, Zella, who with her family had settled in St. Louis County during the disturbance in the Bootheel. In a letter to Cook, dated August 13, 1940, Zella described the birth of a new granddaughter in St. Louis County. In spite of Cook's efforts, the hospital would

24. Cadle, "Cropperville," 28–30.
25. Box 5, folder 2, Cook Papers.
26. Fannie Cook to Edna Gellhorn, April 17, 1939, box 5, folder 2, Cook Papers.
27. Ibid.

not admit "those old no good share croppers," and so they had to go to a "colored doctor." Whitfield's letter expressed gratitude for "your kindness to my family and myself as well as for all kindness and help you are giving to the suffering people in South East Mo."[28]

In *Boot-heel Doctor,* Owen and Zella Whitfield become Reuben and Truth Fielding. Truth remains a minor character, notable mainly for her constancy and stoicism. She is proud of her husband and believes in what he is doing. When he refuses to take charity from the Red Cross or to collect government relief, she accepts it, even though her family goes hungry and one of her babies dies. Her steadfastness contrasts with the bitter defeatism of Della Kennedy, the wife of a white sharecropper who betrays the union. In one of the book's most dramatic scenes, Della simply gives up, refuses to leave her flooding cabin, and drowns herself so her expected baby would never be born and consequently would never be beaten by its father.[29] Truth Fielding, however, never loses her pride in her husband.

The female characters in *Boot-heel Doctor* behave admirably within the limits imposed by the prevailing ideology of gender. Della Kennedy, a poor white woman, is so brutalized by her husband that self-destruction seems the only way to preserve her dignity. Both Della and Truth accept the deaths of their children as a consequence of choices, either noble or ignoble, made by their husbands. The doctor's wife, Hester, remains steadfast, loyal, and kind but lives in her husband's shadow, bravely standing up to her neighbors only when they attack Joel's reputation.

The principal male characters, Joel and Reuben, make choices that place them at the center of the action. During the course of the novel, Reuben develops from a careful, observant man—an African American shrewdly surviving in white society—to the bold leader of a protest movement. In an early chapter, he works quietly at the Red Cross shelter, performing menial tasks for no pay, helping black and white families devastated by a flood. In the aftermath of that natural disaster, he begins to appreciate the extent of the sharecroppers' misery and the relentlessness of the planters' greed. Angered and inspired, he preaches a sermon in a schoolhouse, saying that the flood was bad, but "When trouble comes to black people, the worst kind's usually the kind Man made." Hearing this sermon, Joel Gregory feels frightened as he thinks, "Colored men had been lynched for saying less."[30]

As Reuben emerges to lead a protest movement, Joel admires and even

28. Zella Whitfield to Fannie Cook, August 13, 1940, box 5, folder 5, Cook Papers.
29. Cook, *Boot-heel Doctor,* 141, 28–29.
30. Ibid., 40, 63, 102.

envies him. Reuben is making history, and Joel is ashamed not to be part of that history, ashamed not to be making sacrifices like Reuben's. Joel and Hester receive their share of disapproval for inviting Reuben into their home and being seen with him in public. Hester worries continually about Joel's safety, but it is Reuben who takes the real risks. In the end, Cook's plotting allows Joel to become the hero. When a crowd attempts to lynch the black leader, Joel comes to his rescue.[31] With this plot device, Cook places the white male in control of events that had been set in motion by a black man's courage.

Cook's next novel, *Mrs. Palmer's Honey,* returns to an urban middle-class setting and shifts the focus back to female characters. Honey Hoop, the protagonist, was a citizen of "the Ville," an established, middle-class black neighborhood in segregated St. Louis. Because of her high moral standards, Honey is known as "the virgin of the Ville." In this way, Cook instantly distinguishes her from an earlier African American character, the spicy Moberly, who was the sexually adventurous maid in *The Hill Grows Steeper.*

As the novel opens, Honey's loyalties are divided in several ways. She has a new job in a World War II defense plant, but she still has emotional ties to the Palmers, a white family, who were employing her as a maid. She feels attracted to a rebellious black man named Snake Williams, but she also recognizes the attractions of Ben Boston, a black funeral director and solid middle-class citizen. She loves her mother but rejects the life she had led, bearing fifteen children.

Unlike Reuben, Honey does not openly defy the established order. The choices she makes represent an attempt, perhaps similar to the author's own attempt, to reconcile a settled life with a crusade for social justice. In order to achieve personal independence, Honey must break away from Mrs. Palmer, who continues to view her as a domestic servant. During the course of the novel, she relinquishes her position as servant and caregiver; she finally declares her independence when one of Mrs. Palmer's friends asks if she knows someone to do some cooking, and Honey just laughs.[32]

After a long internal battle, Honey also rejects the wild and dangerous Snake (a name with biblical overtones) and marries Ben Boston, a solid and prosperous man. Although she marries Ben, she keeps a strong sense of herself and continues to support her younger brother's efforts to gain union membership for black people and to integrate the city's neighbor-

31. Ibid., 211, 197, 265.
32. Fannie Cook, *Mrs. Palmer's Honey* (Garden City, N.Y.: Doubleday, 1946), 185.

hoods. By the end of the novel, she is no longer "Mrs. Palmer's Honey"; she is her own person.[33] Unlike Harriet in *The Hill Grows Steeper,* she is able to marry Ben without grieving for a lost part of herself. With her identity intact, she is able to keep her ties with the Palmer family by befriending their daughter, Dorothy Jane. In an interesting twist, Dorothy Jane becomes a supporter of Honey's union activities.

The drama of the Palmer family is a crucial subtext of the novel. Andrew Palmer, head of the household, does not allow racial slurs to be uttered in his presence and speaks out against segregation, even when friends criticize him for his views. He dies violently, struck by a falling object while accepting a medal for good citizenship, and his death throws the family into a tailspin. His widow demands that Honey come back and care for the household. Mrs. Palmer is a simpering woman, who, in Honey's opinion, "always looked too small for her own house."[34] It is her daughter, Dorothy Jane, who follows in her father's footsteps.

Cook's first three novels feature characters who resent or question middle-class privilege and who gravitate toward the labor movement. After leaving her factory job, Harriet Andrews nurses her troubled conscience by lobbying for labor reform. The black labor leader Reuben Fielding inspires the Bootheel doctor Joel Gregory to reexamine his life and values by standing up for the union. In *Mrs. Palmer's Honey,* several characters, including Honey's brother Lamb, find purpose and passion in unionism. Cook herself, the wife of a physician, became involved in labor activities in the 1930s, first supporting the right of domestic workers to organize, then joining an alliance to help the striking sharecroppers.

Despite her own connections with unionism, Cook's portrayals of rebellious workers remained somewhat unconvincing. Some critics who praised Cook's characterization of Honey Hoop in the early chapters of the novel found that the final chapters read more like labor propaganda than well-wrought fiction.[35] The domestic power struggle between Honey and Mrs. Palmer made much more compelling drama than the story of Honey's activism. The worker-heroes in Cook's fiction, including Lamb Hoop, were stereotypical figures, dark and manly proletarians, rather than complex human beings. Reuben Fielding, while much more fully realized than Lamb, remained an admirable enigma, muscular, upright, and visionary, like the figures of labor heroes in New Deal public art.

33. Ibid., 279.
34. Ibid., 61–63, 108, 38.
35. *Current Biography* (1946), 130.

Events in the 1930s and early 1940s caused Cook to consider her own ethnic identity and take a harder look at the issue of racism. Nazi persecution of Jews in Europe had repercussions in St. Louis. In 1933, Cook began supporting the National Committee to Aid the Victims of German Fascism, and in the 1940s she joined the St. Louis Citizens' Committee on Displaced Persons. During World War II, she helped churn out propaganda slogans for the Writers' War Board. Both her sons served in the military, Robert as an army physician, and Howard in the U.S. Air Force.[36]

Jewish characters take center stage for the first time in her 1948 novel *Storm against the Wall*. Essentially it is the story of a Jewish family, the Kleinmans, trying to live decent and useful lives in a world that becomes increasingly hostile and confusing. Even in St. Louis, they cannot escape the rising tide of anti-Semitism in the first half of the twentieth century. The novel's title comes from the book of Isaiah: "When the blast of the terrible ones become as a storm against the wall."[37]

The novel deals effectively with the complex relationships between Jews and blacks in St. Louis. Early in the narrative, Hans Kleinman loses his job as a shoe salesman and feels devastated. Mamie Lee, his African American housekeeper, sympathizes with him but wonders why he had not seen it coming: "What's a little Jew man got to be surprised about when he gets fired? Leastways a colored man knows he gonna get fired, first chance they get."[38] Out of loyalty, Mamie Lee continues to work for the family without pay.

The novel also scrutinizes the relationships between Jews and other Jews. Mr. Kleinman's brother-in-law, Carl Hursch, owns a furniture store that sells poor-quality goods to "schwarzes." Hans accepted a sales position in the store, but finds it morally impossible to push low-quality merchandise on poor people and take their money. He rejects his relative's lack of compunction and finally accepts a much more modest income, once again selling shoes.

Cook used her own personal experiences as the basis for incidents in the novel. As a graduate of the University of Missouri, she reflected on the fact that African Americans were not accepted there. She also deeply regretted her failed attempt to save a black domestic employee from a jail sentence; the man ultimately died of tuberculosis in prison.[39] From these two facts

---

36. Goldman, *Parallel Portraits*, 180–84.
37. Ibid., 165.
38. Cook, *Storm against the Wall*, 34–36.
39. "Cook, Fannie," in *Current Biography* (1946), 130.

of her life, Cook created a fictional episode involving Marc Kleinman, Hans's son, and Orvell, the son of the black housekeeper, Mamie Lee.

Marc learns that it is risky to be a Jew defending a black man. As a student at the University of Missouri, Marc encounters Mamie Lee's son, Orvell, who works as a houseboy for a fraternity. The fraternity rejects Marc because he is Jewish. Orvell runs into trouble with the law. When Marc tries to help, friends advise him to keep quiet and remember he is a Jew. He defies them, saying, "I will not remember that I am a Jew. I will remember only that Orvell Sultan is unjustly jailed." Marc's bravado does no good. Orvell goes to the penitentiary anyway, yet he emerges years later as Otto Street and becomes a lawyer. Meeting him, Marc wonders why he himself had not become a lawyer so that he could help fight injustice.[40]

Marc finds no real solution to the problem of racial prejudice. As a young man trying to make his way in the world, he sees racism and anti-Semitism rising in St. Louis. With his limited financial resources, he tries to help relatives escape from Nazi violence. At one point, feeling overwhelmed, he runs away to a shack in the Ozarks, seriously undermining his marriage. Returning to St. Louis, he attends a film about Buchenwald and finds that he can no longer run away. He goes to work making maps to help the war effort, and his deskmate is a black man.[41] He does the best he can, but his efforts seem pitifully weak against massive forces of evil.

Marc's fictional struggles betray the author's self-doubts. Like Marc, Fannie Cook ran away from her own ethnic identity. Her early novels denied, or masked, her Jewishness. In 1939, while Hitler's aggression escalated, she turned her attention to a crisis in the Missouri Bootheel. By writing *Storm against the Wall,* she came back, like Marc, and confronted anti-Semitism, while trying to maintain her commitment to racial equality between whites and blacks. But she must have felt, like Marc, that the problems were staggering and that her efforts, however earnest, remained small and ineffectual.

Both Marc Kleinman and the Bootheel doctor Joel Gregory occupy fictional worlds battered by real-world catastrophes. They are middle-class men with idealistic spirits, tested by overwhelming events. Despite their desire to actively fight injustice, both remain essentially observers. Joel watches admiringly as Reuben Fielding risks his life standing up for workers' rights. Marc questions his own choices when he sees the persecuted black man, Otto Street, emerge from prison with a law degree, ready to defend his

40. Cook, *Storm against the Wall,* 126, 186.
41. Cook, *Storm against the Wall,* 209, 220, 236–37, 265, 256.

people. Both men's wives stand loyally beside them but fail to understand their need for self-sacrifice. And, in the end, they sacrifice very little, as they continue to live middle-class lives that are productive and altruistic, but hardly heroic.

Harriet Andrews and Honey Hoop also settle for security in traditional marriage after searching for something grander. As a child, Harriet challenges restrictions on her freedom of choice; as a young woman she runs away from marriage and embraces a career, but in the end she accepts the conventional limitations of the female role. Honey Hoop breaks away from her identity as a domestic servant. She flirts with the dangerous and rebellious man named Snake. But in the end she, too, accepts marriage to a steady, solid, middle-class man. Both Harriet and Honey continue, within limits, to work for justice and equality, but neither challenges the gender-based restrictions on their personal freedom.

The characters in Cook's final novel, *The Long Bridge,* turn inward, away from the turmoil of the wider world, to focus on personal fulfillment. Annie Carr, the most interesting of them, defies middle-class norms to become a domestic servant so that her son, Tom, can pursue a career as an artist. Tom, eking out a living in St. Louis during the Depression, sympathizes with the poor, hungry people he sees around him but feels no compunction to take up their cause.[42] His goal is to make money from his art and to marry Dandy, a woman whose devotion to him is selfless in the great tradition of the "perfect wife." These characters are admirable in some ways, but they are strikingly disengaged from the great social questions that troubled Harriet Andrews, Joel Gregory, Reuben Fielding, Lamb Hoop, and Marc Kleinman.

In her fiction, Fannie Cook looked critically at assumptions held by members of her own social stratum, but inevitably she remained a woman of her own place, time, and class. She came to fiction as a woman deeply involved in social-reform activities, but her novels reveal self-doubt about the effectiveness of her participation in social causes. When she went to the Bootheel in 1939, she visited transient camps, but she stayed with a well-to-do family. Her Bootheel hostess, Maude Gilmore, wrote to her on April 27, 1939, inviting her to visit again. In this letter, she described her recent trip to Malden with the Study Club of Charleston. On this outing, she wrote, "We were guests of the Malden Club at an old Colonial home. It is an interesting place to go. They have negro servants, old period furniture and such a large old mansion."[43]

---

42. Fannie Cook, *The Long Bridge* (Garden City, N.Y.: Doubleday, 1949), 34.
43. Maude Gilmore to Fannie Cook, April 27, 1939, box 5, folder 2, Cook Papers.

By the mid-1940s, Cook achieved national prominence as an advocate of racial harmony. In 1946, *Mrs. Palmer's Honey* sold over twenty thousand copies and placed fifteenth on the *New York Times* bestseller list. Her publisher honored her with the George Washington Carver Award for promoting interracial understanding. The *St. Louis Argus* noted her "Out-standing Contribution to Inter-Racial Welfare."[44] She became a sought-after public speaker. While she continued to give aid to Whitfield and the displaced sharecroppers, she moved in circles far removed from their privation and pain.

Josephine Johnson, Cook's compatriot in the struggle to aid the sharecroppers, chose motherhood over social action and career. At the age of twenty-four, in 1934, Johnson won the Pulitzer Prize for her first novel, *Now in November,* a story of rural poverty. Five years later, she supported the sharecroppers' revolt. By the late 1940s, as Mrs. Grant Cannon, she lived in Ohio and struggled with the needs of a growing family. In an undated letter, she commented rather negatively on *Storm against the Wall* and confessed that she was not writing very much because "Every day is so full with just cooking, cleaning, washing, and taking care of the children. (They are wonderful. I feel as though I owned real diamonds!)"[45]

Fannie Cook succeeded in continuing her work as a writer and social activist, despite the demands of motherhood. Edna Gellhorn commented on this feat in an undated letter. Gellhorn described Cook as "the wonder woman who can measure up to and surpass any standard set for wife, mother, homemaker and friend. Then add to all these qualities that add up to a great personality, the gifts of the writer, artist and cook, and one has a faint impression of our Fannie."[46] Cook was a "wonder woman" who combined family and career, but none of the female characters in her novels achieved as much. She was not afraid to write about black labor activists, self-sacrificing male physicians, and out-of-work Jewish shoe salesmen, but she did not write about women like herself.

Like most writers of her generation, she created female characters who conform to traditional images of the woman's role. The hero of her first novel, Harriet Andrews, questions gender stereotypes but ultimately accepts domesticity. In subsequent novels, Cook's female characters struggle with the tension between domestic life and active participation in social causes. Hester Gregory, the Bootheel doctor's wife, retreats into her stark

44. Goldman, *Parallel Portraits,* 156, 163.

45. Josephine Johnson Cannon to Fannie Cook [n.d.], box 18, folder 11, Cook Papers.

46. Edna Gellhorn to Fannie Cook, Fish Creek, May 30 [n.d.], box 3, folder 1, Cook Papers.

and emotionally impoverished home. Honey Hoop finds a way to combine motherly strength with labor activism. Annie Carr sacrifices her own comfort to further the ambitions of her son. These fictional women operate bravely within the restrictions imposed upon them by the conventions of their time.

As a middle-class woman, Cook zealously pursued a literary career and fought for social justice, but as a writer she did not focus her attention on women's issues. During the turbulent decades of the 1930s and 1940s, too many other problems demanded her attention. In her novels, she posed important questions about gender bias, racial prejudice, and economic inequality, but she treated them as separate issues and did not consistently connect them to her own experience. She deserves praise for asking the questions, but at the end of her life she remained a long way from finding answers.

Bibliography of Secondary Works

Allured, Janet L. "Women's Healing Art: Domestic Medicine in the Turn-of-the-Century Ozarks." *Gateway Heritage* 12, no. 4 (spring 1992): 20–32.

Andrews, Gregg. *Insane Sisters: Or, the Price Paid for Challenging a Company Town*. Columbia: University of Missouri Press, 1999.

Baumgarten, Nikola. "Education and Democracy in Frontier St. Louis: The Society of the Sacred Heart." *History of Education Quarterly* 34, no. 2 (summer 1994): 171–92.

Bishop, Beverly D., and Deborah W. Bolas, eds. *In Her Own Write: Women's History Resources in the Library and Archives of the Missouri Historical Society*. St. Louis: Missouri Historical Society, 1983.

Bloom, Harold, ed. *Kate Chopin*. New York: Chelsea House, 1987.

Boren, Lynda S., and Sara de Saussure Davis, eds. *Kate Chopin Reconsidered: Beyond the Bayou*. Baton Rouge: Louisiana State University Press, 1992.

Brandimarte, Cynthia Ann. "Fannie Hurst: A Missouri Girl Makes Good." *Missouri Historical Review* 81, no. 3 (April 1987): 275–95.

Brandon-Falcone, Janice. "'It Pays Me Well and Is a Good Thing': The Club Life of Constance Runcie." *Gateway Heritage* 15, no. 3 (winter 1994–1995): 56–65.

Bruce, Janet. "Of Sugar and Salt and Things in the Cellar and Sun: Food Preservation in Jackson County in the 1850s." *Missouri Historical Review* 75, no. 4 (July 1981): 417–47.

Bundles, A'Lelia. *On Her Own Ground: The Life and Times of Madam C. J. Walker*. New York: Scribner, 2001.

Bundschu, William B. *Abuse and Murder on the Frontier: The Trials and*

Travels of Rebecca Hawkins, 1800–1860. Independence, Mo.: Little Blue Valley, 2003.

Callan, Louise, ed. *Philippine Duchesne: Frontier Missionary of the Sacred Heart, 1769–1852.* Westminster, Md.: Newman Press, 1957.

Cassell, Frank A. "Missouri and the Columbian Exposition of 1893." *Missouri Historical Review* 80, no. 4 (July 1986): 369–94.

Chandler, Kenneth J. "Rose Philippine Duchesne: An American Saint." *Gateway Heritage* 9, no. 1 (summer 1988): 26–31.

Christensen, Lawrence O. "Being Special: Women Students at the Missouri School of Mines and Metallurgy." *Missouri Historical Review* 83, no. 1 (October 1988): 17–35.

Clevenger, Martha R. "From Lay Practitioner to Doctor of Medicine: Woman Physicians in St. Louis, 1860–1920." *Gateway Heritage* 8, no. 3 (winter 1987–1988): 12–21.

Coalier, Paula. "Beyond Sympathy: The St. Louis Ladies' Union Aid Society and the Civil War." *Gateway Heritage* 11, no. 1 (summer 1990): 38–51.

Corbett, Katharine T. "Gratiot Street Prison." *Gateway Heritage* 20, no. 2 (fall 1999): 80–81.

———. *In Her Place: A Guide to St. Louis Women's History.* St. Louis: Missouri Historical Society Press, 1999.

———. "St. Louis Women Garment Workers." *Gateway Heritage* 2, no. 1 (summer 1981): 18–25.

———. "Veuve Chouteau, a 250th Anniversary." *Gateway Heritage* 3, no. 4 (spring 1983): 42–46.

Cottrell, Debbie Mauldin. "Mount Holyoke of the Midwest: Virginia Alice Cottey, Mary Lyon, and the Founding of the Vernon Seminary for Young Ladies." *Missouri Historical Review* 90, no. 2 (January 1996): 187–98.

Cranmer, Catharine. "Little Visits with Literary Missourians: Fannie Hurst." *Missouri Historical Review* 19 (April 1925): 389–96.

Dains, Mary K. "The Congressional Campaign of Luella St. Clair Moss." *Missouri Historical Review* 82, no. 4 (July 1988): 386–407.

———. "Forty Years in the House: A Composite Portrait of Missouri Women Legislators." *Missouri Historical Review* 87, no. 2 (January 1993): 150–67.

———. "Missouri Women in Historical Writing." *Missouri Historical Review* 83, no. 4 (July 1989): 417–28.

———. "Women Pioneers in the Missouri Legislature." *Missouri Historical Review* 85, no. 1 (October 1990): 40–52.

Dains, Mary K., ed. *Show Me Missouri Women: Selected Biographies*. Kirksville, Mo.: Thomas Jefferson University Press, 1989.

Dowl, Aimée. "Fair Ball." *Gateway Heritage* 21, no. 3 (winter 2000–2001): 34–39.

Draper, Arthur G. "Dear Sister: Letters from War-Torn Missouri, 1864." *Gateway Heritage* 13, no. 4 (spring 1993): 48–57.

Fitzwilson, Mary Ann. "'True Confessions': The University of Missouri Sex Questionnaire Incident of 1929." *Gateway Heritage* 17, no. 3 (winter 1996–1997): 4–17.

Fivel, Sharon. "'Disarmingly Simple—Disastrously Chic': Grace Ashley and the Shirt-Stud Dress." *Gateway Heritage* 16, no. 3 (winter 1995–1996): 44–55.

Foley, William E. "The Laclède-Chouteau Puzzle: John Francis McDermott Supplies Some Missing Pieces." *Gateway Heritage* 4, no. 2 (fall 1983): 18–25.

Gilbert, Judith A. "Esther and Her Sisters: Free Women of Color as Property Owners in Colonial St. Louis, 1765–1803." *Gateway Heritage* 17, no. 1 (summer 1996): 14–23.

Goering, Karen Mccoskey. "St. Louis Women Artists, 1818–1945: An Exhibition." *Gateway Heritage* 3, no. 1 (summer 1982): 14–21.

Graham, Margaret Baker. "Stories of Everyday Living: The Life and Letters of Margaret Bruin Machette." *Missouri Historical Review* 93, no. 4 (July 1999): 367–85.

Graves, Karen. *Girls' Schooling during the Progressive Era: From Female Scholar to Domesticated Citizen*. New York: Garland, 1998.

Gregory, Sarah J. "Pioneer Housewife: The Autobiography of Sally Dodge Morris." *Gateway Heritage* 3, no. 4 (spring 1983): 24–33.

Hanley, Marla Martin. "The Children's Crusade of 1922: Kate O' Hare and the Campaign to Free Radical War Dissenters in the Era of America's First Red Scare." *Gateway Heritage* 10, no. 1 (summer 1989): 34–43.

Harris, Charles F. "Catalyst for Terror: The Collapse of the Women's Prison in Kansas City." *Missouri Historical Review* 89, no. 3 (April 1995): 290–306.

Harris, Nini. *A Grand Heritage: A History of the St. Louis Southside Neighborhoods and Citizens*. St. Louis: De Sales Community Housing Corporation, 1984.

Hartmann, Susan M. "Women's Work among the Plains Indians." *Gateway Heritage* 3, no. 4 (spring 1983): 2–9.

Herr, Pamela. *Jessie Benton Fremont*. New York: Franklin Watts, 1987.

Hines, Stephen W., ed. *Little House in the Ozarks: A Laura Ingalls Wilder Sampler: The Rediscovered Writings.* Nashville, Tenn.: Thomas Nelson, 1991.

Hobbs, Lenora. "Sweet Monsters and Kewpies: The Mystery of Rose O'Neill." *Gateway Heritage* 22, no. 1 (summer 2001): 28–36.

Holloway, Marcella M. "The Sisters of St. Joseph of Carondelet: 150 Years of Good Works in America." *Gateway Heritage* 7, no. 2 (fall 1986): 24–31.

Holt, Rev. Earl K., III. "Lengthening Shadows: Mary Institute's 125 Years." *Gateway Heritage* 5, no. 2 (fall 1984): 2–11.

Holtz, William. "Closing the Circle: The American Optimism of Laura Ingalls Wilder." *Great Plains Quarterly* 4 (spring 1984): 79–90.

———. *The Ghost in the Little House: A Life of Rose Wilder Lane.* Columbia: University of Missouri Press, 1993.

Hunt, Marion. "Julia Catherine Stimson and the Mobilization of Womanpower." *Gateway Heritage* 20, no. 3 (winter 1999–2000): 44–51.

———. "Woman's Place in Medicine: The Career of Dr. Mary Hancock McLean." *Missouri Historical Society Bulletin* 26 (July 1980): 255–63.

Jones, Judy Yaeger. "Some Private Advice on Publishers: Correspondence between Laura C. Redden and Samuel L. Clemens." *Missouri Historical Review* 93, no. 4 (July 1999): 386–96.

Kamphoefner, Walter. *The Westfalians: From Germany to Missouri.* Princeton: Princeton University Press, 1987.

Kempker, Erin. "The Union, the War, and Elvira Scott." *Missouri Historical Review* 95, No 2 (April 2001): 287–301.

King, Charles R. "Dr. J. C. Parrish, Frontier Accoucher." *Missouri Historical Review* 85, no. 3 (April 1991): 288–303.

Korner, Barbara O. "Philippine Duchesne: A Model of Action." *Missouri Historical Review* 86, no. 4 (July 1992): 341–62.

Kramer, William A. "The Saxons in Missouri." *Concordia Historical Institute Quarterly* 60 (1987): 2–18.

Kremer, Gary R. "Strangers to Domestic Virtues: Nineteenth-Century Women in the Missouri Prison." *Missouri Historical Review* 84, no. 3 (April 1990): 293–310.

Kremer, Gary R., and Cindy M. Mackey. " 'Yours for the Race': The Life and Work of Josephine Silone Yates." *Missouri Historical Review* 90, no. 2 (January 1996): 199–215.

Kretzmann, P. E. "The Saxon Immigration to Missouri, 1838–1839." *Missouri Historical Review* 33 (1939): 157–70.

Lee, Janice. "Administrative Treatment of Women Students at Missouri

State University, 1868–1899." *Missouri Historical Review* 87, no. 4 (July 1993): 372–86.

Ling, Huping. "Sze-Kew Dun: A Chinese-American Woman in Kirksville." *Missouri Historical Review* 91, no. 1 (October 1996): 35–51.

Mangan, Sister Mary. "Sisters of Loretto, St. Louis: 1847–1997." *Gateway Heritage* 18, no. 3 (winter 1997–1998): 26–35.

Mcintyre, Stephen L. "'Our Schools Are Not Charitable Institutions': Class, Gender, and the Teaching Profession in Nineteenth-Century St. Louis." *Missouri Historical Review* 92, no. 1 (October 1997): 27–44.

McLaurin, Melton. *Celia, a Slave*. Athens: University of Georgia Press, 1991.

McMillen, Margot Ford, and Heather Roberson. *Called to Courage: Four Women in Missouri History*. Columbia: University of Missouri Press, 2002.

Menius, Joseph. *Susan Blow*. St. Clair, Mo.: Page One Publishing, 1993.

Miller, Sally M. *From Prairie to Prison: The Life of Social Activist Kate Richards O'Hare*. Columbia: University of Missouri Press, 1993.

———. "Through Dungeons Dark: The Story of Kate Richards O'Hare." *Gateway Heritage* 13, no. 4 (spring 1993): 58–67.

Moenster, Kathleen. "Jessie Beals: Official Photographer of the 1904 World's Fair." *Gateway Heritage* 3, no. 2 (fall 1982): 22–29.

Mooney, Catherine M. *Philippine Duchesne: A Woman with the Poor*. New York: Paulist Press, 1990.

Moore, Rosa Ann. "Laura Ingalls Wilder and Rose Wilder Lane: The Chemistry of Collaboration." *Children's Literature in Education* 11 (autumn 1980): 101–9.

Morgan, Georgia Cook. "India Edwards: Distaff Politician of the Truman Era." *Missouri Historical Review* 78, no. 3 (April 1984): 293–310.

Morris, Monia Cook. "The History of Woman Suffrage in Missouri, 1867–1901." *Missouri Historical Review* 25 (October 1930–July 1931): 67–82.

Moss, Carolyn J. "Kate Field: The Story of a Once-Famous St. Louisan." *Missouri Historical Review* 88, no. 2 (January 1994): 157–75.

Ohman, Marian M. "Margaret Nelson Stephens." *Gateway Heritage* 18, no. 4 (spring 1998): 44–49.

———. "Missouri's Turn-of-the-Century First Couple: Lawrence 'Lon' Vest and Margaret Nelson Stephens." Pts. 1 and 2. *Missouri Historical Review* 91, no. 3 (April 1997): 250–74; 91, no. 4 (July 1997): 406–30.

Park, Eleanora G., and Kate S. Morrow. *Women of the Mansion*. Jefferson City, Mo.: Midland Printing, 1936.

Pedersen, Sharon. "Married Women and the Right to Teach in St. Louis,

1941–1948." *Missouri Historical Review* 81, no. 2 (January 1987): 141–58.

Pickle, Linda S. *Contented among Strangers: Rural German-Speaking Women and Their Families in the Nineteenth-Century Midwest.* Urbana: University of Illinois Press, 1996.

————. "German and Swiss Nuns in Nineteenth-Century Missouri and Southern Illinois: Some Comparisons with Secular Women." *Yearbook of German-American Studies* 20 (1985): 61–82.

————. "Stereotypes and Reality: Nineteenth-Century German Women in Missouri." *Missouri Historical Review* 79 (April 1985): 291–312.

————. "Women of the Saxon Immigration and Their Church." *Concordia Historical Institute Quarterly* 57 (winter 1984): 146–61.

Porter, Jack Nusan. "Rosa Sonneschein and the American Jewess Revisited: New Historical Information on an Early American Zionist and Jewish Feminist." *American Jewish Archives* 32 (November 1980): 124–31.

Reid, Diane. "Margaret Truman: President's 'Son.'" *Gateway Heritage* 12, no. 4 (spring 1992): 60–67.

Riley, Glenda. *The Feminine Frontier: A Comparative View of Women on the Prairie and the Plains.* Lawrence: University Press of Kansas, 1988.

Ring, Lucile Wiley. *Breaking the Barriers: The St. Louis Legacy of Women in Law, 1869–1969.* Manchester, Mo.: Independent Publishing, 1996.

Robbert, Louise Buenger. "Lutheran Families in St. Louis and Perry County, Missouri, 1839–1870." *Missouri Historical Review* 82 (July 1988): 424–38.

Schroeder, Adolf E., and Carla Schulz-Geisberg, eds. *Hold Dear, as Always: Jette, a German Immigrant Life in Letters.* Columbia: University of Missouri Press, 1988.

Scott, Mary Semple, ed. "History of Woman Suffrage in Missouri." *Missouri Historical Review* 14, nos. 3–4 (April–July 1920): 281–384.

Seyersted, Per. *Kate Chopin.* Baton Rouge: Louisiana State University Press, 1980.

Sherwood, Dolly. *Harriet Hosmer: American Sculptor, 1830–1908.* Columbia: University of Missouri Press, 1991.

————. "Harriet Hosmer's Sojourn in St. Louis." *Gateway Heritage* 5, no. 3 (winter 1984–1985): 42–48.

Sneddeker, Duane R. "Regulating Vice: Prostitution and the St. Louis Social Evil Ordinance, 1870–1874." *Gateway Heritage* 11, no. 2 (fall 1990): 20–47.

Speiss, Lincoln Bunce. "St. Louis Women Artists in the Mid-Nineteenth Century." *Gateway Heritage* 3, no. 4 (spring 1983): 10–23.

Staley, Laura. "Suffrage Movement in St. Louis during the 1870s." *Gateway Heritage* 3, no. 4 (spring 1983): 34–41.

Stepenoff, Bonnie. "Freedom and Regret: The Dilemma of Kate Chopin." *Missouri Historical Review* 81, no. 4 (July 1987): 447–66.

———. "Kate Chopin in 'Out-at-the-Elbows' St. Louis." *Gateway Heritage* 11, no. 1 (summer 1990): 62–67.

———. "Mother and Teacher as Missouri State Penitentiary Inmates: Goldman and O'Hare, 1917–1920." *Missouri Historical Review* 85, no. 4 (July 1991): 402–21.

Stratton, Joanna L. *Pioneer Women: Voices from the Kansas Frontier*. New York: Simon and Schuster, 1981.

Thorne, Tanis. *The Many Hands of My Relations: French and Indians on the Lower Missouri*. Columbia: University of Missouri Press, 1996.

Toth, Emily. *Kate Chopin*. New York: William Morrow, 1990.

Towne, Ruth Warner. "Marie Turner Harvey and the Rural Life Movement." *Missouri Historical Review* 84, no. 4 (July 1990): 384–403.

Tucker, Phillip Thomas. *Cathy Williams: From Slave to Female Buffalo Soldier*. Mechanicsburg, Pa.: Stackpole Books, 2002.

VanderVelde, Lee, and Sandhya Subramanian. "Mrs. Dred Scott." *Yale Law Journal*, 106, no. 1 (October 1996–January 1997): 1033–122.

Waal, Carla, and Barbara Oliver Korner, eds. *Hardship and Hope: Missouri Women Writing about Their Lives, 1820–1920*. Columbia: University of Missouri Press, 1997.

Welsh, Donald H. "Martha J. Woods Visits Missouri in 1857." *Missouri Historical Review* 55 (January 1961): 109–23.

Willett, Julie A. " 'The Prudes, the Public, and the Motion Pictures': The Movie Censorship Campaign in St. Louis, 1913–1917." *Gateway Heritage* 15, no. 4 (spring 1995): 42–55.

William, Christine. "Prosperity in the Face of Prejudice: The Life of a Free Black Woman in Frontier St. Louis." *Gateway Heritage* 19, no. 2 (fall 1998): 4–11.

Wilson, Rodney C. " 'The Seed Time of Gay Rights': Rev. Carol Cureton, the Metropolitan Community Church, and Gay St. Louis, 1969–1980." *Gateway Heritage* 15, no. 2 (fall 1994): 34–47.

Wolfe, Margaret Ripley. "Rumors of a Little Rebellion in Dixie: Real Women and Their Region." *Missouri Historical Review* 92, no. 2 (January 1998): 106–18.

Woods, Harriett. "Stepping Up to Power: The Political Journey of American Women." *Gateway Heritage* 20, no. 3 (winter 1999–2000): 58–60.

————. *Stepping Up to Power: The Political Journey of American Women.* Boulder, Colo.: Westview Press, 2000.

Wuerffel, Stella. "Women in the Saxon Immigration." *Concordia Historical Institute Quarterly* 35 (fall 1962): 81–95.

Young, Dina M. "The Silent Search for a Voice: The St. Louis Equal Suffrage League and the Dilemma of Elite Reform, 1910–1920." *Gateway Heritage* 8, no. 4 (spring 1988): 2–19.

Contributors

Gregg Andrews is a professor of U.S. history and assistant director of the Center for Texas Music History at Texas State University, San Marcos. He is the author of *Insane Sisters: Or, the Price Paid for Challenging a Company Town; City of Dust: A Cement Company Town in the Land of Tom Sawyer;* and *Shoulder to Shoulder: The American Federation of Labor, the United States, and the Mexican Revolution, 1910–1924.* He is currently working on a book manuscript, "Hard Times in Texas: Labor, Culture, and the Great Depression."

Rebekah Weber Bowen holds a master's degree in history from the University of Missouri–Columbia, where her thesis dealt with the impact of the Civil War on gender roles in Saline County, Missouri. She is an archivist for the Missouri State Local Records Preservation Program.

Susan Calafate Boyle received her Ph.D. in American history from the University of Missouri–Columbia. A native of Argentina, she is interested in ethnic minorities and is the author of *Los Capitalistas: Hispano Merchants and the Santa Fe Trail.* She currently works for the National Park Service and specializes in historic trails and cultural landscapes.

Diane Mutti Burke is a doctoral candidate in American history at Emory University in Atlanta. Her dissertation, in progress, is entitled "On Slavery's Border: Slavery and Slaveholding on Missouri's Farms, 1821–1865."

Rhonda Chalfant is completing a Ph.D. at the University of Missouri–Columbia, with a dissertation that focuses on prostitution in Sedalia. She teaches at State Fair Community College in Sedalia and is active in the Pettis County Historical Society.

Carol K. Coburn is an associate professor of American religious history and women's studies at Avila University in Kansas City. She has written two books focused on the interaction of gender, education, ethnicity, and religion in American life: *Spirited Lives: How Nuns Shaped Catholic Culture and American Life, 1836–1945* (coauthored with Martha Smith), and *Life at Four Corners: Religion, Gender, and Education in a German-Lutheran Community, 1868–1945*. She is currently researching the lives and experiences of American Catholic sisters in the post–World War II era.

Judith A. Gilbert is an independent scholar living in Amarillo, Texas. She received a Ph.D. in American history from City University of New York in 1995 and has taught women's history at Kingborough Community College in Brooklyn. She researched "Esther and Her Sisters" on a fellowship from the Missouri Historical Society in St. Louis, and it was originally published in *Gateway Heritage* in 1996.

Gary R. Kremer is a professor of history at William Woods University in Fulton. Prior to joining the faculty at William Woods, Kremer served as director of the Missouri State Archives. He is the author, editor, or coeditor of a number of books on Missouri history, including *Missouri's Black Heritage* and *Dictionary of Missouri Biography*, both available from the University of Missouri Press.

Virginia Laas is a professor of history at Missouri Southern State University in Joplin. She edited *Bridging Two Eras: The Autobiography of Emily Newell Blair* and contributed a chapter, entitled "Reward for Party Service: Emily Newell Blair and Political Patronage in the New Deal," that appeared in *The Southern Elite and Social Change: Essays in Honor of Willard B. Gatewood, Jr.* She is presently at work on a biography of Emily Newell Blair.

Rebecca S. Montgomery received her Ph.D. from the University of Missouri–Columbia and is an assistant professor of history at Georgia Perimeter College in Atlanta. She is the author of "Lost Cause Mythology in New South Reform: Gender, Race, Class, and the Politics of Patriotic Citizenship in Georgia, 1890–1925," which appeared in *Dealing with the Powers that Be: Negotiating the Boundaries of Southern Womanhood;* and the forthcoming *The Politics of Education in the New South: Women and Reform in Georgia, 1890–1930.* She currently is working on a biography of Progressive reformer Celeste Parrish.

Mary C. Neth is an associate professor of history at the University of Missouri–Columbia. She is the author of *Preserving the Family Farm: Women, Community, and the Foundations of Agribusiness in the Midwest, 1900–1940;* "Seeing the Midwest with Peripheral Vision: Identities, Narratives, and Region," which appeared in *The American Midwest: Essays on Regional History;* and other articles on rural women.

Linda Schelbitzki Pickle is professor and chair of the German department at Western Kentucky University. She began her research on rural German immigrants while teaching at Westminster College in Fulton.

De Anna J. Reese is a doctoral candidate in twentieth-century African American, women's, and social history at the University of Missouri–Columbia. Her dissertation, in progress, is on African American women's leadership, activism, and community-building strategies in St. Louis.

Kimberly Schreck is a doctoral student in the history department at the University of Missouri–Columbia. Her dissertation, in progress, focuses on the experiences of mixed-race families in Missouri in the nineteenth century.

Bonnie Stepenoff is a professor of history at Southeast Missouri State University in Cape Girardeau. She is the author of *Thad Snow: A Life of Social Reform in the Missouri Bootheel,* and *Their Father's Daughters: Silk Mill Workers in Northeastern Pennsylvania, 1880–1960.*

LeeAnn Whites is an associate professor of history at the University of Missouri–Columbia. She is the author of *The Civil War as a Crisis in Gender: Augusta, Georgia, 1860–1890,* and many articles concerning the history of women and gender relations in the nineteenth-century South.

Index

Abbot, James Monroe, 67, 78
African Americans, 12, 91; in beauty industry, 11, 169–70, 173, 175; as businesswomen, 10–11, 39, 169; community of, 173–74, 176; Poro College's opportunities for, 175–79; property ownership by women, 29, 32–34, 38, 42–44; relations with Jews, 248–49; and standards of beauty, 168–72, 179; stereotypes of, 146, 148, 150; unemployment of, 237–38; white fears of assertiveness of, 146–47. *See also* Racism; Slaves
Agriculture: brains, not brawn, trend in, 193, 197; education in, 182, 191–93, 195–96, 197; expansion of, 181–82; as male field, 182–83, 196; market-oriented vs. subsistence, 190; New Deal programs in, 238. *See also* Farmers; Farms; Sharecroppers
Andersen, Kristi, 227
Anthony, Susan B.: and Elizabeth Cady Stanton, 103–4; and Virginia Minor, 101, 103, 117
Anti-Semitism, 12, 248–49
Atlas Portland Cement Company: acquiring Ilasco land, 200–201, 208, 210, 215; Koller's suits against, 209–10, 212; paternalism of, 215, 218; role in Koller's commitment, 211, 217–18
Aubuchon, Antoine, 29, 42–44
Authors: Emily Newell Blair as, 220–21; Fannie Cook as, 12, 239–43, 245–51

Banister, Marion, 227, 231
Beauty: African Americans and standards of, 168–72, 179; African Americans in industry of, 10–11, 169–70, 173–75, 178; consumer industries in, 170–73
Beecher, Lyman, 84–85
Bell, David and Partilla, 128–30, 133
Bell, Quentin, 163
Bell, Shannon, 156
Bethel community, 48
Blair, Emily Newell, 12; as Democratic National Committeewoman, 225–27; at Democratic national headquarters, 227–28; drawing women into politics, 219, 226–28; on feminist solidarity, 234–35; goals in Democratic Party, 229–30, 233; and Missouri Democrats, 223–25; in suffrage movement, 221–22; vs. Reed, 222–25; writing by, 220–21
Boot-heel Doctor (Cook), 242–43, 245–47
Bossism, 223, 225
Brackenridge, Henry Marie, 16
Brouillet, Eliza McKenney, 90–91
Brown, Laura, 224, 231
Brown, William Wells, 77, 79–80
Bruns, Henrietta (Jette) Geisberg, 48–51, 57–59, 61–62
Bundles, A'Lelia, 171
Business: African Americans in, 10–11, 39, 169; entrepreneurs in beauty industry, 11, 169–70, 173, 175; and

prostitution, 10, 154–56, 158,
   161–62; and wealth's presumed relation to virtue, 153; widows handling,
   28, 131–32; women running, 25–28,
   36–39, 58, 207. *See also* Property
Bynum, Victoria, 123

Cahokia, Illinois, 87–88
Carondelet, Missouri, 87–90
Cassity, Michael, 153, 164
Catholics, 61; competition with
   Protestants for influence, 84–85,
   98–99; culture of, 97–99; population
   of, 87*n13,* 94; prejudice against,
   84–86; relations with Protestants, 87,
   95. *See also* Nuns; Sisters of St.
   Joseph
Catt, Carrie Chapman, 221–22, 227
Chafe, William, 221
Charity, 164, 179
Child care: by nuns, 97; under slavery,
   69, 76, 78
Children: deaths of, 50, 106; inheritance
   by, 21–22
Cholera, 106
Church: women in, 163–64. *See also*
   Catholics; Religion
Civil War, 9, 93; effects on gender relations, 13, 115–17; effects on gender
   roles, 119–20, 132–33; Missouri's political tightrope during, 119–20; motivations for fighting, 121–22
Clamorgan, Jacques, 32, 36–38, 43–44
Class, 164, 184, 238; black professional,
   169, 175–76, 179; in Cook's novels,
   240–41; in development of Sedalia,
   153–55; of farmers, 190, 197; and
   immigration, 56–57; middle-class
   threatened by prostitutes, 155–56,
   158–59, 161–67; of nuns, 89; prostitutes striving for middle-class status,
   155–56, 162–64
Climate, Missouri, 54–55, 65
Clubs, women's, 184, 195, 224, 232;
   Blair's political support from, 223,
   225; farmers in, 181, 190, 192, 197;
   organizational skills in, 163–64. *See
   also* Organizations, women's
Communities: freed slaves in, 36; immi-

grant, 47–48, 52; Missouri slaves' lack
   of, 80, 137–39, 143, 146–47
Community property (in marriage),
   20–21, 25–26, 33, 35, 39
Cook, Fannie, 12, 162; activism of,
   236–39, 243–45; ambivalences of,
   250; as author, 236–37, 239–43,
   245–51; background of, 237, 248–49;
   causes of, 237–38, 247, 251
Cook, Lizzie, 159–60
Cooper County, 144, 146–48
Corbett, Kathleen T., 7
Credit, 23–24, 161, 198
Cropperville, Butler County, 238, 244
Crowdes, Mrs., 69, 75
Crowdes, Sarah Graves. *See* Graves, Sarah
Culture: German influence on, 63; nuns'
   influence on, 83–84, 97–99

Dains, Mary K., 6–7
Datchurut, Elizabeth, 29, 34, 42–44
Davis, Sam, 138–40
Davis, Sister Mary Borgia, 92
Democratic National Committeewoman,
   Blair as, 225–26, 233–35
Democratic Party: Blair at national head-
   quarters of, 227–28; Blair's attempts
   to draw women into, 226–27,
   231–32; Blair's goals in, 229–30, 233;
   Blair's leadership in, 219, 226; Blair's
   relationship with Missouri, 224–25;
   divisiveness of, 223; women's organi-
   zations within, 226–32
Demuth, I. MacDonald, 153
Depression: Fannie Cook's work in,
   237–38; in Fannie Cook's writing, 12;
   gender roles in novels of, 241–42;
   sharecroppers displaced by, 238,
   243–44
Descoux, Marie, 25, 28
Devolsey, Françoise, 31–32, 40–43
Diefendorf, Barbara, 27–28
Discrimination, 12; against Catholics,
   85–87. *See also* Anti-Semitism; Racism
Domestic ideology, 99–100
Donnelly, Father Bernard, 94, 96
Dreissinger and Achtundvierziger, 47–48
Duden, Gottfried, 47
Dysentery, 50, 54

Easter, Esther, 71, 79
Economy: during Civil War, 124; of
    farming, 73–74, 198; few job options
    and low pay for women, 10, 163, 170;
    gender-defined segments of, 10–11;
    lack of options for freed slaves in, 75,
    141, 143–44, 150–51; Missouri's, dur-
    ing Depression, 237–38; as motivation
    for immigration, 46–47; opportunities
    for women in, 10, 29; plantation vs.
    Missouri small holdings, 73–74; of
    prostitution, 154–56, 158, 160–61; of
    Ste. Genevieve, 23–24; of St. Louis,
    169. *See also* Business; Jobs
Education: agricultural, 11, 182, 184–85,
    191–93, 197; agricultural, for women
    farmers, 185, 191–92, 195–96; con-
    trol of access to, 11, 182, 184, 199,
    206; for the deaf, 82, 88*n*15, 89, 92;
    and German immigrants, 48, 60–61;
    of Koller, 202–3; by nuns, 55–56, 83,
    88–90, 95–97; in politics, 228–29,
    231–32; for rural women, 190
Elites: African American, 34, 174; Koller
    vs., 201–2, 209, 211; Sedalia's ruling
    class, 153–55
Elzea, Samuel, 211, 213–14, 216
Emancipation, 9; effects of, 10, 75,
    134–39; race relations renegotiated
    after, 146–48; relation of women's
    rights to, 102; unclarity about status
    after, 143–44, 146
English language, and immigrants, 61–62
Equality, 12; in inheritance, 19, 22; vs.
    other goals, 235, 237, 241; in prop-
    erty rights, 35 (*see also* French legal
    system); and recognition of difference,
    228
Equal Rights Amendment, 237, 241
Esther, and Jacques Clamorgan, 32,
    36–38, 43–44
Ewens, Mary, 84

Family: closeness of slave and slavehold-
    ing, 64–66, 71, 74–74, 80–81; effects
    of French inheritance laws on, 19;
    emancipated slave's ambiguous status
    in, 145–46, 150–51; emancipated
    slave's exclusion from, 134–36, 138,

142; emancipated slave's inclusion in,
    135–37, 141–42; farming as collective
    enterprise of, 57, 190, 193, 197–98;
    freed slaves' dependence on, 10,
    150–51; immigration by, 45, 57; let-
    ters to and from immigrants, 49–51;
    of slaves, 67, 77–78, 80; strength of
    ties, 43–44; women's attempt to pro-
    tect, 124, 127–31; women's obliga-
    tions to, 203, 221–22
Farmers: clubwomen as, 190, 192, 197;
    women as, 11, 180–81, 184–85, 193.
    See also Sharecroppers
Farms, 23, 33; crops of, 65, 190; as fam-
    ily collective enterprise, 57, 190, 193,
    197–98; female slaves working in
    fields, 66–67, 74; German speakers as
    wives and mothers on, 56–58; inheri-
    tance of, 186–88; ownership of, 11,
    37, 39–40; prosperity of German im-
    migrants', 46, 60; slavery on, 65, 74;
    slaves' resistance on, 65–66, 70–74;
    women managing, 25, 197; women on
    vs. women farmers, 181, 183, 192,
    194–99; workers organizing, 243–44.
    See also Agriculture
Fellman, Michael, 124
Feminist solidarity, through, 234–35
Financial security: of black professional
    class, 169–70; Koller's marginalized,
    213–14; through marriage, 20–23, 29;
    through property ownership, 33, 194
Flannery, Jenny, 127–28, 133
Flint, Timothy, 46
Fournier, Sister St. John, 89, 91
Franciscans, 84
Free-Soilers, 120
Frémont, Jessie Benton, 2, 51, 62–63
French, in deaf education, 92
French colonials, 35, 90; diversity of in-
    terests of, 23–24; settlements of,
    15–16
French legal system, 19; inheritance
    under, 19, 21–23, 29–30; marriage
    contracts under, 20–21; women's busi-
    ness transactions under, 25–29
Frontier: development of institutions on,
    97–99; hard work on, 56–59; Kansas
    City as, 93–94; social welfare work of

nuns in, 82–84, 97–99; women's
power on, 12–13

Gelhorn, Edna, 238, 251
Gender, as relational system, 6
Gender balance, 18, 35, 152
Gender consciousness, 201, 204
Gender differences: in agricultural education, 182, 191–92; in Cook's novels,
239–40; in New Deal programs, 238;
relation to equality, 228; in
stereotypes of African Americans,
147–49
Gender equity, 193; of Minors, 103,
112–15; in property ownership in
marriage, 106–11
Gender ideology, and religious competition, 99–100
Gender politics, in religion, 98
Gender relations: Civil War's effects on,
115–17; between slaves and slaveholders, 71–72; women accused of disrupting, 205
Gender roles, 122, 164, 218; in agriculture, 182–83, 185–86; in Cook's
novels, 242–43, 250–52; effects of
Civil War on, 119–20, 123, 132–33;
in novels of 1930s, 241–42; protecting and being protected in, 122–23,
126–27; in religious women's activities, 98–99; of slaves and slaveholders, 65–67, 74; women's
effectiveness in protection due to,
124, 127–30, 133
German immigrants, 8, 63; diversity
within, 46; English and, 61–62; letters
from, 49–51; nuns, 55–56; population
of, 45, 47; problems of, 49–51,
54–55; prosperity of, 46, 60; religion
of, 52–53, 62; social and political beliefs, 47–48, 121
Gilmore, E. G. and Maud, 244, 250
Glass, Carter, 229, 231
Goltra, Edward, 224–27
Goodwin, J. West, 163–64
Government, 88n15, 89, 191–92, 209
Graves, Sarah, 67, 69, 75, 79
Griswold, Robert, 99–100
Guardianship: Koller opposing, 201–2,

207; and Koller's insanity hearings,
210–12; Koller's money under,
213–14, 216; over Koller's sister, 208;
in Minors' property trustee arrangement, 108–10
Guerrilla warfare, during Civil War,
9–10, 121; effects on protection roles
in, 132–33; view of women in,
123–25; women as protectors in,
123–30

Hapenney, Rebecca, 109–10
Hapke, Laura, 241–42
Hardship and Hope (Waal and Korner),
7
Health care, 172, 214, 244; alternative,
204; nuns working in, 56, 83, 95–96;
of slaves, 76, 143
Heinbach, Mary Alice, 200–201, 205–8,
210
Hermann, Missouri, 47
Hickam, Eda, 144–46; characterizations
of, 147, 150; dependence on white
family, 137–38, 140–41, 143; judge's
compromise for, 138–39; kept in igno-
rance of emancipation, 134–37, 139;
lack of options for, 150–51; viewed as
threat, 147, 149
Hickam, James, 136, 140, 144–45
Hickam, Joseph, 134–36, 139–41, 143
Hickam, Squire, 137–38, 140–41
Hillenkamp, Margaret Blauff and
Frederick, 59–60
Hill Grows Steeper, The (Cook), 239–42,
247
History: changing understandings of, 1,
3–6; women's exclusion from, 13–14
History of Missouri, A, 1
Home industries (sewing, spinning, weav-
ing, etc.), 23, 68
Homesickness, 50–51, 55, 62–63
Horne, Martha and Richard, 125–27,
133
Households: as battleground in Civil
War, 130–31; duties of slaves and
slaveholders in, 65–67, 69; farm, 185,
192; Minors subverting patriarchy of,
106–11; women as protectors of,
9–10; women's power in, 7–9, 12–13;

women's responsibility for, 116, 123–24, 163
Hull, Cordell, 226–27, 230, 231

Ilasco, Missouri, 200–201; Atlas getting land of, 208, 210, 215; Koller acting as legal representative for, 205–6; Koller living in, 213–15; and Koller's commitment, 217–18
Illinois Country, 15, 17, 27–28
Illness: caused by women disrupting gender relations, 205; cholera, 106; dysentery, 50, 54; venereal diseases, 158–59. *See also* Insanity
Immigrants, 13, 63, 201; culture of, 47, 62–63; failure of, 53, 57; nuns teaching, 91, 97; population in Kansas City, 97; religion of, 84. *See also* German immigrants
Industrialization, 9, 183–84
Influence, 10; becoming power, 12–13; vs. power, 3–5, 9, 108–9
Ingels, Rosa Russell, 184, 195
Inheritance: by black women, 39–43; of farms, 186–87; under French legal system, 19, 21–23, 29–30; Koller acting as sister's representative in, 205–7; by males, 112, 183; Minors challenging tradition in, 112–14, 117–18; by slaves, 75
In Her Place (Corbett), 7
Insanity, 11; involuntary commitment for, 215–17; Koller accused of, 201–2, 210–11, 212, 216–17; Koller's sister accused of, 206–7; Koller vs. accusations of, 212–13
Internationalism, 223
Isaacs, Sue, 122–23, 133
Ivory, Sister Francis Joseph, 94–95

Jackson, Bart, 160–61
Jackson, Claiborne Fox, 121–22
Jaulin, Jean, 24–25
Jeannette, 31–32, 38–40, 43–44
Jesuits, 84
Jews: African Americans' relations with, 248–49; Cook as, 239–40, 249
Jobs, 169, 182, 237; for black women, 144, 175–79, 246; discrimination in,

11; lacking during Depression, 237–38; options for women, 10, 163
Johnson, Josephine, 238, 243–44, 251

Kansas, vs. Missouri slaveholders, 120
Kansas City: 93–97
Kansas-Nebraska Act (1854), 120
Kendley, Manie, 68–69
Kenrick, Peter Richard, 93
Kinney, Alice E., 187, 198
Know-Nothing Party, 87
Koller, Euphemia B., 11; vs. Atlas Cement Company, 200–201, 205–6, 210, 215, 218; challenging paternalism, 207, 218; insanity hearings of, 210–12, 216; land of, 207–8, 210, 215; money under guardianship, 216; obituary of, 200; ordered to State Hospital, 216–17; sources of empowerment of, 202–6; suits about property ownership, 208–10, 212
Korner, Barbara Oliver, 7
Ku Klux Klan, 87

LaBastille, Marie, 34, 43
Labor movement: agriculture workers organizing, 243–44; vs. Atlas Cement Company, 201; in Cook's novels, 242–43, 245–47; Cook's support for, 238, 247
League of Nations, 223, 225
Lectures, 174, 190
Legal system, 211; involuntary commitment in, 210–12, 215–16; Koller's insanity hearings in, 210–13; Koller's suits in, 200–201, 208–10, 212–13; lack of opportunities for women in, 205–6, 217; prostitutes' participation in, 159–62; women's transactions in, 18–19, 25–27, 42–43. *See also* French legal system
Legislature, 101, 109, 116–17
Letters, from immigrants, 53, 59–60
Lewis, J. Hamilton, 222–23
Logan, Cynthy, 72, 78
Long Bridge, The (Cook), 250
Lynchings, 149, 170, 174, 246

Magazines, Blair's articles in, 220–21
Malone, Annie Turnbo, 10–11, 168–70,
    173, 175–79
Marriage, 29; contracts under French
    legal system, 20–21, 35; in Cook's
    novels, 241–43, 245–47, 250; French,
    16–18; property ownership and con-
    trol in, 39, 106–10, 109–11; slaves',
    36, 77, 80; women's lack of rights in,
    101–2
Martin, Katherine, 223–24
Mauro, Philip, 110–11
McReynolds family, 130–32
McRoberts, Mollie, 131–32
Megown, Benton B., 208, 210–11
Megown, John E., 208–9
Men: absence of, 12–13, 24–25, 28, 116;
    involvement in women's rights move-
    ment, 104–5, 118; supporting
    women's political activism, 221
Minor, Francis Gilman, 106, 112
Minor, Virginia and Francis: background
    of, 106, 114–15; gender equity of,
    112–15; partnership of, 103–4,
    106–11; subverting patriarchy of
    households, 106–12; support for
    Union, 115–16; in women's rights
    movement, 101–5, 117
Minorities, in state histories, 4
Minor v. Happersett (Supreme Court),
    101, 102n3, 104, 116
Missouri Compromise (1820), 120
Missouri Suffrage Association, 101, 116
Missouri Women Farmers' Club
    (MWFC): formation of, 180–81,
    184–85, 190–91; goals of, 194–95;
    membership of, 186–90, 193–96; mo-
    tives for, 185–86, 191; obstacles to
    growth of, 196–99; struggles of,
    183–84
"Missouri Women in Historical Writing"
    (Dains), 6–7
Mitchell, Frances Pearle, 180, 190; back-
    ground of, 186–87; and Missouri
    Women Farmer's Club, 194, 196; on
    women farmers, 184, 193
Mrs. Palmer's Honey (Cook), 246–47,
    251
Muench, Friedrich, 56–57

Napton, Melinda, 67–68, 71, 75
Native Americans, 84
Nativists, 85, 87, 201
Nazis, Cook's concern about, 248
New Deal programs, 235, 238
Newspapers: beauty ads in, 170–73; dis-
    crimination in, 87, 148; on Euphemia
    Koller, 200, 211; on prostitution,
    158–59, 162, 164–66; on Virginia
    Minor, 118
Novels, 12; Cook's, 239–43, 245–51
Nuns, 8–9, 87; discrimination against,
    85–86; German-speaking, 45, 52–53,
    55–56, 61–62; influence in the West,
    97–99; in Kansas City, 95, 97; work
    of, 82–84. See also Sisters of St.
    Joseph

Old Lutheran communities, 48, 52, 62
O'Neill, Mother Evelyn, 97
Organizations, women's, 220, 238–39;
    within Democratic Party, 226–31; for
    reforms, 183–84; for women farmers,
    190–91. See also Clubs, women's
Orphans, nuns caring for, 83, 90–92, 96

Paternalism, of Atlas Concrete, 215, 218
Patriarchy, 113, 115, 182, 215; and
    emancipated slaves, 136–38; on farms
    and farm households, 192, 194; gen-
    der and race differences in power,
    149–50; Minors subverting
    household, 106–12; women's passivity
    under, 123–24
Patton, Priscilla, 74, 76–77
Peiss, Kathy, 171
Pendergast political machine, 222,
    225–26
Perry County, 48, 52
Peters, Mary Estes, 77–78
Peyroux, Isabel Rodríguez, 25–26
Plea for the West, A (Beecher), 84–85
Political parties, 12. See also Democratic
    Party
Politics, 174, 219, 225; and Fannie
    Cook, 12, 238–39; men's response to
    women in, 226–27; as motivation for
    immigration, 46–47; participation in,
    183, 221–22, 226–28, 231–32; power

through, 7–8, 12, 147–48, 233–34;
women's role in, 227–28, 233
*Politics and Poetics of Transgressions,
The* (Stallybrass and White), 156
Pommerel, Mother Celestine, 89–91
Poro College, 174–78
Poro products, 173–74
Poverty, 251; and charity in Sedalia,
164–65; during the Depression, 238,
243–44; Fannie Cook's work against,
12, 237–38; Koller's under guardianship, 214; of nuns in Carondelet,
87–88; slaves' after emancipation, 75,
144
Power, 7; gender and race differences in,
149–50; vs. influence, 3–5, 9, 108–9;
influence becoming, 12–13; sources of,
12, 202–6, 234–35; women's, 10, 25,
224; women's in politics, 224, 227,
233–34
Professions: farming as, 11, 182, 190,
192, 194; men's power over, 184,
198–99, 206. *See also* Class, black
professional
Progressive Era reforms, 183–84
Prohibition, 63
Property: by African American women,
32–34, 37–38, 42–44, 176–77; benefits of ownership, 8, 33, 194; difficulty
determining from records, 33–34; in
French marriages, 16–17, 20–21; inheritance under French legal system,
19, 21–23; Koller and Heinbach's
joint ownership, 207–8; Koller's, 203;
Koller's lawsuits about, 208–10;
Minors' innovations in ownership,
106–10, 112, 114–15; ownership presumed to be male, 11, 183, 192; patriarchy in, 112–14, 194; by prostitutes,
10, 154, 159; women protecting, during Civil War, 124–27; women's ability to manage, 185–87, 194; women's
struggle to control, 11, 192; women
transacting business about, 25–27,
109–11, 185–87
Prostitutes, 10, 154–58, 160; business's
relations with, 161–62; middle-class
threatened by, 155–56, 158–59,
161–67; social ostracism of, 164–65

Protection, 237; Civil War's effects on
gender roles of, 121, 132–33; as male
role, 119–20, 122–23; prostitutes'
lack of, 160–61; women's failure in,
130–31; women taking on role, 121,
123–29
Protestants: Catholic relations with, 87,
95; competition with Catholics for
influence, 84–85, 98–99; prejudice
against nuns, 85–86
Public sphere. *See* Spheres, public and
domestic
Public women, 9–10

Race politics, 174
Race relations, 8, 149–50, 251; Cook's
involvement in, 239; in Cook's novels,
245–46, 247, 248–49; renegotiating
after emancipation, 146–48
Racism: Cook's concern about, 12, 248;
gender differences in, 149–50; post\-
Civil War, 146–48; and standards of
beauty, 168–70
Railroads, 93–94, 152, 181–82
Ralls County, 203, 209; Atlas Cement
Company in, 201, 215; Koller's lawsuits against, 201, 209, 212–13; and
Koller's sanity hearings, 213, 216; and
State Hospital in Fulton, 214–15
*Reading, Writing, and Rewriting the
Prostitute Body* (Bell), 156
Reed, James A., 222–25, 230–31
Reforms, women advocating, 183–84
Religion: churches excluding prostitutes,
165; and clergy, 83, 117–18; gender
politics in, 98; of German speakers,
48, 52–53, 62; nuns' influence vs.
clergy's, 83–84; Protestant/Catholic
relations, 84–87, 95, 98–99; and
wealth's presumed relation to virtue,
153. *See also* Catholics
Rendlen, Charles E., Sr., 207–8, 214–15
*Report of a Journey to the Western States
of North America* (Duden), 47
Republicans, 214–15
Respectability: 10, 166–67
Rhineland, Missouri's, 63
Ridre, Marie Magdeleine, 25–26
Rights. *See* Suffrage; Women's rights

Roosevelt, Eleanor, 235
Roosevelt, Franklin Delano, 235, 238
Rosati, Bishop Joseph, 82, 87n13, 89,
    92–93

Saline County, during Civil War, 120–22,
    124–28, 132–33
Salvation Army, 165
Sanity. See Insanity
Scharf, Lois, 235
Science, in agriculture, 181–82
Scott, Anne Firor, 226
Scott, Elvira Weir, 68, 78, 125, 127, 133
Scott, Mary Semple, 224–25, 230
Sedalia: development of, 152–53; prosti-
    tution in, 10, 154, 161; repression of
    prostitution in, 158–61
Segregation, 11, 156, 238
Sexual abuse, of slaves, 77–78
Sharecroppers, 12, 238, 243–44. See also
    Agriculture; Farmers
Simonson, Emma E. (Cortelyou), 188–90
Sirbu, Petru, 207–8
Sisters of St. Joseph of Carondelet (CSJs),
    82, 100; caring for orphans, 90–92; in
    deaf education, 92–93; finances of,
    88–90; growth of order, 89–91; in
    Kansas City, 94–97; and male clerics,
    94, 98; Motherhouse of, 93
Sisters of St. Mary, 56
Slavery: divisiveness over, 93, 120–21;
    and emancipation, 10, 115; household
    relations in, 8, 64, 66, 69–77, 79–81;
    mistresses under, 65, 67–68, 70–73,
    79; plantation vs. Missouri smallhold-
    ing, 65, 73–74, 80; resistance to,
    65–66, 70–74, 76–77, 81
Slaves, 88n16, 91; abuse of, 77–80; defi-
    nition of, 141–42; dependence on for-
    mer owners, 10, 144; kept in
    ignorance of emancipation, 134–36,
    139; lack of clarity in emancipation,
    143–44, 146; lack of family and com-
    munity support for, 66, 80, 137–39,
    143, 146–47; population of, 105,
    120–21; poverty after emancipation,
    75; treatment of, 36, 76, 78
Social activism, 12; in Cook's novels,

249–50; by Emily Newell Blair, 221;
    by Fannie Cook, 236–37, 243–45
Social mobility, 34–35, 168
Social status, 49, 60–61
Social welfare: as Cook's priority, 241;
    Madam C. J. Walker's contributions
    to, 174–75; nuns working in, 9, 56,
    82–84, 92–93, 95–96
South: migrants from, 121; replication of
    planter class in St. Louis, 105–6, 112
Spain, 16; property rights under, 33, 35,
    38–39, 42–43
Spheres, public and domestic, 6; women
    challenging, 163, 183–84, 205;
    women expanding, 164, 221
Spiritualism, 203–4, 212–13
Stallybrass, Peter, 156
Stanton, Elizabeth Cady, 101, 103–4
State histories, women in, 2–4
State Hospital in Fulton, 200, 214–17
Ste. Genevieve, 15–16; economy of,
    23–24; farms around, 23; population
    of, 16, 18, 51; women's rights in, 17,
    21, 29. See also French legal system
Stephens, Minnie, 160, 164
Stereotypes, of African Americans, 146,
    148, 150
Stevens, Mayor, 158, 165
St. Joseph, Sisters of (CSJs). See Sisters of
    St. Joseph
St. Joseph's Academy, 90
St. Joseph's Girls Home, 96
St. Joseph's Home for Boys, 92
St. Joseph's Hospital, 95
St. Joseph's Institute for the Deaf, 89,
    92–93
St. Louis, 105; African American busi-
    nesswomen in, 10–11; African
    American community in, 173–74;
    African American population in, 105,
    169; black beauty culture in, 168–69;
    nuns in, 52, 87; property ownership
    by African American women in,
    32–34, 38, 42; Sisters of St. Joseph in,
    82–83, 89–93; social activism in, 102,
    112–13, 115–16, 236–39; social mo-
    bility in, 34–35; social relations in, 87,
    170, 248–49

Stoddard, Amos, 16–17
Storm against the Wall (Cook), 239, 248–50
Stratton, Paulina, 64*n1*, 67–68, 70–72, 75–78
St. Teresa's Academy, 95–97
St. Vincent de Paul, 91
Suffrage: activists for, 101, 112–13, 221–22, 237; Blair's political support from movement, 223, 225; effects of, 219, 233–34; movement, 116, 221–23; and women's power in political parties, 12; women's right to as citizens, 116. *See also* Women's rights
Symanski, Richard, 156

Thompson, James, 161–62
Trade: preferred over farming, 33; in Ste. Genevieve economy, 23–24; by women, 27–28. *See also* Business
Transportation, 82, 93–94. *See also* Railroads

Union, the, 48, 120–21, 126, 152
Urbanization, 9, 183–84
Ursuline order, 52, 82, 86

Valle, Marie Louise, 25, 28
Veblen, Thorstein, 166–67
Victims, women seen as, 124–25, 132

Waal, Carla, 7
Walker, Madam C. J., 10–11, 168–70, 173–75, 179
Wars, 13. *See also* Civil War
Wealth, 29, 30, 153
Weaver, Harry G., 211, 213–14, 216–17
Weitbrecht, Sophie Luise Duensing and Gotthilf, 53–54

West, the, 84–85
Western Sanitary Commission, 115–16
White, Allon, 156
Whitfield, Owen and Zella, 243–45, 251
Widows: and control over property, 28, 114–15; farm management by, 185, 189; inheritance by, 20–22; running businesses, 27–28, 29, 58–59, 131–32; in Ste. Genevieve, 18–19
Wilson, Mrs. Halsy, 231–32
Wives and mothers: compared to widows, 18–19, 29; in Cook's novels, 251–52; farm management by, 188–89; under French legal system, 16–17, 26; German immigrants as, 45–46, 49–50, 56; legal status of, 107–11; nuns symbolically, 8–9; protection as, 237; transacting business, 27–28; women on farms as, 11, 181, 183, 192, 194–95, 197; women's obligations as, 251; women's role as, 3–5. *See also* Marriage
Woman's National Democratic Club, 233
Women: in Civil War rhetoric, 122–23; evaluation of contributions of, 3–4; in histories, 1–3; as legally dead, 107–8
Women's Democratic State Committee, 224–25
Women's history, development of, 6–7
Women's rights, 102, 184, 241; under French legal system, 29, 35; lacking in marriage, 101–2; leaders of movement for, 103–4; men's involvement in movement for, 104–5, 117–18. *See also* Suffrage
Wood, Maude M. Griffith, 188, 193–94
World's Fair (1904), 169–70, 174

Photo Credits

All are left to right. **Page i**—Opal Denton Whitley (collection of Irene Whitley Marcus); female pilot and her plane (Missouri State Archives); and Business Women's Week, ballot box, 1951 (Hazel Palmer Collection, Missouri State Archives). **Page ii**—Mary Frances Gentry Holliway and others giving cookies to World War II GIs at Jefferson City train station (collection of Mary Frances Gentry Holliway); Mrs. Leonard Stephens, feeding chickens, Middle Grove, Mo., 1923 (Missouri State Archives); and log cabin and family (DNR Land Survey Collection, Missouri State Archives). **Page iii**—telephone office, Lancaster, Mo., ca. 1921; women and children soaking their feet in Lost Creek, Seneca, Mo.; and Business and Professional Women's Club event, 1936 (Hazel Palmer Collection), all in Missouri State Archives. **Page viii**—ferry at Rocheport, Mo., Maclay family, September 28, 1898; woman and her gun (Ed Gill Collection); Lebanon High School Home Economics Class, 1956 (Gerald Massie Collection), all in Missouri State Archives. **Page ix**—family picking cotton, Pemiscot County, Mo. (Gerald R. Massie Collection, Missouri State Archives); friends of Pauline Dallmeyer and Alvin Dallmeyer meeting a state official at capitol (collection of Dorothy Summers Dallmeyer); Anne Edwards, Francille Bailey, and Marge Guemmer of the Business and Professional Women's Club (Hazel Palmer Collection, Missouri State Archives). **Page x**—Nun, Sisters of St. Mary, Jefferson City, Mo. (Ann Noe Collection); two women in Pomme de Terre River, 1923 (Paul Doll Collection); and women working, Cabool Shoe Plant (Gerald R. Massie Collection), all in Missouri State Archives.